YEAR B ▪ 2009

workbook
FOR LECTORS AND GOSPEL READERS

Mary A. Ehle

LTP

LITURGY
TRAINING
PUBLICATIONS

Workbook for Lectors and Gospel Readers 2008, United States Edition © 2007 Archdiocese of Chicago. All rights reserved.

Liturgy Training Publications, 1800 North Hermitage Avenue, Chicago IL 60622; 1-800-933-1800, fax 1-800-933-7094, orders@ltp.org, www.ltp.org

Editor: Donna Crilly
Production Editor: Kris Fankhouser
Typesetter: Jim Mellody-Pizzato
Original book design: Jill Smith
Revised design: Anna Manhart and Jim Mellody-Pizzato
Cover art: Barbara Simcoe
Interior art: Anna Manhart

Printed in the United States of America.

ISBN 978-1-56854-676-6
WL09

The paper used to print this year's *Workbook for Lectors and Gospel Readers* was carefully chosen with our customers in mind and with a commitment to the environment. After extensive searching, we found a highly opaque paper that fits both of those needs. The 40# Remarque Offset paper that this book is printed on is 100% recycled and contains a minimum of 40% postconsumer waste. The non-postconsumer portion consists of pre-consumer recycled fiber. Although many de-inking processes use highly toxic bleach, this paper was processed using PCF (Processed Chlorine Free) technologies. This paper is also acid-free to reduce yellowing as it ages.

CONTENTS

The Author

Mary A. Ehle is an editor at Liturgy Training Publications. She holds a doctorate in Religious Studies from Marquette University as well as degrees from St. John's University in Collegeville, Minnesota, and St. Norbert College in De Pere, Wisconsin. Mary is an experienced liturgist, pastoral musician, and director of faith formation. She continues to give workshops on a variety of pastoral and theological topics in which she draws insights from scripture and liturgy and relates them to the life of the Church.

Dedication

This book is dedicated to John Craghan and Carol Stockhausen, two professors of Sacred Scripture who instilled in the author, a systematic and pastoral theologian, an excitement for and a desire to delve deeply into the word of God. Thank you for helping me to love the study of scripture and, more importantly, to love scripture itself. May Christ's presence in the word continue to nourish us all.

Nihil Obstat

Reverend Brian J. Fischer
Censor Deputatus
December 19, 2007

Imprimatur

Reverend John F. Canary, STL, DMin
Vicar General
Archdiocese of Chicago
December 31, 2007

The *Nihil Obstat* and *Imprimatur* are official declarations that a book is free of doctrinal and moral error. No implication is contained therein that those who have granted the *Nihil Obstat* and *Imprimatur* agree with the content, opinions, or statements expressed. Nor do they assume any legal responsibility associated with publication.

INTRODUCTION

The liturgy is the public prayer of the Church. Prayer itself involves a relationship—a relationship between God and you, the person praying. In public prayer such as the liturgy, the relationship also includes members of the assembly, those present and those not present. The *Catechism of the Catholic Church* (CCC) states that the liturgy is "a participation in Christ's own prayer addressed to the Father in the Holy Spirit. In the liturgy, all Christian prayer finds its source and goal" (CCC, #1073).

As a lector, your ministry helps to facilitate the public prayer of the Church in the Liturgy of the Word. This is a tremendous responsibility, but one which you do not need to take on by yourself. There are other lectors who proclaim the Word in your parish; the ordained ministers and lay ecclesial ministers in your parish community are present to help form you so that you might better be able to carry out your ministry of proclamation and prayer. You also belong to a church community that has called you forth and recognized that you have either the gift of public speaking or are a person of prayer—or perhaps both. Through your continued participation in the Church's liturgy, your involvement in workshops for lectors, your own preparation, and above all the willingness to grow in your relationship with God, you will hone you skills and gifts as a lector. And in this day and age, where people are often more comfortable interacting with each other through e-mail or on a cellular phone, you will make possible genuine human interaction through the sharing of God's word when you lector to the best of your ability.

The Liturgy of the Word as Prayer

The Second Vatican Council's Dogmatic Constitution on Divine Revelation, or *Dei Verbum* (DV), makes it clear that the Liturgy of the Word and the Liturgy of the Eucharist are to be regarded with the same reverence: "The Church has always venerated the divine Scriptures as she venerated the Body of the Lord, in so far as she never ceases, particularly in the sacred liturgy, to partake of the bread of life and to offer it to the faithful from the one table of the Word of God and the Body of Christ" (DV, #21). In imparting the word of the Lord in the scriptures to your assembly, you are feeding them with the Bread of Life, and providing nourishment for them to continue their life of prayer and to develop further their relationship with the Lord.

Yet how the Liturgy of the Word is celebrated has the ability to foster or not a deepening of one's relationship with God. You have an important role to play in this. But first, as a lector, you need to be mindful that the Liturgy of the Word is prayer, a dialogue between God and his people. Aware of this, your presence and how you proclaim the word will nurture the assembly's prayer. In the Introduction to the Lectionary (#28), we read of the Liturgy of the Word as meditation, a form of prayer:

> The liturgy of the word must be celebrated in a way that fosters meditation; clearly, any sort of haste that hinders recollection must be avoided. The dialogue between God and his people taking place through the Holy Spirit demands short intervals of silence, suited to the assembled congregation, as an opportunity to take the word of God to heart and to prepare a response to it in prayer.

In the beginning was the Word, and the Word was with God, and the Word was God.

The *General Instruction of the Roman Missal* (#29) also reflects on the dialogue of prayer that occurs in the Liturgy of the Word:

> When the Sacred Scriptures are read in the Church, God himself speaks to his people, and Christ, present in his own word, proclaims the Gospel.

The Holy Spirit works through the words you proclaim and in the hearts of believers recalling the saving works of God in history (CCC, #1103). Your presence, the variations in tone and volume you use, and the different paces and rhythms you employ all serve to provide room for the Spirit to work in people's hearts, leading them to prayer. Depending on the time in the liturgical year, the events of a person's life, and world events, this prayer might be one of praise, thanksgiving, desire, forgiveness, pleading, or joyful expectation. No matter the prayer, you will have succeeded in your ministry if you have stepped aside and not drawn attention to yourself. For your part, any barriers to the dialogue that is prayer, of remembering and making present God's marvelous deeds through the Spirit, will have been removed.

You have been called forth to serve as a lector, proclaiming God's word. In speaking about immersing oneself into the scriptures through study, reflection, or during the proclamation at Liturgy, remember that "prayer should accompany the reading of sacred Scripture, so that a dialogue takes place between God and man" (DV, #25). Your communication of God's word during the public prayer of the Church is proclamation, but it is also proclamation in the context of prayer. This sometimes is forgotten. One way to be attentive to your proclamation as prayer is to center your preparation on prayer—on your conversation with God.

Preparation as Prayer

Saint Augustine in one of his sermons spoke of the necessity of coming to the ministry of the word from one's personal prayer. Although he was referring to clergy, his thought can be extended today to include all who proclaim the word of God. He asserted that one is "an empty preacher of the Word of God to others, not being a hearer of the Word in his own heart" (*Sermon*, #179). This translates in the contemporary

> God so loved the world that he gave his only Son, so that everyone who believes in him might not perish but might have eternal life.

idiom for lectors as "you have to listen to God through the prayer of your heart, lest you be a disingenuous proclaimer of the Word on Sunday." You might want to ask yourself: "How can I better hear the Word of God in my own heart so I can better communicate the Word to the assembly gathered before me to pray?"

Spiritual preparation as a lector is essential. Because of the weightiness of the ministry the lector performs, the preparation that is required is both spiritual and technical. The Introduction to the Lectionary describes the lector's preparation as "above all" spiritual. This spiritual preparation "presupposes at least a biblical and liturgical formation." According to paragraph 55 of the Introduction,

> The biblical formation is to give readers the ability to understand the readings in context and to perceive by the light of faith the central point of the revealed message. The liturgical formation ought to equip the readers to have some grasp of the meaning and structure of the liturgy of the word and of the significance of its connection with the liturgy of the Eucharist.

If you are a veteran lector, you might have already developed a method of spiritual preparation that works well for you. Newcomers to the ministry might want to experiment with different methods of preparation. Whatever the method you choose, it is important to have a regular manner in which you prepare. Moreover, the spiritual preparation must be centered on prayer, your own dialogue and conversation with God as to how best you can be the conduit for the presence of God to your assembly. Some parishes provide opportunities for their lectors—even all their liturgical ministers for a given Sunday—to come together during the week prior to the Sunday to pray and reflect on the readings and the Gospel for the Sunday on which they will be serving. You might choose to participate in these sessions or to suggest that this type of gathering of liturgical ministers take place at your parish. If you do not have the time to commit to participating in a group like this, you might center your spiritual preparation on reflection questions on the readings and the Gospel. Very often, parishes print reflection questions for next week in the current week's bulletin or they publish them on the parish Web site. If you are unsure of where to find reflection questions on the readings, you might ask a member of the parish staff.

The preparation you as a lector need to do before a Sunday celebration is more involved than the preparation of some of your other liturgical ministry colleagues. While it would be good for all liturgical ministers to prepare spiritually for the liturgy at which they will serve, your spiritual preparation goes beyond simple reflection on the readings. As the last quote from the Introduction to the Lectionary mentioned, spiritual preparation also involves biblical and liturgical formation. The biblical preparation entails developing an understanding of the readings in context. For this, some tools of the lector's ministry are essential. Try preparing with a copy of the Bible and a copy of *Workbook* at your side. With the Bible you will be able to read the readings in the context of the entire chapter or book in which they are contained. Sometimes the introductions at the beginning of each book of the Bible also provide beneficial information. Frequently, the footnotes are useful in developing a better understanding of the meaning of a passage.

This is my commandment: love one another as I love you.

The commentaries in *Workbook* aid in both your biblical and liturgical formation. The commentaries beneath the readings provide historical-critical background to assist you in understanding the reading in its original context. They also draw connections between the readings and the time in the liturgical year, so that the lector is better able to appreciate why particular readings are proclaimed on the days they are. Furthermore, the commentaries offer pastoral suggestions for helping you to make connections between the reading and our world and Church today. Both understanding the original intention of the author in writing the inspired words of scripture and relating them to the contemporary context will allow you to communicate God's presence in the word to your assembly. Your ministry will then effectively deepen your own prayer and that of those present in your community.

One way of looking at the goal of the spiritual preparation of the lector is in the language of some of the early Church fathers and mothers of the desert. These men and women of prayer were so devoted to cultivating their relationship with God through the scriptures that they simply wanted to "become prayer," a phrase used by Olivier Clément, a well-respected theologian.[1] They wanted their entire life—their presence and their actions to show forth the presence of God. But what does it mean for a minister of the word to "become prayer" in the twenty-first century? First, it entails openness to the Spirit of the Lord working in your own life. In your preparation time, as well as in the ordinary events of your life, cultivate an awareness of the presence of God in yourself and in others you meet. The direction with which you live your life is both inward and outward toward God—the Spirit of God within you and in others.

Second, immerse yourself in the practice of your faith. Participate consistently in the Sunday eucharistic prayer of the Church. Pray as a conversation with God, but also with the traditional prayers of the Church. Third, let the scriptures be your guide in talking with God. God never stops inviting us to closer union with him through the word.

As you prepare the readings, perhaps you will want to start out the Monday of the Sunday before you are scheduled to be a lector simply by reading over the passages from scripture, getting a sense of their main theme or point. You will want to read through both the first and second readings (not only the reading you will proclaim) and the Gospel. As you go through your life during week, perhaps there is a phrase that you will want to remember and draw on during the week. Let this be your prayer every time it comes to mind. Use it as the direction for living your life during the week. The word of God is living and active—it's not meant to be kept by us on the written page. Because of circumstances in the parish community, occasionally lectors struggle with living out the word of God in their own ministry. Sometimes our human nature, which naturally dislikes change, takes over and the lectors become a clique, an elite group, unwillingly to welcome newcomers to the ministry. If lectors truly work at "becoming prayer," however, there will be no room in the ministry for excluding those who are gifted and talented in public speaking, and who are willing to be formed liturgically and biblically, to become persons of prayer themselves. Lectors, too, must be willing to be greeters and ministers of hospitality to those they come across before and after the liturgy, welcoming those they know and reaching out to those who are newcomers or clearly need their assistance. Consonance between the word of God the lector proclaims and the word of God lived out is, in the end, what it means to "become prayer."

When we are able to witness to the word of God in our words and actions, then we are closer to "becoming prayer" in our day and age. Then your proclamation of the word of God in the context of the Church's public prayer, the liturgy, will be a proclamation filled with integrity. The assembly gathered to worship with you will sense the genuineness of your proclamation. They will know you have prepared both technically as well as spiritually.

Prayerfulness and Practical Matters

The spirit of prayerfulness in the Liturgy of the Word is reflected both in the way the minister of the word presents himself or herself and in the manner in which he or she proclaims the word of God. There are many practical matters in relation to the lector that effect the celebration of the Liturgy of the Word. Even for the seasoned minister of the word, a reminder every so often about some of these matters is helpful. As you read through these comments, please be mindful of the fact that there will be issues and concerns regarding carrying out the ministry of the word that are specific to the parish to which you belong, particularly matters concerning the sound system and microphones. In order to address issues such as these, many parishes already have implemented yearly or semiannual formational gatherings with all the ministers of the word.

When you are scheduled to be a minister of the word, make sure to arrive early, at least 20 minutes or so. You do not want to be rushing out the door and arriving at the last minute. This creates unnecessary anxiety both for you, and for those who are expecting you to be present. You do not want to leave anyone wondering whether or not you are coming. Arriving early also gives you time to check the Lectionary, making sure your reading is marked correctly so that you do not need to turn pages, trying to locate the reading after you approach the ambo. Before the liturgy begins, you will also want to find out if there are any additional rites taking place during the Mass that affect the time when you need to approach the ambo, for example, dismissal for Children's Liturgy of the Word, Rite of Acceptance, Baptism, and so on. Being aware of any changes will help you to keep the flow of the liturgy going; then no one will be left waiting for the lector to come to the ambo at the appropriate time.

Magnify the LORD with me; let us exalt his name together.

Blessed are the poor in spirit, for theirs is the kingdom of heaven.

Some lectors will want to sit in silence and prayer either in the sacristy or in the church before the celebration of the liturgy begins. Others will want to be greeting members of the assembly or welcoming other liturgical ministers. For some, this sense of community enables them to remember that the faith we profess and the God we worship in the liturgy is present among us, in each other. Find a method of immediate preparation that works best for you and lets you center yourself before the liturgy. No matter the method of immediate preparation you chose, you'll want to be focused once the liturgy begins.

Your posture is very important—both when you are proclaiming the word of God and during the rest of the liturgy when you are not carrying out your specific ministry. As you approach the ambo, make sure you are standing tall and erect. You want to exude confidence, but not overconfidence or arrogance. The manner in which you carry yourself will let the assembly know you have something important to tell them. When you are seated in the assembly or the sanctuary area, sit upright, actively listening and responding, involving yourself in the prayer of the liturgy. As a minister of the word, you also have the role of being an example for the rest of the community. People will recognize you before, during, and after the liturgy. How you present yourself at times other than when you are proclaiming the word is as important as how you appear in front of the assembly when it is your turn to execute your ministry. So sing, pray, and listen attentively throughout the liturgy as part of the assembly. Through your Baptism you are first a part of the assembly, then you are called forth from the assembly because you have a specific gift you and the church recognize. But you remain part of the assembly. Anything that would set you apart as "better than" others or not in unity with those in the assembly will detract from your ministry. Conversely, your full, conscious, and active participation will help lead others to the same. So, even though your gift might be in public speaking and not public singing, still participate in the sung prayer of the community!

After you arrive at the ambo, take a brief moment to focus yourself. Many ministers of the word are nervous when they read. This energy, if channeled correctly, can help to convey the message of the reading. One way that works for some lectors is to take an unnoticeable breath after arriving at the ambo. While taking that breath, you might want to say a short prayer offering the proclamation of the reading to God. Doing so reminds you that the reading is not about you, but about God. When you are focused, begin with the announcement of the reading in a confident, strong tone of voice. Both the announcement at the beginning of the reading and the acclamation at the end of the reading are important liturgically. Sometimes they are glossed over, but a strong pronouncement of them while making eye contact with the assembly engages those present.

If you make a mistake when you are proclaiming the word, keep your composure. You do not want to laugh and draw attention to yourself. Depending on the mistake, you might want to return to the beginning of the sentence. The assembly's comprehension of the reading will be aided with this method. If you clearly mispronounce or stumble over a word, simply restate that word and proceed. You do not want work out how to say the word at the ambo by saying it over and over again, trying to get the pronunciation correct. This makes it obvious to everyone that you have not prepared. More than that, however, it shows a lack of reverence for the word you proclaim. Because we're human beings, we all make mistakes. Your ability to maintain your composure in itself reverences the word of God.

Our natural human anxiety causes us to read faster when we are in front of people. Indeed, most lectors tend to proclaim the word too fast; some even race, wanting to finish the reading quickly. Many whose pace is rapid are not even aware that this is the case. A good reminder for most lectors, then, is slow down, slow down, slow down. A slower pace will help the assembly to understand the reading. In a culture that has so much visual stimulation, we are becoming less and less auditory in how we process information. This challenges you as a lector always to be aware of your pace, to take your time communicating the word to the assembly.

Your appearance or how you present yourself also reflects the reverence you have for the word of God and for the worship of God in the midst of the assembly. Although different parishes have different guidelines for dress, your appearance needs to speak of the importance of the liturgy itself and your particular ministry. Choose attire that is neither flashy

The LORD's word is true; all his works are trustworthy.

nor shabby so as not to make yourself the center of attention. In addition, choose attire that is practical—especially shoes. You probably should not lector in big winter boots or shoes with high or clunky heels. People in the assembly will be looking at what you are wearing, rather than listening to what you are proclaiming. Regarding your appearance, take a quick look in the mirror before the liturgy to avoid having the assembly focus on your hair if it has not been combed. This is particularly important for those ministers of the word who gratefully serve at the very early morning Masses and sometimes have to trudge through inclement weather to do so!

In addition to its role in spiritual formation—liturgical and biblical formation—that was previously discussed, *Workbook for Lectors* is also meant assist you in the practical matters concerning your ministry. The words in bold in the text of the readings indicate emphasis on particular words. They provide suggestions for which words should be stressed, though not all to the same degree. The margin notes on the left side of the readings provide pro-

nunciations for difficult or uncommon words and names, explanations of certain words or phrases from the reading, and suggestions for how to proclaim the reading such as when to take pauses and what tone of voice to use. Use *Workbook for Lectors* as a guide, not as a manual with definitive pronouncements as to how to proclaim the readings. Your own technical preparation and the feedback you receive from the assembly and parish staff regarding your proclamation can also assist you in becoming a better lector.

When you have addressed the practical matters, you will then be able to concentrate more readily on praying with the community. You will be able to remember your proclamation of the word is part of the public prayer of the Church's liturgy. It serves to deepen your relationship with God and move those in the assembly to grow in theirs as well. Through your ministry, then, you will offer praise to God and draw others to that same praise in the liturgy and in the ordinary events of their lives. You will have helped to lead the assembly to the full, active, and conscious participation the Church desires. You and the assembly will have "become prayer" and God will have been glorified because of the ministry you do.

Pronunciation Key

Most consonants in the pronunciation key are straightforward: The letter B always represents the sound B and D is always D, and so on. Vowels are more complicated. Note that the long I sound (as in kite or ice) is represented by *ī* while the long A (as in skate or pray) is represented by *ay*; long A followed by an R (as in prayer or Samaritan) is represented by *ai*. Long E (as in beam or marine) is represented by *ee*; long O (boat, coat), *oh*; long U (sure, secure) by *oo* or *yoo*. Short A (cat), E (bed), I (slim), and O (dot) are represented by *a, e, I,* and *o* except in an unstressed syllable, when E and I are signified by *eh* and *ih*. Short U (cup) is represented by *uh* or sometimes *u*. An asterisk (*) indicates the *schwa* sound, as in the last syllable of the word "stable." The letters *oo* and *the* can each be pronounced in two ways (as in *cool* or *book*; *thin* or *they*); underlining differentiates between them. Stress is indicated by the capitalization of the stressed syllable in words of more than one syllable.

bait = bayt
cat = kat
sang = sang
father = FAH-ther
care = kair
paw = paw
jar = jahr
easy = EE-zee
her =her
let = let
queen = kween
delude = deh-LOOD
when = hwen
ice = is
if = if
finesse = fih-NES

thin = thin
vision = VIZH*n
ship = ship
sir = ser
gloat = gloht
cot = kot
noise = noyz
poison = POY-z*n
plow = plow
although = ahl-THOH
church = cherch
fun = fun
fur = fer
flute = floot
foot = foot

Recommended Works

Church Documents

Catechism of the Catholic Church. United States Catholic Conference, Inc., 1994.

Dei Verbum (Dogmatic Constitution on Divine Revelation). In *Vatican II: The Conciliar and Post Conciliar Documents,* edited by Austin Flannery, OP, Northport, New York: Costello Publishing Company, Inc., 1992.

"Introduction to the Lectionary." In *Lectionary for Mass: Study Edition.* Chicago, Illinois: Liturgy Training Publications, 1998.

Guides for Proclaiming God's Word

Connell, Martin. *Guide to the Revised Lectionary.* Chicago, Illinois: Liturgy Training Publications, 1998.

Meyers, Susan E. *Pronunciation Guide for the Sunday Lectionary.* Chicago, Illinois: Liturgy Training Publications, 1998.

Rosser, Aelred R. *Guide for Lectors.* Chicago, Illinois: Liturgy Training Publications, 1998.

_____. *A Well-Trained Tongue: Formation in the Ministry of the Reader.* Chicago, Illinois: Liturgy Training Publications, 1996.

_____. *A Word That Will Rouse Them: Reflections on the Ministry of Reader.* Chicago, Illinois: Liturgy Training Publications, 1996.

General Reference Works on the Bible

Boadt, Lawrence. *Reading the Old Testament: An Introduction.* New York, New York/Mahwah, New Jersey: Paulist Press, 1984.

Brown, Raymond E. *An Introduction to the New Testament.* The Anchor Bible Reference Library. New York, New York: Doubleday, 1997.

The New Jerome Biblical Commentary. Raymond E. Brown, Joseph Fitzmyer and Roland E. Murphy, eds. Englewood Cliffs, New Jersey: Prentice Hall, 1990.

Perkins, Pheme. *Reading the New Testament: An Introduction.* New York, New York/Mahwah, New Jersey: Paulist Press, 1988.

Commentaries on the Gospel of Mark

Donahue, John R. and Harrington, Daniel J. *The Gospel of Mark.* Sacra Pagina Series. Collegeville, Minnesota: The Liturgical Press, 2005.

LaVerdiere, Eugene. *The Beginning of the Gospel: Introducing the Gospel of Mark.* Collegeville, Minnesota: The Liturgical Press, 1999.

Marcus, Joel. *The Gospel according to Mark (Mark 1—8).* Anchor Bible Commentary, vol. 27. New York, New York: Doubleday, 2000.

Senior, Donald. *The Passion of Jesus in the Gospel of Mark.* Wilmington, Delaware: Michael Glazier, 1984.

Van Linden, Philip A. *The Gospel according to Mark.* Collegeville Bible Commentary, vol. 2, New Testament. Collegeville, Minnesota: The Liturgical Press, 1985.

Notes

1. *The Roots of Christian Mysticism: Texts from the Patristic Era with Commentary.* Translated by Theodore Berkeley, OCSO, and Jeremy Hummerstone. Hyde Park, New York: New City Press, 1993.

1ST SUNDAY OF ADVENT

Lectionary #2

READING I   Isaiah 63:16b–17, 19b; 64:2b–7

Isaiah = ī-ZAY-uh

Beginning with the question "Why do you let us wander . . . ?" speak in a questioning tone of voice. As you impart the words "Return for the sake of your servants" and continue through the prophet's appeal to the Lord to "rend the heavens and come down," shift to a tone of pleading.

A reading from the Book of the Prophet Isaiah

> **You**, LORD, are our **father**,
>   our **redeemer** you are named **forever**.
> Why do you let us **wander**, O LORD, from your ways,
>   and harden our **hearts** so that we fear you not?
> **Return** for the sake of your **servants**,
>   the tribes of your **heritage**.
> Oh, that you would **rend** the heavens and come **down**,
>   with the mountains **quaking** before you,
> while you wrought **awesome** deeds we could not **hope** for,
>   such as they had not heard of from of **old**.
> No **ear** has ever **heard**, no **eye** ever **seen**, any God but **you**
>   doing such deeds for those who **wait** for him.
> Would that you might meet us doing **right**,
>   that we were **mindful** of you in our ways!

READING I The message of the prophet Isaiah has been understood as an "Advent message" throughout the history of the Church. However, regular churchgoers in your assembly may not remember this selection. The reading begins with a statement of Advent hope in the Lord who is forever acclaimed as redeemer. Yet the greater part pleads for the Lord to come and meet the sinful people again in hope of finding them changed from their old ways.

The *General Norms for the Liturgical Year and Calendar* refers to Advent as a period of "devout and joyful expectation." In preparing to remember Christ's first coming, we also await Christ's second coming at the end of time (#39). The joyful expectation of Advent distinguishes it from the penitential character of Lent. However, part of our preparation for Christmas entails recognizing that we are sinful. Just as Israel owned her sinfulness and professed the Lord's constancy in the midst of her failures, we are called to do the same. Our "devout and joyful expectation" for Christmas places a twofold responsibility on us: to change from our sinful ways and to celebrate God as our Father, who continues to draw us to him.

The readings for the first three Sundays of Advent this year come from Isaiah 40—66, which scholars believe was written by a different author or authors than Isaiah 1—39. This latter section emphasizes the eschatological hope offered to the people of Israel.

After being taken over by its enemies, Israel will once again be restored. This is the reason for the sense of optimism in today's reading from Isaiah. The prophet begs the Lord to return to his people. As a

Shift the tone in your voice to one filled with some remorse, as the past is remembered beginning with the prophet's words "Behold, you are angry, and we are sinful." Read the last verse with a sense of relief in your voice. It offers the hope of faith that flawed human persons do not have the final word: the Lord, the potter, is also our redeemer.

Behold, you are **angry**, and we are **sinful**;
   all of us have become like unclean people,
   all our **good** deeds are like polluted **rags**;
we have all **withered** like **leaves**,
   and our **guilt** carries us away like the **wind**.
There is **none** who calls upon your name,
   who **rouses** himself to cling to you;
for you have hidden your **face** from us
   and have **delivered** us up to our **guilt**.
Yet, O LORD, **you** are our **father**;
   we are the **clay** and **you** the **potter**:
   we are all the **work** of your **hands**.

people, the Israelites are sinful, withered, and no longer call on the Lord's name. The prophet, however, still believes that the Lord calls his people back, expressing this belief in the beloved imagery of the clay and potter.

Both individuals and Church communities, like the Israelites, need to confess that they, too, have not always been faithful to the Lord. The prophet's emotions and those he attributes to the Lord are ordinary human emotions of longing and disappointment, even anger. Practice this reading so

that the different sentiments come through in your tone of voice and are not overstated.

Leave the assembly with the heartfelt sense that while Advent is a season of hope, we must also repent and turn back to the Lord. We only need to cooperate and open ourselves to be formed by his hands.

READING II   Offer the opening greeting as a prayer for those gathered in the assembly before you today. Taking time with these words will also enable them to recognize that this verse

from Paul is the basis for the greetings in the liturgy we celebrate today.

Although the Corinthians struggle among themselves, Paul is affirming them in this greeting and thanksgiving. God is always present, even in the midst of divided communities. But we Christians today need to be reminded to keep ourselves firm in the faith until the day of the Lord, just as Paul was reminding the Corinthians. This is the Advent message of the reading. God will be faithful until the end and if we put our trust in God, we too will be kept firm until the end. Remember,

A reading from the first Letter of Saint Paul to the Corinthians

Brothers and sisters:
Grace to you and **peace** from God our **Father**
   and the Lord Jesus **Christ**.

I give **thanks** to my God **always** on your account
   for the grace of God **bestowed** on you in Christ **Jesus**,
   that in him you were enriched in **every** way,
   with all **discourse** and all **knowledge**,
   as the **testimony** to Christ was **confirmed** among you,
   so that you are not lacking in **any** spiritual gift
   as you **wait** for the revelation of our Lord Jesus **Christ**.
He will keep you **firm** to the end,
   irreproachable on the day of our Lord Jesus **Christ**.
God is **faithful**,
   and by him you were **called** to fellowship with his **Son**,
   Jesus **Christ** our **Lord**.

Corinthians = kor-IN-thee-unz

Look up and make eye contact with the assembly, addressing Paul's customary greeting to them.

Pause slightly after the greeting and before continuing Paul's message of thanksgiving with the words "I give thanks" before you continue with Paul's message. Offer the thanksgiving with warmth. This long, complex sentence explains why Paul is thankful to God.

Pause before the last sentence begins. Fill your voice with confidence and assurance as you proclaim God's faithfulness until the "day of our Lord Jesus Christ," a reference to the day of judgment at the end of time.

on this First Sunday of Advent, we have the opportunity to stand firm in our faith again, ready to deepen our relationship with God and one another as we celebrate the unfolding of the Paschal Mystery over the course of the new liturgical year.

When you proclaim this reading, reflect on the grace God bestowed on your faith community in the past, and on that which God continues to bestow. Think of the many ways in which your community already gives testimony to Christ. Let thanksgiving to God for all the goodness in your community be heard in your

voice as you read Paul's thanksgiving to the Corinthians.

Finally, while it is important to practice every reading you will proclaim out loud, this is particularly the case when you have to proclaim a reading that is composed of Paul's long sentences. Try practicing out loud with someone listening. Ask the hearer what he or she understood to be the essence of the reading to check whether you tackled Paul's lengthy sentence structure accurately.

GOSPEL   Today's Gospel message is unambiguous: watch, be vigilant. We live in a society that has been criticized for its "hyper-vigilance." On the First Sunday of Advent, this short Gospel from Mark—the evangelist who likes to be brief and to the point—calls us to reflect on whether we are really "watching."

The first two weeks of Advent focus on watching for the Lord's coming at the end of time, and the last weeks on Jesus coming as Messiah at a particular time and place in history. The earliest followers of Jesus believed that his second coming

Proclaim the introductory phrase ("Jesus
said to his disciples") to the assembly
by making eye contact with them before
beginning the parable.

Note the repetition of the word "watch."
Each time it occurs, increase the intensity in your voice slightly.

Pause before the last verse ("What I say
to you . . ."). Memorize it if you are able
and deliver it looking directly at the
assembly. State the command with
strength and insistence, but do not shout.

GOSPEL   Mark 13:33–37

A reading from the holy Gospel according to Mark

Jesus said to his **disciples**:
"Be **watchful**! Be **alert**!
You **do** not know when the time will **come**.
It is like a man traveling **abroad**.
He leaves **home** and places his **servants** in charge,
    each with his own **work**,
    and orders the **gatekeeper** to be on the **watch**.
Watch, therefore;
    you do not **know** when the **lord** of the house is **coming**,
    whether in the **evening**, or at **midnight**,
    or at **cockcrow**, or in the **morning**.
May he not come **suddenly** and find you **sleeping**.
What I say to **you**, I say to **all**: 'Watch!' "

---

was imminent. Certainly, this passage from Mark does not tell us when Jesus will return. However, its urgent message is found in the repetition of the call to be watchful, alert, and awake.

This parable is part of an eschatological discourse in Mark that immediately precedes the Passion narrative. Jesus' cross is always before us, even in the season of Advent. For Mark, a Gospel without an infancy narrative, the Passion and death of Jesus are primary. Jesus is first and foremost the suffering Son of God, who is

the Messiah. As Christians, we believe it is through Jesus' Passion, death, and Resurrection that he can be seen as the Messiah. Jesus is the Messiah at his birth because of the cross. Our wait for the second coming of Christ—our role as gatekeepers—is made easier because of his triumph on the cross.

Unlike our early Christian ancestors who believed that Christ's return would happen within their lifetime, during Advent we remind ourselves that our preparations for Christ's return need to be ongoing. We joyfully prepare for the *parousia*, Christ's

second coming in glory at the end of time, although we do not know how soon it will occur. We are like the gatekeeper—on watch for Jesus' coming again. By the way in which you proclaim this Gospel—adding more emphasis each time the words connoting watchfulness occur—you will help those gathered for worship to understand their role to wait patiently, but vigilantly, for the Messiah.

2ND SUNDAY OF ADVENT

Lectionary #5

READING I   Isaiah 40:1–5, 9–11

Isaiah = ĭ-ZAY-uh

This first address, beginning "Comfort, give comfort to my people" and concluding with "double for all her sins," is from God to a heavenly council or a group of prophets. Though it's in the imperative, let your voice still convey tender mercy. Pause after this section.

Note the switch in voices that the words "A voice cries out" signifies.

Read through this passage slowly, as if painting the images of wastelands, valleys, mountains, rugged land, and rough country. The voice tells us that the glory of the Lord—seen metaphorically in these landscape changes—will triumph over sorrow and redeem the people of Israel. When you proclaim the words "Then the glory of the Lord shall be revealed," do so with kingly majesty in your tone of voice. Pause after these words before the next section.

The voice switches back to God with the words "Go up on a high mountain." Your tone needs to be one of command in contrast to tender mercy, which was the tone you used when you conveyed the first section of the reading.

A reading from the Book of the Prophet Isaiah

Comfort, give **comfort** to my people,
   says your God.
Speak **tenderly** to **Jerusalem**, and proclaim to her
   that her **service** is at an **end**,
   her **guilt** is **expiated**;
indeed, she has received from the hand of the LORD
   double for all her **sins**.

   A **voice** cries out:
In the **desert prepare** the way of the LORD!
   Make **straight** in the **wasteland** a **highway** for our **God**!
Every **valley** shall be filled **in**,
   every **mountain** and **hill** shall be made **low**;
the **rugged** land shall be made a **plain**,
   the **rough** country, a broad **valley**.
Then the **glory** of the LORD shall be **revealed**,
   and all **people** shall see it **together**;
   for the **mouth** of the LORD has **spoken**.

Go **up** on to a high **mountain**,
   Zion, herald of glad **tidings**;
cry **out** at the top of your **voice**,
   Jerusalem, herald of good **news**!

READING I   Today's passage is taken from part of the book of Isaiah referred to as the Book of Consolation (40:1—55:13). Israel is to be consoled because the exile is almost at an end. The Lord's coming will bring redemption; God's justice will triumph. This is the good news that Zion is to proclaim.

For the minister of the word, this selection from Isaiah poses many challenges. There are a number of switches in the voice that is speaking. These are noted in the margin notes above. There are also a number of different modulations or inflections needed to convey adequately the meaning of this passage. Practice the reading often, perhaps recording yourself or proclaiming it to another person before you do so in front of the assembly. Ask yourself or the person with whom you practiced: Was the shift in speakers understood? How well was the sense of comfort and consolation expressed? How was the enthusiasm of the command of the voice crying, "Prepare the way of the Lord" heard? Did you make the transition from the Lord coming with power to the gentleness of the shepherd well?

The comfort and hope offered by the prophet Isaiah is what you offer the assembly before you. There are many places and peoples in the world in need of this message. Many who sit before you on the Second Sunday of Advent desire a message of consolation. You stand in the place of Isaiah and have the privilege of offering this gift to them. Through your practice and personal prayer, prepare yourself to impart

Fear **not** to cry out
   and say to the cities of **Judah:**
   Here is your **God!**
Here comes with power
   the Lord **GOD**,
   who **rules** by his strong arm;
here is his **reward** with him,
   his **recompense** before him.
Like a **shepherd** he feeds his **flock**;
   in his **arms** he gathers the **lambs**,
carrying them in his **bosom**,
   and leading the **ewes** with **care**.

Pause before the verse that begins "Like a shepherd he feeds his flock." Bring your voice down in tone and volume as you come to this verse. The tender mercy the Lord asks of us in the first verse of this reading is only that which he himself gives as a shepherd.

READING II   2 Peter 3:8–14

A reading from the second Letter of Saint Peter

Do **not** ignore this one **fact**, beloved,
   that with the Lord one **day** is like a thousand **years**
   and a thousand **years** like one **day**.
The Lord does not **delay** his promise, as **some** regard "delay,"
   but he is **patient** with you,
   not wishing that **any** should perish
   but that **all** should come to **repentance**.
But the day of the **Lord** will come like a **thief**,
   and then the **heavens** will pass away with a mighty **roar**
   and the **elements** will be dissolved by **fire**,
   and the **earth** and everything **done** on it will be found **out**.

If you are able, memorize the "one fact": "that with the Lord one day is like a thousand years," and make eye contact throughout your presentation of it.

In your voice, contrast the patience of the Lord in the line "but he is patient with you" with the suddenness reflected in the line "the day of the Lord will come like a thief."

---

consolation to them so that they will recognize the Lord's presence as a shepherd-king. This will help to make the celebration of Christmas after the four weeks of Advent a genuine celebration of the Lord coming in our midst.

READING II You have an opportunity with the opening address of this reading to gain the assembly's attention. They may be surprised to hear the announcement because of the infrequency with which they hear from the letter of Saint Peter in the Sunday assembly.

The main theme of the letter, written by an elder in Rome (most probably not Peter), is the author's defense of the Christian belief in the second coming of the Lord, the *parousia*. Though early believers thought the second coming was imminent, the author finds himself arguing that, despite the delay in the second coming, Christian belief in the second coming is still justifiable. The Lord's promise will still be fulfilled—new heavens and a new earth will appear.

On the Second Sunday of Advent, this reading provides us an opportunity to ponder how we understand our belief in the second coming. As your study this reading, spend some time thinking about the second coming and how our faith understands it. The *Catechism of the Catholic Church* (#668–682) is a good place to begin.

The images of the apocalypse in the passage can be disconcerting for some people; try to hold back so as not to over-emphasize these images. What is more important is the obligation Christians have to live ethically and morally in the

The sentence beginning with "Since everything is to be dissolved in this way" contains both harsh images of the judgment day and an appeal to Christians to behave in a manner that reflects their belief in the Lord. Speak to the assembly with a sense of urgency and seriousness in your voice.

Pause before the section that begins with the words "But according." Offer the hope of Advent—the hope of the coming of new heavens and a new earth—as you proclaim these final verses. You will want to replace the seriousness in your voice with calmness. Remember, though, calmness does not necessarily mean softer. Your words still need to be delivered clearly and audibly.

Since **everything** is to be dissolved in this way,
　　what sort of persons ought you to **be**,
　　conducting yourselves in **holiness** and **devotion**,
　　waiting for and **hastening** the coming of the day of **God**,
　　because of which the **heavens** will be dissolved in **flames**
　　and the **elements** melted by **fire**.
But according to his **promise**
　　we await **new** heavens and a **new** earth
　　in which **righteousness** dwells.
Therefore, beloved, since you **await** these things,
　　be **eager** to be found without **spot** or **blemish** before him,
　　　at **peace**.

GOSPEL　Mark 1:1–8

Look up at the assembly in your announcement: "The beginning of the gospel of Jesus Christ the Son of God." Clearly emphasize the word "beginning." Pause after the statement that identifies from where in the Gospel according to Mark this reading is taken.

A reading from the holy Gospel according to Mark

The **beginning** of the gospel of Jesus **Christ** the Son of **God**.

As it is **written** in Isaiah the **prophet**:
　　*Behold, I am sending my **messenger** ahead of you;*
　　　he will prepare your way.
　　*A **voice** of one crying out in the **desert***:
　　　"***Prepare** the way of the **Lord**,*
　　　*make **straight** his **paths**."*
John the **Baptist** appeared in the **desert**
　　proclaiming a baptism of **repentance** for the forgiveness of **sins**.

Use a narrative tone of voice—such as that of a new commentator—as you describe John the Baptist and his ministry. The narrative section begins "John the Baptist appeared in the desert" and concludes with "He fed on locusts and wild honey."

time before Christ comes again in glory. Throughout the history of Christian belief, the followers of Jesus had to be reminded continuously of their responsibility to live uprightly. Moving away from the belief in the imminent *parousia* did not excuse them from this obligation, nor does it excuse those in the assembly before you today.

Your own mindfulness of the connection between ethical behavior and the Lord's coming at the end of time will serve you well as you proclaim the passage from the letter of Saint Peter today. We still must wait patiently for the Lord's coming.

We must also recognize the day of the Lord will come like a thief in the night. But all is not up to the Lord. We are called to respond to the Lord's grace acting in our lives—to choose to cooperate with the promptings of the Spirit and announce the coming day of the Lord by the way we live. Our lives are an Advent—a time of preparation and waiting for the coming of this day.

GOSPEL　We hear of John the Baptist on the Second and Third Sundays of Advent. On this Second Sunday,

we are introduced to the Baptist with the prophet Isaiah's words that begin the Gospel according to Mark. They are some of the most familiar "Advent words," recognized by many from either Handel's *Messiah* or the musical *Godspell*. After citing Isaiah's words, Mark introduces John the Baptist and describes his ministry in brief as a ministry of baptism with water.

During Advent we can focus on "three comings": the coming of God in the Incarnation (past), the coming of Christ in our hearts (today), and the second coming of the Lord in glory (future). The emphasis

Judean = <u>joo</u>-DEE-un

Jerusalem = juh-R<u>OO</u>-suh-lem

Jordan = JOR-d*n

Look up and make eye contact with the assembly as much as possible as you state John the Baptist's proclamation: "One mightier than I is coming after me." Pause before you convey the difference between John's baptism and the Baptism of the one coming after him. The last verse ("I have baptized you with water; he will baptize you with the Holy Spirit") is the culmination of the Gospel passage. Read this sentence slowly and emphatically with the faith of someone who has experienced the coming of the Messiah and the gift of Baptism he offers now through the Church.

People of the **whole** Judean countryside
    and **all** the inhabitants of **Jerusalem**
    were going **out** to him
    and were being **baptized** by him in the Jordan **River**
    as they acknowledged their **sins**.
John was clothed in **camel's** hair,
    with a leather **belt** around his waist.
He fed on **locusts** and wild **honey**.
And **this** is what he **proclaimed**:
    "One **mightier** than I is coming **after** me.
I am not worthy to **stoop** and loosen the **thongs** of his **sandals**.
I have baptized you with **water**;
    he will baptize you with the Holy **Spirit**."

during the first weeks of Advent is traditionally on the second coming of the Lord. Yet, with the introduction of John the Baptist, the relationship between the coming of the Messiah in history, the coming of Jesus in the midst of the Christian community today, and the second coming of the Lord begins to unfold. These three comings are related through Baptism.

Most often we think of Lent as *the* season of preparation for the celebration of the sacraments of initiation—and Baptism, in particular. This is, in fact, the case, but Advent also is a time to appreciate how the sacrament of Baptism welcomes new members into the community of believers, the Church. The Church chooses to express its anticipation of the second coming by celebrating its faith in God—Father, Son, and Holy Spirit—gathering Sunday after Sunday at the eucharistic table. The Holy Spirit—the Spirit of Christ—now lives in the midst of the eucharistic assembly whose members were welcomed through the sacrament of Baptism. It is, however, by virtue of our Baptism that we are to "prepare the way of the Lord." John the Baptist's mission becomes ours.

Impart this Gospel reading to your assembly by enunciating clearly the words of the prophet Isaiah. Proclaim the words with an understanding of how John the Baptist fulfilled them and how we are to fulfill them today as we in the Church prepare for the Lord's second coming and the celebration of the Lord's coming in the hearts of all who believe.

IMMACULATE CONCEPTION

Lectionary #689

READING I   Genesis 3:9–15, 20

A reading from the Book of Genesis

After the man, **Adam**, had eaten of the **tree**,
  the LORD God **called** to the man and **asked** him,
    "Where **are** you?"
He answered, "I **heard** you in the garden;
  but I was **afraid**, because I was **naked**,
  so I **hid** myself."
Then he asked, "Who **told** you that you were **naked**?
You have eaten, then,
  from the **tree** of which I had **forbidden** you to eat!"
The man replied, "The **woman** whom you put here with me—
  she gave me **fruit** from the tree, and so I **ate** it."
The LORD God then asked the **woman**,
  "Why did **you** do such a thing?"
The **woman** answered, "The **serpent** tricked me into it,
    so I ate it."

Then the LORD God said to the **serpent**:
  "Because you have **done** this, you shall be **banned**
    from **all** the animals
    and from **all** the wild **creatures**;
  on your **belly** shall you **crawl**,
    and **dirt** shall you **eat**
    all the **days** of your **life**.

The entire reading is familiar; be sure to take your time in order to express the human character of the discussion among God, Adam, and Eve.
Read Adam's words with a little self-consciousness in your voice, not in a direct manner.

As you impart God's words of accusation, let sternness be heard in your voice. The Lord was probably slightly angry, as a parent would be with a disobedient child.
Speak Adam's reply ("The woman whom you put here with me") with a bit of childlike anxiety in your voice.
Give the woman's response ("The serpent tricked me into it, so I ate it") in a tentative tone of voice.

Read the punishment given by the Lord to the serpent, beginning with the words "Because you have done this" in a stern, firm tone of voice.

READING I   Today we celebrate Mary's preservation from original sin from the moment of her conception. This doctrine developed over time in the Church and was proclaimed infallibly by Pope Pius IX in 1854 after much consultation with bishops and theologians.

Mary stands in stark contrast to Adam and Eve in the story from Genesis. While Adam tried to blame Eve for his wrongdoing and Eve tried to blame her poor choice on the serpent, Mary chose to say "yes" to God's will. In so doing, she became the "new Eve," the Mother of God, and the Mother of the Church. Through Mary, the "new mother of all the living," the possibility of an intimate relationship with God through Christ is offered to all. She helped changed the course of history by choosing life (God) and not sin as Eve had done.

What a choice to celebrate in this Advent season! Mary's choice, which was the opposite of Eve's, gave hope that the Savior indeed would come. Her choice continues to give hope that we can be like her, and not like Eve, in choosing to give birth to God in our own lives. Through the intercession of Mary, may we make this choice as Christmas approaches. With God's help and our cooperation, enmity will be overcome. Proclaim this reading with the Christian hope that, though we are sinful like Adam and Eve, sin no longer has the last word. Life in Christ, whose birth was made possible by Mary's obedience, does.

enmity = EN-mih=tee

Pause before the concluding verse that begins "The man called his wife Eve." Read it as the conclusion of the narrative, but emphasize the words "mother of all the living." The last line is not one of total despair.

> I will put **enmity** between **you** and the **woman**,
>   and between **your** offspring and **hers**;
> **he** will strike at your **head**,
>   while **you** strike at his **heel**."

The man called his wife **Eve**,
    because she became the **mother** of **all** the **living**.

READING II Ephesians 1:3–6, 11–12

A reading from the Letter of Saint Paul to the Ephesians

Brothers and sisters:
Blessed be the **God** and **Father** of our **Lord** Jesus **Christ**,
    who has **blessed** us in **Christ**
    with **every** spiritual blessing in the **heavens**,
    as he **chose us** in him, before the foundation of the world,
    to be **holy** and without **blemish** before him.
In **love** he destined us for **adoption** to himself
        through Jesus **Christ**,
    in accord with the **favor** of his **will**,
    for the **praise** of the **glory** of his **grace**
    that he granted **us** in the **beloved**.

In **him** we were also **chosen**,
    destined in accord with the **purpose** of the One
    who accomplishes **all** things according to the intention
        of his **will**,
    so that we might **exist** for the praise of his **glory**,
    we who **first hoped** in **Christ**.

Proclaim the line "Blessed be . . ." with profound joy and praise. Raise your voice a bit. Pause slightly after the words "Jesus Christ." Let wonder and awe be heard in your voice until the sentence concludes "without blemish before him." Pause after this line.
Pause slightly after the words "In love." Lower the tone of your voice as you recount what God has done: "he destined us for adoption." Pause at the end of this sentence before beginning the next section.
Pause slightly again after the words "In him."

Make the tone of your voice for the last phrases match the tone of praise with which you started.

READING II This reading is from the great blessing at the beginning of the letter of Saint Paul to the Ephesians. Praise, wonder, awe, gratitude, and joy come through these words. The blessing begins with a formula known from the Old Testament and common in Jewish and early Christian prayers: "Blessed be . . . ." The author then explains why God is blessed and to be praised.

God is to be blessed and praised because of his plan to form a new people, made up of both Jew and Gentile. This people, the body of the Church, will have Christ for its head and Savior (see Ephesians 5:22). In God's plan, Mary played an indispensable role. Through her openness to the working of God's grace in her life, Mary gave birth to the Son of God, the Savior of the world, the head of the Church.

The use of the word "beloved" in verse six is a strong baptismal reference and is connected to the Marcan account of the Baptism of Jesus in which the voice from the heavens addresses Jesus as his "beloved Son" (Mark 1:11). Through Baptism we are brought into the visible communion of persons under the headship of Christ. Baptism also includes an element of forgiveness of sins. Incorporation into the visible communion of persons and the forgiveness of sins are both ways in which the divine plan for all to be in union with God is realized. Be grateful to God for his plan of salvation in Christ and for Mary's role in leading you and others into the body of the Church through the sacrament of Baptism. This will help you to offer this reading as the great blessing that the author intended it to be.

GOSPEL Luke 1:26–38

A reading from the holy Gospel according to Luke

The angel **Gabriel** was sent from **God**
　　to a town of **Galilee** called **Nazareth**,
　　to a virgin betrothed to a man named **Joseph**,
　　of the house of David,
　　and the virgin's name was **Mary**.
And coming to her, he said,
　　"**Hail**, full of **grace**! The **Lord** is with you."
But she was greatly **troubled** at what was said
　　and **pondered** what sort of greeting this might be.
Then the angel said to her,
　　"Do not be **afraid**, **Mary**,
　　for you have found **favor** with God.
Behold, you will conceive in your womb and bear a **son**,
　　and you shall **name** him **Jesus**.
He will be **great** and will be called **Son** of the **Most High**,
　　and the Lord God will give him the **throne** of **David** his
　　　　father,
　　and he will **rule** over the house of **Jacob forever**,
　　and of his Kingdom there will be **no end**."
But **Mary** said to the **angel**,
　　"How can this **be**,
　　since I have **no** relations with a **man**?"
And the angel said to her in reply,
　　"The **Holy Spirit** will come upon you,
　　and the **power** of the Most **High** will **overshadow** you.
Therefore the **child** to be **born**
　　will be called **holy**, the Son of **God**.

Slow down and look up as you speak Mary's name.

The angel Gabriel's response to Mary's perceived anxiety is calming. Reflect this by speaking the angel's words ("Do not be afraid, Mary") in a reassuring voice.

Slow down again as you speak Jesus' name. In Hebrew, Jesus means "God saves."

Let the ordinariness of Mary's question be heard in your voice by asking the question "How can this be, since I have no relations with a man?" in a reserved manner. Mary is profoundly human in her confusion in the dialogue with the angel.

GOSPEL ┃ In today's Gospel, we hear the Lucan account of the annunciation of the birth of Jesus to Mary. Often we focus on the greatness of Mary's "yes" to do the will of God and rightly honor her for that choice that we are to emulate today. However, Mary's "yes" is not an end in itself; it is only a beginning. It paves the way for God to be active in history in a new way.

The solemnity of the Immaculate Conception celebrates Mary's conception in the womb of her mother, Saint Ann, *not*

Jesus' conception in Mary's womb. Yet we hear the Lucan account of the annunciation of Jesus' birth on this solemnity not only in order to show how God is present from the very beginning of life, but also to emphasize the intimate, unique relationship between Mary and Jesus.

The intimacy of the relationship that was to be between Mary and Jesus comes through in the details provided by Luke in this Gospel. The Gospel according to Luke is one in which details, especially names, are important. Many of the details in the annunciation of the birth of Jesus parallel

Luke's account of the annunciation of the birth John the Baptist in 1:5–25 (for example, the angel came to Zechariah/Mary; Zechariah was startled/Mary was startled; the angel's message to both was not to be afraid; Elizabeth and Mary both questioned the angel). In the end, the compositional details are meant to convey the fact that God's grace is present and active everywhere, in all people, no matter how significant or insignificant they might be. The names of Joseph, Mary, and Jesus in this Gospel are important. Joseph means

And **behold**, **Elizabeth**, your relative,
    has **also** conceived a son in her old age,
    and this is the **sixth** month for her who was called **barren**;
    for **nothing** will be **impossible** for **God**."
Mary said, "**Behold**, I am the **handmaid** of the Lord.
May it be **done** to me according to your **word**."
Then the angel **departed** from her.

Pause before your give the concluding line ("Then the angel departed from her"). The angel departing does not signify an end, but rather a beginning that will culminate in the Savior's birth, death, and Resurrection. Salvation history will be forever changed. Thus, do not lower your voice on this line. Read it in a clear tone of voice so it does not get lost.

"May Yahweh add," Mary means "excellence," and Jesus means "God saves."

Whether Mary understood that she was to give birth to the divine Son, the second person of the Trinity, is not addressed by Luke in this passage. The Gospel itself was written approximately 80–90 AD and the author's main point in writing was to present how salvation was present "today" in the person of Jesus, the Spirit-filled Savior of the world. From the moment of conception, Luke has the Holy Spirit present. It was by the creative work of the Spirit that Mary conceived the child who was destined to be the Son of God and whom some three centuries later would be understood as the second person of the Trinity in the Nicene Creed.

Celebrating the solemnity of the Immaculate Conception during the season of Advent serves to focus us on how—through the Holy Spirit—God has always been present in human history. In a particular way, through the conception, birth, and life of Mary, the mother of Jesus and the Mother of the Church, we see how God's plan of salvation continued to unfold.

As we prepare to celebrate the birth of the Savior at Christmas, let this Gospel remind us of how God's grace is available to human persons, waiting for us to respond as Mary did. While we will not give birth to the Savior in history as Mary did, through our lives we too are called to make Christ present to others.

3RD SUNDAY OF ADVENT

Lectionary #8

READING I   Isaiah 61:1–2a, 10–11

Isaiah = ī-ZAY-uh

In the Gospel according to Luke, Jesus proclaims the words "The spirit of the Lord God is upon me" to announce a "year of favor from the Lord and a day of vindication by our God" in the synagogue at the beginning of his public ministry. Mention of the "spirit" points to God's marvelous works.

Pause before the new section begins ("I rejoice heartily"). Let your voice be filled with joy and happiness as you proclaim the prophet's words.

As you deliver the phrase about "justice and praise," let your voice exude the confidence that God will bring about this joyful reality.

A reading from the Book of the Prophet Isaiah

The **spirit** of the Lord GOD is upon me,
   because the LORD has **anointed** me;
he has sent me to bring glad **tidings** to the **poor**,
   to **heal** the **brokenhearted**,
to proclaim **liberty** to the **captives**
   and **release** to the **prisoners**,
to announce a year of **favor** from the LORD
   and a day of **vindication** by our **God**.

I rejoice **heartily** in the LORD,
   in my **God** is the joy of my **soul**;
for he has **clothed** me with a robe of **salvation**
   and **wrapped** me in a mantle of **justice**,
like a **bridegroom** adorned with a **diadem**,
   like a **bride** bedecked with her **jewels**.
As the **earth** brings forth its **plants**,
   and a **garden** makes its **growth** spring up,
so will the Lord GOD make **justice** and **praise**
   spring **up** before all the **nations**.

READING I How often do we take time to rejoice in God and to celebrate with joy all that God has done for us? The Third Sunday of Advent is traditionally known as Gaudete Sunday (*gaudete* means "rejoice" in Latin). On this Sunday we pause to mark the midpoint of our Advent journey. We are given the time to "rejoice heartily in the Lord" and to look forward to all the ways in which the Lord will "make justice and praise spring up" in the future.

The four verses you will proclaim are the beginning and the end of a poem from Isaiah 61. Familiarize yourself with the entire poem. This will help you to understand the context for the joy that abounds in the words and images you are tasked with reading. Observe also that Jesus quoted the words from Isaiah 61:1–2 in the synagogue as he began his public ministry in the Gospel according to Luke.

At the time of the composition of this passage from Isaiah, a new Jerusalem was arising from the ruins of her fall in 587 BC. In this poem, the prophet identifies himself with Jerusalem and speaks for her in the final two verses. His joy is that of Jerusalem whom the Lord will save. Jerusalem will be restored. Just as the earth brings forth life and gardens grow, so Jerusalem will come to life again. Her hope is in a messiah who will deliver salvation to her. This messiah will come from the earth and will be one with human beings. It is in the second half of the final verse ("so will the Lord God make justice and praise spring up before all the nations") that the prophet reminds us that God is the source of any and all salvation that comes.

Thessalonians = thes-uh-LOH-nee-unz

Match the tone of your voice to each specific command: "Rejoice," "pray," and "give thanks." Pause after the words "for you in Christ Jesus" before you begin the negative commands. Deliver the negative commands ("Do not . . .") with insistence in your voice.

Pause before you pray this prayer for the assembly before you, taking time to sense God's presence among you.

READING II   1 Thessalonians 5:16–24

A reading from the first Letter of Saint Paul to the Thessalonians

Brothers and sisters:
Rejoice **always**. Pray without **ceasing**.
In **all** circumstances give **thanks**,
    for this is the will of **God** for you in Christ **Jesus**.
Do not **quench** the Spirit.
Do not **despise** prophetic **utterances**.
Test everything; **retain** what is **good**.
Refrain from every kind of **evil**.

May the God of **peace** make you **perfectly** holy
    and may you **entirely**, **spirit**, **soul** and **body**,
    be preserved **blameless** for the coming of our Lord Jesus **Christ**.
The one who **calls** you is **faithful**,
    and he will also **accomplish** it.

The Israelites understood that the salvation God would bring on "the day of vindication" *(nāqām)* would be total. Jerusalem would be wholly repaired—physically, individually, corporately, and spiritually. This is the marvelous work of God that the presence of the Spirit working in the messiah would bring about.

As our focus in Advent turns more toward waiting to remember and celebrate the Messiah's coming in history in the person of Jesus Christ, seize the opportunity you have as a minister of the word this

Sunday to enable your community to rejoice—to celebrate that the spirit of the Lord is upon each and every one of them. They are now to continue the mission of the Messiah who came as Lord and Savior. The Lord works through you in your ministry of reader to bring rejoicing to your community. Let this poem from Isaiah also remind you that just as God is the source of life and messianic glory, God is also the source of your ministry.

READING II Paul loved the community of Christians at Thessalonica. It was one of the first communities he founded. However, this community—as ours today—was not without its troubles. Yet Paul urged the people to rejoice always and pray without ceasing even in the midst of their difficulties. They were to rejoice because the Lord was going to come again.

Christians at Thessalonica struggled with questions about the date for the *parousia* and what happened to loved ones

GOSPEL   John 1:6–8, 19–28

A reading from the holy Gospel according to John

A man named **John** was sent from **God**.
He came for **testimony**, to testify to the **light**,
    so that all might **believe** through him.
He was **not** the light,
    but came to **testify** to the light.

And **this** is the testimony of John.
When the Jews from Jerusalem sent **priests** and **Levites** to him
    to ask him, "Who **are** you?"
    he **admitted** and did not **deny** it,
    but admitted, "I am **not** the Christ."
So they asked him,
    "What **are** you then? Are you **Elijah**?"
And he said, "I am **not**."
"Are you the **Prophet**?"
He answered, "**No**."
So they said to him,
    "Who **are** you, so we can give an **answer** to those who **sent** us?
What do you have to **say** for yourself?"

Emphasize that John was "sent from God." This gives credibility and importance to John's role.

Levites = LEE-vits

The phrase "the Jews" is used to refer primarily to the leadership of the Jewish community in Jerusalem. In the dialogue that follows, let tension be heard in your voice.

Note the repetition of the words "I am not." State both of John the Baptist's replies to the questions of the priests and Levites emphatically, and the second one more emphatically than the first. The question posed to John is the same one asked of Jesus two other times in the Gospel according to John: 8:25 and 21:12.

after they died. Paul urged the community neither to "quench the Spirit" nor to "despise prophetic utterances." Your task as a minister of the word is to help the assembly before you realize that Paul's instructions are offered to them today, and fittingly so.

As we move toward Christmas when we remember Jesus' coming in the past and look forward to his coming again, we also celebrate his present coming in us. This latter coming is one that is sometimes neglected in our church communities and one of the places where we would do well to contemplate Paul's instructions about

not quenching the Spirit and despising prophetic utterances. Always, though, we must not forget Paul's call to test everything and only retain what is good.

On this Gaudete Sunday, rejoice and be thankful for the ways your community already proclaims the presence of the Lord in its midst. Realize also the ways in which the community before you needs to work at following the commands you impart and offer Paul's prayer for them. Let the assembly hear rejoicing and confidence in your

voice as you let them know God is faithful and is with them this Advent as they approach Christmas trying to be the best Christians they can be.

GOSPEL   Last Sunday we were introduced to John the Baptist as a messenger who was preparing the way of the Lord. The brief description of the Baptist and his ministry of baptizing with water offered in the Gospel according to Mark left us with a clear message: the one whose way the Baptist was preparing

John gives another clear admission in his response to the Pharisees' question. Fill your voice with both the certainty of faith and humility (John understood he was not the Messiah, and we today understand we are not modern-day messiahs).

Bethany = BETH-uh-nee

He said:
"I am *the **voice** of one crying out in the **desert**,*
*'Make **straight** the way of the **LORD**,'*
as Isaiah the **prophet** said."
Some **Pharisees** were **also** sent.
They asked him,
"Why then do you **baptize**
if you are not the **Christ** or **Elijah** or the **Prophet**?"
John **answered** them,
"**I** baptize with **water**;
but there is one **among** you whom you do not **recognize**,
the one who is coming **after** me,
whose **sandal** strap I am not worthy to **untie**."
This happened in **Bethany** across the **Jordan**,
where John was **baptizing**.

was mightier than him. On this Third Sunday of Advent, we hear the description of John the Baptist from the Gospel according to John. In years when the Lectionary cycle of readings is A or C, the Gospel on the Third Sunday of Advent is a continuation from the Second Sunday. Presumably because of the brevity of Mark's account of the Baptist, it was necessary to draw from the Gospel according to John for this Third Sunday.

How appropriate is John the Baptist's testimony about the light for Gaudete Sunday! The Light, the Word made flesh who was God in the Gospel according to

John, is our reason to rejoice! We do not rejoice in John the Baptist as our savior, though we reverence the ministry he carried out and the testimony he gave. John the Baptist is himself our example as he is unambiguous about where he stands in relation to the Light even in the face of confrontation from the priests and Levites sent on behalf of the Jewish leaders (the Jews from Jerusalem).

When asked to name a symbol of Advent and Christmas used in worship or in our homes, most of us would probably say "light" and think of the candles on the

Advent wreath, the indoor Christmas lights hung on our tree, or the outdoor lights that illuminate our homes. As you proclaim this Gospel, pray for yourself and your assembly that, in our service in the Church and in the world, we may give testimony to the true Light—always being as clear and unequivocal about our identity in relation to the Light as John the Baptist was about his. May the lights of our testimony brighten the way toward the celebration of the true Light of the World this Christmas.

4TH SUNDAY OF ADVENT

Lectionary #11

READING I 2 Samuel 7:1–5, 8b–12, 14a, 16

Samuel = SAM-yoo-ul

Second Samuel is one of the historical books, and readings from these books are often difficult for the assembly to understand. Make sure you understand who is speaking to whom so you can convey the story clearly to the assembly by the tone of your voice. You will be able to relate this clearly to the assembly by taking your time with the narrative lines that identify the speaker and not rushing through them. Then, after the narrative lines, pause slightly before stating the words of the one speaking.

A reading from the second Book of Samuel

When King **David** was settled in his **palace**,
    and the LORD had given him **rest** from his **enemies** on
        every **side**,
    he said to **Nathan** the **prophet**,
    "Here **I** am living in a house of **cedar**,
    while the ark of **God** dwells in a **tent**!"
Nathan answered the king,
    "Go, do **whatever** you have in mind,
    for the LORD is with you."
But that night the LORD **spoke** to Nathan and said:
    "**Go**, tell my servant **David**, '**Thus** says the LORD:
    Should **you** build **me** a house to dwell in?

" 'It was **I** who took you from the **pasture**
    and from the care of the **flock**
    to be **commander** of my people **Israel**.
I have **been** with you **wherever** you went,
    and I have destroyed all your **enemies** before you.

READING I Even from this First Reading from the second book of Samuel, we can sense the nearness of celebration of the Nativity of the Lord. The Lord's promise that a messiah will be raised from the lineage of David is reflected in this passage. For Christians, this promise is fulfilled in the person of Jesus of Nazareth, who came at a particular time and in a particular place. Through this historical figure, whom Christians believe to be the Son of God, the Davidic dynasty indeed lives on forever.

In this passage, taken from the oracle (or prophecy) of Nathan (2 Samuel 7:1–29), King David is concerned that the ark of God dwelled only in a tent while his palace was a house. David's vision, however, was limited. In the word of the Lord spoken through Nathan, we hear that the Lord's dwelling place is neither confined to the ark of the covenant nor to any palace a king might build him. King David is not to build him a dwelling place, because the Lord himself will make David's house a dynasty, a perpetual dwelling place for him. The Lord will dwell within a people,

the people of Israel, and in their descendents. As Christians, our identity is forever linked to this Chosen People. The Messiah, the Son of God, has come down to us through David, whose kingdom continues both in the Jews and in the Christian Church today.

The lengthy quote from "It was I who took you from the pasture" through the end of the reading is from the Lord. Nathan is told by the Lord to tell David these words. The words are meant to reassure David that the Lord has always been with him.

And I will make you **famous** like the **great** ones of the **earth**.
I will fix a place for my people **Israel**;
   I will **plant** them so that they may **dwell** in their place
   without further **disturbance**.
Neither shall the **wicked** continue to **afflict** them as they did
     of **old**,
   since the time I first appointed **judges** over my people Israel.
I will give you **rest** from all your enemies.
The LORD **also** reveals to you
   that **he** will establish a **house** for you.
And when your **time** comes and you rest with your **ancestors**,
   I will raise up your **heir** after you, sprung from your **loins**,
   and I will make his kingdom **firm**.
I will be a **father** to him,
   and he shall be a **son** to me.
Your **house** and your **kingdom** shall endure **forever** before me;
   your **throne** shall stand firm **forever**.' "

The climax of the Lord's promise begins with the words "And when your time comes." Build in confidence and hope as you come to the final line of the promise: "your throne shall stand firm forever." The Lord extends this same promise to us today.

And, just as important, the message of the Lord that Nathan conveys to David includes a promise, which is summarized in the final verse: "Your house and your kingdom shall be made sure forever before me; your throne, David, shall be established forever."

Your task as the one who proclaims this reading is to let the assembly know that the kingdom of the Lord continues on in their presence as the Church in the world today and in the presence of our Jewish brothers and sisters. Yes, the Lord resides in the ark of the covenant and in tabernacles in our synagogues and churches, but the Lord also resides in the hearts of his chosen people. At Christmas, we celebrate this along with remembering Jesus' birth and looking forward to his coming at the end of time.

READING II At first glance, it might not be obvious why this reading from the end of the letter of Saint Paul to the Romans is read on the Fourth Sunday of Advent. A closer look reveals a major theme of Paul in Romans is found in these two short verses. God's promise of salvation through Jesus Christ is available to all people, Jew and Gentile alike. All Advent prepares us to celebrate this truth.

These concluding verses from Paul's letter are both a doxology and a benediction offered in praise and blessing of God. According to custom, Paul ends his letter thanking specific people by sending his greetings to them. Paul then praises and blesses God, who is the giver of all gifts and ministries. Most importantly, praise is due to God because what was revealed by the prophets has been fulfilled in Jesus Christ.

READING II   Romans 16:25–27

A reading from the Letter of Saint Paul to the Romans

Brothers and sisters:
To him who can **strengthen** you,
    according to my **gospel** and the proclamation of Jesus **Christ**,
    according to the revelation of the **mystery** kept **secret**
      for long ages
    but now **manifested** through the prophetic **writings** and,
    according to the **command** of the eternal **God**,
    made known to all nations to bring about the **obedience**
      of **faith**,
to the only **wise** God, through Jesus **Christ**
be **glory** forever and **ever. Amen.**

Romans = ROH-munz

Look up at the assembly as you proclaim the opening address and pause significantly after it. You want to make sure you have the assembly's attention because the reading is only one sentence.
The words of the doxology refer to God.

Increase the energy and volume in your tone as you build to the climax of the doxology ("be glory forever and ever"). Don't be surprised if people in the assembly respond "Amen" with you!

Paul is concerned throughout this letter—and the final verses are no exception—that the Church at Rome understands the connection between the proclamation of Jesus Christ and the message of the prophets in the Old Testament.

Practice this passage carefully. Its main point is praise of God, though it is basically one long sentence. Everything between the words "To him who can strengthen you" and "be glory forever and ever" is parenthetical. You are giving glory to God and recounting reasons why God deserves

praise. For Paul—and for us—this praise is due because God's saving power has been revealed to all nations in Jesus Christ. If you think of proclaiming these verses as a prayer of praise, then the appropriate pauses will come more naturally.

GOSPEL   Luke's narrative of the conception of Jesus is the same Gospel we heard on the solemnity of the Immaculate Conception (see that commentary for more background). Its message to us on the Fourth Sunday of Advent

emphasizes how close we are to Christmas. In fact, if we were to ask Mass-goers to name an Advent reading or Gospel, this is the one they would probably mention most frequently.

The last weeks of Advent center on Jesus' coming in the past as one of us. The two previous weeks of Advent we have come to know John the Baptist and his ministry in relation to the one who was coming after him. Now, this last Sunday of Advent, we root ourselves even more

Offer this Gospel to the assembly with gentleness and with a careful, reserved pace. The annunciation of the birth of Jesus is a cherished narrative in the Catholic tradition.

The dialogue between Gabriel and Mary is intimate and personal. Reflect this in your tone of voice. Speak the words of dialogue as if you were talking one to one with another person and not addressing an entire assembly.

The angel Gabriel describes who Mary's son will be with titles that reference his salvific role ("Jesus," "Son of the Most High"). When speaking the angel's words, place solemnity and honor for whom Mary's child will be in your voice.

GOSPEL   Luke 1:26–38

A reading from the holy Gospel according to Luke

The angel **Gabriel** was sent from God
  to a town of **Galilee** called **Nazareth**,
  to a **virgin** betrothed to a man named **Joseph**,
  of the house of **David**,
  and the **virgin's** name was **Mary**.
And coming to her, he said,
  "**Hail**, full of **grace**! The **Lord** is with you."
But she was greatly **troubled** at what was said
  and **pondered** what sort of **greeting** this might be.
Then the angel said to her,
  "Do not be **afraid**, Mary,
  for you have found **favor** with God.

"**Behold**, you will **conceive** in your womb and bear a **son**,
  and you shall name him **Jesus**.
He will be **great** and will be called Son of the Most **High**,
  and the Lord God will give him the **throne** of David his **father**,
  and he will **rule** over the house of Jacob **forever**,
  and of his **kingdom** there will be no **end**."
But Mary said to the angel,
  "How can this **be**,
  since I have no **relations** with a man?"
And the angel said to her in **reply**,
  "The Holy **Spirit** will come **upon** you,
  and the power of the Most **High** will **overshadow** you.

deeply in history. The house and the kingdom promised to David in the today's First Reading from 2 Samuel will endure forever because the person of Jesus, conceived in the womb of Mary, is the Messiah.

Luke's Gospel is the only one that includes an annunciation narrative of the birth of Jesus. The Lucan account of the annunciation of Jesus' birth closely parallels the Gospel's account of the annunciation of the birth of John the Baptist (Luke 1:5–25), which is also only contained in the Third Gospel. One of the similarities

between these narratives is that an intimate conversation takes place in both. In the annunciation of the birth of John the Baptist, the angel of the Lord (Gabriel) appeared to Zechariah, calming his fear and imparting to him the news that in his old age and that of his wife, Elizabeth, they would be the parents of John, a man who would prepare a people for the Lord (see Luke 1:17). In today's Gospel, the largest section of the narrative is the conversation between Gabriel and Mary. The angel calms Mary's fear as the angel attempted

to soothe Zechariah's fear. Mary, like Zechariah, questions the angel's announcement of the birth of a child to her, but unlike Zechariah she opens herself to the Spirit of God working in her to give birth to Jesus.

In both annunciation narratives, Luke tells us that the Spirit is present from conception. In the case of John the Baptist, the angel informs Zechariah that John "will be filled with the holy Spirit even in his mother's womb" (Luke 1:15) and in the case of Jesus the angel responds to Mary's

Therefore the **child** to be born
   will be called **holy**, the Son of **God**.
   And **behold**, Elizabeth, your relative,
   has **also** conceived a son in her old **age**,
   and this is the sixth month for her who was called **barren**;
   for **nothing** will be impossible for **God**."
Mary said, "**Behold**, I am the **handmaid** of the Lord.
May it be **done** to me according to your word."
Then the angel **departed** from her.

Communicate Mary's fiat ("Behold, I am the handmaid of the Lord") with the fledgling trust and openness to God that she must have had. Mary has made a decision to do God's will. Let the release and freedom that comes from making a decision be heard in your voice. Pause before the words "Then the angel . . . ."

question ("How can this be, since I have no relations with a man?") that "the Holy Spirit will come upon you, and the power of the Most High will overshadow you" (verse 35). Through the working of the Holy Spirit in the intimate and personal encounter with Mary, "the time of the fulfillment of God's promises and preparations" began (*Catechism of the Catholic Church* [CCC], #484). The Holy Spirit came upon her and was with Jesus, God's Son, from the moment of his conception. We believe as Catholics that "the mission of the Holy Spirit is always conjoined and ordered to that of the Son" (CCC, #485).

On this Fourth Sunday of Advent, the proclamation of this Gospel bids us remember what the working of the Spirit in the lives of Mary and Jesus signified in history. As a minister of the Gospel, the Spirit also works in your life. And the Spirit continues to work in the lives of those in the assembly gathered to worship. The more we assist each other in affirming this, the more we, like Mary, will be able to open ourselves to Jesus' presence with and in us now and at his coming again in glory.

Before this Christmas comes, we have four more days to follow Mary's example and say, "Behold, I am the handmaid of the Lord. May it be done to me according to your word."

NATIVITY OF THE LORD: VIGIL

Lectionary #13

Isaiah = ī-ZAY-uh

As the prophet will be neither silent nor quiet, let your voice too be neither silent nor quiet; let it come across with confidence, loud and clear, as you state the line "For Zion's sake I will not be silent."

diadem = DĪ-uh-dem

Make the contrast clear between the names "Forsaken" and "Desolate" and "My Delight" and "Espoused."

Pause slightly before the verses "For the Lord delights in you . . . so shall your God rejoice in you." They are full of beautiful wedding imagery. Let the refrain of the Responsorial Psalm that follows this reading give you the sense of intimate joy and overwhelming gratitude with which this last section needs to be read. The refrain is from Psalm 89: "For ever I will sing the goodness of the Lord."

READING I   Isaiah 62:1–5

A reading from the Book of the Prophet Isaiah

For **Zion's** sake I will **not** be silent,
    for **Jerusalem's** sake I will **not** be quiet,
until her **vindication** shines forth like the dawn
    and her **victory** like a burning **torch**.

Nations shall **behold** your vindication,
    and **all** the kings your **glory**;
you shall be called by a **new** name
    pronounced by the mouth of the LORD.
You shall be a **glorious crown** in the hand of the LORD,
    a royal **diadem** held by your **God**.
No **more** shall people call you "**Forsaken**,"
    or your land "**Desolate**,"
but you shall be called "My **Delight**,"
    and your land "**Espoused**."
For the LORD **delights** in you
    and makes your land his **spouse**.
As a **young man** marries a **virgin**,
    your **Builder** shall marry **you**;
and as a **bridegroom** rejoices in his **bride**
    so shall **your** God rejoice in you.

READING I | Jerusalem's restoration and the return of the Hebrew people from exile are meant for all to see. Our path to glory begins with the birth of Jesus, the one we call "Messiah." It is the beginning of an intimate relationship with God in Jesus through the Church.

The contrast between the old and new names testifies to the significance and depth of what is transpiring in the relationship between God, Jerusalem, and its people. Names like "Forsaken" and "My Delight" are present elsewhere in Israelite history (1 Kings 22:42; 2 Kings 21:1). In the past Israel and her people had been associated with fertility cults; the name "Espoused" means Israel has been forgiven.

These are not minor changes in the relationship between God and Israel; they are life-altering. In human history, what transpired with the birth of the Messiah gave witness to how much God wants to bring the world close. The entire song from which these five verses come is found in Isaiah 62:1–12. The last two verses are the reading for the Mass at Dawn on Christmas (see that commentary for more insights into the passage). In fact, these latter two verses are the climax of the song. This is the conclusion you do not read, and therefore the assembly does not hear it at the Christmas Vigil Mass.

The spousal imagery in verse five ("As a young man marries a virgin, your Builder shall marry you . . .") occurs in other places in Isaiah (Isaiah 49:14; 50:1). Yet what is new in this instance is that all of Israel will be brought back to that time when she was the virgin spouse of the Lord.

A reading from the Acts of the Apostles

When **Paul** reached **Antioch** in Pisidia and entered
 the **synagogue,**
 he **stood** up, **motioned** with his hand, and **said,**
 "Fellow **Israelites** and you others who are God-fearing, **listen.**
The God of this people **Israel** chose our ancestors
 and exalted the people during their **sojourn**
 in the land of **Egypt.**
With **uplifted** arm he **led** them out of it.
Then he removed **Saul** and raised up **David** as king;
 of him he **testified,**
 'I have found **David,** son of **Jesse,** a man after my own **heart;**
 he will carry out my **every** wish.'
From this man's **descendants** God, according to his promise,
 has brought to Israel a **savior, Jesus.**
John heralded his coming by proclaiming a **baptism** of **repentance**
 to all the people of **Israel;**
 and as John was completing his course, he would say,
 '**What** do you suppose that I **am?** I am **not** he.
Behold, one is coming **after** me;
 I am not **worthy** to unfasten the **sandals** of his **feet.'"**

Antioch = AN-tee-ahk
Pisidia = pih-SID-ee-uh

Pause noticeably after "said," so as to make it obvious that what follows is Paul's speech. Paul is proud of the history of the Israelites. Convey his pride in the strength of your voice as you proclaim the words "The God of this people Israel chose our ancestors . . . led them out of it."

Speak Jesus' name clearly and with reverence in the line "has brought to Israel a savior" as we celebrate the Vigil of Christmas.

We heard John's words ("Behold, one is coming after me; I am not worthy to unfasten the sandals of his feet") during Advent. Proclaim them again with humbleness. As John knew his place, recognize your role to proclaim the coming of Jesus with humility.

The Church has been understood for centuries as the bride of Christ, with Christ as her bridegroom. It is an image through which the unity of Christ and the Church is expressed. This image conveys the deep, personal relationship between Christ and the Church, as well as the distinction between Christ and the Church (*Catechism of the Catholic Church,* #796).

READING II It seems strange to be proclaiming a passage from the Acts of the Apostles at the Christmas Vigil liturgy because we usually hear from Acts. This reading in particular focuses on the Jewish heritage of our Christian belief in Jesus as the Savior. The text is a few verses from Paul's sermon in the Jewish synagogue at Antioch in Pisidia, the administrative center for the Roman province of Galatia, and is found in the section of the Acts that narrates the extension of Paul's mission beyond the Jerusalem community.

Look at the entire speech Paul gave (Acts 13:16–41). You will find that the verses are from a section that gives more detail than what we have here. The missionary discourse is Paul's first in Acts and meant to persuade the Jewish audience that God has sent Israel a savior in the person of Jesus. Masterfully crafted, the discourse shows Paul reverencing the Jews as "fellow Israelites," a title that not only shows his oneness with them (as Paul is a Jew), but also honors the history of salvation already begun in the Chosen People. The section of the speech after these verses shows how Jesus is the fulfillment

GOSPEL Matthew 1:1–25

Practice the names so that the assembly can sense the importance of history. Read the genealogy with care as if it were that of your own family or one of your parishioners. Pace yourself, not rushing, but not reading too slowly either.

A reading from the holy Gospel according to Matthew

The book of the **genealogy** of Jesus **Christ**,
    the son of **David**, the son of **Abraham**.

Abraham became the father of **Isaac**,
    Isaac the father of **Jacob**,
    Jacob the father of **Judah** and his brothers.
Judah became the father of **Perez** and **Zerah**,
    whose **mother** was **Tamar**.
Perez became the father of **Hezron**,
    Hezron the father of **Ram**,
    Ram the father of **Amminadab**.
Amminadab became the father of **Nahshon**,
    Nahshon the father of **Salmon**,
    Salmon the father of **Boaz**,
    whose **mother** was **Rahab**.
Boaz became the father of **Obed**,
    whose **mother** was **Ruth**.
Obed became the father of **Jesse**,
    Jesse the father of **David** the king.

David became the father of **Solomon**,
    whose mother had been the **wife** of **Uriah**.
Solomon became the father of **Rehoboam**,
    Rehoboam the father of **Abijah**,
    Abijah the father of **Asaph**.
Asaph became the father of **Jehoshaphat**,
    Jehoshaphat the father of **Joram**,
    Joram the father of **Uzziah**.

Perez = PAIR-ez

Tamar = TAY-mahr

Hezron = Hez-ruhn

Ram = ram

Amminadab = uh-MIN-uh-dab

Nahshon = NAH-shuhn

Salmon = SAL-muhn

Boaz = BOH-az

Rahab = RAY-hab

Obed = OH-bed

Uriah = yoo-RĪ-uh

Rehoboam = ree-huh-BOH-uhm

Abijah = uh-BĪ-juh

Asaph = AY-saf

Jehoshaphat = jeh-HOH-shuh-fat

Joram = JOHR-uhm

Uzziah = uh-ZĪ-uh

of the promise to the Hebrew people, and the conclusion calls the people in the synagogue to faith, recounting all that God has done through the death and Resurrection of Jesus.

For Christians, salvation history can neither be understood apart from the history of the Chosen People of Israel nor apart from the birth, life, death, and Resurrection of Jesus. Although Jews do not profess faith in Jesus as their Messiah, this passage enables us to reflect on the intimate faith connection we have with Jews. God was active in history and in the lives of

people before the birth of the Messiah and God is still active in the lives of those who do not profess Jesus as the Messiah.

We Christians have an obligation, like Paul, to evangelize and spread the Good News of salvation. Paul taught Jews and Gentiles alike, affirming the presence of God in history before the coming of the Messiah and then sharing the joy of the union of the divine and human in Jesus Christ.

GOSPEL The genealogy of Jesus presents us with a core truth of our faith: Jesus Christ, Emmanuel—God with us—born of the Virgin Mary through the creative act of God, enters into human history, indeed the history of the world. Jesus is fully human and fully divine. Here, the author of Matthew offers us a similar theological truth as the author of Acts in this evening's Second Reading about God's presence in history: God works through human persons, men and women who sometimes have faith and sometimes do not.

Jotham = JOH-thuhm

Ahaz = AY-haz

Hezekiah = hez-eh-KĪ-uh

Manasseh = muh-NAS-uh

Amos = AY-m*s

Josiah = joh-SĪ-uh

Jechoniah = jek-oh-NĪ-uh

Shealtiel = shee-AL-tee-uhl

Zerubbabel = zuh-ROOB-uh-b*l

Abiud = uh-BĪ-uhd

Eliakim = ee-LĪ-uh-kim

Azor = AY-zohr

Zadok = ZAY-dok

Achim = AH-kim

Eliud = ee-LĪ-uhd

Eleazar = el-ee-AY-zer

Matthan = MATH-uhn

Take a deep, but inaudible, breath before the announcement of the birth of Jesus ("Of her was born Jesus who is called the Christ"). Read the announcement slowly and with solemnity.

Take another deep breath (though inaudible) after the phrase "fourteen generations," as you have finished the genealogy. The pause will also make apparent the beginning of a new section of the Gospel.

Uzziah became the father of **Jotham,**
    Jotham the father of **Ahaz,**
    Ahaz the father of **Hezekiah.**
Hezekiah became the father of **Manasseh,**
    Manasseh the father of **Amos,**
    Amos the father of **Josiah.**
Josiah became the father of **Jechoniah** and his brothers
    at the time of the **Babylonian exile.**

After the **Babylonian exile,**
    Jechoniah became the father of **Shealtiel,**
    Shealtiel the father of **Zerubbabel,**
    Zerubbabel the father of **Abiud.**
Abiud became the father of **Eliakim,**
    Eliakim the father of **Azor,**
    Azor the father of **Zadok.**
Zadok became the father of **Achim,**
    Achim the father of **Eliud,**
    Eliud the father of **Eleazar.**
Eleazar became the father of **Matthan,**
    Matthan the father of **Jacob,**
    Jacob the father of **Joseph,** the **husband** of **Mary.**
Of her was born **Jesus** who is called the **Christ.**

Thus the **total** number of generations
    from **Abraham** to **David**
    is **fourteen** generations;
    from **David** to the **Babylonian exile,**
    fourteen generations;
    from the **Babylonian exile** to the **Christ,**
    fourteen generations.

Although from God, it is into and also from the ordinariness of human life that Jesus comes. The genealogy is intentionally composed of three sections of 14 names: from Abraham to David; David to the Babylonian; and the exile to Jesus, who is called the Christ. Both men and women (Tamar, Rahab, Ruth, Bathsheba, and Mary) are included as those who were responsible for both good and evil. Most of us are familiar with the good reputations of Abraham, Isaac, and Jacob, but perhaps not as much with the less-than-stellar Tamar, who deceived her father-in-law Judah into an incestuous relationship, and Bathsheba, who was the wife of Uriah and committed adultery with David. The inclusion of Ruth shows that the ancestry of Jesus is not exclusively Jewish; Ruth was a Moabite who joined the Israelite community. All this is to affirm that Jesus came to save his people (for the author of Matthew, this includes Jews and Gentiles alike) from their sins. Jesus' people include those of every race, nation, culture, gender, age, and background. For Matthew, Jesus is the Messiah-King of Israel, the son of David, the son of Abraham, and the son of Mary.

After the genealogy, Matthew's focus on Joseph in the story of Jesus' birth provides us with a model of how we can share the Good News of Christmas with others. Joseph, like Mary in Luke's Gospel, listens to the voice of God in the angel and is obedient to God's will. He trusted that God would be with him as he took care of Mary. We can see Joseph's adherence to the will

Express the care and concern of Joseph for Mary as you read about his unwilling-ness to expose her to shame ("Joseph her husband, since he was a righteous man").

Emphasize the name "Jesus" and what it means by taking your time proclaiming the line "She will bear a son and you are to name him Jesus, because he will save his people from their sins." This is what Christmas is all about.

"When Joseph awoke, he did as the angel of the Lord had commanded him . . . he named him Jesus." These words describe Joseph's fiat, his own obedience to the will of God. Utter these narrative words with the placid-ness Joseph must have felt when he, like Mary, opened himself to doing the will of God.

Now **this** is how the **birth** of Jesus Christ came about.
When his mother **Mary** was betrothed to **Joseph**,
   but **before** they lived together,
   she was found with **child** through the Holy **Spirit**.
Joseph her **husband**, since he was a **righteous** man,
   yet unwilling to expose her to **shame**,
   decided to divorce her quietly.
Such was his intention when, **behold**,
   the **angel** of the Lord **appeared** to him in a **dream** and said,
   "**Joseph**, son of **David**,
   do **not** be afraid to take Mary your **wife** into your home.
For it is through the Holy **Spirit**
   that this child has been **conceived** in her.
She will bear a **son** and you are to name him **Jesus**,
   because he will save his **people** from their **sins**."
All this took place to **fulfill**
   what the **Lord** had said through the **prophet**:
     *Behold, the **virgin** shall **conceive** and bear a **son**,*
     *and they shall name him **Emmanuel**,*
   which means "**God** is **with** us."
When Joseph **awoke**,
   he did as the angel of the Lord had **commanded** him
   and took his wife into his home.
He had **no** relations with her until she bore a **son**,
   and he **named** him Jesus.

[Shorter: Matthew 1:18–25]

of God in the way he respected Mary's human dignity as created by God. In the lifetimes of Joseph and Mary, a betrothed Jewish woman who was unfaithful would be stoned as Jewish law dictated. But Joseph, despite thinking that Mary had not been loyal to him, chose to listen to God's will rather than bring shame upon her.

Offer the genealogy as a testimony to the magnificence of God choosing to be born among us, becoming human like us. Offer it also as a reminder that we are to live Christmas as Joseph did, by reverenc-ing the presence of Emmanuel in all those with whom we come in contact, whether they are intimate spouses, close friends, or merely acquaintances. Mary and Joseph exemplify what it means to trust that God is present at turning points in life's jour-ney. Like Mary and Joseph, may we trust that God is with us as we live Christmas in the ordinariness, messiness, and beauty of human life.

NATIVITY OF THE LORD: MIDNIGHT

Lectionary #14

Isaiah – ī-ZAY-uh

Express the lines in the first section "The people who walked in darkness have seen a great light" and "land of gloom a light has shone" with contentment. Relief from the darkness has come.

Pause before the section that begins "For the yoke that burdened them," which recounts the difficulties that the Israelites faced and that have now been resolved because the light has shone on them. Put a little tension in your voice as you recall the oppression the Israelites faced.

Midian = MID-ee-uhn

READING I   Isaiah 9:1–6

A reading from the Book of the Prophet Isaiah

The people who walked in **darkness**
    have seen a great **light**;
upon those who **dwelt** in the land of **gloom**
    a **light** has **shone**.
You have brought them **abundant** joy
    and great **rejoicing**,
as they **rejoice** before you as at the **harvest**,
    as people make **merry** when dividing spoils.
For the **yoke** that **burdened** them,
    the **pole** on their **shoulder**,
and the **rod** of their **taskmaster**
    you have **smashed**, as on the day of Midian.
For **every** boot that tramped in **battle**,
    every cloak rolled in **blood**,
    will be burned as **fuel** for **flames**.

READING I The term "oracle" is used to refer to prophetic statements that relate to a judgment or the future. An oracle is often preceded by the words "Thus says the Lord," a formula that indicates that what follows is a divine message communicated by a go-between such as a prophet. In its historical context this messianic oracle, today's First Reading, seems to suggest the triumph of light over darkness and gloom. The Israelites faced much darkness and gloom in their history. In this selection from Isaiah the yoke, pole, and rod are symbols of their oppression by the Assyrians. But for Isaiah, a prophet of hope, this oppression will be overcome. God will never abandon the Israelites even in their darkest moments. A child will be born who will have the characteristics such that he can be named Wonder-Counselor, God-Hero, Father-Forever, and Prince of Peace. This child will come from the line of David and so will continue the Davidic monarchy, another concrete way Isaiah shows that God is faithful to the Chosen People.

Outside of the birth narratives this is one of the most well-known scripture readings of Christmas. For Christians, the child in this hymn of faith is believed to be the Savior, Jesus. Jesus is the great light that has come once and for all to overturn the darkness and gloom of world history. No longer do we need to live in the hopelessness of oppression or the sadness of the gloom often evident in our world. Rather, the coming of the Messiah in Jesus offers Christians the opportunity to see that the course of history has been changed. We live in hope, at once already fulfilled and yet to come again.

For a **child** is **born** to us, a **son** is **given** us;
   upon his shoulder **dominion** rests.
They name him Wonder-**Counselor**, God-**Hero**,
   Father-**Forever**, Prince of **Peace**.
His dominion is **vast**
   and forever **peaceful**,
from David's **throne**, and over his **kingdom**,
   which he confirms and sustains
by **judgment** and **justice**,
   both now and **forever**.
The **zeal** of the LORD of **hosts** will **do** this!

Read each of the titles with different expression: 1) Wonder-Counselor with awe, 2) God-Hero with strength, 3) Father-Forever with confidence and assurance, and 4) Prince of Peace with gentleness. Pause after the last title. Convey the characteristics of the royal Messiah's dominion in the same way as you spoke the titles (although the structure is not exactly parallel): 1) vast with awe, 2) peaceful with gentleness, 3) confirms and sustains with confidence and assurance, and 4) judgment and justice with strength.

READING II   Titus 2:11–14

A reading from the Letter of Saint Paul to Titus

Beloved:
The **grace** of **God** has **appeared**, saving **all**
   and training us to reject **godless** ways and **worldly** desires
   and to live **temperately**, **justly**, and **devoutly** in this age,
   as we await the **blessed** hope,
   the **appearance** of the **glory** of our great **God**
   and savior Jesus **Christ**,
   who gave himself for us to **deliver** us from all **lawlessness**
   and to **cleanse** for himself a people as his own,
   eager to do what is **good**.

Titus = TĪ-tus

Proclaiming a one-sentence reading is difficult. Thinking more about the meaning of the sentence in terms of the past, present, and future will be more helpful than following the punctuation exactly.

While biblical scholars discuss whether this passage represents an account of a coronation of a king or an actual birth of a child, no matter which interpretation is given, for the Israelites, the passage represents the hope for a better life through a new leader. Jews today still hold out the messianic hope of this passage. And though the Christian belief that the messianic hope has been fulfilled in Jesus distinguishes us from our Jewish brothers and sisters, still together we can hold onto a common joy and rejoicing when we see darkness and gloom overcome in

individual hearts and in the world. Let joy reign in your heart, be seen in your eyes, and be heard in your voice as you proclaim this reading to the assembly. Even those who may only come to church on Christmas should be able to sense the extraordinariness of this joy proclaimed in the dark of night during this late-night liturgy!

READING II   One sentence! At first glance this is all this short reading from Titus, one of the three pastoral epistles (1 and 2 Timothy are the others),

seems to be. But it is so much more. In one sentence, the author of this letter discloses the grace of God active in the past, present, and future. As we celebrate Christmas we not only remember Jesus' first coming in history, his birth in Bethlehem (past), we also affirm how he is God-with-us today (present), and we look forward in blessed hope to his appearance again as the glory of God (future).

According to the author of Titus, when we celebrate Jesus' coming as the grace of God in history, Jesus' saving works accomplished through his life, death, and

GOSPEL Luke 2:1–14

Take your time with this familiar story.

**Caesar Augustus =
SEE-zer aw-GUHS-tuhs**

Quirinius = kwih-RIN-ee-uhs

Syria = SEER-ee-uh

Judea = joo-DEE-uh

A reading from the holy Gospel according to Luke

In those days a **decree** went out from Caesar **Augustus**
    that the whole **world** should be **enrolled**.
This was the **first** enrollment,
    when **Quirinius** was governor of **Syria**.
So all went to be enrolled, each to his own town.
And **Joseph** too went up from **Galilee** from the town of **Nazareth**
    to **Judea**, to the city of **David** that is called **Bethlehem**,
    because he was of the house and family of **David**,
    to be enrolled with **Mary**, his **betrothed**, who was with **child**.
While they were there,
    the **time** came for her to **have** her child,
    and she gave **birth** to her **firstborn son**.
She **wrapped** him in **swaddling** clothes and **laid** him in a **manger**,
    because there was no **room** for them in the **inn**.

Now there were **shepherds** in that region living in the **fields**
    and keeping the **night** watch over their **flock**.
The **angel** of the Lord **appeared** to them
    and the **glory** of the Lord shone **around** them,
    and they were struck with great **fear**.
The **angel** said to them,
    "Do **not** be **afraid**;
    for **behold**, I proclaim to you good **news** of great **joy**
    that will be for **all** the **people**.
For **today** in the city of **David**
    a **savior** has been born for you who is **Christ** and **Lord**.

Contrast the fear that the shepherds feel with the comfort that the angel's words provide in the section beginning with the words "The angel of the Lord appeared to them . . . and they were struck with great fear . . . . The angel said to them, 'Do not be afraid.' "
Emphasize the word "today" in "For today in the city of David." Look up and convey this line to the assembly as a solemn proclamation. While Jesus was born in Bethlehem some 2,000 years ago, he is present today in the assembly, in the word, in the celebrant, and in the Eucharist.

Resurrection must be as near to our minds as his birth as an infant. He is the "savior Jesus Christ" who through his life showed us how to live; he gave himself for us through his death to deliver us from sin; in his death and Resurrection he washed us clean and took us as his own people. The totality of Jesus' first coming encompasses all of his life, death, and Resurrection—from birth to death to new life.

We, who accept as true the Savior's first coming in history, have ethical responsibilities, for Christ now lives in us. Often the Christmas season is the time of year

when we take these ethical responsibilities seriously. However, for the author of Titus, the concern is the eagerness with which we are *always* ready to do what is good. We move forward from the celebration of Christmas, renewed as Christ's people and sent forth with fervor to do good every day. Jesus Christ has taught us to do this through his own life. Our eagerness to do good can lead those around us to inquire into why we live the way we do. Our good actions can be the source of evangelization. We just might be called upon to share our belief in Jesus Christ as the Messiah

and our blessed hope in his second coming. Finally, take an opportunity to reflect prayerfully on how you as a lector live the ethical demands in this reading.

GOSPEL Luke's account of the birth of Jesus calls out the truth that we are a graced humanity. For years people have been moved by this story. Many have passed the Lucan story on by oral tradition to their children, and this is the narrative that is often dramatized at Christian pageants. Why? While we adhere to details

And **this** will be a **sign** for you:
> you will find an **infant** wrapped in **swaddling** clothes
> and **lying** in a **manger**."
And **suddenly** there was a multitude of the heavenly **host**
> with the angel,
> praising **God** and saying:
>> "**Glory** to God in the **highest**
>>> and on earth **peace** to those on whom his favor **rests**."

End on a very joyful note as you proclaim the praises of the heavenly host with the angel. We have already sung the Gloria, so read the praises with the same exuberance with which the Gloria was sung. A look of joy reflected on your face is more than appropriate.

that may or may not be true historically, nonetheless they convey a profound truth of faith: God chose to come as one of us, to be among us and with us in the world. God graced humanity with divinity.

While Luke emphasizes God's coming to all of humanity, he often gives particular attention to the poor. In this story his focus on the swaddling clothes in which the infant Jesus is wrapped and the shepherds being the first to hear the news of Jesus' birth and to visit the infant shows that God

graces the lowly and poor of humanity. One of the scriptural foundations for the Catholic teaching regarding concern for the poor is found in this Lucan story.

Having Jesus born in the lowly and inhospitable circumstances of a stable, being placed in a manger, and recognizing shepherds as the first visitors of Jesus provides a stark contrast to the power of the Roman ruler Caesar Augustus. Seemingly having little power based the circumstances of his birth, Jesus will give testimony throughout his entire life to a new kind of power, a power that affirms the

goodness of God in all of humanity. In his own life, death, and Resurrection he will be the salvation of humanity. Present this Christmas Gospel with reverence and awe at the momentous change the course of human history took some 2,000 years ago. Proclaim it with the belief of Christmas that "Today is born our Savior, Christ the Lord" (Psalm 98).

Lectionary #15

READING I   Isaiah 62:11–12

Isaiah = ī-ZAY-uh

Zion refers to Jerusalem.

Look up as you proclaim the words "See, the Lord proclaims to the ends of the earth." "To the ends of the earth" also includes all sides of the assembly, even the back rows and those standing!

Soften your voice on the name "holy people." Speak the title "redeemed of the Lord" with confidence. State the name "Frequented," which means "sought out," with reassurance, for Zion—and we—will not be forsaken.

A reading from the Book of the Prophet Isaiah

See, the LORD proclaims
    to the **ends** of the **earth**:
say to daughter **Zion**,
    your **savior** comes!
Here is his **reward** with him,
    his **recompense** before him.
They shall be called the **holy** people,
    the **redeemed** of the LORD,
and you shall be called "**Frequented**,"
    a city that is **not forsaken**.

READING I The end of the Babylonian exile and the joyful return of the Israelites to Jerusalem is the historical context for this reading. While the Israelites were not always faithful to God, God was always with them. Imagine the joy of the Israelites returning in procession to Jerusalem. In later times the joy of this reading is seen in the procession on the first day of major pilgrimage feasts such as the feast of Tabernacles.

This reading's announcement of salvation extends beyond Jerusalem and its people. All the ends of the earth will know the newness of life that has come upon Jerusalem. As dawn breaks on Christmas morning, Christians once again proclaim with conviction that the fullness of salvation has come through Jesus Christ, who himself was of Jewish descent. Just as the members of the community at Jerusalem could now be called "the holy people" and the "redeemed of the Lord" and Jerusalem called "Frequented," Christian communities also claim these titles, but in a new way. Jesus Christ makes us the redeemed of the Lord. Make this announcement of salvation resound throughout the church as if the doors were opened wide for the whole neighborhood to hear the joyful news!

If you're able, this would be a good text to commit to memory. However, it would not be wise to try and proclaim a text from memory for first time at a Christmas liturgy.

READING II   Titus 3:4–7

Titus = TĪ-tus

The phrase "When the kindness and generous love of God our savior appeared" refers to Jesus Christ. Emphasize this as the main point by reading it more slowly than what follows.

The second point is "he saved us through the bath of rebirth." Read a little slower through "Holy Spirit."

Speak with warmth the words "so that we might be justified . . . become heirs in hope of eternal life."

A reading from the Letter of Saint Paul to Titus

Beloved:
When the **kindness** and **generous** love
   of **God** our savior **appeared**,
not because of any righteous deeds **we** had done
   but because of his **mercy**,
he **saved** us through the **bath** of rebirth
   and **renewal** by the Holy **Spirit**,
whom he **richly** poured out on us
   through Jesus Christ our **savior**,
so that we might be **justified** by his **grace**
   and become **heirs** in **hope** of eternal **life**.

READING II   Christmas and Easter come together once again! From birth to Resurrection we learn that Jesus Christ saves. These four short verses from the letter to Titus deal directly with the central question for Christians: salvation.

Some in the community on Crete, for which Titus was responsible, believed they could earn their salvation by good deeds. From the authentic Pauline letters through the later pastoral epistles (1 and 2 Timothy, Titus) and up to the present day, the Christian tradition has been clear that

salvation is a gift from God. Today, we would say that God sent the Savior because God loved humanity unconditionally. No deeds or actions on our part can earn us salvation.

Yet we are called to respond to our gift of salvation by living our lives in a certain way. In the two verses that precede this selection from Titus, we hear Christians called to perform honest work, live in gentle obedience, respect authority, speak no evil, and be kind to all. During this time of year we may find it difficult to respond in love to others, especially family members

and close friends. As you prepare this reading, reflect on how God's example of gratuitous self-giving in Jesus Christ provides an example for us to live out our baptismal commitment.

GOSPEL   The Gospel this Christmas morning begins where the Gospel for the Mass at Midnight ended. At the end of the latter Gospel, the heavenly hosts and angel praise God saying, "Glory to God in the highest." At the end of this passage, the shepherds, after listening to

GOSPEL   Luke 2:15—20

A reading from the holy Gospel according to Luke

When the **angels** went away from them to **heaven**,
    the **shepherds** said to one another,
    "Let us go, then, to **Bethlehem**
    to see this thing that has taken place,
    which the **Lord** has made known to us."
So they went in haste and found **Mary** and **Joseph**,
    and the **infant** lying in the **manger**.
When they saw this,
    they made known the **message**
    that had been told them about this **child**.
All who heard it were **amazed**
    by what had been told them by the **shepherds**.
And **Mary** kept all these things,
    reflecting on them in her **heart**.
Then the shepherds returned,
    glorifying and **praising** God
    for all they had **heard** and **seen**,
    just as it had been told to them.

Let eagerness be heard in your voice as you speak the shepherds' words

Pause after "Mary and Joseph." They are not lying in the manger with the infant!

Lower your voice and speak gently and slowly about Mary ("And Mary kept all these things, reflecting on them in her heart"). Pause after describing Mary's response. Then raise your voice and speak excitedly to convey the shepherds' response ("Then the shepherds returned, glorifying and praising God . . . told to them").

the angel's message about the birth of a savior, praise God for what they had seen in the manger, while Mary reflects in her heart on what has taken place. Both are on their own, distinct faith journeys, as we are today. In their own ways, the shepherds and Mary are both responding to the amazing news that a savior has been born who is Christ and Lord. They simply express their amazement differently.

Some in your assembly will be natural evangelizers like the shepherds and will want to go out into the world announcing the Good News of the Savior's birth. Others,

like Mary, will take the Good News into their hearts, reflecting on what it means for them and for the world. While our tendency might be to proclaim this Gospel emphasizing the exuberance of the shepherds, this could overshadow Mary's response. A balanced proclamation, which contrasts the two responses, can affirm both responses in Christians today. It might also call those who are more introspective to evangelization and those who are more evangelical to prayerful reflection.

This brief Gospel is packed with meaning, so take your time communicating

it. Many will unconsciously stop listening after the first few lines because they are familiar with the story. Fill your voice with the reverence, eagerness, and joy that permeate Luke's account of the Savior's birth. This will help many to hear the Gospel anew this Christmas and lead them to express amazement at the Savior's birth through their unique personalities and gifts in unity with the whole Church!

NATIVITY OF THE LORD: DAY

Lectionary #16

READING I   Isaiah 52:7–10

A reading from the Book of the Prophet Isaiah

How **beautiful** upon the **mountains**
    are the **feet** of him who brings glad **tidings**,
announcing **peace**, bearing good **news**,
    announcing **salvation**, and saying to **Zion**,
    "Your God is **King!**"

Hark! Your **sentinels** raise a cry,
    together they shout for **joy**,
for they see **directly**, before their eyes,
    the LORD **restoring** Zion.
Break out together in **song**,
    O **ruins** of Jerusalem!
For the LORD **comforts** his people,
    he **redeems** Jerusalem.
The LORD has **bared** his holy arm
    in the sight of all the nations;
all the **ends** of the **earth** will **behold**
    the **salvation** of our God.

Isaiah = ī-ZAY-uh

Speak the opening lines slowly and serenely as if painting a picture for the assembly. Raise your voice incrementally as you come to the announcement of the King in the words "Your God is King!" Pause significantly after the announcement.

Sentinels = SEN-tih-nuls

A new section begins with "Hark!" Now a group of people—the guards on the towers—shout the news of God the King coming to Jerusalem. Look up and around, reaching everyone, even those in the back rows and those standing in the church today, on the words "for they see directly, before their eyes, the Lord restoring Zion."

Memorize the last line ("all the ends of the earth will behold the salvation of our God") if you can do so with ease.

READING I   You are the messenger in this reading who is announcing peace and salvation. Picture an image in your mind of the messenger running along the mountaintops proclaiming that "God is King!" To the Hebrew people who sometimes forgot God and failed to live up to their part of the covenant, it must have seemed that God also had forgotten them, especially during the long days of the Babylonian exile. The traditional role of the messenger was to announce the advent of the king. And this messenger had news: the Babylonians had been defeated by the Persians. A new day was dawning; it seemed like God was back in power and was once again watching out for the people of Jerusalem.

Consistent in this reading is the affirmation that God is King; God is leading the people. It is neither the exiles returning home nor the city of Jerusalem that attracts the writer's attention; the Lord is his focus. On Christmas Day, too, we are mindful of God's divine initiative in sending Jesus Christ to be King, the bringer of peace and salvation. We are followers of Jesus Christ and praise God because God took the lead in offering us salvation. Just as the author of this passage draws attention to the Lord, your challenge is to proclaim this reading with the same focus. Leave the assembly ready to break out together in song (like the ancient ruins) with a psalm of praise ("All the ends of the earth have seen the saving power of God") by the way your words exude gratitude and praise for all that God has done throughout history and especially in Jesus Christ.

READING II Hebrews 1:1–6

A reading from the Letter to the Hebrews

Brothers and sisters:
In times **past**, God spoke in partial and various ways
    to our **ancestors** through the **prophets**;
in these **last** days, he has spoken to us through the **Son**,
    whom he made **heir** of all things
    and **through** whom he created the **universe**,
    who is the **refulgence** of his **glory**,
        the very **imprint** of his **being**,
        and who **sustains** all things by his mighty **word**.
    When he had accomplished **purification** from **sins**,
        he took his **seat** at the right hand of the **Majesty** on high,
    as far **superior** to the **angels**
        as the **name** he has inherited is more **excellent** than theirs.

For to **which** of the angels did God ever say:
    You are my son; *this* day I have **begotten** you?
Or again:
    I will be a **father** to him, and *he* shall be a **son** to me?
And again, when he leads the **firstborn** into the world, he says:
    Let all the **angels** *of God* **worship** *him.*

In the lines "In times past . . . in these last days," make sure and observe the commas to differentiate between how God spoke in the two different times.

By pausing significantly after the colons in the phrases "For to which of the angels did God ever say" and "Or again," you will make it clear that the author is offering three distinct quotations. The assembly will not be aware they are from the Old Testament, but they are from Psalm 2:7, 2 Samuel 7:14, and Deuteronomy 32:43. The first two the author writes in the form of a question, and the third as a strong affirmation of the Son's identity. Let the difference be heard in the inflection of your voice.

READING II Why do we read this passage on Christmas Day? The short answer to this question is because on Christmas Day we assert with utmost conviction what we believe about Jesus Christ, the Son of the Father: that he is fully divine and fully human. Often, and rightly so, on Christmas we focus on the fullness of Jesus' humanity. But the second part of our Christian belief about the identity of Jesus Christ is that he is himself fully divine. The two together comprise our belief in the Incarnation of God in Jesus Christ.

As an apologetic for Christian belief in the Son's divinity, the author of Hebrews develops the theme of the high priesthood of Jesus. The Son is different from and superior to past prophets because God spoke completely through him (1:1–2); the Son is superior to the angels because he sacrificed himself for the purification of sins (1:4–5); the Son is the "reflection of God's glory"—he is the only begotten Son of God (1:3).

Early Christians needed to defend their belief in the preexistence and divinity of Jesus Christ because they were challenged by Jews and others who did not believe that God could become human like us while retaining the fullness of divinity and being the Messiah. But the truth for Christians is that God did do this in and through the person of the Son. The later articulation of our beliefs about the Son's relationship to God will find many of its roots in the letter to the Hebrews.

GOSPEL   John 1:1–18

A reading from the holy Gospel according to John

In the **beginning** was the **Word**,
    and the Word was **with God**,
    and the Word **was** God.
He was in the **beginning** with God.
All things came to be **through** him,
    and **without** him **nothing** came to be.
What came to be through him was **life**,
    and this life was the **light** of the human **race**;
the **light** shines in the **darkness**,
    and the **darkness** has not overcome it.

A man named **John** was sent from God.
He came for **testimony**, to testify to the **light**,
    so that **all** might **believe** through him.
He was **not** the light,
    but came to **testify** to the light.
The **true** light, which enlightens **everyone**,
    was coming into the world.

He was **in** the world,
    and the world came to be **through** him,
    but the world did not **know** him.
He came to what was his own,
    but his **own** people did **not** accept him.

This passage is complex. Read the section "In the beginning was the Word, and the Word was with God, and the Word was God" as if you were telling a story and not teaching philosophy. Everything depends on these opening lines that recall the creation story in Genesis.

The Word is life and light, not darkness. Accentuate these images by putting lightness in your voice with life and light, and heaviness with darkness.

Pause before "A man named John was sent by God." As John becomes the focus, you are doing a little less theology and philosophy, so you can read a bit more quickly and with less earnestness.

The Gospel transitions again beginning with the words "The true light, which enlightens everyone." Pause before these words and then return to your original tone and tempo. There is both sadness and hope in this section.

We worship the Son as God! Let the last line of this reading be filled with your own conviction that Jesus Christ is the Son of God, the very reflection of God's glory—indeed, fully divine. Only because Jesus Christ is fully divine as well as fully human were we purified from our sins. Through our participation in the Eucharist we share in Jesus' high priesthood of the new covenant. This, too, we celebrate on Christmas.

GOSPEL   There is a lot of complicated theology and philosophy behind the prologue to the Gospel according to John, but you needn't be completely familiar with it nor comprehend it to communicate the prologue's fundamental meaning. In an age when some were denying the humanity of Jesus and others were rejecting his divinity, John begins his Gospel with this hymn that we now proclaim on Christmas Day. These verses are an incarnation hymn, a profound description of the divine becoming human.

John wrote in a time when most believed that the material world was evil and the spirit world was good. The two worlds could never be bridged, lest the divine be contaminated with the vices of nature. While we are separated from John's day by thousands of years, many today speak of the wickedness of the flesh and the evilness of human nature. Some even teach that to know God we must leave behind the flesh. These people disrespect humanity. How contrary to the truths of

But to those who **did** accept him
    he gave **power** to become **children** of **God**,
    to those who believe in his name,
    who were born not by **natural** generation
    nor by **human** choice nor by a **man's** decision
    but of **God**.

And the Word became **flesh**
    and made his **dwelling** among us,
    and we saw his **glory**,
    the glory as of the Father's only **Son**,
    full of **grace** and **truth**.

John **testified** to him and cried out, saying,
    "**This** was he of whom I said,
    'The one who is coming **after** me ranks **ahead** of me
    because he existed **before** me.'"
From his **fullness** we have **all received**,
    grace in place of **grace**,
    because while the **law** was given through **Moses**,
    grace and **truth** came through Jesus **Christ**.
No one has ever **seen** God.
The only **Son**, God, who is at the Father's **side**,
    has **revealed** him.

[Shorter: John 1:1–5, 9–14]

This is Christmas: "And the Word became flesh!" Communicate the joy and wonder of this in your voice.

Pause again before the words "John testified to him and cried out." This is the second time the author deviates to narrate John's story and role. Return to the tone you used in the first section that dealt with John.

This, too, is Christmas: no one has seen God until the Son revealed God. State the lines "No one has ever seen God. The only Son, God, who is at the Father's side, has revealed him" with faith and conviction, reading them slowly.

John's prologue and the truth of Christmas for Christians!

In the Word made flesh, the same Word who existed with God and was God from the very beginning, and through whom the world was created, God chose to bridge the chasm between the material and spiritual worlds. God, as John tells us, chose to give out of God's own grace, the fullness of God—the Son, the Word. No longer would the physical world, of which we human persons are a part, be separated from the true face of God. Through the Incarnation of the Word, this has been changed forever. We can know God in and through our human nature—for the world has come to see God through the revelation of the Son, the Word made flesh.

Humanity and divinity were united in a new way different from the grace given through the law of Moses. This new way allows for a relationship between all creation and its Creator that was never before possible. While it builds on the relationship God had with God's people as recounted in the Old Testament, it also changes that relationship, because all flesh has now seen the glory of God! As Saint Athanasius, an early Church Father put it, "God became human so that we could become divine." The beauty of the Incarnation and the possibilities it holds out for us are what this passage from John's Gospel discloses and what we come together to be eternally grateful for on Christmas.

HOLY FAMILY OF JESUS, MARY, AND JOSEPH

Lectionary #17

READING I   Genesis 15:1–6; 21:1–3

Abram = AY-br*m
Be clear and direct as you introduce the Lord's words at the beginning of the reading.

Pause after each speaker. Also, lower your tone of voice as you read the narrative lines that identify the next speaker, such as "But Abram said" and "Abram continued."

Eliezer = el-ee-AY-zer

A reading from the Book of Genesis

The word of the LORD came to **Abram** in a **vision**, saying:
  "Fear **not**, Abram!
    I am your **shield**;
    I will make your **reward** very **great**."
But **Abram** said,
  "O Lord GOD, what **good** will your gifts be,
  if I keep on being **childless**
  and have as my **heir** the **steward** of my house, **Eliezer**?"
Abram continued,
  "**See**, you have given me no **offspring**,
  and so one of my **servants** will be my heir."
Then the word of the LORD came to him:
  "**No**, that one shall **not** be your heir;
  your own **issue** shall be your heir."
The Lord took Abram **outside** and said,
  "Look up at the **sky** and count the **stars**, if you can.
Just so," he added, "shall your **descendants** be."
Abram put his **faith** in the LORD,
  who **credited** it to him as an act of **righteousness**.

The LORD took note of **Sarah** as he had **said** he would;
  he **did** for her as he had **promised**.

Express beauty, wonder, and joy in your voice as you tell Abram of the Lord's promise to him. Imagine yourself outside looking at the sky on a starry evening as you speak the Lord's words: "Look up at the sky and count the stars, if you can." Pause after these lines and before the section beginning with the words "The Lord took note of Sarah."

Narrate the section beginning with the words "The Lord took note of Sarah" with a sense of fulfillment; God has been faithful to Abraham and Sarah.

READING I The Introduction to the Lectionary tells us that the first two readings on the feast of the Holy Family were chosen to disclose the virtues of family life (#95). Aside from the last section of this passage, the entire reading is a dialogue between the Lord and Abram/Abraham. The family virtue of faithfulness is at the heart of this dialogue (for more on understanding the virtues of the Christian family, see the *Catechism of the Catholic Church,* #2201–2233).

Abram's questions and concerns in this reading are very human; he is not angry or upset or distrustful of the Lord, but simply trying to understand how the Lord can fulfill what he has promised. Abram's concern is natural because he is worried about carrying on his family name. Despite Abram's anxieties, and those of Sarah, their relationship with the Lord bears fruit in the promise of descendants fulfilled in the birth of Isaac. In this reading

we hear the Lord's promise of descendants to Abram and Abram's trust in that promise, but there is more to the Lord's covenant with Abram. The second story in Genesis 15 is that of God's promise of the land to Abram and the sealing of this promise in the covenant (15:7–20). Only after noting Abram's own confession of faith in the Lord and that the Lord accepted it as an "act of righteousness" (15:6) does the author detail God's promise of land to Abram. Abram's faith, affirmed by the Lord

Abraham = AY-bruh-ham

Sarah became **pregnant** and bore Abraham a **son** in his old **age**,
    at the set **time** that God had **stated**.
Abraham gave the name **Isaac** to this son of his
    whom Sarah **bore** him.

Or:

READING I   Sirach 3:2–6, 12–14

A reading from the Book of Sirach

God sets a **father** in **honor** over his **children**;
    a **mother's authority** he **confirms** over her **sons**.
Whoever honors his **father** atones for **sins**,
    and **preserves** himself from them.
When he **prays**, he is **heard**;
    he stores up **riches** who reveres his **mother**.
Whoever honors his **father** is gladdened by **children**,
    and, when he **prays**, is **heard**.
Whoever reveres his **father** will live a long **life**;
    he who **obeys** his father brings **comfort** to his **mother**.

My son, take **care** of your father when he is **old**;
    grieve him **not** as long as he **lives**.
Even if his **mind** fail, be **considerate** of him;
    revile him **not** all the days of his **life**;
kindness to a **father** will not be **forgotten**,
    firmly **planted** against the debt of your **sins**
    —a house raised in **justice** to you.

as an act of righteousness meant that Abram was in right relationship with the Lord; Abram's faith was in the Lord's promise and this outweighed his human concerns.

Note that after the dialogue between the Lord and Abram, the reading skips over many chapters in Genesis. The final section of the reading is taken from the beginning of chapter 21 and recounts the birth of Isaac. In one of the chapters that is omitted, Abram's name is changed to Abraham to signify the he will be "the father of a host

of nations." Sarah's name was changed, too—originally it was Sarai. While no explanation is given for her name change, presumably it occurs because she, too, will share in the blessings of the covenant. Name changes in ancient times signified a new way of life—that the person was heading in a new direction. Abram-Abraham and Sarai-Sarah are a few of the most famous name changes, but recall also that Jacob's name was changed to Israel ("one

who struggles with God"), and Simon to Peter ("rock"), the latter one in the New Testament. Abraham's name change is significant because he goes from Abram, which means "exalted father," to Abraham, which means "father of a multitude." Sarai and Sarah both mean "princess." One of the reasons why one might choose to take a new name for the celebration of the sacrament of Confirmation is to signify a commitment to a reordering of one's relationship with God and to one's renewed commitment to the new covenant with the Lord.

Note the repetition of "by faith" at the beginning of each new section. Pause before the beginning of each section. Each time you begin with the words "by faith," be more deliberate and determined in your delivery of them. Also, pause slightly after the words "by faith" each time you deliver them. This draws attention to the fact that Abraham and Sarah lived these experiences with trust and fidelity in the Lord.

Christ's Resurrection is represented by the gift of Isaac back to Abraham mentioned in the final verse ("He reasoned that God was able to raise").

READING II   Hebrews 11:8, 11–12, 17–19

A reading from the Letter to the Hebrews

Brothers and sisters:
By *faith* Abraham *obeyed* when he was called to go out to a place
 that he was to **receive** as an **inheritance**;
 he went out, not **knowing** where he was to **go**.
By **faith** he received *power* to **generate**,
 even though he was **past** the normal age
 —and Sarah **herself** was **sterile**—
 for he thought that the one who had made the **promise** was
 trustworthy.
So it **was** that there came forth from **one man**,
 himself as good as **dead**,
 descendants as **numerous** as the stars in the **sky**
 and as **countless** as the **sands** on the **seashore**.

By **faith** Abraham, when put to the **test**, offered up **Isaac**,
 and he who had received the **promises** was ready to offer
 his only **son**,
 of whom it was said,
 "Through **Isaac** descendants shall bear your **name**."
He reasoned that **God** was able to raise even from the **dead**,
 and he received Isaac **back** as a **symbol**.

Or:

The call to faithfulness of both Jewish and Christian families today is rooted in the faithfulness of Abraham and Sarah. Like Abraham and Sarah, even though we might not understand how something is going to happen because of our family's situation, God will provide; God is faithful to his covenantal promise. The example of Abraham and Sarah shows that we also must only be faithful, trying never to let go of our relationship with the Lord, always remaining open to dialogue with him to learn his ways.

READING II Like the First Reading, this reading shows forth virtues of family life. It is directly linked with the First Reading in that it recounts the experience of Abraham and Sarah in faith. To assist in your preparation, read through the First Reading at the same time you are practicing this one.

This reading from the letter to the Hebrews is from the chapter that begins with one of the most familiar lines from scripture in the New Testament: "Faith is the realization of what is hoped for." The chapter itself contains references to those who were faithful in the Old Testament, among them Isaac (11:20), Jacob (11:21), Joseph (11:22), and Moses (11:23–30). The faithfulness of this "cloud of witnesses," as Hebrews 12:1 refers to them, climaxes

READING II   Colossians 3:12–21

A reading from the Letter of Saint Paul to the Colossians

Brothers and sisters:
Put **on**, as God's **chosen** ones, **holy** and **beloved**,
  heartfelt **compassion**, **kindness**, **humility**, **gentleness**,
    and **patience**,
  bearing with one another and **forgiving** one another,
  if one has a **grievance** against another;
  as the Lord has forgiven **you**, so must you **also** do.
And over **all** these put on **love**,
  that is, the **bond** of **perfection**.
And let the **peace** of Christ **control** your hearts,
  the **peace** into which you were **also** called in one **body**.
And be **thankful**.
Let the **word** of Christ *dwell* in you **richly**,
  as in all **wisdom** you **teach** and **admonish** one another,
  singing **psalms**, **hymns**, and spiritual **songs**
  with **gratitude** in your hearts to **God**.
And **whatever** you do, in **word** or in **deed**,
  do **everything** in the name of the Lord **Jesus**,
  giving **thanks** to God the **Father** through **him**.

Wives, be **subordinate** to your husbands,
  as is **proper** in the Lord.
Husbands, **love** your wives,
  and avoid any **bitterness** toward them.
Children, obey your **parents** in **everything**,
  for this is **pleasing** to the Lord.

---

in the faithfulness of Christ in his sacrifice on the cross. Reading through this chapter and the one that follows it will help provide you with some of the context for the passage you proclaim.

The last line that you will proclaim in this reading is the most powerful because the author of Hebrews understands the faith of Abraham to prefigure Christ's Resurrection. The Greek (*en parabolē*), translated as "symbol," seems to imply

that God sparing Isaac from death points to or prefigures the Resurrection of Christ when one interprets the Old Testament through the lens of the New Testament.

In delivering this line, you are calling yourself and the assembly, which you are a part of, to practice the virtue of faithfulness in the God of our ancestors who has gifted us with his Son, Jesus Christ. We practice faithfulness, not alone, but in the communion of the Church founded on the witness of those who have been faithful before us. Our Christian faithfulness

is rooted in the covenant of Abraham and sealed by Jesus' sacrifice and his Resurrection from the dead—the center of the new covenant.

GOSPEL   When the feast of the Holy Family entered the Roman liturgical calendar for universal observance in the twentieth century, it was celebrated on the Sunday after Epiphany. Because the new calendar was developed after the

Fathers, do not **provoke** your children,
so they may not become **discouraged**.

[Shorter: Colossians 3:12–17]

GOSPEL   Luke 2:22–40

A reading from the holy Gospel according to Luke

When the days were completed for their **purification**
according to the law of **Moses**,
they took him up to **Jerusalem**
to **present** him to the **Lord**,
just as it is **written** in the **law** of the Lord,
*Every **male** that opens the **womb** shall be **consecrated***
*to the **Lord***,
and to offer the **sacrifice** of
*a pair of **turtledoves** or two young **pigeons***,
in accordance with the **dictate** in the law of the **Lord**.

Now there was a man in Jerusalem whose name was **Simeon**.
This man was **righteous** and **devout**,
awaiting the consolation of Israel,
and the Holy **Spirit** was upon him.
It had been **revealed** to him by the Holy Spirit
that he should not see **death**
before he had seen the **Christ** of the **Lord**.
He came in the *Spirit* into the **temple**;
and when the **parents** brought in the child **Jesus**
to perform the custom of the **law** in regard to him,
he took him into his **arms** and blessed **God**, saying:

Joseph and Mary were faithful Jews taking Jesus to the Temple to take part in the rituals prescribed by the law. The plural "their" in the narrative verse ("When the days were completed for their purification") suggests that Mary and Joseph might have participated with Jesus in the rituals.

Simeon = SIM-ee-uhn

Second Vatican Council, the feast now falls on the Sunday between Christmas and Epiphany. Having closer proximity to Christmas shows that God's presence was not only manifested in Jesus, who was an infant lying in a manger, but that God was also manifested in Jesus through his childhood (although we know little about this), in adulthood as he was baptized by John, and as he began his mission to preach the Good News that salvation was at hand.

On this feast of the Holy Family, the Gospel reading for each of the three years is about Jesus' childhood. Because Mark, the primary Gospel read during Year B of the Lectionary cycle of readings, does not have an infancy narrative or any descriptions of events that happened during Jesus' childhood, we hear the beloved narrative of Jesus' presentation in the Temple from the Gospel according to Luke today.

This is a rather lengthy Gospel, which you will want to practice proclaiming out loud in order to work on the pacing of your delivery. Most of the material is narrative in form, meaning that as you read you will be relating the details of the story to your assembly. Both Simeon's words of blessing to God and to Joseph and Mary need to be highlighted in your presentation. They express the identity of Jesus, predicting the role he will play in the salvation of all peoples.

Simeon was a watchman at the Temple. His words of blessing ("Now Master . . . |and glory for your people Israel") are known to us today as the Nunc Dimittis and are prayed as part of Compline, the final prayer of the day in the Divine Office. Nunc Dimittis is so-called because it comes from the first two words of the Latin translation of Simeon's words. Simeon leaves his post at the Temple after praying these words. Speak them with a sense of peacefulness in your own voice.

Anna = AN-uh
Phanuel = FAN-yoo-el or fun-NYOO-uhl
Asher = ASH-er

Take your time with this concluding remark ("The child grew and became strong, filled with wisdom; and the favor of God was upon him"). It was necessary that Jesus grow from infancy to childhood to adulthood, thus sharing our human experience of maturing. Luke tells us he was filled with wisdom so that we might know that God's salvation touches all periods of human life.

"**Now**, Master, you may let your servant **go**
  in **peace,** according to your **word,**
for my eyes have **seen** your **salvation,**
  which you prepared in sight of all the **peoples,**
a light for **revelation** to the **Gentiles,**
  and **glory** for your people **Israel.**"
The child's *father* and *mother* were **amazed** at what was said
  about him;
and Simeon **blessed** them and said to **Mary** his **mother,**
  "**Behold**, this child is destined
for the **fall** and **rise** of **many** in Israel,
and to be a **sign** that will be **contradicted**
—and you **yourself** a **sword** will pierce—
so that the thoughts of **many** hearts may be **revealed.**"
There was also a **prophetess**, **Anna,**
  the daughter of **Phanuel,** of the tribe of **Asher.**
She was **advanced** in years,
  having lived **seven** years with her husband after her **marriage,**
  and then as a **widow** until she was **eighty-four.**
She never **left** the temple,
  but worshiped **night** and **day** with **fasting** and **prayer.**
And coming **forward** at that very **time,**
  she gave **thanks** to God and **spoke** about the child
  to **all** who were awaiting the **redemption** of **Jerusalem.**

When they had **fulfilled** all the prescriptions
  of the law of the Lord,
  they returned to **Galilee,**
  to their **own** town of **Nazareth.**
The child **grew** and became **strong,** filled with **wisdom;**
  and the favor of **God** was upon him.

[Shorter: Luke 2:22, 39–40]

The Lucan account of Jesus' presentation emphasizes not only the faithfulness of Joseph and Mary in presenting Jesus for the purification rituals prescribed according to the law of Moses, but also the faithfulness of Anna, a prophetess. Prophetesses were known for their faithfulness to God's will; holiness was clearly discernible in their lives. In your proclamation give as much attention to this section as you do to the previous ones. Anna's example bears witness that faithfulness is a virtue to be espoused throughout one's entire life. In the end, the faithfulness of Mary and Joseph, and Simeon and Anna, does not stop with themselves; while their example teaches us about faithfulness, what is most important is the identity of Jesus as Savior.

MARY, THE MOTHER OF GOD

Lectionary #18

READING I   Number 6:22—27

A reading from the Book of Numbers

The LORD said to **Moses**:
    "**Speak** to **Aaron** and his sons and **tell** them:
    This is how you shall **bless** the **Israelites**.
Say to them:
    The LORD **bless** you and **keep** you!
    The LORD let his face **shine** upon you,
        and be **gracious** to you!
    The LORD look upon you **kindly**
        and give you **peace**!
So shall they invoke my **name** upon the **Israelites**,
    and I will **bless** them."

Identify the speaker clearly: "The Lord said to Moses."
Moses = MOH-ziz
Aaron = AIR-un
Israelites = IZ-ree-uh-līts
Pray the blessing ("The Lord bless you . . . and give you peace") slowly and with care, line by line, as if you were blessing your assembly. You are asking the Lord to take care of his people.

Pause at the end of the blessing before the Lord's words that are not a part of the actual blessing: "So shall they invoke my name upon the Israelites, and I will bless them."

READING I   Our liturgical celebration today focuses on Mary, the Mother of God. We are still in the Christmas season and our world is marking the beginning of a new year. In the book of Numbers, the brief passage we read today comes at the end of a section on laws and regulations that the Hebrew people were to follow. One of the reasons we read this passage today on the solemnity of Mary, the Mother of God, is that is attests to her roots in the ancient traditions of the Hebrew people. Mary, as we see also in today's Gospel, was a faithful Jew. This blessing probably was not far from her heart, as it is still near and dear to many Jews and Christians today.

The three lines of the blessing ask that God take care of his people, reveal himself to them, and grant them peace. The expression "let his face shine" in Hebrew corresponds to our word "smile." To ask the Lord to let his face shine upon us means to see God happy. God has divine pleasure and contentment because he is in relationship with us. Even though he does not need us for companionship, he chooses to be in relationship with us. The Hebrew word for "peace" (shalom) includes not only the sense of serenity, of which we usually think, but also happiness and prosperity. The peace that comes from God reaches into all areas of our life, so that we too can experience the pleasure that comes from living life in God.

Offer this blessing as a prayer for the community before you. In your preparation, think about the ways in which the Lord has blessed you and given you peace. This will help you to achieve a tone of prayerfulness in your voice.

READING II Galatians 4:4–7

A reading from the Letter of Saint Paul to the Galatians

Brothers and sisters:
When the **fullness** of time had **come**, **God** sent his **Son**,
    born of a **woman**, born under the law,
    to **ransom** those under the law,
    so that **we** might receive **adoption** as sons.

As **proof** that you are sons,
    God sent the **Spirit** of his **Son** into our **hearts**,
    crying out, "**Abba**, **Father**!"
So you are no longer a **slave** but a **son**,
    and if a **son** then also an **heir**, through **God**.

Paul captures the entire Paschal Mystery in a single sentence: "When the fullness of time had come . . . adoption as sons." The commas are a good guide for your proclamation. "God sent his Son" is the main clause.

"Abba, Father!" are the same words that Jesus used while praying in Gethsemane (Mark 14:36). Abba is an Aramaic term that connotes a childlike intimacy between father and child. Note the mention of God, the Spirit, and the Son in the phrase "God sent the Spirit of his Son into our hearts," which introduces the prayer address.

READING II This reading expresses all the joy that comes from a life-giving transition. Paul wrote in a society in which slavery was a reality, so he employed that image in making his point about the new position of Christians in relation to God. Prior to the Son's coming, the Galatians were slaves to sin. Paul often characterized this slavery as being bound by all the details of the Jewish law. When Jesus Christ came, everything changed. Faith—and not deeds of the law—was required in order to inherit the promises of Abraham.

Christ took on our humanity, being born of a woman and under the law. It was necessary that he take upon himself our human condition in order that we might be able to call ourselves adopted sons and daughters of God. We can use the Son's words—"Abba, Father!"—in our prayer to God. We no longer have to follow the letter of the law in order to be in right relationship with God.

Try to convey in your reading of this passage the dynamic movement from constraint to freedom that is behind Paul's words. In order to do this, it might be helpful to reflect on a time when you experienced a change from an old way of life to a new way. How did it feel to be set free from the old to embrace the new? Consider this change as living life more deeply in the Spirit of the Son whom God sent. You are realizing more your identity as an adopted son or daughter of God; this is what you are calling the assembly to realize today as well.

GOSPEL Luke 2:16–21

A reading from the holy Gospel according to Luke

Pause at the comma after "Mary and Joseph." They are not lying in the manger with the infant!

The **shepherds** went in **haste** to **Bethlehem**
    and found **Mary** and **Joseph**,
    and the **infant** lying in the **manger**.
When they saw this,
    they made **known** the message
    that had been **told** them about this child.

Let amazement be in your voice for "all who heard" the news felt the same.

All who **heard** it were **amazed**
    by what had been **told** them by the **shepherds**.

Speak gently and unhurriedly, describing Mary's response in the words "And Mary kept all these things, reflecting on them in her heart." Speaking slowly and admiring her response allows people to hear it as if for the first time.

And **Mary** kept all these things,
    reflecting on them in her **heart**.
Then the **shepherds** returned,
    glorifying and **praising** God
    for all they had **heard** and **seen**,
    just as it had been told to them.

Pause before the final verse ("When eight days were completed for his circumcision"). It is important, so do not rush through it. Jesus is the fulfillment of Jewish law. In Hebrew, Jesus means "he will save" or "God saves." The verse brings Jesus and Mary together in relationship: Jesus is son of Mary and Son of God.

When **eight** days were completed for his **circumcision**,
    he was named **Jesus**, the name given him by the **angel**
    before he was **conceived** in the womb.

GOSPEL   This is the same Gospel proclaimed during the Christmas Mass at Dawn, except it begins a verse later and ends with an additional verse. Today, we read this Gospel from the perspective of the solemnity of Mary, the Mother of God.

Early Church leaders debated how Christians should refer to Mary. Should she be called the "Mother of Christ" (*Christotokos*) or the "Mother of God" (*Theotokos*)? Calling Mary the "Mother of Christ" emphasizes that she gave birth to the human Jesus. On the other hand, the title "Mother of God" stresses the divine nature of the one she bore as a human but who still retained his divinity. The Council of Ephesus in 431 decided that Mary was to be referred to as the "Mother of God." At its core, this title of Mary affirms the truth about the Christian belief of who Jesus Christ was and is: God incarnate.

As in the First and Second Readings for today, the addition of the verse at the end of the Gospel is significant. Jesus was born at a particular time in history and in a particular religious tradition. Mary and Joseph raised him to be faithful to its laws and customs. For Luke, Jesus is the fulfillment of the hopes of the Chosen People for a messiah—the fulfillment of the law. May we, like Mary, reflect in our hearts on who Jesus is for us and for the world. Knowing, then, that Jesus is the Savior of the world, may we go faithfully in prayer to God through his Son in the Holy Spirit and through the intercession of Mary, the Mother of God.

EPIPHANY OF THE LORD

Lectionary #20

READING I   Isaiah 60:1–6

A reading from the Book of the Prophet Isaiah

Let the ups and downs of this first section be heard in your voice. Raise your voice at first, then lower it as your speak of darkness, and then raise it again as you state with joy that the Lord shines over Jerusalem.

Rise up in **splendor**, **Jerusalem**! Your **light** has come,
the **glory** of the **Lord** shines upon you.
See, **darkness** covers the earth,
and **thick** clouds cover the **peoples**;
but upon you the LORD **shines**,
and over **you** appears his **glory**.
Nations shall **walk** by your **light**,
and **kings** by your **shining** radiance.
Raise your **eyes** and look **about**;
they all **gather** and come to you:
your **sons** come from afar,
and your **daughters** in the arms of their **nurses**.

Raise your eyes and look to different sides of the assembly as you proclaim "Raise your eyes and look about; they all gather and come to you: your sons . . . and your daughters." Everyone here has gathered and come to worship the Lord. When you turn to make eye contact with different sections of the assembly, be careful not to move away from the microphone.

Then you shall be **radiant** at what you see,
your **heart** shall **throb** and **overflow**,
for the **riches** of the sea shall be emptied **out** before you,
the **wealth** of nations shall be **brought** to you.
Caravans of **camels** shall **fill** you,
dromedaries from Midian and Ephah;
all from Sheba shall come
bearing **gold** and **frankincense**,
and **proclaiming** the **praises** of the **LORD**.

Midian = MID-ee-uhn
Ephah = EE-fah
Sheba = SHEE-buh

The last phrase captures the main point of the passage. It is also the reason why both Jews and Christians continue to gather in prayer.

READING I   Today we celebrate the solemnity of the Epiphany of the Lord. The Baptism of the Lord ends the Christmas season next Sunday. Epiphany and the Baptism of the Lord, along with Christmas, are the three "manifestation" feasts. Epiphany was the original feast of God's manifestation and was a celebration of both Jesus' birth and Baptism. The inclusion of Christmas came later, and in the West became the principal celebration of Jesus' birth.

When most people in your assembly think of Epiphany, they will imagine the magi coming to glorify Jesus. The reading from Isaiah, as well as the example of the magi, teaches that those who see the glory of the Lord are accountable for what they see. Just as Jerusalem was called to "rise up" and be a light for other nations, we need to proclaim God's glory beyond our church buildings and into the streets and neighborhoods of our cities.

The First Reading provides us with a description of the new Jerusalem. The Israelites return from the exile with the Lord's light shining on them and their city. More than the Israelites, though, other nations and kings, indeed, sons and daughters from afar, also gather in Jerusalem. The Lord's glory is so impressive that others want to join in singing God's praises.

Proclaim this reading with joy and excitement, praising God for the many ways in which he is present in your life, your parish community, the universal Church, and the world itself. Just as we hear of Israel's duty to be the light of the Lord to the world, through your own joy extol the assembly to reflect on the Lord's shining glory.

Ephesians = ee-FEE-zhunz

Address the "You have heard" directly to the assembly by looking up and making eye contact.

Pause significantly after the colon in the line "to his holy apostles and prophets by the Spirit." State the mystery "that the Gentiles are coheirs . . . in the promise in Christ Jesus through the gospel" firmly, but with contentment because you believe in it.

Gentiles = JEN-tils
coheirs = co-airs

READING II   Ephesians 3:2–3a, 5–6

A reading from the Letter of Saint Paul to the Ephesians

Brothers and sisters:
You have **heard** of the **stewardship** of God's **grace**
    that was given to me for your **benefit**,
        namely, that the **mystery** was made **known** to me
            by **revelation**.
It was not made known to people in **other** generations
    as it has **now** been revealed
        to his **holy** apostles and **prophets** by the **Spirit**:
        that the **Gentiles** are **coheirs**, **members** of the **same body**,
        and **copartners** in the **promise** in Christ **Jesus**
            through the **gospel**.

READING II   When Paul spoke of the "stewardship of God's grace," he was referring to the realization of God's plan in history. The fullness of this realization occurred in the person of Jesus Christ, who in Paul's time both Jews and Gentiles adored.

Through Christ, God manifested himself to all. Paul understood the primary purpose of his ministry was to bring Jews and Gentiles together around Christ Jesus. Both are heirs to his promise. Both are members of the same body, the body of Christ. For Paul, Christ's own body is the source of unity among Jews and Gentiles; it is what binds them together.

The challenge for us today is to bring Christ to the world in a way that respects the many, diverse religious and cultural traditions of the world's peoples. Our mission obligates us to spread the message of Christ and to live in imitation of him, welcoming others into the body of Christ. In its Decree on the Church's Missionary Activity (*Ad gentes divinitus* [AG]), the Second Vatican Council taught that the spread of the Gospel, just as in the early Church, develops through the local cultures. Young churches today "borrow from the customs, traditions, wisdom, teaching, arts and sciences of their people everything which could be used to praise the glory of the Creator, manifest the grace of the saviour, or contribute to the right ordering of Christian life" (AG, #22; see LG, #13.) Furthermore, the Council's Declaration on the Relation of the Church to Non-Christian Religions (*Nostra aetate* [NA]) taught that "the Catholic Church rejects nothing of what is true and holy" in others religions,

GOSPEL   Matthew 2:1–12

A reading from the holy Gospel according to Matthew

Bethlehem = BETH-luh-hem
Judea = joo-DEE-uh
Herod = HAIR-ud

When **Jesus** was born in **Bethlehem** of Judea,
   in the days of King **Herod**,
   behold, **magi** from the **east** arrived in **Jerusalem**, saying,
   "**Where** is the newborn **king** of the Jews?
We saw his **star** at its **rising**
   and have **come** to do him **homage**."

As you proclaim the section that begins with "When King Herod heard this," express in your tone of voice that King Herod is conniving. He is up to something here as he assembles the chief priests and the scribes together.

Observe the repetition of "Bethlehem of Judea" as the place of Jesus' birth. It occurred at the beginning of the Gospel as well. Bethlehem was the place of David's birth. The repetition serves to point out Jesus' Davidic ancestry.

When King **Herod** heard this,
   he was greatly **troubled**,
   and **all Jerusalem** with him.
Assembling all the chief priests and the scribes of the people,
   he inquired of them where the **Christ** was to be **born**.
They said to him, "In **Bethlehem** of Judea,
   for **thus** it has been **written** through the **prophet**:
     And **you**, **Bethlehem**, *land of Judah*,
       *are by no means **least** among the **rulers** of **Judah**;*
     *since from you shall **come** a **ruler**,*
      *who is to **shepherd** my people **Israel**."*

King Herod really does not want to offer the child true homage. Try adding a little sarcasm to your voice so that Herod's deceptive character comes through.

Then Herod **called** the **magi** secretly
   and ascertained from them the **time** of the star's **appearance**.
He sent them to **Bethlehem** and said,
   "**Go** and search **diligently** for the **child**.
When you have found him, **bring** me word,
   that I **too** may go and **do** him **homage**."
After their **audience** with the **king** they set **out**.

Pause slightly before and after the line "After their audience with the king they set out." Impart the joy and relief of the magi in the lines "They were overjoyed at seeing the star, and on entering the house they saw the child with Mary his mother."

And **behold**, the **star** that they had **seen** at its **rising**
   preceded them,
   until it **came** and **stopped** over the place where the **child** was.

yet she is still "duty bound to proclaim without fail, Christ who is the way, the truth and the life" (NA, #2; John 1:6).

The Jews and Gentiles in early Christian communities did not always see eye to eye or want to accept each other fully into the body of Christ. In Christ, we are to work through our differences, accepting what is true, good, and beautiful in all religious traditions, cultures, and peoples. As Paul found out, working to bring people together as the body of Christ was a lifelong endeavor. This endeavor, which is now ours, is possible for us to

undertake because God is faithful—the Spirit of Christ remains with us in the work we do.

| GOSPEL | The story of the magi is rightly beloved by Christians; it is the story associated with the solemnity of Epiphany, the day many think of as the day of the three kings. However, if we think of this day only in terms of the three kings, we miss its broader meaning, a meaning that Matthew captured in his Gospel.

The word epiphany means "manifestation." Recall that Luke had the shepherds at the scene of Jesus' birth as the first to pay him homage. In today's passage from Matthew, we learn that the magi, Gentiles, were the first to adore Jesus. Yet the magi observed Jesus' star and went to King Herod because they wanted to pay the child who was born king of the Jews homage. In observing a particular star and wanting to follow it, the magi were acting on the popular belief at the time that each person was represented by a star at their birth. When some of the Jews, including

Take your time with the lines that tell us how the magi offered homage to the Christ child. Read them with homage in your own voice.

frankincense = FRANK-in-sens

myrrh = mer

They were **overjoyed** at seeing the **star**,
    and on entering the house
    they saw the **child** with **Mary** his **mother**.
They **prostrated** themselves and did him **homage**.
Then they **opened** their **treasures**
    and **offered** him gifts of **gold**, **frankincense**, and **myrrh**.
And having been **warned** in a dream **not** to return to **Herod**,
    they **departed** for their **country** by another **way**.

King Herod, were notified, they remained unmoved, even disturbed. Matthew's main point in this narrative is that, in Jesus, God is made manifest to the whole world. God's promises are not reserved to a select few. They are available to all, there to be accepted in faith just as the magi who were Gentiles did.

At the end of today's Gospel the magi go back to their home country. They did not remain basking in the excitement from their adoration of Christ. This would have been selfish. Rather, their mission to the world began as they journeyed back home to share their joy of seeing the Christ child. One could say their own birth as followers of Jesus occurred as they offered homage to Jesus, God's definitive epiphany to the world.

The U.S. Bishops referenced Guerric of Igny, a twelfth-century French abbot, in their explanation of the relationship between Christmas and Epiphany: "That which we have celebrated up to today is the birth of Christ, that which we celebrate today is our own birth" (Sermon 14, cited in Study Text 9, *The Liturgical Year*). We are born as Christians in our act of giving homage to Christ and bringing his presence to the world. By the way you emphasize the importance of the last line in this Gospel, the assembly will know praise of God can never be separated from continuing to make Jesus manifest in our cities, towns, and villages. If we separate our faith from our mission in the world, then we have not been truly born as Christians.

BAPTISM OF THE LORD

Lectionary #21

READING I   Isaiah 55:1–11

A reading from the Book of the Prophet Isaiah

Be direct as you identify the speaker in the opening line ("Thus says the Lord"). Note the repetition of the word "come" in the reading. Start off with a quiet but clearly audible invitation to your assembly to "come." Each time you repeat the Lord's invitation to "come," place a little more excitement in your voice.

Thus says the LORD:
All you who are **thirsty**,
    come to the **water**!
You who have no **money**,
    come, receive **grain** and **eat**;
come, without **paying** and without **cost**,
    drink **wine** and **milk**!
Why spend your **money** for what is not **bread**,
    your **wages** for what fails to **satisfy**?
Heed **me**, and you shall eat **well**,
    you shall delight in **rich** fare.
Come to me **heedfully**,
    listen, that you may have **life**.
I will **renew** with you the everlasting **covenant**,
    the **benefits** assured to **David**.

The verses "As I made him a witness to the peoples" contain a personal comparison with David and show how God has been faithful in the past and will continue to be faithful. Use a more narrative tone of voice.

As I made him a **witness** to the *peoples*,
    a **leader** and commander of **nations**,
so shall **you** summon a nation you knew **not**,
    and nations that knew **you** not shall **run** to you,
because of the **LORD**, your **God**,
    the **Holy** One of **Israel**, who has **glorified** you.

Pause before the section that begins with "Seek the Lord while he may be found." Return again to an invitational tone of voice, though somewhat stronger than the first invitation to "come."

Seek the LORD while he may be **found**,
    call him while he is **near**.

READING I Today we celebrate the Baptism of the Lord; thus, the reason for the choice of this beautiful reading from Isaiah could not be clearer. This reading also is fifth among the seven readings from the Old Testament proclaimed at the Easter Vigil. As you prepare, you might also want to turn to that commentary.

Throughout this reading is an invitation from the Lord to come to the banquet feast. The author of this passage understands that the exile is almost at an end

and Israel will be restored; the Lord will be faithful to the covenant. Yet the people need to repent of their ways that have separated them from God. We, like Israel, also need to seek the Lord, turning from our wicked ways back to God, who forgives. The Church's theology of Baptism and Eucharist has been informed by this reading; welcome and invitation, as well as the forgiveness of sins, have always been a part of our understanding of both sacraments.

Once we accept the Lord's call to "come to the water," we are not left on our own. We journey together with our brothers and sisters in faith who also have accepted the invitation. And when we gather together as the community of the faithful, we celebrate the Eucharist. This eschatological banquet that the author of Isaiah is inviting all of Israel to is fulfilled for Christians in the eucharistic banquet—a new eschatological banquet.

Phrases such as "Let the scoundrel forsake his way and the wicked man his thoughts" imply a responsibility to change on the part of those who choose to accept the invitation to turn to the Lord. A stronger, more self-assured voice will help the sense of responsibility.

"For just as from the heavens . . . achieving the end for which I sent it" is a lengthy sentence. Take your time as you convey the Lord's promise. Use a gentle and lighter tone of voice through the words "that goes forth from my mouth." After the semicolon, speak the words "my word shall not return to me void" with conviction. You know this promise has already been fulfilled in Jesus.

Let the scoundrel **forsake** his way,
    and the wicked man his **thoughts**;
let him **turn** to the LORD for **mercy**;
    to our **God**, who is **generous** in **forgiving**.
For **my** thoughts are not **your** thoughts,
    nor are **your** ways **my** ways, says the LORD.
As high as the **heavens** are above the **earth**
    so high are **my** ways above **your** ways
    and **my** thoughts above **your** thoughts.

For just as from the **heavens**
    the **rain** and **snow** come down
and do not **return** there
    till they have **watered** the earth,
    making it **fertile** and **fruitful**,
giving **seed** to the one who **sows**
    and **bread** to the one who **eats**,
so shall my **word** be
    that goes forth from my **mouth**;
my **word** shall **not** return to me **void**,
    but shall **do** my will,
    achieving the **end** for which I **sent** it.

Or:

READING I   Isaiah 42:1–4, 6–7

A reading from the Book of the Prophet Isaiah

Thus says the LORD:
Here is my servant whom I **uphold**,
    my **chosen** one with whom I am **pleased**,

For Christians, the promise of the Lord in the final sentence is fulfilled in Jesus. He is the Word who has gone forth from the Lord's mouth and has not returned to him without effect. Through our hearing the word of the Lord proclaimed and our participation in the eucharistic banquet, we are nourished to go forth, bringing others to the Lord. In others words, we follow the example of Jesus, who went forth from his own Baptism to do God's will. Through your ministry as a lector, the word of the Lord is going out from God through you,

reaching others in the assembly. Your preparation of the reading and the skill and the sincerity with which you proclaim it will help attract others more deeply to their faith. Though you may not personally hear or see its effects, the word will not be without effect.

READING II   Our Second Reading today, like the First Reading, is proclaimed during Easter (turn to the commentary for the Second Sunday of Easter for more background). The three epistles

of John are seen as part of the Johannine tradition because they contain some of the same themes as the Gospel according to John (read the prologue to the Gospel of John and the first chapter of 1 John to see the theme of light and darkness in both), although they probably were not written by the same author.

Just as the Christian community at the time of the writing of the Gospel according to John was divided, the Johannine Church of the epistles is also divided over false

upon whom I have put my **spirit**;
    he shall bring forth **justice** to the nations,
not crying out, **not** shouting,
    not making his voice heard in the **street**.
A **bruised reed** he shall not **break**,
    and a smoldering **wick** he shall not **quench**,
until he establishes **justice** on the earth;
    the **coastlands** will **wait** for his **teaching**.

I, the LORD, have **called** you for the victory of **justice**,
    I have grasped you by the **hand**;
I **formed** you, and set you
    as a **covenant** of the people,
    a **light** for the **nations**,
to open the eyes of the **blind**,
    to bring out **prisoners** from **confinement**,
    and from the **dungeon**, those who live in **darkness**.

READING II   1 John 5:1–9

A reading from the first Letter of Saint John

Beloved:
Everyone who **believes** that **Jesus** is the **Christ** is **begotten** by **God**,
    and everyone who loves the **Father**
    loves **also** the one **begotten** by him.
In **this** way we **know** that we love the **children** of God
    when we love **God** and obey his **commandments**.
For the *love* of God is **this**,
    that we **keep** his commandments.

Be sure to proceed slowly as you proclaim the opening line ("Everyone who believes that Jesus is . . . and everyone who *loves* the Father *loves* also the one begotten by him") so as not to get tangled up with the repetition of the word "loves."

teachings. Some believed Jesus was not truly the Son of God from the Father—the Messiah. Others failed to see the necessity of loving one another. For the author of the epistle, the way in which Christians loved one another testified to their belief in Jesus Christ. Those who believed in Jesus' atoning sacrifice on the cross would no longer sin; their lives would witness to their belief.

Observe that the Spirit is present at Jesus' Baptism, explicitly in the Gospel and implicitly in this reading. The presence of the Spirit witnesses to the Son of God, testifying to the water and the blood. It is this same Spirit who continues to be present in the Church. In the sacrament of Baptism (water), the Spirit is present as new members witness to their faith in the Son of God and are incorporated into the community of believers. In the sacrament of the Eucharist (blood), which recalls Jesus' sacrifice, the Spirit is also present, making us a living memorial of that sacrifice.

Your goal in the proclamation of this reading is to show the relationship between love of God and love of the children of God. Paying close attention to the Lectionary divisions of the reading will help you to understand the author's line of reasoning and achieve this goal. Also, reflect on how you give witness to Jesus as the Son of God in the way you love others. Your personal reflection will give your proclamation more integrity.

"And his commandments are not burdensome . . . is our faith" are hopeful, positive words. Offer them with a lighter tone of voice. This will help the assembly hear that God's commands are not overly weighty.

In the words "This is the one who came through water and blood . . . but by water and blood," water refers to the Baptism of Jesus and the blood to the cross.

Give God's testimony found in the words "that he has testified on behalf of his Son" with certainty: you know that Jesus is the Son of God.

And his commandments are **not burdensome**,
    for whoever is begotten by **God** conquers the **world**.
And the **victory** that conquers the world is our **faith**.
Who indeed is the **victor** over the world
    but the one who **believes** that Jesus is the Son of God?

This is the one who came through **water** and **blood**, Jesus **Christ**,
    not by water **alone**, but by water and **blood**.
The **Spirit** is the one who **testifies**,
    and the **Spirit** is **truth**.
So there are **three** that testify,
    the **Spirit**, the **water**, and the **blood**,
    and the **three** are of **one accord**.
If we accept **human** testimony,
    the testimony of **God** is surely **greater**.
Now the testimony of **God** is **this**,
    that he has testified on **behalf** of his Son.

Or:

READING II   Acts 10:34–38

A reading from the Acts of the Apostles

Peter proceeded to speak to those gathered
    in the house of **Cornelius**, saying:
    "In **truth**, I see that **God** shows no **partiality**.
Rather, in **every** nation whoever **fears** him and acts **uprightly**
    is **acceptable** to him.

GOSPEL   When we arrive at the celebration of the Baptism of the Lord, our society has long since moved on from Christmas, but for us this celebration marks the day when we officially end the Christmas season and begin to look forward to the short period of Ordinary Time before Lent. Yet Christmas never really ends. Over 20 years ago in its study text on the liturgical year, the Bishops' Committee on the Liturgy in the United States wrote the following: "The Baptism of the Lord does not conclude Christmas by putting it away until next year. The evangelists place the baptism of Jesus at the start of his public ministry, with the narrative details manifesting his identity. Thus Christmas ends with the scene set for the retelling of Jesus' life" (Study Text 9, p. 45).

Mark uses the revelation of God (theophany) that Jesus saw to reveal his identity in four ways: 1) that the "heavens being torn open" is a reference to Isaiah 64:1, the beginning of a prayer that for God to reveal himself at the dawn of a new age; 2) the "Spirit . . . descending upon him" alludes to Isaiah 63:11, 14, which recounts the Lord's Spirit coming down on the Israelites during the Exodus; 3) the dove is often used as a symbol for Israel in the Old Testament (Hosea 11:11; Psalm 68:13; 74:19) and rabbinical commentaries; and 4) "a voice came from heaven" suggests a reference to Isaiah 42:1, the first suffering servant song. Put together, these four elements show that Jesus is, for Mark, the Son of God, the suffering servant in whom the Spirit dwells and in whom a new age has dawned.

You **know** the word that he sent to the **Israelites**
   as he proclaimed **peace** through Jesus **Christ**, who is Lord of **all**,
   what has happened all over **Judea**,
   beginning in **Galilee** after the baptism
   that **John** preached,
   how God anointed **Jesus** of **Nazareth**
   with the Holy **Spirit** and **power**.
He went about doing **good**
   and **healing** all those oppressed by the **devil**,
   for **God** was with him."

GOSPEL   Mark 1:7–11

A reading from the holy Gospel according to Mark

This is what John the **Baptist** proclaimed:
   "One **mightier** than I is coming **after** me.
I am **not worthy** to stoop and loosen the **thongs** of his **sandals**.
I have baptized you with **water**;
   he will baptize you with the Holy **Spirit**."

It **happened** in those days that **Jesus** came from **Nazareth**
      of **Galilee**
   and was **baptized** in the **Jordan** by **John**.
On coming up out of the **water** he saw the **heavens** being
      torn **open**
   and the **Spirit**, like a **dove**, **descending** upon him.
And a **voice** came from the *heavens*,
   "**You** are my beloved **Son**; with **you** I am well **pleased**."

Look up as you state the phrase "One mightier than I is coming after me." Having recently heard John the Baptist's proclamation in Advent, the assembly is familiar with his message. Use patience as you proclaim his words so they will be heard in the new context of the celebration of the Baptism of the Lord.

Pause before the section that begins with the words "It happened in those days." A narrative tone of voice is more suitable for describing Jesus' Baptism.

The climax of the Gospel comes in the declaration from the voice: "You are my beloved Son; with you I am well pleased."

On this third "manifestation" feast—Christmas and Epiphany being the other two—the revelation of Jesus' identity in his Baptism provides us with a sense of our identity as well. Yet Mark does not come right out and tell us who Jesus is. By having only Jesus see the vision of God, Mark is able to keep Jesus' identity hidden. In contrast to Matthew and Luke, Jesus' Baptism is a personal experience in this Gospel. For example, the statement "You are my beloved Son; with you I am well pleased" is addressed personally to Jesus; it is seemingly inaudible to others. Yet for us, the baptized, Jesus' identity is no longer hidden. The statement from the voice reveals Jesus' identity as the beloved Son of God and attests to his intimate relationship with the Father. Through our Baptism, we too are claimed by God as his beloved sons and daughters and sent forth to begin our public ministry in the name of Jesus and the Church. Let this Gospel serve as a reminder of our own Baptism and our election by God to manifest Christ in all we do. Even though the Christmas season ends today, in reality Christmas will never end.

2ND SUNDAY IN ORDINARY TIME

Lectionary #65

READING I   1 Samuel 3:3b–10; 19

A reading from the first Book of Samuel

Samuel was **sleeping** in the temple of the LORD
　　where the **ark** of God was.
The LORD called to Samuel, who answered, "**Here** I am."
Samuel ran to **Eli** and said, "**Here** I am. You **called** me."
"I did **not** call you," Eli said. "Go back to **sleep**."
So he went back to sleep.
Again the LORD called **Samuel**, who **rose** and went to **Eli**.
"**Here** I am, " he said. "You **called** me."
But Eli answered, "I did **not** call you, my **son**. Go back to **sleep**."

At **that** time **Samuel** was not **familiar** with the LORD,
　　because the LORD had not **revealed** anything to him as yet.
The LORD called Samuel **again**, for the **third** time.
Getting **up** and going to **Eli**, he said, "**Here** I am. You **called** me."
Then Eli understood that the LORD was calling the youth.
So he said to Samuel, "Go to **sleep**, and **if** you are called, reply,
　　'**Speak**, LORD, for your servant is **listening**.'"
When Samuel went to **sleep** in his place,
　　the LORD **came** and **revealed** his presence,
　　calling out as **before**, "**Samuel**, **Samuel**!"
Samuel answered, "**Speak**, for your servant is **listening**."

Samuel grew **up**, and the LORD was with him,
　　not permitting any **word** of his to be without **effect**.

Think of this reading in terms of scenes.
Scene one begins with the words
"Samuel was sleeping" and continues
through "So he went back to sleep."
Pause before the next scene.

Scene two begins with "Again the Lord
called Samuel" and concludes with
Eli's response "I did not call you." Pause
again before the next scene.

Eli = EE-lī

Scene three begins "At that time Samuel
was not familiar with the Lord" and ends
with Eli's advice to Samuel ("Go to sleep,
and if you are called . . .").

Scene four includes Samuel's recognition of the Lord and his response. Speak
Samuel's words with a sense of self-
confidence, for he now truly knows who
is calling and how to respond.

Pause before "Samuel grew up . . .
without effect." Impart it while making
eye contact with the assembly.

READING I　This Sunday, we begin the short period of Ordinary Time between the end of the Christmas season and Ash Wednesday.

　　Today's First Reading from 1 Samuel is the story the prophetic call of Samuel. In this narrative (3:1–21) there are two main themes: the call of Samuel and the col-lapse of Eli's household. Some verses not included in the First Reading help form the context: verses 11–18 and verses 20–21. Do not read these verses when you pro-claim the reading, but read them as you prepare. They detail the difficult message about the downfall of Eli's family that Samuel will have to reveal to Eli after accepting God's call.

　　Though influential in the community because he was the priest serving the ark of the covenant, Eli was not a strong leader and his sons were evil. After Samuel rec-ognizes that it is the Lord calling him, and he responds to the Lord by saying, "Speak, for your servant is listening," the Lord tells Samuel that he is going to condemn Eli's family because his sons were blasphem-ers. Thus, Samuel's acceptance of the Lord's call meant sharing a difficult mes-sage with Eli, but Samuel was also to serve God by anointing of the first two kings of Israel, Saul and David.

　　Jesus' acceptance of God's call did not mean everything would go smoothly, nor does our acceptance of God's call. But, as the narrative tells us, the Lord was with Samuel as he fulfilled his role (3:19). In your proclamation, you will want the assem-bly to come away with the sense that the Lord is also always with them as they live out God's call, a call that can mean pro-claiming difficult messages or making dif-ficult decisions. Your proclamation can

READING II   1 Corinthians 6:13c–15a, 17–20

Corinthians = kor-IN-thee-unz

Follow the punctuation carefully in the first sentence ("The body is not for immorality, but for the Lord . . . by his power").

Raise the inflection in your voice at the end of "Do you not know that your bodies are members of Christ?" Pause at the end of the questions, allowing people time to ponder the question.

The second question begins like the previous one. Wait until the last phrase to change the inflection in your voice.

"Therefore glorify God in your body" is a positive restatement of the previous negative command ("avoid immorality"). Be resolute, but not harsh, when you deliver the command. Address it looking at the assembly. You're commanding your community—which is one and has members—to glorify God as one body.

A reading from the first Letter of Saint Paul to the Corinthians

Brothers and sisters:
The **body** is not for **immorality**, but for the **Lord**,
    and the **Lord** is for the **body**;
    God raised the **Lord** and will **also** raise **us** by his **power**.

Do you not **know** that your **bodies** are members of **Christ**?
But whoever is **joined** to the Lord becomes one **Spirit** with him.
Avoid immorality.
Every **other** sin a person commits is **outside** the body,
    but the **immoral** person sins against his **own** body.
Do you not **know** that your body
    is a **temple** of the Holy **Spirit** within you,
    whom you have from **God**, and that you are not your **own**?
For you have been **purchased** at a price.
Therefore **glorify** God in your **body**.

---

also reveal the Lord's call to the assembly to journey once again through Ordinary Time on the way to Lent and Easter.

READING II We now begin Ordinary Time with Paul's instruction to the Corinthians to care for their bodies because the body itself is "for the Lord" and "a temple of the Holy Spirit." This is one of the earliest books in the New Testament, written around the year 56, about two decades before any of the four Gospels. Paul addressed the letter to a community notorious for its immorality.

In the letter Paul is persistent in his efforts to call the Corinthians to change their behavior, especially those who professed faith in Jesus Christ. While our society is far removed in time and place from the Corinthian community Paul addressed, the human penchant for immorality still exists.

Paul's letter shows that the belief in reverencing the body developed early in Christian communities. This attests to the fact that from the beginning Christianity was an incarnational faith: the Word became flesh in the person of Jesus. Therefore, if followers of Christ denigrate

their own bodies, they harm not only themselves, but also others who belong to the body of Christ, the Church. That, for Paul, is as much as blaspheming Christ.

Paul's message to the Corinthians translated for us today is that Christmas must live on in the followers of Christ in the way we respect one another's humanity. Christ, born as an infant in a manger, lives on today in the Church, his body. As we Christians make decisions about our ethical behavior each day, the relevant Pauline principle from this passage is that our actions impact not only our individual bodies, but

A reading from the holy Gospel according to John

John was standing with **two** of his disciples,
    and as he watched **Jesus** walk by, he said,
    "Behold, the **Lamb** of God."
The two disciples **heard** what he said and **followed** Jesus.
Jesus **turned** and **saw** them following him and said to them,
    "What are you **looking** for?"
They said to him, "**Rabbi**"—which translated means **Teacher**—,
    "where are you **staying**?"
He said to them, "**Come**, and you will **see**."
So they **went** and **saw** where Jesus was staying,
    and they **stayed** with him that day.
It was about four in the afternoon.
Andrew, the brother of Simon **Peter**,
    was **one** of the two who heard **John** and **followed** Jesus.
He **first** found his own brother Simon and told him,
    "We have found the **Messiah**"—which is translated **Christ**—.
Then he **brought** him to Jesus.
Jesus looked at him and said,
    "You are **Simon** the son of **John**;
    you will be called **Cephas**"—which is translated **Peter**.

Beginning with the phrase "The two disciples heard what he said and followed Jesus," note the theme of following in this Gospel. Highlight each form of the word "follow."

Offer Jesus' question to the two disciples in a personal and inviting manner. This is also an invitation to your community to journey with Jesus through Ordinary Time, Lent, and Easter—once again recounting the stories, teachings, and mysteries of our faith.

Pause and look up when you tell the assembly what Andrew told Simon. Add some excitement as you speak these words. The assembly will then understand his proclamation to others as a result of his encounter with Jesus.

Cephas =SEE-fus

Cephas in Aramaic and *Petros* (Peter) in Greek mean "rock." Narrate the last section of the Gospel not as the conclusion many have heard before, but as a climax.

the corporate body of the Church, in particular the body of believers with whom we worship every Sunday.

GOSPEL   Today's Gospel is in the section of John after the prologue and before most of the signs of Jesus are narrated. Johannine scholars have noted how, from the testimony of John the Baptist through the first miracle at Cana (2:1–11), Jesus' identity is progressively revealed with different titles, each heightening the importance of who Jesus is. Jesus' identity moves from John the

Baptist's recognition of the one who is to come after him whose sandal strap he is not worthy to untie (1:27) to "the Lamb of God" to the one who is teacher and Messiah and has disciples to one who continues to gain more followers and is called the Son of God and the King of Israel (1:49). John lets his readers know that the disciples will believe not only on the basis of their initial encounter with Jesus, but because of greater things: they will see "the heaven opened and the angels of God ascending and descending upon the Son of Man" (1:51). As believers, then, they will be com-

pelled to call others to faith, to follow the Messiah.

As you proclaim the scriptural passage, visualize yourself as John the Baptist, the one who announces Jesus as the Lamb of God. Through your proclamation of this Gospel, the assembly is called to follow Jesus. Imagine yourself also offering Jesus' invitation of "Come, and you will see" to them and inviting them to extend the invitation to others, especially those who might be interested in inquiring into the Catholic Church and participating in the Rite of Christian Initiation of Adults.

3RD SUNDAY IN ORDINARY TIME

Lectionary #68

READING I   Jonah 3:1–5, 10

Jonah = JOH-nuh

Pause before and after "Set out for the great city of Nineveh . . . I will tell you."

Nineveh = NIN-uh-vuh

A reading from the Book of the Prophet Jonah

The **word** of the LORD came to **Jonah**, saying:
"Set out for the great city of **Nineveh**,
and **announce** to it the message that I will tell you."
So Jonah made **ready** and went to **Nineveh**,
according to the LORD's bidding.
Now **Nineveh** was an **enormously** large city;
it took three days to go through it.
Jonah **began** his journey through the city,
and had gone but a single day's **walk** announcing,
"**Forty** days more and **Nineveh** shall be **destroyed**,"
when the **people** of Nineveh **believed** God;
they proclaimed a **fast**
and **all** of them, **great** and **small**, put on **sackcloth**.

Put across Jonah's prophecy to the people of Nineveh ("Forty days more and Nineveh shall be destroyed") with sternness and urgency in your voice. Capture the almost instantaneous repentance of the people of Nineveh described in the words "when the people of Nineveh . . . put on sackcloth" by relaxing the tension in your voice.

Pause before you describe God's forgiveness ("When God saw by their actions . . . he repented . . . he did not carry it out") with compassion.

When God **saw** by their actions how they **turned** from their
evil way,
he **repented** of the evil that he had **threatened** to do to them;
he did **not** carry it out.

READING I This is the only Sunday in all three years of the Lectionary cycle of readings on which a passage from the book of Jonah is read.

The book of Jonah is only four short chapters long. The first two chapters describe Jonah's call by God and his rebellion; the story of Jonah and the big fish is in these chapters. The last two chapters narrate the "second chance" that God gives Jonah.

After he offers a prayer of thanksgiving and is spewed out of the fish, Jonah is sent on a second prophetic mission to Nineveh. This is where today's reading begins. Jonah is now charged with bringing the mercy that the Lord offered to him to Nineveh. His prophetic message is one of repentance and change. The Ninevites seem to accept this message immediately, like the first disciples in today's Gospel.

Jonah himself might have rescinded his own offer of mercy and remained an obstinate prophet, but God remained merciful. The last verse in the reading tells us even God repented of the evil he had threatened to do to the Ninevites.

This is a challenging reading for those of us who profess to follow the Lord. Your task as a minister of this word is to convey both the conversion the Lord demands and the loving mercy that follows. The Lord's kindness will prevail even when we who follow his ways fall short. Jonah himself experienced this truth.

Corinthians = kor-IN-thee-unz

Make eye contact as you state the opening fact of the reading ("the time is running out") with conviction and fervor.

READING II 1 Corinthians 7:29–31

A reading from the first Letter of Saint Paul to the Corinthians

I **tell** you, brothers and sisters, the **time** is running **out**.
From now **on**, let those having **wives** act as **not** having them,
    those **weeping** as **not** weeping,
    those **rejoicing** as **not** rejoicing,
    those **buying** as not **owning**,
    those **using** the world as not using it **fully**.
For the world in its **present** form is passing **away**.

READING II This reading is centered on Paul's conviction, and that of the early Christians, that the *parousia*, Christ's second coming, was imminent. We heard many readings with this theme in Advent, but why would we hear one again on the Third Sunday in Ordinary Time?

    The Gospel reading is Mark's account of the call of the first disciples. The call of any disciple of Christ involves turning away from the world. Although we continue to proclaim in the Memorial Acclamations after the consecration at Mass that "Christ will come again," we—like the Corinthian community—need to be reminded that the ways of the world are not wholly our ways. Only faith in Jesus Christ is lasting for those who choose to be his followers.

    The two verses that form today's epistle are part of a larger section of 1 Corinthians in which Paul responds to questions from the community. Chapter seven focuses on questions of marital and social status. Paul's main concern is the Corinthians' attachment to the world. He counsels them to remain in their present social and marital state. Ultimately, it does not matter whether we are married or single, weeping or rejoicing. Paul's message—and your message to the present-day disciples in your assembly—is not to be deceived by the allure of this world. The world is good, but only insofar as it leads us closer to the Lord, so we might be ready when he comes again in glory.

GOSPEL   Mark 1:14–20

A reading from the holy Gospel according to Mark

After **John** had been **arrested**,
  Jesus came to **Galilee** proclaiming the gospel of **God**:
  "**This** is the time of **fulfillment**.
The kingdom of **God** is at **hand**.
Repent, and **believe** in the **gospel**."

As he passed by the Sea of **Galilee**,
  he saw **Simon** and his brother **Andrew** casting their **nets**
    into the sea;
  they were **fishermen**.
Jesus said to them,
  "Come after **me**, and **I** will make you fishers of **men**."
Then they **abandoned** their nets and **followed** him.
He walked along a little farther
  and saw **James**, the son of **Zebedee**, and his brother **John**.
They **too** were in a boat mending their nets.
Then he **called** them.
So they **left** their father **Zebedee** in the boat
  along with the hired men and **followed** him.

Fill your voice with strength, confidence, conviction, and sincerity as you proclaim Jesus' message. The strength of your voice will make evident the authority with which Jesus teaches.

Pause noticeably after the proclamation of Jesus' words and before the narrative picks up with "As he passed by the Sea of Galilee."

Enunciate clearly Jesus' invitation: "Come after me, and I will make you fishers of men." It is the second week in a row we hear this call.

Pause after narrating the response of Simon and Andrew to Jesus' call. This will help make clear that in the next section Jesus calls again, this time James and John.

Zebedee = ZEB-eh-dee

GOSPEL   Mark's portrait of Jesus is clear from the very beginning: Jesus is the Son of God, a powerful teacher and healer, a person with authority.

Simon, Andrew, James, and John respond without hesitation and in a radical way to Jesus' command. As the Gospel reading shows us, being disciples of Jesus entails some kind of break with the past, perhaps reordering family relationships and life priorities. In the last verse (1:20), the reference to the "hired men" in the boat with James and John and their father,

Zebedee, could point to the fact that Zebedee's family had a fishing business. It seems, then, that James and John left their economic stability behind as well. While presumably they would still have to be concerned about how they were going to make it financially, their choice to follow Jesus shows they were choosing to center their lives around a person and a message of Good News. This person and his message would now be the ordering principle for their lives—economic decisions and decisions about relationships would follow from their commitment to Jesus.

You and the assembly accepted Jesus' call to discipleship in the sacrament of Baptism. For most of us, our parents responded to this call for us. This Gospel is a helpful reminder to us to evaluate our lives to see how we can best be faithful to Jesus' message of repentance and belief in the Good News. In this way, we will renew our baptismal commitment to be disciples of Jesus.

4TH SUNDAY IN ORDINARY TIME

Lectionary #71

READING I   Deuteronomy 18:15–20

Deuteronomy = doo-ter-AH-nuh-mee

Pause after the first line of the reading. The rest of the reading is either words that Moses himself speaks or words that the Lord speaks to Moses. Moses now speaks to the people.

Horeb = HOH-reb

In the words "This is exactly what you requested of the Lord, your God," Moses is reminding the people what they asked of God. Emphasize that these are the people's words Moses is reciting back to them.

Let slight trepidation be heard in your voice as you speak the consequences for false prophecy described in the words of the final section ("But if a prophet presumes . . . he shall die"). Do not be overly ominous at the end, because no matter whether the prophet is true or false, the salvation offered by the Lord will prevail.

A reading from the Book of Deuteronomy

Moses spoke to **all** the people, saying:
  "A **prophet** like me will the LORD, your **God**, raise **up** for you
  from among your own **kin**;
  to **him** you shall **listen**.
This is **exactly** what you **requested** of the LORD, your God,
    at **Horeb**
  on the **day** of the assembly, when you **said**,
  'Let us not **again** hear the voice of the LORD, our **God**,
  nor see this great **fire** any more, lest we **die**.'
And the LORD said to me, 'This was **well** said.
I will **raise** up for them a **prophet** like you from among their **kin**,
  and will put my **words** into his **mouth**;
  he shall tell them **all** that I **command** him.
Whoever will **not** listen to my words which he speaks
    in my **name**,
  I **myself** will make him **answer** for it.
But **if** a prophet presumes to speak in my name
  an **oracle** that I have **not** commanded him to **speak**,
  or **speaks** in the name of **other** gods, he shall **die**.' "

READING I | The book of Deuteronomy is the fifth book of the Pentateuch, the first five books of the Old Testament, also known as the Torah or the Law. In particular, it details how the people are to renew their covenant with God and order their lives.

For the Israelites, Moses is first among prophets. His words and the words of the Lord he announces, like the Advent readings, predict the coming of another prophet. Unlike the readings in Advent, however, this reading includes a warning to the people and to any who would presume to be a prophet.

At the time of Moses, true and false prophets were distinguished by their word. Moses was a true prophet because he conveyed the word of the Lord to the Israelites (18:18); Moses delivered God's promise to raise up another prophet, a promise that for Christians would be fulfilled in Jesus. (The promise was also understood in a messianic sense by Jews.) Fulfillment of a prophetic message was another test of a true prophet (18:21). A false prophet would speak his own message or that of other gods (18:20).

Christ is the prophet par excellence, but by virtue of our Baptism we also share in his prophetic role through our proclamation of the word of God. For us today the word of God in scriptures, which you proclaim in your ministry as a lector, and the tradition of the Church as discerned by the magisterium—the Church's teaching office—provide norms by which we can

Corinthians = kor=IN-thee-unz

Read "I should like you to be free of anxieties" directly to the assembly.

Note the parallel structure in the next section: unmarried man/married man and unmarried woman/married woman. Emphasize which you are talking about. This will help to give structure to the reading as the assembly listens to it. Look up and around at various people in the assembly as you deliver these lines.

Paul explains himself in the final verse ("I am telling you this for your own benefit"). Try using a didactic tone to communicate these lines. You want to assist the assembly in hearing that the Lord is to be the center of their lives.

READING II   1 Corinthians 7:32–35

A reading from the first Letter of Saint Paul to the Corinthians

Brothers and sisters:
I should like you to be free of **anxieties**.
An **unmarried** man is anxious about the things of the **Lord**,
    how he may please the **Lord**.
But a **married** man is anxious about the things of the **world**,
    how he may please his **wife**, and he is **divided**.
An **unmarried** woman or a **virgin** is anxious about the things
        of the **Lord**,
    so that she may be **holy** in both **body** and **spirit**.
A **married** woman, on the other hand,
    is anxious about the things of the **world**,
    how she may please her **husband**.
I am telling you this for your own **benefit**,
    not to impose a **restraint** upon you,
    but for the sake of **propriety**
    and **adherence** to the Lord without **distraction**.

judge between true and false prophets, thus continually renewing our covenant with God and ordering our lives appropriately.

READING II   This passage continues where last Sunday's reading ended. Paul is responding to questions from the Corinthian community dealing primarily with practical issues. Today's verses focus on the issues of marriage and virginity.

In this passage, Paul counsels that an unmarried man or woman is concerned about "the things of the Lord," and a married man or woman is anxious about the "things of the world." This seems to say that the unmarried life is better than the married life, which divides a person's loyalty. Paul's teaching on the value on marriage and virginity can only be appreciated in connection to his belief about the *eschaton*, the end times. Paul is so concerned that time will run out before the Lord returns (see last Sunday's epistle), he does not want people changing their social positions, thus creating more anxiety. He would prefer that people prepare themselves for the Lord's coming in their current situation. Thus, while virginity may be preferable to the married life, he does not advise people not to marry. He merely wants the Corinthians to remain as they are because the Lord's return is imminent.

Notice the parallel structure in the middle section of the reading. Paul has often been charged unjustly with being a chauvinist. The parallel structure in this reading shows how Paul often placed the same demands on both men and women in terms of their relationship with the Lord.

GOSPEL Mark 1:21–28

A reading from the holy Gospel according to Mark

Capernaum = kuh-PER-n*m

The opening lines ("then they came to
Capernaum . . . and not as the scribes")
provide background. Read them in a
descriptive tone of voice, one that simply
passes on information.

Do not over-dramatize, but put some
expression in your voice, especially
when speaking the words of the man
with an unclean spirit and the commands
of Jesus.

Convey the description of the people's
reaction with surprise and wonder.
Let these sentiments be heard in their
question ("What is this?"). As you
give their reply to their own question
("A new teaching with authority . . .
they obey him"), try putting a little
nervousness in your voice. They are
unsure of what has happened and what
its implications might be. Pause again
before you narrate Mark's conclusion,
found in the words "His fame spread
everywhere through the whole region of
Galilee," with confidence and pride.

Then they came to **Capernaum**,
　　and on the **sabbath** Jesus entered the **synagogue** and **taught**.
The people were **astonished** at his teaching,
　　for he taught them as one having **authority** and not as
　　　　the **scribes**.
In their synagogue was a man with an **unclean** spirit;
　　he cried out, "What have you to do with **us**, Jesus of **Nazareth**?
Have you come to **destroy** us?
I know who **you** are—the **Holy** One of **God**!"
Jesus **rebuked** him and said,
　　"**Quiet**! Come **out** of him!"
The unclean spirit **convulsed** him and with a loud cry
　　came **out** of him.
All were **amazed** and asked one another,
　　"What **is** this?
A new teaching with **authority**.
He commands even the **unclean** spirits and they **obey** him."
His **fame** spread **everywhere** throughout the **whole** region
　　of **Galilee**.

GOSPEL　Mark made readers of his
Gospel aware of Jesus' full
identity in 1:1, but to those who followed
Jesus or witnessed his actions, the fullness of his identity remains hidden. Showing
that only the demon recognized Jesus'
identity is part of Mark's literary technique,
which we will see again in next Sunday's
Gospel. The title "the Holy One of God,"
although not a common messianic title,
names Jesus as one in whom God works in
a distinctive manner.

We know that good often comes from
evil. This is the case in today's Gospel. At
the time of the writing, common sicknesses
were often referred to as demons or unclean
spirits. The analogy is clear. Anything that
separates us from God is unclean, harmful,
and destructive. Sickness, disease, vio-
lence, and evil lead us away from what gives
life. Yet out of these struggles new life
can come. Through the demon's recognition of Jesus and his consequent antago-
nism toward Jesus, others were led to faith.

As a minister of the Gospel, read this
narrative with the tension inherent in it.
Our human nature teaches us to dislike
conflict, and there is a high degree of conflict in this story. Try and capture that in
your voice without over-dramatizing. If
you succeed, you will achieve a goal for
today—leading others to faith. Jesus' first
miracle could be a miracle in someone's
life today, bringing him or her to confess
Jesus as "the Holy One of God."

5TH SUNDAY IN ORDINARY TIME

Lectionary #74

Job = johb

Job's speech throughout this reading is sorrowful. Ask his questions and convey his thoughts with some of the emotion he experienced.

A reading from the Book of Job

Job spoke, saying:
    Is not man's life on **earth** a **drudgery**?
        Are not his **days** those of **hirelings**?
    He is a **slave** who longs for the **shade**,
        a **hireling** who waits for his **wages**.
    So I have been assigned months of **misery**,
        and troubled **nights** have been **allotted** to me.
    If in **bed** I say, "When shall I **arise**?"
        then the night **drags** on;
        I am filled with **restlessness** until the **dawn**.
    My days are **swifter** than a weaver's **shuttle**;
        they come to an end without **hope**.
    Remember that my life is like the **wind**;
        I **shall** not see **happiness** again.

Pause before the final verse. Job addresses God directly here. Let despair be heard in your voice, especially in the second half of the sentence. Read the second half of the sentence in a slightly slower than normal tempo.

READING I The book of Job is one of the poetical books in the Old Testament. It tells the story of a man named Job, who through much suffering holds onto his faith in God. Job does not answer the question "Why does God permit suffering?" but through his experiences teaches us that God is faithful and only asks us to be faithful to him in the midst of suffering.

This reading might be hard to proclaim well, especially if you have had a fairly easy life. You might want to skim through the book of Job to get a sense of the troubles Job faced. Prayerfully consider the tragedies that befall people every day to help you get a sense of how Job must have felt when he spoke these words.

You stand in the place of Job and everyone who has ever been affected by sorrow in life and who has wondered where to find meaning in life. In the end, Job's faith prevailed. As Christians, we believe that Jesus conquered the drudgery of life once and for all, gifting his followers with the happiness Job felt he would never see again.

Your spiritual preparation for the proclamation of this reading will be as important—if not more important—than your practical preparation. The former will allow you to read Job's words with compassion and respect human suffering and despair. The latter will help you proclaim the words with an understanding of their poetical nature.

Corinthians = kor-IN-thee-unz

Recompense = REH-kum-pens
Proclaim the line "If I do so willingly, I have recompense, but if unwillingly, then I have been entrusted with a stewardship" carefully so the contrast between "willingly" and "unwillingly" comes across clearly.

Paul never waivers: everything he does (and that we do) must be for the sake of the Gospel. State the first half of the verse "All this I do for the sake of the gospel" with conviction and the latter half ("so that I too may have a share in it") with hope in the reward of the Gospel.

READING II   1 Corinthians 9:16–19, 22–23

A reading from the first Letter of Saint Paul to the Corinthians

Brothers and sisters:
If I preach the **gospel**, this is no **reason** for me to **boast**,
    for an obligation has been **imposed** on me,
        and **woe** to me if I do **not** preach it!
If I do so **willingly**, I have a **recompense**,
    but if **unwillingly**, then I have been entrusted with
        a **stewardship**.
What then is my **recompense**?
That, when I **preach**,
    I **offer** the gospel **free** of charge
        so as not to make full use of my **right** in the gospel.

Although I am **free** in regard to all,
    I have made myself a **slave** to all
        so as to win over as many as **possible**.
To the **weak** I became **weak**, to win **over** the weak.
I have become all things to all, to save at least **some**.
All this I do for the sake of the gospel,
    so that I **too** may have a **share** in it.

READING II This is a complex passage to proclaim. Paul himself was a complex person whose writing often lacked clarity. In order to understand the words you will be reading, some sense of the context is necessary.

Paul believes he deserves no reward for preaching the Gospel. He prided himself on providing for himself in the communities to whom he preached the Gospel. He would take no payment from the communities in exchange for his preaching.

Moreover, Paul has no obligations to anyone. He is bound only to the Gospel.

Some scholars suggest that Paul was a bit of an egotist and perfectionist. Paul tried to justify his actions in service of the Gospel. While this, too, can be a skewed understanding of how to proclaim the Gospel, Paul's point is clear: Christians must proclaim the Gospel to everyone, everywhere, especially to the weak—those most vulnerable to scandal.

You are Paul's voice in this passage, which reads almost like a soliloquy. Practice it often so you will be able to leave the members of the assembly asking themselves if they preach the Gospel willingly or unwillingly—simply out of a sense of obligation. Paul acknowledges he preaches both willingly and unwillingly, often like we participate in the Sunday liturgy. He teaches that if we proclaim the Gospel willingly (and if we fulfill our Sunday obligation willingly), we will receive a reward from the Lord. Let your assembly experience the joy in this as you proclaim the last line of the passage.

Mark's use of time references such as "evening, after sunset" and "Rising very early before dawn" helps to keep the narrative moving as it transitions from an individual healing in a private setting to multiple healings in a communal setting to Jesus' preaching and healing outside of Capernaum. A lengthy pause before each section and before the beginning of the next will assist those who are listening to understand the progression of the narrative.

Lower your voice slightly to convey the tranquility of prayer. Jesus' going off to pray as described in the verse "Rising early . . . he prayed" reminds us of him praying in Gethsemane.

Jesus' response to the disciples ("that I may preach there also. For this purpose have I come") is the main point of this Gospel. Emphasize Jesus' statement about his purpose by looking up at the assembly as if they were the disciples to whom he was responding.

GOSPEL   Mark 1:29–39

A reading from the holy Gospel according to Mark

On leaving the **synagogue**
　　Jesus entered the house of **Simon** and **Andrew**
　　　　with **James** and **John**.
Simon's **mother**-in-law lay sick with a **fever**.
They **immediately** told him about her.
He **approached**, **grasped** her hand, and helped her **up**.
Then the fever **left** her and she **waited** on them.

When it was **evening**, after **sunset**,
　　they brought to him all who were **ill** or possessed by **demons**.
The whole **town** was gathered at the **door**.
He cured many who were **sick** with various **diseases**,
　　and he drove out many **demons**,
　　not **permitting** them to speak because they **knew** him.

Rising very **early** before dawn, he **left**
　　and went off to a **deserted** place, where he **prayed**.
Simon and those who were with him **pursued** him
　　and on **finding** him said, "**Everyone** is **looking** for you."
He **told** them, "Let us go **on** to the nearby **villages**
　　that I may preach **there also**.
For this purpose have I **come**."
So he went into their **synagogues**,
　　preaching and driving out **demons** throughout the **whole**
　　　　of Galilee.

GOSPEL This Sunday's Gospel continues our journey through the first chapter of Mark. Though Mark does not elaborate when describing an event, he does include the most important facts. Mark uses these facts, such as Jesus' withdrawal to a deserted place mentioned this in the passage, to provide continuity in the story of faith he develops in his Gospel.

The passage you proclaim this Sunday reveals the rapid expansion of Jesus' ministry. From Jesus' cure of Simon's mother-in-law (an individual healing) to his cure of "many who were sick" and his driving out of "many demons," Jesus' healing works are no longer reserved for a few, but are available to all. Jesus, like those of us who work long hours, needs to retreat, to spend time alone in prayer. But he finds there are many who still need him and track him down—not unlike parents, priests, or lay ministers in a parish. Jesus realizes that his message needs to be heard. He continues on his mission, willingly accepting that his work is not done.

Pausing between the sections and not glossing over the time references will help give a sense of the movement in the narrative. This will enable you to build toward the culmination that what is most important is not the work Jesus does, but rather the message he preaches. This message he lives out in his actions. We are called to do the same, so in the end it will not only be the demons who know Jesus' identity, but we who profess him as the Holy One of God. You probably work tirelessly, so as you prepare to proclaim this Gospel, take some time alone to renew yourself for your own ministry of proclaiming the Good News in your parish.

6TH SUNDAY IN ORDINARY TIME

Lectionary #77

READING I   Leviticus 13:1–2, 44–46

A reading from the Book of Leviticus

The LORD said to **Moses** and **Aaron**,
    "If someone has on his **skin** a **scab** or **pustule** or **blotch**
    which **appears** to be the sore of **leprosy**,
    he shall be brought to **Aaron**, the priest,
    or to one of the priests among his **descendants**.
If the man is **leprous** and **unclean**,
    the priest shall **declare** him unclean
    by reason of the **sore** on his **head**.

"The one who **bears** the sore of leprosy
    shall keep his **garments** rent and his head **bare**,
    and shall muffle his **beard**;
    he shall cry **out**, '**Unclean, unclean**!'
As long as the **sore** is on him he shall **declare** himself unclean,
    since he **is** in fact unclean.
He shall dwell **apart**, making his abode **outside** the camp."

Leviticus = lih-VIT-ih-kus

Aaron = AIR-un

The Hebrew word translated as "leprosy" includes a variety of skin diseases. When a skin disease was active and infectious, a person was considered "unclean."

When you read the verse "The one who bears . . . he shall cry out, 'Unclean, unclean!' ", do not shout the words that the leper must say. Remember, the leper is not actually speaking, but you are passing on what "The Lord said to Moses and Aaron."

The passage ends without much hope. Impart the conclusion to this reading ("He shall dwell apart, making his abode outside the camp") as the fact and law that it was.

READING I The book of Leviticus serves as a "how-to" book for the Levitical priests who ministered in the sanctuary. It contains laws and rituals regarding how to conduct worship. The purpose of these rubrics is to lead not only the Levitical priests, but also all of the Israelites toward holiness, thus allowing them to live uprightly before God.

The passage for this Sunday comes from a section of Leviticus that explains the purity codes relating to clean and unclean animals, childbirth, leprosy, and bodily cleanness. It is important to know that, while this reading focuses on the uncleanness of the leper, the story does not end with ostracizing the leper. The ritual for the cleansing of a leper is found in the next chapter of Leviticus. The Lord wants people to be healed, to be brought to fullness of life in relation to him and to others. Although the assembly will not hear about the cleansing of the leper in Leviticus, they will hear the story of Jesus healing the leper in the Gospel.

We in North America do not often see "lepers," but we do have people that are often considered "unclean" or "unworthy." Perhaps we might even consider ourselves "unclean" at times. As a society we do not always offer compassion to those in need. Although the reading you proclaim does not include words about the Lord's compassion, you still have a chance to reach out to those whom society shuns. Greet the people you see before and after the liturgy knowing the Lord is present in them regardless of their need. Doing this is also part of being a minister of the word.

Corinthians = kor-IN-thee-unz

There are three statements Paul makes in this reading that summarize his conclusion to the question of whether Christians may partake of food that has been sacrificed to idols. The first statement is in the first verse: "whether you eat or drink . . . do everything for the glory of God." Emphasize the latter half of this first statement ("do everything for the glory of God") by reading it slowly and authoritatively. "Avoid giving offense" is the second summary statement. Take your time with these three words to stress their importance. Then read the rest of the sentence parenthetically, following the punctuation given. Paul's remarks come together in this third and final statement: "Be imitators of me, as I am of Christ." Pause before and after your proclamation of it. Put more emphasis on Paul's imitation of Christ. Christians ultimately are to imitate Christ, not Paul.

READING II   1 Corinthians 10:31—11:1

A reading from the first Letter of Saint Paul to the Corinthians

Brothers and sisters,
whether you **eat** or **drink**, or **whatever** you do,
    do **everything** for the glory of **God**.

Avoid giving **offense**, whether to the **Jews** or **Greeks** or
        the church of **God**,
    just as **I** try to please **everyone** in **every** way,
    not seeking my **own** benefit but that of the **many**,
    that they may be **saved**.
Be imitators of **me**, as **I** am of **Christ**.

READING II   Saint Paul teaches us that, as members of the body of Christ, we are to watch out for each other. While we cannot please everyone, we are to keep others in mind as we make decisions.

The Corinthians asked if one could eat meat sacrificed to idols if it was served at a friend's table. Paul never responds with a definitive "yes" or "no." Rather, he responds, "Whatever you do, do everything for the glory of God." Part of giving glory to God, for Paul, means respecting our neighbors

and not giving offense to them. For some Corinthians who were looking for a black-and-white response to the question of whether or not it was permissible to eat "idol meat," Paul's response undoubtedly fell in the gray area, leaving some perplexed.

In the social, religious, and historical context of this reading, Paul was concerned that the Corinthians respect their own consciences as well as those of others. Impart this section of the reading with the awareness of who we need to take into account today so we better reflect the image of the one body of Christ. How can

we respect Paul's teaching to be mindful of others when we make decisions?

You stand in the place of Paul in this reading. Memorize the last line of this passage and offer it with confidence in yourself and your own Christian vocation. This might mean spending some of your preparation time reflecting on how you imitate Christ in your own life. The challenge you leave the assembly is to always keep Christ as the focus of their lives, striving to imitate him as much as possible.

The leper's words to Jesus ("If you wish, you can make me clean") and Jesus' nonverbal and verbal responses ("he stretched out his hand . . . 'I do will it. Be made clean'") reflect the personal encounter that took place between them. A loving and caring tone of voice is appropriate.

Offer Jesus' instruction not to publicize the miracle, but follow the prescribed rituals "sternly," as Mark's narrative states.

Pause after Jesus' stern instruction and before the conclusion ("The man went away and began to publicize . . ."). Read this section as if it began with the word "But." You want the assembly to be surprised and perplexed as to why the man disregarded Jesus' command.

GOSPEL   Mark 1:40–45

A reading from the holy Gospel according to Mark

A **leper** came to Jesus and kneeling down **begged** him and said,
"If you **wish**, you can make me **clean**."
Moved with **pity**, he **stretched** out his hand,
touched him, and said to him,
"I **do** will it. Be made **clean**."
The **leprosy** left him **immediately**, and he was made **clean**.
Then, warning him **sternly**, he **dismissed** him at **once**.

He said to him, "See that you tell **no** one **anything**,
but **go**, show yourself to the **priest**
and **offer** for your cleansing what Moses prescribed;
that will be **proof** for them."

The man went **away** and began to **publicize** the whole matter.
He **spread** the report abroad
so that it was **impossible** for Jesus to enter a town **openly**.
He remained **outside** in **deserted** places,
and people kept **coming** to him from **everywhere**.

GOSPEL   After the narratives of the call of the disciples from both John and Mark, the past few weeks of Ordinary Time have concentrated on Jesus' exorcisms and healings. The power and authority with which Jesus teaches and acts has been clearly evident. Today's Gospel is no exception. Chosen to coincide with the First Reading, this Gospel completes the story. Jesus' healing touch replaces the rejection faced by the unclean lepers.

As members of a sacramental Church, we are brought close to the Lord through our experience of him in the sacraments.

The leper's experience of Jesus' healing in this Gospel was a personal experience. So, too, are the sacraments for us. And, while they are personal experiences for each individual, they are not meant to be private. The Second Vatican Council taught that the liturgy and the sacraments are meant to be celebrated in common, thus acknowledging the presence of Christ in the community (see the Constitution on the Sacred Liturgy, #27).

We know the leper defied Jesus' command not to tell anyone of his healing and publicized it. Through the healed man's words and presence, others were led to seek out Jesus. We have all had experiences we could not wait to tell someone else about. With excitement and joy in your voice as you narrate the actions of the healed leper, extend to your assembly the invitation to be a sacramental people—announcing the Good News of their healing relationship with Christ to everyone they meet, especially those who are outcasts and may feel they are forgotten by society or the Church.

7TH SUNDAY IN ORDINARY TIME

Lectionary #80

READING I Isaiah 43:18–19, 21–22, 24b–25

A reading from the Book of the Prophet Isaiah

Thus says the LORD:
Remember **not** the events of the **past**,
   the things of **long** ago **consider** not;
see, I am doing something **new**!
   Now it springs forth, **do** you not perceive it?
In the **desert** I make a **way**,
   in the **wasteland**, **rivers**.
The **people** I formed for **myself**,
   that they might **announce** my praise.
Yet you **did** not call upon me, O **Jacob**,
   for you grew **weary** of me, O **Israel**.
You **burdened** me with your **sins**,
   and **wearied** me with your **crimes**.
It is I, **I**, who wipe out,
   for my **own** sake, your **offenses**;
   your **sins** I remember no **more**.

Isaiah = i-ZAY-uh

Make eye contact with the assembly as you proclaim the words "Thus says the Lord."

Place excitement, enthusiasm, and joy in your voice as you call your assembly to see the new thing the Lord is doing.

Change the tone of your voice to one of disappointment as you read the Lord's words.

Disappointment turns to hope as the Lord's mercy continually reveals itself as the new, redemptive power in life in the final verse. Include a significant pause after the first "I" and a slight pause after the second "I."

READING I | With its emphasis on the Lord's mercy in light of Israel's sinfulness, this passage teaches us that despite our offenses God will remain faithful. God will do "something new."

Historically, the "something new" is Israel's return to Palestine. Chapter 43 of Isaiah and the beginning of the chapter that follows speak about Israel's redemption and restoration. Read over these sections of Isaiah. This will help you better understand the context of this passage.

In the Hebrew, this passage builds toward the final verse in the reading ("It is I, I, who wipe out . . ."). Note the movement from what the Israelites did *not* do to what the Lord *does* in verse 25.

Both the Israelites and the Lord are weary: the Israelites because they are no longer able to offer Temple sacrifice and the Lord because he is constantly listening to their complaints and being burdened by their sins. It is the Lord who steps forward, who makes the move, willing to blot out their transgressions and start anew.

Christians understand the newness that springs forth to be the gift of the Messiah in the person of Jesus Christ. Read and reflect on the Gospel for today. In it, those gathered around Jesus also witnessed a marvelous healing. At the sight of this, their words witnessed to the joy of "something new" occurring—"We have never seen anything like this." Apply the joy, astonishment, and excitement in their words to the promise of the Lord that you proclaim in the First Reading. Healing and forgiveness have become a reality once and for all in Jesus.

Corinthians = kor-IN-thee-unz

Silvanus = sil-VAY-nus

Whether or not Paul was vacillating, indecisiveness is something that people in the assembly will be able to relate to. Your clear emphasis on the "yes" and "no" statements will help them make the connection.

Proclaim the words "But the one who gives security with you in Christ . . . hearts as a first installment" in a reassuring tone of voice.

Capernaum = kuh-PER-n*m

READING II   2 Corinthians 1:18–22

A reading from the second Letter of Saint Paul to the Corinthians

Brothers and sisters:
As God is **faithful**,
    our word to you is not "**yes**" and "**no**."
For the Son of **God**, Jesus **Christ**,
    who was **proclaimed** to you by us, **Silvanus** and
        Timothy and **me**,
    was **not** "yes" **and** "no," but "**yes**" has been in him.
For **however** many are the promises of **God**, their **Yes** is in **him**;
    therefore, the **Amen** from us **also** goes through him to God
        for **glory**.
But the one who gives us **security** with you in **Christ**
    and who anointed **us** is God;
he has **also** put his **seal** upon us
    and given the **Spirit** in our **hearts** as a first **installment**.

GOSPEL   Mark 2:1–12

A reading from the holy Gospel according to Mark

When Jesus returned to **Capernaum** after some days,
    it became **known** that he was at **home**.
Many gathered **together** so that there was no longer **room**
        for them,
    not **even** around the **door**,
    and he preached the word to them.

READING II Over the past five Sundays in Ordinary Time, we have read from Paul's first letter to the Corinthians. By the time of the writing of his second letter, support for Paul in the Corinthian community seems to have waned. In today's passage Paul seems defensive. There appear to be charges that the collection for the poor at Jerusalem had been kept by the apostle. The words "Our word to you is not 'yes' and 'no' " suggest that some accused Paul of being indecisive about whom he was planning to visit.

Paul must have had a good amount of strength and conviction in order to stand up for himself and his ministry. This passage plainly tells us that the source of Paul's ministry was always Jesus Christ, God's complete and total "yes." It was in Jesus Christ that God's promises were fulfilled; in Jesus was their "yes." The Greek verb *gegonen* used in the phrase "but 'yes' has been in him" is in the perfect tense, signifying that the action of God's "yes" in Jesus Christ has happened and continues to happen. God's promises were fulfilled once and for all in Jesus Christ, and we

today continue to be blessed by Jesus' "yes." Paul himself performed his ministry with the conviction that the "yes" of Jesus lived on in him. Strive to imitate Paul's faithfulness to God—which was rooted in God's faithfulness to him in Jesus Christ—with your own "yes" to God as you perform your ministry of the word.

GOSPEL Over the past three Sundays in Ordinary Time, we have heard the Marcan narratives of exorcisms

Offer the first words of dialogue you speak in this Gospel ("Child, your sins are forgiven") compassionately.

They came **bringing** to him a **paralytic** carried by **four men**.
Unable to get near **Jesus** because of the **crowd**,
    they opened up the **roof** above him.
After they had broken **through**,
    they let down the **mat** on which the paralytic was **lying**.
When **Jesus** saw their **faith**, he said to the **paralytic**,
    "**Child**, your sins are **forgiven**."
Now some of the **scribes** were sitting there **asking** themselves,
    "**Why** does this man **speak** that way? He is **blaspheming**.
Who but God **alone** can forgive **sins**?"
Jesus immediately knew in his mind
    what they were thinking to themselves,
    so he said, "Why are you **thinking** such things in your **hearts**?
Which is **easier**, to say to the paralytic,
    'Your **sins** are forgiven,'
    or to say, '**Rise**, pick up your **mat** and **walk**'?
But that you may **know**
    that the Son of Man has **authority** to forgive sins on **earth**"
    —he said to the **paralytic**,
    "**I say** to you, **rise**, pick up your **mat**, and go **home**."
He **rose**, picked up his mat at **once**,
    and went **away** in the sight of **everyone**.
They were all **astounded**
    and **glorified** God, saying, "We have **never** seen **anything**
        like this."

Jesus is concerned in his response to the scribes ("Why are you thinking such things . . . ?"). His words are not harsh, but simply authoritative. The evangelist wants the scribes to understand who the Son of Man is.

The narration at the end provides a statement of faith both in the action of the healed paralytic man and in the words of the witnesses. Voice the fledgling words of faith of the witnesses ("We have never seen anything like this") with confidence and hope.

and healings performed by Jesus, and today is no exception. This passage is part of a larger section in which we see growing tension and controversy between Jesus and the Pharisees, out of which the plot to kill Jesus develops.

As you prepare to proclaim this Gospel, notice it is the faith of the people who carried the paralytic that is the prerequisite for the miracle. "Jesus saw their faith" and forgave the sins of the paralytic.

Like many of the Gospel narratives proclaimed during the liturgical year, this one can be divided into sections. The first begins by setting the scene. Read this in a more narrative tone of voice. The second and lengthiest section tells of the healing of the paralytic who is surrounded by the community of his friends. Finally, we have the tension-filled dialogue between Jesus and the scribes. Most scholars believe "But that you may know" is a later insertion, probably not addressed to the scribes.

In the final line of the Gospel, Easter faith prevails. The astonishment of the people gathered is the same as ours when we see that God has done something new in Jesus, the Messiah, and continues through us and our faith to do something new today. Look up at your assembly and state with the conviction of faith that "We have never seen anything like this." In faith, this coming Wednesday, you will walk again with Jesus on the road to his Passion, death, and Resurrection.

ASH WEDNESDAY

Lectionary #219

READING I   Joel 2:12–18

A reading from the Book of the Prophet Joel

Even **now**, says the LORD,
  return to me with your whole **heart**,
    with **fasting**, and **weeping**, and **mourning**;
Rend your **hearts**, not your **garments**,
    and **return** to the LORD, your **God**.
For **gracious** and **merciful** is he,
    slow to **anger**, **rich** in **kindness**,
    and **relenting** in punishment.
Perhaps he will again relent
    and leave behind him a **blessing**,
Offerings and **libations**
    for the LORD, your **God**.

Blow the **trumpet** in **Zion**!
    proclaim a **fast**,
    call an **assembly**;

Joel = JOH-*l

Speak the words "Even now" slowly and deliberately, making eye contact with the assembly so that the connection with the present time can be made.

Take your time with the line "For gracious and merciful is he." This will give the assembly the opportunity to hear of God's loving kindness as they turn back to the Lord this Lent.

Pause before you begin the section filled with the commands ("Blow the trumpet, proclaim a fast, call an assembly . . ."). Impart the commands with a strong voice and with increasing momentum: you are calling the assembly to begin once again the season of Lent.

READING I   With the words of this First Reading from the minor prophet Joel, we begin the Lenten season of penitence and renewal. Although Ash Wednesday is not a holy day of obligation, traditionally the imposition of ashes on this day has made it more popular than some holy days.

The name "day of ashes" *(dies cinerum)* is in the earliest existing copies of the Gregorian Sacramentary and probably dates from the eighth century. On this day, the ashes used are made by burning the palms from Palm Sunday of the previous year. The ordinary minister, a priest or deacon, blesses the ashes and then marks all present with the sign of the cross on the forehead, saying, "Turn away from sin and be faithful to the Gospel" (Mark 1:15) or "Remember, man, you are dust and to dust you shall return" (Genesis 3:19). Other people—for example, extraordinary ministers of communion—may assist with the imposition of ashes where there is genuine need, especially for the sick and the shut-ins. Whenever people are marked with ashes, the symbolism is clear: during the Lenten season they are to turn their hearts back to God, repent of their sinful ways, and embrace the way of the Lord.

The prophet Joel wrote his message during a time when Israel faced a harsh locust plague and severe drought. The first two chapters of the book of Joel deal with these crises. The following two chapters of Joel are often referred to as "eschatological" because they depict the coming of the day of the Lord, a day when God's judgment will rain down on the people. In today's passage we hear the Lord's call to the people of Israel to repent, to return to the Lord.

Gather the **people**,
   notify the congregation;
Assemble the **elders**,
   gather the **children**
   and the **infants** at the **breast**;
Let the **bridegroom** quit his room,
   and the **bride** her **chamber**.

Between the porch and the altar
   let the **priests**, the **ministers** of the LORD, **weep**,
And say, "**Spare**, O LORD, your **people**,
   and make not your **heritage** a **reproach**,
   with the nations **ruling** over them!
Why should they say among the **peoples**,
   '**Where** is their **God**?'"

Then the LORD was stirred to concern for his land
   and took pity on his people.

Lower your voice as you convey the call for priests and ministers of the Lord to weep. Put some pleading in your voice as you say, "spare, O Lord, your people."

The last line is a narrative one. Pause significantly before you state it, and then deliver it with compassion: the Lord's mercy prevailed over the Israelites as it will for us this Lent.

This call to repentance is written in language that shows Joel is knowledgeable about the Temple in Jerusalem and its priesthood. Notice in particular the language of "blessing" (verse 14), notifying the congregation, and the references to the "priests, the ministers of the Lord." While the entire assembly is called together—the aged, infants, children, men, and women—the priests are called upon to lead the congregation in prayer, entreating God to "spare, O Lord, your people."

As we begin once again the solemn season of Lent, we are given the opportunity once again to begin a serious journey of fasting, weeping, mourning, and repenting, like the people of Israel. We undertake this Lenten journey with the assurance that the Lord is always with us, answering our prayers for new life, conversion, and restoration.

The last verse of this reading informs us that the Lord "took pity on his people" (verse 18). With this verse, a turning point in the book of Joel is reached; the Lord has answered the prayer of his people. Just as

he responded to the prayers of the people of Israel in the face of the locust plague and drought, we believe that he will respond to our Lenten prayers as well, bringing new life to us personally, to our world, and to our church communities.

READING II   We hear from Paul's second letter to the Corinthians much less often in the three-year Sunday Lectionary cycle than we do his first letter. In 1 Corinthians, Paul was addressing a community noted for its internal divisions.

Corinthians = kor-IN-thee-unz

Look up at the assembly as you "implore" them to be "reconciled to God."

Proclaim these words at a moderate pace, adding a slight pause after them.

State the quotation from Isaiah 49:8 ("In an acceptable time . . .") with confidence.

Pause before the high point of the reading in the final two lines. Memorize these lines if you are able to do so without difficulty. Then, emphasizing the word "now," look up at the assembly and proclaim them with the utmost confidence.

READING II   2 Corinthians 5:20—6:2

A reading from the second Letter of Saint Paul to the Corinthians

Brothers and sisters:
We are **ambassadors** for **Christ**,
  as if God were **appealing** through us.
We **implore** you on behalf of Christ,
  be **reconciled** to God.
For our sake he made him to **be** sin
    who did not **know** sin,
    so that we might become the **righteousness**
    of God in him.

Working **together**, then,
  we appeal to you **not** to receive the grace
    of God in **vain**.
For he says:

  *In an **acceptable** time I **heard** you,
    and on the day of **salvation** I **helped** you.*

Behold, **now** is a very acceptable time;
  behold, **now** is the day of salvation.

As such, Paul made the theological argument that each member of the community, whether weak or strong, was important because all are members of the body of Christ. His presentation of this point climaxed in his statement directly to the Corinthians that "you are the body of Christ" (1 Corinthians 12:27). In contrast, while clearly the Corinthian community at the time of Paul's writing of 2 Corinthians was still divided, factionalism was not primary on Paul's mind in this letter. Rather, Paul was concerned about his own credibility, which had deteriorated in the face of challenges from "false apostles" (11:5, 13) and a lack of internal support from the community (2:5–11; 7:8–12).

While the authenticity of 2 Corinthians remains unquestioned, many scholars do believe that it is a compilation of letters written by Paul. The letter from which today's reading comes is seen as the earliest (2 Corinthians 2:14–7:4, excluding 6:14–7:1), probably written only a year after 1 Corinthians, c. 55 AD. The short passage you proclaim this Ash Wednesday is Paul's attempt to call the Corinthians to reconciliation to God. In it, Paul makes the argument that, since he and his coworkers Timothy and Apollos are ambassadors for Christ, the only way for the Corinthians to be reconciled to God is through reconciliation with them. Thus, Paul beseeches them "not to receive the grace of God in vain" (6:1). Paul and his fellow workers are attempting to make Christ present to those to whom they proclaim the Gospel. In their lives they are attempting to "become the very holiness of God."

As a lector, you stand in the place of Paul and those who ministered with him, pleading with the assembly before you to

GOSPEL Matthew 6:1–6, 16–18

A reading from the holy Gospel according to Matthew

Jesus said to his **disciples**:
    "Take care **not** to perform righteous deeds
    in order that people may **see** them;
    otherwise, you will have **no** recompense
        from your heavenly **Father**.
When you give **alms**,
    do not blow a **trumpet** before you,
    as the **hypocrites** do in the **synagogues**
        and in the **streets**
    to win the praise of others.
Amen, I say to you,
    they have **received** their reward.
But when **you** give alms,
    do not let your **left** hand know what your **right** is doing,
    so that your almsgiving may be **secret**.
And your Father who **sees** in secret will **repay** you.

"When **you** pray,
    do not be like the **hypocrites**,
    who love to stand and pray in the **synagogues**
        and on **street corners**
    so that others may see them.
Amen, I say to you,
    they have **received** their reward.
But when **you** pray, go to your inner **room**,
    close the **door**, and pray to your Father in **secret**.
And your Father who **sees** in secret will **repay** you.

Look at the assembly as you deliver the opening words of the Gospel: "Jesus said to the disciples."

Pause before the beginning of each section. The sections outline the importance of the traditional Lenten practices of almsgiving, praying, and fasting. As you proclaim the opening line of each section (for example, "When you give alms"), do so clearly, making eye contact. This will help the assembly to make the connection between Jesus' instructions to his disciples and their meaning for us today.

hypocrites = HIP-uh-crits

Note the repetition of the line "Amen, I say to you, they have received their reward" three times. Each time it occurs, pause slightly before and after it. This will highlight it and its meaning: the reward of Jesus' disciples will come from the Father, not from others.

be reconciled to God during the season of Lent. The Lenten road will lead us to Holy Week, and the celebration of the Passion, death, and Resurrection of the one through whom we are able to become the holiness of God. Through your proclamation of this reading you offer the opportunity for reconciliation with God in Christ to others. As Paul tells the Corinthians by quoting the prophet Isaiah, "Now is the acceptable time! Now is the day of salvation!" your proclamation of these words lets the assembly know there is no better time to be reconciled with God than now. Because

you are a lector, you are a public face in your church community. If there is anyone in the community with whom you need to be reconciled, now is the acceptable time to reconcile with them in Christ.

GOSPEL In reference to the practice of penance in the Christian life, the Catechism states that "the interior penance of the Christian can be expressed in many and various ways. Scripture and the Fathers insist above all on three forms, *fasting*, *prayer*, and *almsgiving*, which express conversion in relation to oneself, to God,

and to others" (#1434). The Gospel reading on Ash Wednesday provides the scriptural reference for the Church's teaching about fasting, prayer, and almsgiving—practices that are also traditional practices of the Jewish people (see Deuteronomy 6:5).

Coming from Matthew's Sermon on the Mount (4:23—7:29), this Gospel reflects the evangelist's concern about pretentiousness and overtly pious acts. The Gospel according to Matthew was probably written around 80–90 AD for Jews who believed in Jesus Christ as the Messiah. It is possible that the community for whom Matthew

"When **you** fast,
    do not look **gloomy** like the **hypocrites**.
They neglect their **appearance**,
    so that they may **appear** to others to be fasting.
Amen, I say to you, they have **received** their reward.
But when **you** fast,
    anoint your **head** and wash your **face**,
    so that you may **not** appear to be fasting,
    except to your **Father** who is hidden.
And your Father who **sees** what is hidden will **repay** you."

**Offer the final line with reassurance;
God will reward those who do good.
For followers of Jesus, this is all that
matters; the world's payment for good
deeds is not lasting.**

was writing had been separated from the mainstream of Judaism by a ban called *birkat hammînîm* imposed by the rabbis of Jamnia. This would provide one explanation for the growing polemic between the Matthean community of Christians who still understood themselves to be Jewish and the larger Jewish community as represented by the leaders of the synagogue, in particular those represented by the rabbis of Jamnia in chapter 23.

The tension is evident in today's Gospel in Jesus' criticism of the hypocrites and the contrast he develops between their need for attention and the appropriate way in which the practices of prayer, fasting, and almsgiving are to be carried out. Private, personal observance of these traditions is seen to be the proper manner in which to develop one's relationship with God.

While we each individually observe Lent, we also do so as a Christian community. Together, we will hear the Lenten Gospels that challenge us to a deeper faith in the Paschal Mystery. The Gospel according to Matthew offered at the beginning of Lent is meant to challenge us, personally and as a Christian community, not to fail in our responsibility to draw closer to God through prayer, fasting, almsgiving, and other works of penance. When you proclaim this Gospel you are encouraging your community to accept their Lenten responsibility. In so doing they will be distinguished from the hypocrites, because they have returned to God as the center of their lives and repented of arrogance or self-centeredness. All who proclaim the Gospel are called to be examples to the assembly of this repentance.

1ST SUNDAY OF LENT

Lectionary #23

READING I Genesis 9:8–15

Genesis = JEN-uh-sis

Be clear as you announce the opening line ("God said to Noah and to his sons with him"). The line identifies the words that follow as God's words.

A reading from the Book of Genesis

God said to **Noah** and to his **sons** with him:
"**See,** I am now establishing my **covenant** with you
 and your descendants **after** you
 and with every living **creature** that was **with** you:
 all the **birds,** and the various tame and wild **animals**
 that were **with** you and came out of the **ark.**
I will establish my **covenant** with you,
 that never **again** shall all bodily creatures be **destroyed**
 by the waters of a **flood;**
 there shall not be another **flood** to devastate the **earth.**"
God added:

Pause after the words "devastate the earth" and before the next section begins with "God added."

"**This** is the **sign** that I am **giving** for all ages to come,
 of the covenant between **me** and **you**
 and **every** living creature **with** you:

bow = boh

I set my **bow** in the clouds to serve as a **sign**
 of the covenant between **me** and the **earth.**
When I bring **clouds** over the earth,
 and the **bow** appears in the clouds,
 I will **recall** the covenant I have made

Speak the words that describe the rainbow as a sign of God's promise to his people ("I set my bow in the clouds") with warmth. You might want to remember a time when you have seen the beauty of a rainbow and felt the contentment it brings.

between **me** and **you** and **all** living beings,
 so that the **waters** shall **never** again become a flood
 to destroy **all** mortal **beings.**"

READING I The description of the Lord's covenant with Noah follows after the story of the Great Flood, when Noah, his family, and all the animals in the ark came forth to see a new day. God had preserved life despite the flood. This covenant is a sign that God will continue to do so.

The description of the Lord's covenant with Noah is significant for two reasons: 1) Usually covenants entail promises made by each of the two parties, even if the promise made by one is simply to be faithful to what is asked of them by the other, in this case the Lord. However, Noah does not respond to the Lord's promise; his affirmation of the covenant is assumed. 2) The promise the Lord makes to Noah and his sons extends to "every living creature" (verses 9–10). Noah's sons are the ancestors of all the nations and symbolic of this covenant's universality (see 10:1).

As we begin Lent, this reading is a reminder of God's covenant fulfilled in Jesus—one rooted in those made with Noah, Abraham, and Moses. The waters of the flood, through which Noah, his family, and the animals with him survived because of God's goodness, symbolize the waters of Baptism, through which Christians are brought through death to new life. In Jesus, the new covenant was extended to all. For the elect among us, Lent is a time to consider the covenantal relationship they will enter through the waters of Baptism at the Easter Vigil. Like Noah, our response to the new covenant in Jesus need not be evident; rather, the way in which we live should be evidence of our solemn promise to the Lord.

Look up at the assembly as your give the opening address: "Beloved."

The reading begins with a narrative section about Christ's suffering, death, and Resurrection ("Christ suffered . . . life in the Spirit"). Notice that the verbs in this section are in the past tense.

Note the verse about Noah ("while God patiently waited . . .") is also in the past tense.

In the next section, the connection between Noah and the flood and Christian Baptism is made clear. Impart the explanation of Baptism as an "appeal to God for a clear conscience" with strength in your voice.

READING II   1 Peter 3:18–22

A reading from the first Letter of Saint Peter

Beloved:
Christ **suffered** for sins **once**,
      the **righteous** for the sake of the **unrighteous**,
      that he might lead you to **God**.
Put to **death** in the **flesh**,
      he was brought to **life** in the **Spirit**.
In it he **also** went to preach to the spirits in **prison**,
      who had once been **disobedient**
      while God **patiently** waited in the days of Noah
      during the **building** of the **ark**,
      in which a **few** persons, **eight** in all,
      were **saved** through **water**.
This prefigured **baptism**, which saves you **now**.
It is not a removal of **dirt** from the body
      but an **appeal** to God for a clear **conscience**,
      through the **resurrection** of Jesus **Christ**,
      who has gone into **heaven**
      and is at the right hand of **God**,
      with **angels**, **authorities**, and **powers** subject to him.

READING II With the prefigurement of Baptism in God's saving Noah and his family from the Great Flood, the Second Reading today highlights the baptismal character of Lent, drawing our attention to Lent as a season of immediate preparation of the elect for Baptism and in which Christians prepare to renew their own baptismal covenant.

First Peter was probably written between 70–90 AD by a disciple of Peter in Rome who wanted to carry on Peter's legacy. While there was no state-sponsored persecution of Christians in Asia Minor at

that time, it is clear that Christians were vulnerable (4:14, 16). The letter calls on those Christian to remain faithful despite the fact that they are "aliens" (paroikoi, 2:11) in their own land.

Why would the Christians feel like they did not belong? The list of vices in 4:3–4 shows that the Christians no longer participated in pagan feasts. Their sufferings are united with Christ. Because Christ suffered for sins once being put to death in the flesh and having been given life in the Spirit, the righteous too will share in this life.

This passage recalls God's saving a few people in Noah's time from the flood. The destructive waters of the flood contrast with the waters of Baptism through which Christians are saved. Through the grace of Baptism, Christians participate in the Resurrection of Christ. They will be given the strength to persevere in their Christian vocation. As you proclaim this reading, be conscious of the fact that you offer Christians hope that they are one with Christ as they strive to be faithful to the baptismal commitment that they will renew at Easter.

GOSPEL   Mark 1:12–15

Pause after the announcement of the
Gospel from Mark. Make sure you have
the assembly's attention before
proceeding because the Gospel is brief.

Lower your tone of voice slightly as you
state "the angels ministered to him."
Even Jesus needed to get away and have
others "take care of him."

Pause before the narrative line "After
John had been arrested." The Gospel
shifts its focus here.

Pause again before you proclaim Jesus'
words ("This is the time of fulfillment . . .")
with strength and conviction in your voice.

A reading from the holy Gospel according to Mark

The **Spirit** drove **Jesus** out into the **desert**,
    and he remained in the desert for **forty** days,
        tempted by **Satan**.
He was among wild **beasts**,
    and the angels **ministered** to him.

After John had been **arrested**,
    Jesus came to **Galilee** proclaiming the gospel of **God**:
    "**This** is the time of **fulfillment**.
The **kingdom** of God is at **hand**.
Repent, and **believe** in the gospel."

GOSPEL   **Each year on the First Sunday of Lent the Gospel** is one of the synoptic accounts of the temptation of Jesus in the desert by Satan. The choice of story coincides with the Christian community's beginning its wandering in the desert during the Forty Days of Lent.

Jesus' temptation in the desert immediately follows the account of his Baptism at the Jordan by John (1:9–11). The Spirit "immediately" *(kai euthys)* drove Jesus out into the desert. For Mark, the immediacy and the "here and now" of these events is

significant. The temptation of Jesus needed to take place at this time to hasten the beginning of his public ministry in which he would proclaim that the kingdom of God has come near, a statement affirming that in his own person the kingdom of God is present at this very moment (1:14–15).

Mark, in his concise account, simply states that Jesus was tempted by Satan. The Greek verb *peirazō,* used by Mark in the passive voice and translated "tempted," means "to be put to the test." The basics are enough for Mark—the Spirit drove Jesus into the desert (Jesus did not seem

to have much of a choice in the matter) and Jesus was tested.

With our hectic pace, sometimes we need to have the Spirit drive us into the desert. Once in the desert we reflect on those areas in our lives in which we are thirsting for God. In your proclamation of this Gospel, you have the opportunity to instill in the assembly the desire to remain with Jesus in the desert, so that they might be open to celebrating their new life at Easter.

2ND SUNDAY OF LENT

Lectionary #26

Genesis = JEN-uh-sis

Abraham = AY-bruh-ham

Pause slightly after God's words, allowing the significance of what God is commanding Abraham to do to sink in.

Moriah = moh-RĪ-uh

The section beginning with the words "When they came to the place" narrates Abraham's obedience to God's commands. A matter-of-fact tone of voice is probably best here.

Place strength in your voice in delivering the call and willingness in your voice as you convey Abraham's answer.

READING I   Genesis 22:1–2, 9a, 10–13, 15–18

A reading from the Book of Genesis

God put **Abraham** to the **test**.
He called to him, "**Abraham!**"
"**Here** I am!" he replied.
Then God said:
    "Take your son **Isaac**, your **only** one, whom you **love**,
        and **go** to the land of **Moriah**.
There you shall **offer** him up as a **holocaust**
    on a height that I will point **out** to you."

When they **came** to the place of which God had told him,
    Abraham built an **altar** there and arranged the **wood** on it.
Then he reached **out** and took the **knife** to **slaughter** his son.
But the LORD's **messenger** called to him from **heaven**,
    "**Abraham, Abraham!**"
"**Here** I am!" he answered.
"Do not lay your **hand** on the **boy**," said the messenger.
"Do not do the least **thing** to him.

READING I During the season of Lent, the Old Testament readings on Sundays are about the history of salvation; they present "the main elements of salvation history from its beginning until the promise of the New Covenant" (Introduction to the Lectionary, #97). On the First Sunday of Lent we heard the story of God's grace active in saving all living creatures from the flood. Today, the First Reading tells us of God's blessings to Abraham, our father in faith, because of his unconditional response to God's testing.

The account of God's putting Abraham to the test by calling for the sacrifice of his son Isaac is part of the story of Abraham and Sarah contained in Genesis 11:27—25:18. Within this narrative, Abraham and Sarah endure ten trials (12:1–4, 7; 12:10—13:1; 13:2–18; 14—15; 16—17; 18:1–15; 18:16—19:29; 20:1—21:7; 21:8–34; 22) and receive seven blessings from the Lord (12:2–3, 7; 13:14–17; 15; 17; 18; 22:16–18). God's command to sacrifice Isaac is the most difficult trial Abraham faced. It ends, however, with the seventh and climactic

blessing, a blessing that repeats the great promises of land, prosperity, and progeny.

Unlike in some of the other trials, in this one Abraham does not outwardly question what God is asking of him, nor does he try and find his way around the demand. Although God's demands appear harsh and unreasonable—especially in an Israelite society that no longer practiced human sacrifice, Abraham responds unconditionally, without giving much thought to carrying out what God asks of him—the sacrifice of his son Isaac. Abraham's trust in God appears complete and total. The words the

I **know** now how **devoted** you are to God,
    since you did not **withhold** from me your **own** beloved son."
As Abraham looked **about**,
    he spied a **ram** caught by its **horns** in the **thicket**.
So he went and took the **ram**
    and offered it up as a holocaust in place of his son.

Again the LORD's messenger called to Abraham
        from heaven and said:
    "I **swear** by **myself**, declares the LORD,
    that **because** you acted as you **did**
    in not **withholding** from me your beloved **son**,
    I will **bless** you **abundantly**
    and make your **descendants** as countless
    as the stars of the **sky** and the sands of the **seashore**;
    your descendants shall take **possession**
    of the gates of their **enemies**,
    and in your **descendants** all the nations of the earth
        shall find **blessing**—
    all this because you **obeyed** my command."

Build in intensity and excitement as you come to the climax of the great blessings the Lord bestows upon Abraham in the final speech from the Lord's messenger ("I swear by myself . . .").

angel speaks to Abraham after he comes to the precipice of sacrificing his son bear witness to this. After commanding Abraham not to lay his hand on the boy, the angel recognizes Abraham's devotion to God in the words "I know now how devoted you are to God, since you did not withhold from me your own beloved son" (verse 12).

For us today, this story reminds us how God is present through the trials of our lives. Our Baptism did not take away the problems we face; rather, the baptismal covenant we entered took away original sin, but also welcomed us into a community of faith that professes God's ongoing presence in its midst through the working of the Holy Spirit. Let your narration of Abraham's experience serve as a reminder of the generous blessing God bestows on us who obey his commands. All nations and peoples were forever changed because of Abraham's response to God. So, too, Christians are forever changed by the love of the God of Abraham, Isaac, and Jacob—God, who is also the Father of Jesus Christ.

READING II This reading comes from Romans 8, the chapter in which the response to the question ("Who will deliver me from this mortal body?") posed in 7:24 is found.

The questions in the reading are rhetorical in nature. Both Paul and the Romans know the answer. But Paul uses the questions as a tool to remind the Romans how great God's love is for them that he would give his Son. Surely, God will not abandon the Christians at Rome in the face of the difficult challenge to live according to the Spirit. But the Christians at Rome

Romans = ROH-munz

Beginning with the question "Who will bring a charge against God's chosen ones?" increase the confidence and intensity in your tone of voice.

The questions build to the conclusion of the reading ("Christ Jesus it is who died . . ."). State this line emphatically, in a way that is as absolute as the covenant between God and us in Jesus Christ.

READING II   Roman 8:31b–34

A reading from the Letter of Saint Paul to the Romans

Brothers and sisters:
If God is **for** us, who can be **against** us?
He who did not **spare** his own Son
    but handed him **over** for us **all**,
    how will he not **also** give us **everything** else along with him?

Who will bring a **charge** against God's **chosen** ones?
    It is God who **acquits** us, who will **condemn**?
Christ **Jesus** it is who **died**—or, rather, was **raised**—
    who also is at the right hand of **God**,
    who indeed **intercedes** for us.

---

struggled, and thus Paul encouraged them not to be compromised by the flesh even in the face of harassment and sometimes even outright persecution for their beliefs. Paul makes clear the extent of God's support for Christians in 8:32: "He who did not spare his own Son." This verse might also be a reference to Abraham who was willing to sacrifice his son Isaac, hence the connection between today's First and Second Readings.

In your preparation, read at least the entire subsection in chapter 8 (verses 31–39) from which this reading comes. The

final verses (37–38) function as a summary for the entire eighth chapter, describing in powerful and expressive language the strong bond between God and his children forged by his love manifest in Christ Jesus. *Nothing* can separate those justified through faith in Jesus Christ—"who died— or, rather, was raised."

During Lent, we pause to consider the many different kinds of sins that separate us from our own true nature and cause harm to our relationship with God and others (see the Catechism, #1849–1876). We,

also, as the choice of the reading evidences, never lose sight of Easter, and God's gift of everlasting love for us through the Resurrection of his Son.

| GOSPEL | Mark's Transfiguration narrative follows the first of three predictions of Jesus' Passion (8:31–38; 9:30–50; 10:32–34), in which Jesus teaches the disciples that the Son of Man will have to undergo great suffering, be put to death, and will rise again after three days. After this prediction, which Peter, probably speaking for most of the disciples, did not

GOSPEL   Mark 9:2–10

A reading from the holy Gospel according to Mark

Jesus took **Peter**, **James**, and **John**
and led them up a **high** mountain apart by **themselves**.
And he was **transfigured** before them,
and his **clothes** became dazzling **white**,
such as no fuller on earth could **bleach** them.
Then **Elijah** appeared to them along with **Moses**,
and they were **conversing** with Jesus.
Then **Peter** said to Jesus in **reply**,
"**Rabbi**, it is **good** that we are **here**!
Let us make three **tents**:
one for **you**, one for **Moses**, and one for **Elijah**."
He hardly knew what to say, they were so **terrified**.
Then a **cloud** came, casting a **shadow** over them;
from the cloud came a **voice**,
"**This** is my beloved **Son**. **Listen** to him."
Suddenly, looking **around**, they no longer saw **anyone**
but Jesus **alone** with them.

As they were coming **down** from the mountain,
he **charged** them not to relate what they had seen to **anyone**,
except when the Son of **Man** had **risen** from the **dead**.
So they **kept** the matter to **themselves**,
questioning what rising from the dead **meant**.

Pause after the introductory sentence ("Jesus took Peter, James and John . . ."). Then convey the excitement evident in the description of the Transfiguration in your voice.

Elijah = ee-LĪ-juh

Pause before the words "Then a cloud came." Speak in a normal tone of voice as you deliver the words of the voice, not pretending to be a "godly" voice.

Narrate the line "questioning what rising from the dead meant" slowly, as if you are pondering what it means yourself.

understand, Jesus invites the disciples and the surrounding crowd with them to take of their cross and follow him (8:34).

Mark's placement of the Transfiguration account after this first Passion prediction reveals to his readers that, while Jesus is the Messiah, he will not come to reign in glory as expected of a royal messiah. Rather, his triumph will come through his suffering and death. The cross will not have the final word though; Jesus will reign in glory because of his Resurrection.

In this Gospel, Peter, James, and John are given a glimpse of what the glory of

Jesus will look like. What the disciples observed was Jesus in his heavenly state, clothed in "dazzling white." The description of Jesus' clothes as such was familiar in Jewish thought. In the book of Daniel, God, the "Ancient One," wears clothing that is "snow bright" (Daniel 7:9), signifying his heavenly origin.

As those who hear the Gospel today, we know and understand the story of Jesus' life, Passion, death, and Resurrection. Yet as you proclaim this story, remember that some in the assembly need to see a glimpse of Jesus' glorious identity. Your

proclamation of the Transfiguration serves as a reminder to them that Easter comes at the end of Lent. Even though we who are disciples of Jesus today often want to have Easter before Holy Week, let this Gospel serve to teach you and your community that together you must come down the mountain with Jesus and follow him to Jerusalem. There you will see him, too, as the Son of God, the fulfillment of the law and the prophets (Moses and Elijah).

3RD SUNDAY OF LENT

Lectionary #29

READING I Exodus 20:1–17

Exodus = EK-suh-dus

Proclaim the first commandment ("I, the Lord, am your God . . .") with firmness and strength in your voice. Lower your tone of voice to deliver its explanation ("who brought you out of the land of Egypt . . ."). Repeat the same vocal pattern for the other commandments that include a commentary.

A reading from the Book of Exodus

In **those** days, God **delivered** all these **commandments**:
  "**I**, the LORD, am your **God**,
    who **brought** you out of the land of **Egypt**, that place
      of **slavery**.
You shall not have **other** gods besides **me**.
You shall not carve **idols** for yourselves
    in the shape of **anything** in the sky **above**
    or on the earth **below** or in the waters **beneath** the earth;
    you shall not bow **down** before them or **worship** them.
For **I**, the LORD, your **God**, am a **jealous** God,
    inflicting **punishment** for their fathers' **wickedness**
    on the **children** of those who **hate** me,
    down to the **third** and **fourth** generation;
    but bestowing **mercy** down to the **thousandth** generation
    on the children of those who **love** me
      and keep my **commandments**.

"You shall **not** take the name of the LORD, your God, in **vain**.
For the LORD will **not** leave **unpunished**
    the one who **takes** his name in **vain**.

"Remember to keep **holy** the **sabbath** day.
Six days you may **labor** and do all your **work**,
    but the **seventh** day is the **sabbath** of the LORD, your **God**.

READING I No explanation is needed for the content of this First Reading. Clearly, it is the version of the Ten Commandments given to Moses on Mount Sinai found in Exodus. A second description of the Ten Commandments is found in Deuteronomy 5:6–21 with only two slight differences: 1) The reason that Deuteronomy provides for the observance of the Sabbath is that the Lord had brought the Israelites out of the land of Egypt where they were slaves and in doing so he commanded them to keep the Sabbath (5:12–15). On the other hand, Exodus 20:8–11 gives the Creation of heaven, earth, and all that is in them as the explanation for keeping the Sabbath holy. 2) The last commandment differs in the ordering of the neighbor's wife and the neighbor's house. In Deuteronomy, the instruction not to covet your neighbor's wife appears before the one not to covet your neighbor's house (5:21), whereas in Exodus 20:17 the neighbor's house is listed first, then the neighbor's wife.

The reading from the Old Testament on the first three Sundays of Lent has had a covenant theme. On the First Sunday of Lent, we heard of the Lord's covenant with Noah and his sons (and all living creatures) after the flood; on the Second Sunday, the reading was God's promise to Abraham after he asked Abraham to sacrifice Isaac; and today we hear of the response God asks from the Israelites to the covenant he formed with Moses on Mount Sinai. Both the covenant with Noah and Abraham were fairly simple and direct in form. But the description of the covenant made with the Israelites through Moses is more complex,

No **work** may be done then either by **you**, or your
    son or **daughter**,
  or your **male** or **female** slave, or your **beast**,
  or by the **alien** who lives with you.
In **six** days the LORD made the **heavens** and the **earth**,
  the **sea** and all that is **in** them;
  but on the **seventh** day he **rested**.
That is why the LORD has **blessed** the sabbath day and
    made it **holy**.

"Honor your **father** and your **mother**,
  that you may have a long life in the land
  which the LORD, your **God**, is **giving** you.
You shall not **kill**.
You shall not commit **adultery**.
You shall not **steal**.
You shall not bear false **witness** against your **neighbor**.
You shall not **covet** your neighbor's **house**.
You shall not **covet** your neighbor's **wife**,
  nor his male or female **slave**, nor his **ox** or **ass**,
  nor anything **else** that **belongs** to him."

[Shorter: Exodus 20:1–3, 7–8, 12–17]

Beginning with "You shall not kill," commandments 6–10 are simply listed. Communicate them directly and with authority. Add a considerable pause after each commandment, giving the assembly time to internalize the meaning of each one.

following in accord with political covenants of the Ancient Near East. These covenants usually began with a description of what the political power had done for the people with whom the covenant was being made. In this case, the covenant with the Israelites begins with a statement of how the Lord has brought the Israelites out of the land of Egypt (20:2). The covenant then stated a response that was to be given by the people for the gift they had received. The Ten Commandments are the response asked of the Israelite people to their gift of freedom. Finally, covenants were usually sealed with a ritual. In the case of the Mosaic covenant, Exodus 24 describes the animal sacrifice and Moses reading the law of the Lord. It also presents the people's response to the ordinances of the Lord: "All the words that the Lord has spoken we will do."

The Ten Commandments, also referred to as the Decalogue (literally, "ten words"), have held pride of place in the moral code of the Jewish and Christian religious traditions for centuries. While Christians share this moral code with Jews, we also see in Jesus the fulfillment of the law. Your proclamation of the Decalogue this Lent provides something akin to an examination of conscience for the assembly as they look at where they have failed to be faithful to their covenant with God. Our living out of the Ten Commandments, while not always the easiest responsibility to follow, is done in response to God's loving initiative to enter into a covenant with us. God's loving

Corinthians = kor-IN-thee-unz

Follow the punctuation closely in the section "Jews demand signs . . . and the wisdom of God."
Gentiles = JEN-tils

Pay close attention to the words marked for emphasis in the phrase "For the foolishness of God." This is a difficult verse to understand because of Paul's use of paradox. Your emphasis of the keys words ("foolishness," "wisdom," "weakness," and "strength")—along with the measured pace with which you deliver these lines—will aid in the assembly's understanding of the text.

READING II 1 Corinthians 1:22–25

A reading from the first Letter of Saint Paul to the Corinthians

Brothers and sisters:
Jews demand **signs** and Greeks look for **wisdom**,
    but we proclaim Christ **crucified**,
    a **stumbling** block to **Jews** and **foolishness** to **Gentiles**,
    but to those who are **called**, Jews and Greeks **alike**,
    Christ the **power** of God and the **wisdom** of God.
For the **foolishness** of God is **wiser** than human **wisdom**,
    and the **weakness** of God is **stronger** than human **strength**.

---

kindness *(hesed)* is steadfast (Exodus 20:6) as we strive to respond in faithfulness: "All the words that the Lord has spoken we will do."

READING II Saint Paul is writing to a Corinthian community that is arguing about to whom they give allegiance (1:11–12). Some profess to belong to Paul, others to Apollos, others to Cephas, and yet others to Christ. Paul's response is to ask rhetorically whether Christ has been divided or whether one of the others to

whom they pledge allegiance to has been crucified for them (1:13).

For Paul, salvation comes through the cross, as "foolish" as this might sound. For the Jews who demand signs and the Greeks who look for wisdom, that the cross is a pathway to salvation was absurd and unreasonable. The Jews insisted on miracles from God, thus showing a lack of trust. Similarly, the Greeks insistence on finding wisdom through the construction of their own religious systems showed their desire

to find God solely through reason. Both of the ways of approaching God seem reasonable. Yet Paul eloquently argues for belief in the foolishness of the cross (verse 25).

Proclaim this passage as one of hope for Christians everywhere. In acknowledging Christ crucified and the new life that came through the cross, we let go of our human need to take control of everything—our human need to "be God." While to many in our highly technological society the cross may still be foolishness, to Christians it is a testimony of God's strength and our

GOSPEL John 2:13–25

A reading from the holy Gospel according to John

Since the **Passover** of the Jews was **near**,
  Jesus went up to **Jerusalem**.
He found in the **temple** area those who sold **oxen**,
    sheep, and **doves**,
  as well as the **money** changers seated there.
He made a **whip** out of **cords**
  and **drove** them all **out** of the temple area,
    with the **sheep** and **oxen**,
  and **spilled** the coins of the **money** changers
  and **overturned** their **tables**,
  and to those who sold **doves** he said,
  "Take these **out** of here,
  and **stop** making my Father's **house** a **marketplace**."
His **disciples** recalled the words of **Scripture**,
  Zeal for your house will **consume** me.
At **this** the Jews answered and said to him,
  "What **sign** can you show us for **doing** this?"
Jesus answered and said to them,
  "**Destroy** this temple and in **three** days I will raise it **up**."
The Jews said,
  "This **temple** has been under construction for **forty-six years**,
  and **you** will raise it up in **three days**?"
But **he** was speaking about the temple of his **body**.

The first section of the narrative ("The Passover of the Jews was near . . .") describes the scene in the Temple. In communicating these lines to the assembly you are drawing a picture for them; the details are important, so proceed unhurriedly.

Use a firm tone in your voice as you impart Jesus' words ("Take these things out of here").

zeal = zeel

Make sure to differentiate in your tone of voice between Jesus' words ("Destroy this temple . . .") and the response of the Jews ("This temple has been under construction . . ."). Jesus' words are a direct statement to be delivered with certainty and the Jews' words end in a question. Remember to raise your voice at the end of the question.

---

desire to use our human strength to cooperate with God's grace, not to try to save the world on our own.

GOSPEL John's account of the cleansing of the Temple is near the beginning of Jesus' public ministry, whereas in the synoptic Gospels, the event takes place in closer proximity to Jesus' Passion and death (Mark 11:15–19; Matthew 21:12–13; and Luke 19:45–48). This leaves the raising of Lazarus to be the primary motive for putting Jesus to death

in John's account, or at least the sign that caused an increase in momentum toward his Passion. John's narrative that is read today combines both the scene in the Temple with the one at the Sanhedrin trial on the night before Jesus' Crucifixion. During this trial, witnesses testify falsely that Jesus himself said he would destroy the Temple (Mark 14:58; Matthew 26:61). Observe that in this Johannine passage, Jesus does not say, "*I* will destroy" this Temple, but rather addressing the Jews (in John, this title was used for the Jewish leaders) says, "*[You]* destroy this temple."

Moreover, the action that ensues following the destruction of the Temple is different in John. Jesus himself will raise up the new Temple, his own body. For John, Jesus is the true Light of the World because in his body is "the glory as of a father's only son, full of grace and truth" (1:14).

Notice the connection between the final verses of the Gospel and the Second Reading. During the Lenten season, the Second Reading and the Gospel (as well as the Old Testament reading) are related. In

Communicate the words "While he was in Jerusalem . . ." at a moderate pace, not in a rush.

Therefore, when he was raised from the **dead**,
    his disciples **remembered** that he had said this,
    and they came to believe the **Scripture**
    and the **word** Jesus had **spoken**.

While he was in **Jerusalem** for the feast of **Passover**,
    many began to believe in his **name**
    when they saw the **signs** he was doing.
But Jesus would not **trust** himself to them because he **knew**
        them all,
    and did not need **anyone** to testify about human **nature**.
He **himself** understood it **well**.

both Paul's letter to the Corinthians and the Gospel according to John, those who demand signs and based their faith on signs are criticized and rejected (1 Corinthians 1:22; John 2:23–25). A faith based on "signs" or miracles is not a lasting faith. Rather, a faith based on the resurrected Jesus as the true dwelling place and temple of God is eternal. The disciples in today's Gospel realize this only after Jesus was raised from the dead, when they remembered what Jesus had said about raising the Temple in three days.

Just as Paul in his letter to the Corinthians tried to unite believers in the one body of Christ, so too the evangelist John emphasized the center of the Christian faith in the new Temple, the body of Christ. For John, the image was not a corporate one—he did not understand the community as the new Temple. While Paul was to tell the Corinthian community, "You are the body of Christ" (1 Corinthians 12:27), still, for him, the body was one and it was Christ's. In the Church, believers are united with Christ's body through Baptism in which they share in Christ's death and

Resurrection and the Eucharist in which they participate in communion with him and one another (see the Catechism, #790; *Lumen Gentium*, #7).

3RD SUNDAY OF LENT, YEAR A

Lectionary #28

READING I   Exodus 17:3–7

Exodus = EK-suh-dus

A reading from the Book of Exodus

In those days, in their thirst for **water**,
   the people **grumbled** against Moses,
   saying, "**Why** did you ever make us leave **Egypt**?
Was it just to have us **die** here of **thirst**
   with our **children** and our **livestock**?"
So Moses cried out to the LORD,
   "What shall I **do** with this people?
A little **more** and they will **stone** me!"
The LORD answered Moses,
   "Go over there in front of the **people**,
   along with some of the **elders** of Israel,
   holding in your hand, as you go,
   the **staff** with which you struck the **river**.
I will be standing there in **front** of you on the rock in Horeb.
Strike the rock, and the **water** will flow from it
   for the people to drink."
This Moses **did**, in the presence of the **elders** of Israel.
The place was called Massah and Meribah,
   because the Israelites **quarreled** there
   and **tested** the LORD, saying,
   "Is the LORD **in** our midst or **not**?"

Express the people's grievance to Moses ("Why did you ever make us leave Egypt . . . ?") with some frustration in your voice.

Convey the Lord's words in response to Moses ("Go over there in front . . .") with a sense of calm. They are simply a set of instructions needed in an intense situation.
Horeb = HOH-reb

Pause after the Lord's words and before the words "This Moses did . . . ."
Massah = MAS-ah
Meribah = MAIR-ih-bah

Ask the question "Is the Lord in our midst or not?" very deliberately.

READING I   Both the Israelites in today's First Reading and the Samaritan woman in the Gospel desire water so that they might not be thirsty—the Israelites thirst for water to quench their thirst in the wilderness, and the Samaritan woman thirsts for the water of eternal life about which Jesus speaks. In the renewal of the liturgy, *Sacrosanctum Concilium* (SC), Vatican II's Constitution on the Sacred Liturgy, called for more emphasis to be given to the recollection of Baptism and the preparation for Baptism during Lent (SC, #109). One of the ways the baptismal character of Lent has been restored is through the celebration of the scrutinies on the Third, Fourth, and Fifth Sundays in parishes where there are elect. Because of their importance in regard to Christian initiation, the readings for Year A may be used each year in places where there are catechumens. In Year A, the image of water is central on the Third Sunday of Lent.

   In this reading from Exodus, the Israelites encounter their third test as they journey in the wilderness to Sinai and Canaan after the Egyptians have been conquered. The first test involved bitter water they could not drink and about which they grumbled to Moses (15:22–27). Their second test regarded quail and manna, the food that the Lord provided in response to their hunger and their complaints against Moses and Aaron. In the third test, the Lord sees if the Israelites can follow his instructions. As in the previous two tests, the Israelites grumbling to Moses is really their way of testing the Lord. God does not chastise the Israelites for their grumbling;

READING II   Romans 5:1–2, 5–8

A reading from the Letter of Saint Paul to the Romans

Brothers and sisters:
Since we have been justified by **faith**,
    we have **peace** with God through our Lord Jesus **Christ**,
    through whom we have gained **access** by faith
    to this **grace** in which we stand,
    and we **boast** in **hope** of the glory of **God**.

And **hope** does not **disappoint**,
    because the love of **God** has been poured **out** into our **hearts**
    through the Holy **Spirit** who has been **given** to us.
For **Christ**, while we were still **helpless**,
    died at the appointed **time** for the **ungodly**.
Indeed, only with difficulty does one die for a **just** person,
    though perhaps for a **good** person one **might** even
        find courage to **die**.
But God **proves** his love for us
    in that while we were still **sinners** Christ **died** for us.

rather, he simply gives instructions to Moses to resolve the situation. Moses' faithfulness in following the Lord's instructions is an example to the Israelites: no matter how often they would quarrel with God, God would always be faithful.

Like the Israelites, the people in your assembly have places in their lives where they have thirsted for God, saying, "Is the Lord in our midst or not?" God, however, always responds with life-giving water. At Easter, as we renew our baptismal covenant, we will once again "drink" of the life-giving water God offers to us.

READING II   This reading begins with a synopsis of one of the fundamental truths of the Christian faith expounded on in Paul's letter to the Romans: "we have been justified by faith" (verse 1). Then Paul describes three of the effects of justification by faith: peace, hope, and love. Peace or reconciliation with God comes only "through our Lord Jesus Christ" (see 5:2, 9, 11, 17, 21). The use of *dia* ("through") in the Greek signifies that Christ's role is one of mediating this peace through the salvation he brings. And the use of the present

indicative, *echomen* ("we have"), affirms Christ's present influence in mediating peace now.

The hope that comes from justification is not deceptive or unreal; hence, in Paul's words it "does not disappoint" (verse 5). The reason that hope "does not disappoint" is the third effect of justification: the love of God for us. God's love makes hope a genuine reality.

While Paul was speaking to members of the Church at Rome, through your ministry as a lector, his words are addressed to us today. They are meant to encourage us

GOSPEL John 4:5–42

A reading from the holy Gospel according to John

Samaria = suh-MAIR-ee-uh

Sychar = SĪ-kar

Jesus came to a town of **Samaria** called **Sychar**,
    near the plot of land that **Jacob** had given to his son **Joseph**.
Jacob's **well** was there.
Jesus, tired from his **journey**, sat down there at the **well**.
It was about noon.

Pause after setting the scene and before the line "A woman of Samaria . . . ." Read this line slowly.

A woman of **Samaria** came to draw **water**.
Jesus said to her,
    "**Give** me a drink."
His disciples had gone into the town to buy food.
The Samaritan woman said to him,

Samaritan = Suh-MAIR-uh-tun

    "How can **you**, a **Jew**, ask **me**, a **Samaritan** woman,
        for a **drink**?"
—For Jews use **nothing** in common with Samaritans.—
Jesus answered and said to her,
    "If you knew the **gift** of God
    and who is saying to you, '**Give** me a drink,'
    you would have asked him
    and he would have given you **living** water."
The woman said to him,
    "**Sir**, you do not even have a **bucket** and the cistern is **deep**;
    where then can you **get** this living water?
Are you greater than our father **Jacob**,

Express some concern in your voice as you speak the woman's question ("Are you greater than our father Jacob . . . ?").

    who **gave** us this cistern and **drank** from it **himself**
    with his **children** and his **flocks**?"

to know that, through our faith claimed in Baptism, we were justified. Thus, the peace, hope, and love of God that come through Christ are present in our lives today through the working of the Spirit who has been given to us (verse 5). These effects or gifts of justification were freely given through Christ in his death on the cross for us who were once unjustified. Your proclamation today can serve to lead the assembly to offer thanksgiving to God for his love, given to us through Jesus Christ and present now in our hearts through the Spirit.

GOSPEL On this Sunday and the next two Sundays, the narratives from the Gospel according to John about the Samaritan woman, the man born blind, and the raising of Lazarus may be read in parishes where there are elect because of their importance in relation to Christian initiation (Introduction to the Lectionary, #97). The Gospel of the Samaritan woman is replete with meaning, both literal and symbolic. On many levels this moving narrative is intended to call the elect—indeed, the entire parish

community—to a deeper conversion to Jesus Christ as they approach the celebration of the Easter sacraments.

This narrative falls in John at a point where Jesus has withdrawn to Galilee to remove himself from the growing hostility of the Pharisees. On Jesus' way to Galilee, he had to pass through Samaria. In Sychar of Samaria is where the encounter with the woman at the well occurs. Here, Jacob's well lies at a fork in the road; in one direction was western Galilee, and in the other the Lake of Gennesaret. That Jacob's well lay at a fork in the road could

Offer the solemn promise in Jesus' answer to the woman's question ("Everyone who drinks this water . . .") with sincerity and assurance.

Pause after the woman's acceptance of Jesus' promise and before the next section begins with the words "Jesus said to her." Try lowering your tone of voice slightly as you read this section.

Jesus answered and said to her,
  "Everyone who drinks **this** water will be thirsty **again**;
  but whoever drinks the water **I** shall give will **never** thirst;
  the water I shall give will become in him
  a **spring** of water welling up to eternal **life**."
The woman said to him,
  "Sir, **give** me this water, so that **I** may not be thirsty
  or have to keep coming **here** to draw **water**."

Jesus said to her,
  "**Go** call your **husband** and come **back**."
The woman answered and said to him,
  "I do not **have** a husband."
Jesus answered her,
  "You are **right** in saying, 'I do not have a husband.'
For you have had **five** husbands,
  and the one you have now is **not** your husband.
What you have said is **true**."
The woman said to him,
  "Sir, I can see that you are a **prophet**.
Our **ancestors** worshiped on this **mountain**;
  but you people say that the place to worship is in **Jerusalem**."
Jesus said to her,
  "**Believe** me, woman, the hour is coming
  when you will worship the Father
  neither on this mountain **nor** in Jerusalem.
You people worship what you do not understand;
  we worship what we understand,
  because **salvation** is from the **Jews**.
But the hour is **coming**, and is now **here**,
  when **true** worshipers will worship the Father
    in **Spirit** and **truth**;
  and indeed the Father seeks such people to worship him.

be symbolic of the choice that the Samaritan woman and all who meet Jesus have to make. Will she believe in Jesus? Will we? Traditionally, Jacob's well is a place where a man would court his bride. Perhaps it is symbolic of Jesus' courting the Samaritan woman to a new relationship with him, or of God's invitation to Samaria to be his bride again.

Jesus' literal request of the woman for a drink is disconcerting on a number of accounts. In even speaking with the Samaritan woman he is breaking down humanly created social barriers of nationalities, sexes, and religious traditions. In terms of their religious traditions, Jews believed that salvation would come from them and Samaritans believed that later traditions such as worship in Jerusalem were unnecessarily added to the faith, eroding its true meaning. Jews and Samaritans also had distinct messianic expectations. The Jews expected their messiah to come from the David's lineage, and the Samaritans were waiting for a prophet like Moses (Deuteronomy 18:15).

From the initial discussion between Jesus and the woman comes the first Christological insight of the passage. On the basis of Jesus' offer of "living water," the woman senses that Jesus might be greater than Jacob (4:12). To her question, Jesus replies with a statement that conveys the power of the water he will give to continuously quench one's thirst. This water, like the waters of Baptism, leads to eternal life because its source is the Father of the risen Jesus.

After the woman expresses her desire for the water Jesus offers, the dialogue

Express the woman's faith evident in the line "I know that the Messiah is coming . . ." with a confident tone of voice in contrast to a moderate tone of voice for the words of Jesus ("I am he").

God is **Spirit**, and those who worship him
    must worship in **Spirit** and **truth**."
The woman said to him,
    "I know that the **Messiah** is coming, the one called the **Christ**;
    when he **comes**, he will tell us **everything**."
Jesus said to her,
    "**I** am he, the one **speaking** with you."

At that moment his disciples returned,
    and were **amazed** that he was talking with a **woman**,
    but still no one said, "What are you **looking** for?"
    or "Why are you talking with **her**?"
The woman **left** her water jar
    and went into the town and said to the people,
    "Come see a man who told me **everything** I have **done**.
Could he possibly be the **Christ**?"
They went out of the town and came to him.
Meanwhile, the disciples urged him, "Rabbi, **eat**."
But he said to them,
    "I have food to eat of which you do not know."
So the disciples said to one another,
    "Could someone have **brought** him something to eat?"
Jesus said to them,
    "**My** food is to do the will of the one who **sent** me
    and to finish his **work**.
Do you not say, 'In four months the harvest will be here'?
I tell you, look **up** and see the fields ripe for the **harvest**.
The **reaper** is already receiving **payment**
    and gathering **crops** for eternal **life**,
    so that the **sower** and **reaper** can rejoice **together**.
For here the saying is verified that '**One** sows and **another** reaps.'

Pause before beginning the section in which Jesus uses the images of harvesting, reaping, and sowing. The connection between this section and the verses that have preceded it is not easy to make. Take your time as you proclaim these verses, even near the end of an already lengthy Gospel.

switches to a more personal subject, the number of husbands she has had in her life. In this intimate conversion, the woman comes to the second Christological affirmation of the Gospel. She identifies Jesus as a prophet (verse 19). Through Jesus' response, we learn that, in Jesus, worship is no longer connected with a particular place as it was for Samaritans who worshipped on a mountain (Genesis 28:16–18) or for Jews who worshipped in Jerusalem. Rather, worship is connected to a person, Jesus, through whom salvation comes.

The third Christological affirmation comes at the end of this section of the dialogue, when the woman affirms her belief that the Messiah, the Christ, is coming and Jesus responds that indeed he is the one about whom she speaks (verses 25 and 26). The return of the disciples then interrupts the conversation between the woman and Jesus. While the disciples were amazed that Jesus was even speaking with a woman, the woman left and proclaimed her new but still fledgling and tentative faith to the townspeople.

Remaining behind, the disciples misunderstand Jesus' words about the food they will have to eat. This food is doing the Father's will, which culminates in his death and exaltation. As the water Jesus offers to the woman is clearly a symbol of the waters of Baptism, this food that Jesus speaks about suggests a reference to the Eucharist and its connection to the Paschal Mystery.

The lengthy Gospel concludes with a discussion of the harvest, which at first glance seems quite disparate from the rest

I sent you to **reap** what you have not **worked** for;
    others have done the work,
    and **you** are sharing the **fruits** of their work."

Many of the Samaritans of that town began to **believe** in him
    because of the word of the woman who testified,
    "He told me **everything** I have done."
When the Samaritans **came** to him,
    they invited him to **stay** with them;
    and he stayed there two days.
Many more began to believe in him because of his **word**,
    and they said to the **woman**,
    "We no longer believe because of **your** word;
    for we have heard for **ourselves**,
    and we know that this is **truly** the savior of the **world**."

[Shorter: John 4:5–15, 19b–26, 39a, 40–42]

Proclaim the final words in this Gospel, the words of the Samaritans ("We no longer believe . . ."), as if the elect themselves were saying these words to your church community, whose evangelization initially introduced them to Jesus.

of the narrative. Yet the harvest is a sign of the new age inaugurated by Jesus and fulfilled in his obedience to the Father's will, the glorious result of which will be the reconciliation of all to the Father through Jesus. Thus, the sower and reaper will rejoice together (verse 36).

The evangelist never tells whether or not the Samaritan woman actually gives Jesus the drink of water he requested. Perhaps leaving this unknown is a literary device of the evangelist. It focuses us on Jesus' own actions of reconciliation, which

offer hope to those who drink of his life-giving waters. Through the water Jesus shows barriers can be broken down, not only through our encounter with one another in Christ, but eternally. Thus, no earthly water that the woman could provide as drink is necessary, for Jesus provides all.

Through our personal relationship with Jesus, as evidenced by the relationship of the woman at the well with Jesus, we are led to faith and to insights into who Jesus is. Through our sharing of this faith, following the example of the Samaritan woman, we can bring others to Jesus. Their own

personal experience with Jesus, then, will lead them to a deeper belief in Jesus. The final and climactic christological claim made by the people who have heard Jesus' word for themselves ("we know that this is truly the savior for the world") witnesses to this. Your proclamation of this narrative, then, can lead the assembly to consider both the impact their own confession of faith has in their life, and their role in evangelizing others—as they have done with the elect in their midst.

4TH SUNDAY OF LENT

Lectionary #32

READING I 2 Chronicles 36:14–16, 19–23

A reading from the second Book of Chronicles

In **those** days, all the **princes** of Judah, the **priests**, and the **people**
    added **infidelity** to **infidelity**,
    practicing **all** the abominations of the **nations**
    and **polluting** the LORD's **temple**
    which he had **consecrated** in Jerusalem.

Early and **often** did the LORD, the God of their **fathers**,
    send his **messengers** to them,
    for he had **compassion** on his people and his **dwelling** place.
But they **mocked** the messengers of God,
    despised his warnings, and **scoffed** at his prophets,
    until the **anger** of the LORD against his people was so **inflamed**
    that there was no **remedy**.
Their enemies **burnt** the house of God,
    tore **down** the walls of **Jerusalem**,
    set all its **palaces** afire,
    and **destroyed** all its precious objects.
Those who escaped the **sword** were carried **captive** to **Babylon**,
    where they became **servants** of the king of the **Chaldeans**
        and his **sons**
    until the **kingdom** of the **Persians** came to power.

Chronicles = KRAH-nih-k*ls

Judah = JOO-duh

Narrate the first section ("In those days . . .") with disappointment in your voice because the focus is on the infidelity of the princes, the priests, and the people.

Convey the Lord's kindness evident in the section beginning "Early and often did the Lord . . ." with genuine concern in your voice. Then express the Israelites' response ("But they mocked . . .") with disdain, and the Lord's answer ("until the anger of the Lord . . .") in a firm tone of voice.

A lower tone of voice that reflects some sadness is appropriate in delivering the consequences of the Israelites' failure to turn back to the Lord in the section beginning with the words "Their enemies burnt . . . ."

Babylon = BAB-ih-lon

Chaldeans = kal-DEE-unz

READING I The first and second books of Chronicles describe the history of Israel from Creation to the beginnings of the Persian Empire. First Chronicles 1—9 covers the span of time from Creation through the reign of David. Second Chronicles continues the history from the reign of Solomon through the destruction of Judah by the Babylonians (Chaldeans) and the exile of her people, until the king of Persia, Cyrus, permits the exiles to return (2 Chronicles 36:22–23).

Today's reading begins with a description of the infidelity and sinfulness of seemingly everyone in Judah. Despite the fact that the Lord sent messengers, the people fail to heed the words of the prophets leading to the destruction of Jerusalem and the Temple by the Babylonians and the exile to Babylon of those who survived.

Surprisingly a pagan king, Cyrus of Persia, served as a messenger of hope with his edict allowing the exiles to return (verses 22 and 23). During the Lenten season we reflect our sinful actions that have resulted in our being exiled from God. As we are honest this Lent about our own infidelity, we live in the Easter hope of our salvation that came through the Son. Be watchful, though. This Easter hope may be shown to you and your parish community in unexpected ways—as unexpected as a pagan king proclaiming God's word welcoming his people home!

READING II This brief passage from Ephesians deals with God's plan for salvation as it relates to all humanity. Ephesians was probably not written

Jeremiah = jair-uh-MĪ-uh

All this was to fulfill the **word** of the LORD spoken by **Jeremiah**:
  "Until the land has retrieved its lost sabbaths,
    during all the time it lies **waste** it shall have **rest**
  while **seventy** years are **fulfilled**."

Cyrus = SĪ-rus

In the first year of **Cyrus**, king of **Persia**,
  in order to fulfill the **word** of the LORD spoken by **Jeremiah**,
  the LORD **inspired** King Cyrus of **Persia**
  to issue this **proclamation** throughout his **kingdom**,
  both by word of **mouth** and in **writing**:

Proclaim the edict of Cyrus ("All the kingdoms of the earth . . .") in a confident, optimistic voice.

  "Thus says **Cyrus**, king of **Persia**:
  All the kingdoms of the **earth**
  the LORD, the God of **heaven**, has **given** to me,
  and he has **also** charged me to build him a **house**
  in **Jerusalem**, which is in **Judah**.
Whoever, therefore, among you belongs to **any** part of his **people**,
  let him go **up**, and may his **God** be **with** him!"

READING II   Ephesians 2:4–10

Ephesians = ee=FEE-zhunz

A reading from the Letter of Saint Paul to the Ephesians

Practice the sentence that begins with the words "God, who is rich in mercy" out loud, lowering your tone of voice for the parenthetical clauses and strengthening it on the main clauses ("God . . . brought us to life with Christ").

Brothers and sisters:
God, who is rich in **mercy**,
  because of the great **love** he had for us,
  even when we were **dead** in our **transgressions**,
  brought us to life with **Christ**—by **grace** you have
    been **saved**—,
  raised us **up** with him,

---

by Paul, but Pauline themes are evident, although in a manner that reveals some development from the earlier, authentic letters of Paul. Four primary examples of this development are as follows: 1) in Ephesians, the Church is understood as a universal, spiritual, and heavenly phenomenon, whereas in the undisputed Pauline letters the view of the Church as a local community predominates; 2) in Ephesians, Christ is understood as the head of the Church, which is his body, and in the authentic Pauline letters, the Church is the body of

Christ with many members; 3) in Ephesians, the dispute between Jew and Gentile regarding conversion is missing—they are reconciled to God through the cross (2:16); and 4) in Ephesians, direct references to the *parousia*, the second coming of Christ, as something that will occur soon are lacking; rather, as evidenced in today's reading, the emphasis of Ephesians is on Christians being *presently* united with Christ and each other through Christ's Resurrection: God "raised us up with him and seated us with him in the heavens in Christ Jesus" (verse 4).

Although the Second Reading is often not clearly related to the First Reading, during Lent, the connection is more direct. Today, both readings speak of God's mercy. In the First Reading, God uses Cyrus to call his people back home, letting them know that the Lord has not abandoned them despite their infidelity. And in the Second Reading the Ephesians hear that, despite their being dead because of their trespasses, God still loved them, making them alive together with Christ (verse 5).

and **seated** us with him in the **heavens** in Christ **Jesus**,
that in the ages to **come**
He might show the **immeasurable** riches of his **grace**
in his **kindness** to us in Christ **Jesus**.
For by **grace** you have been **saved** through **faith**,
and this is not from **you**; it is the **gift** of God;
it is not from **works**, so no one may **boast**.
For we are his **handiwork**, created in Christ **Jesus** for the
good **works**
that God has prepared in **advance**,
that we should **live** in them.

Take your time proclaiming the line "For by grace . . . ." You are delivering an important teaching here. Place happiness and gratitude in your voice as you communicate to the assembly that God's grace that saves through faith is a "gift of God."

GOSPEL John 3:14–21

A reading from the holy Gospel according to John

Nicodemus = nik-oh-DEE-mus

Jesus said to **Nicodemus**:
"Just as **Moses** lifted up the **serpent** in the **desert**,
so must the Son of **Man** be lifted up,
so that **everyone** who **believes** in him may have eternal **life**."

For God so **loved** the world that he gave his only **Son**,
so that everyone who **believes** in him might not **perish**
but might have eternal **life**.
For God did **not** send his Son into the world
to **condemn** the world,
but that the world might be **saved** through him.
Whoever **believes** in him will not be condemned,
but whoever does **not** believe has **already** been condemned,
because he has not believed in the name of the only Son of **God**.

Give emphasis to Jesus' words ("so that everyone who believes . . ."). These words are at the heart of the Gospel. Note their repetition in the following verse. Offer them as words of hope and evangelization.

Practice the line "Whoever believes in him . . ." carefully so you don't stumble over the multiple occurrences and forms of the words "believe" and "condemned." Use a measured pace in your delivery.

Thus, for the author of Ephesians God's plan for salvation is carried out through the Resurrection of Christ. As in the authentic Pauline letters, this salvation is pure gift, pure grace (verse 8). But, in Ephesians, with salvation comes the responsibility to do good works. These works do not earn us salvation. Thus, the ministry that you as a lector and others in the Church perform is not carried out to gain salvation, but rather it is seen as a thanksgiving for the gift of salvation in

Christ already received. Such is also true of the works of penance we perform during the season of Lent.

GOSPEL Nicodemus was a Pharisee and a leader in the Jewish community, perhaps a member of the ruling Sanhedrin. According to the evangelist, he comes to Jesus "at night" (3:2), probably because he does not yet belong to the light. Nicodemus, although not yet in the light, comes inquiring of Jesus, the one he addresses as "Rabbi" or "Teacher" who

has come from God. Jesus responds to Nicodemus by noting to him the necessity of being "born from above" if one is to see the kingdom of God (verse 3).

For Jesus' part, he reveals to Nicodemus how his life has to change; at this point his faith is incomplete for he has yet to be baptized in water and receive God's Spirit. Nicodemus is probably thinking of natural birth when he asks Jesus how an old person can be born again, because surely he cannot reenter the womb (verse 4). Birth

Pause before the words "And this is the verdict" to mark the movement toward a climax in Jesus' words. Pause again before the words "But whoever lives the truth." Try making eye contact with the assembly for as much of this verse as you can.

And **this** is the **verdict**,
    that the **light** came into the world,
    but **people** preferred **darkness** to **light**,
    because their works were **evil**.
For **everyone** who does **wicked** things **hates** the light
    and does not come **toward** the light,
    so that his **works** might not be **exposed**.
But whoever lives the **truth comes** to the light,
    so that his **works** may be clearly seen as done in **God**.

from a Jewish mother automatically made one a member of God's Chosen People, but now through Jesus membership in the Chosen People does not entail being born in the flesh to someone of the same lineage. Rather, in Jesus, the Word made flesh, the Son of Man who came down from heaven and has gone up to heaven (verses 13 and 14), being a child of God now involves being born again through water and the Spirit. One must believe in him to have eternal life (verse 15).

Today's Gospel picks up the scene with Nicodemus after his dialogue with Jesus is finished. The remainder of the passage consists of Jesus' words to Nicodemus, with no response on Nicodemus' part. Included in Jesus' reflection to Nicodemus is a frequently quoted verse, John 3:16: "For God so loved the world that he gave his only Son, so that everyone who believes in him might not perish but might have eternal life."

These words focus on a similar theme as the First Reading: God invites his exiled people home to him. We, as Christians,

come home to God to share in his life through Jesus Christ, who offered salvation through his death and Resurrection. The words of John 3:16 summarize the main point of the Second Reading as well: by God's love Christians have been raised up with Christ through their faith in him. Both the epistle and the Gospel end with the responsibility placed on those who believe in Jesus to see that their works reflect their belief. Through believers, others will be brought to faith in the true light.

4TH SUNDAY OF LENT, YEAR A

Lectionary #31

READING I   1 Samuel 16:1b, 6–7, 10–13a

A reading from the first Book of Samuel

The LORD said to **Samuel**:
    "Fill your horn with **oil**, and be on your **way**.
I am sending you to **Jesse** of Bethlehem,
    for I have chosen my **king** from among his **sons**."

As Jesse and his sons came to the **sacrifice**,
    Samuel looked at **Eliab** and thought,
    "**Surely** the LORD's **anointed** is here before him."
But the LORD said to Samuel:
    "Do not judge from his **appearance** or from his lofty **stature**,
    because I have rejected him.
Not as **man** sees does **God** see,
    because **man** sees the **appearance**
    but the LORD looks into the **heart**."
In the same way Jesse presented **seven** sons before Samuel,
    but Samuel said to **Jesse**,
    "The LORD has not chosen **any** one of these."
Then Samuel asked Jesse,
    "Are these **all** the sons you **have**?"
Jesse replied,
    "There is still the **youngest**, who is tending the **sheep**."
Samuel said to Jesse,
    "**Send** for him;
    we will not begin the sacrificial **banquet** until he arrives **here**."

Proclaim the Lord's announcement to Samuel that he has chosen a king ("Fill your horn with oil . . .") with confidence.

Eliab = ee-LĪ-ub

Deliver the Lord's advice to Samuel ("Do not judge from his appearance"), making eye contact with the assembly because it is practical advice for us today as well.

Offer Jesse's response to Samuel's question ("There is still the youngest . . .") with reticence in your voice.

READING I "Not as man sees does God see." Today's readings all emphasize the images of light and sight— seeing with the eyes of faith. On the Fourth Sunday of Lent those parishes with elect celebrate the second scrutiny. All the readings were chosen to emphasize the connection with this rite of Christian initiation that is "meant to uncover, then heal all that is weak, defective, or sinful in the hearts of the elect; and to bring out, then strengthen all that is upright, strong, and good" (RCIA, #141).

This First Reading from Samuel gives an account of David's anointing by Samuel. The Lord knows from the beginning whom he has chosen to be king. Yet Samuel—and presumably also Jesse and his sons—are seeing with human eyes. According to their eyes, the king should have a physical appearance that conveys importance, even a sense of arrogance or control. But the Lord makes his decision on other qualities, judging according to the heart of a person. Thus, David is the Lord's chosen one, anointed by Samuel as king.

Interestingly, the anointing of David described in this reading is understood as a "secret anointing" because later in the next chapter of Samuel it is unknown to David's brother Eliab (1 Samuel 17:28). Moreover, in the second book of Samuel there are two other accounts of David's anointing. The first describes David's anointing after Saul's death by the "men of Judah" in a location near Hebron (2 Samuel 2:4). The second portrays David's anointing by the elders after he made an agreement with

Jesse sent and had the young man brought to them.
He was **ruddy**, a youth **handsome** to behold
and making a **splendid** appearance.
The LORD said,
"There—anoint **him**, for **this** is the one!"
Then **Samuel**, with the horn of oil in **hand**,
anointed **David** in the presence of his **brothers**;
and from that day **on**, the spirit of the LORD
rushed upon David.

State the Lord's command to Samuel ("There—anoint him") slowly and with enthusiasm. This line is the heart of the reading.

READING II   Ephesians 5:8–14

Ephesians = ee=FEE-zhunz

A reading from the Letter of Saint Paul to the Ephesians

Brothers and sisters:
You were once **darkness**,
but **now** you are **light** in the **Lord**.
Live as children of **light**,
for **light** produces every kind of **goodness**
and **righteousness** and **truth**.
Try to learn what is **pleasing** to the Lord.
Take no part in the **fruitless** works of **darkness**;
rather **expose** them, for it is **shameful** even to **mention**
the things done by them in **secret**;
but **everything** exposed by the **light** becomes **visible**,
for **everything** that becomes visible is **light**.
Therefore, it says:
"**Awake**, O sleeper,
and **arise** from the **dead**,
and Christ will give you **light**."

Begin the opening line ("You were once darkness . . .") in a lower tone of voice. Then increase the volume slightly as you proclaim the second half of the sentence ("but now you are light"). Make eye contact with the assembly throughout the entire line if you can do so with ease.

Proclaim the words "Awake, O sleeper" as an urgent imperative to the community by increasing the volume in your tone of voice, making eye contact with the assembly.

---

them that acknowledged him as head of the northern and southern kingdoms (5:1–5). David is identified by the Lord as both the shepherd and commander of the people of Israel. As the king chosen by God, he is to be both a pastoral leader and a political leader.

That David's first anointing went unrecognized by some teaches us that God's choices may not always be human choices. God's ways may or may not be confirmed by others. For those who see with the heart as God sees, the approval of others is of little consequence. Like David,

though, those who see with the eyes of faith often are called to accept a role as pastoral leaders in their faith community. By virtue of our Baptism, every Christian has been anointed for service to God. While the type of leadership roles Christians undertake varies, all are chosen to lead by the way they see—with their faith. In doing so, they will be mediators of the presence of God to others as David was in his role as king. They will help others to see.

| READING II | "You have been enlightened by Christ. Walk always as children of the light and keep the flame of faith alive in your hearts. When the Lord comes, may you go out to meet him with all the saints in the heavenly kingdom" (RCIA, #579). |

Through Baptism, we become children of the light, not of the darkness as this prayer spoken after the presentation of the baptismal candle, which was lit from the paschal candle, to the newly baptized attests.

GOSPEL John 9:1–41

A reading from the holy Gospel according to John

As Jesus passed by he saw a man **blind** from **birth**.
His disciples asked him,
   "**Rabbi**, who **sinned**, this **man** or his **parents**,
   that he was born **blind**?"
Jesus answered,
   "**Neither** he **nor** his parents sinned;
   it is so that the works of **God** might be made **visible**
      through him.
We have to do the works of the one who sent me while it is day.
Night is coming when **no** one can work.
While I am in the **world**, I am the **light** of the world."
When he had said this, he **spat** on the ground
   and made **clay** with the **saliva**,
   and **smeared** the clay on his **eyes**, and said to him,
   "Go **wash** in the Pool of Siloam"—which means **Sent**—.
So he **went** and **washed**, and came back able to **see**.

His **neighbors** and those who had seen him earlier
   as a **beggar** said,
   "Isn't **this** the one who used to sit and **beg**?"
Some said, "It **is**,"
   but **others** said, "**No**, he just **looks** like him."
He said, "I **am**."
So they said to him, "How were your eyes **opened**?"
He replied,
   "The man called Jesus made **clay** and **anointed** my eyes
   and told me, 'Go to Siloam and **wash**.'
So I **went** there and **washed** and was able to **see**."

Pause after the phrase "While I am in the world." Then look up at the assembly as you proclaim Jesus' self-identification ("I am the light of the world").

Siloam = sih-LOH-um

Be direct in your tone of voice in communicating the now-healed blind man's response ("I am") to those who were questioning his identity.

Reading this passage from Ephesians during Lent, when many prepare for Baptism and all the baptized are called to reflect more deeply on their baptismal commitment, provides a reminder of the difference between living as children of the light and children of darkness.

   This reading is part of a larger section of Ephesians that discusses Christian and non-Christian conduct (4:17—5:20). The dualism between light and darkness that the author describes is an ethical and moral dualism related to a person's behavior.

Behavior that made one a child of darkness included licentiousness (4:19), deceitful desires (4:22), speaking falsehoods (4:25), immorality and obscenity (5:3–4), and greed (5:5). In contrast, children of the light are imitators of God, living in love as Christ loved them (5:1). As members of the one body of Christ (4:26), children of the light have the responsibility to make another aware of his or her sin (5:13), thus helping each other to produce goodness, righteousness, and truth (5:9).

   Often in our society today, our lives are kept private; our focus is on ourselves as individuals and how we can be self-sufficient. Yet our life as children of the light in the Christian community instills in us the virtue of mutuality and interdependence. We need each other to be faithful in our Christian commitment. As the early baptismal hymn quoted at the end of the reading states, "Arise from the dead, and Christ will give you light." Often this light comes through other children of the light—and sometimes through those whose actions

And they said to him, "Where **is** he?"
He said, "I don't know."

They brought the one who was once blind to the **Pharisees**.
Now Jesus had made clay and opened his eyes on a **sabbath**.
So then the Pharisees **also** asked him how he was able to see.
He said to them,
    "He put **clay** on my eyes, and I **washed**, and now I can **see**."
So some of the Pharisees said,
    "This man is **not** from God,
    because he does not keep the **sabbath**."
But **others** said,
    "How can a **sinful** man do such signs?"
And there was a division among them.
So they said to the blind man **again**,
    "What do you have to say about him,
    since he opened your eyes?"
He said, "He is a **prophet**."

Now the Jews did not believe
    that he had been **blind** and gained his **sight**
    until they summoned the **parents** of the one
        who had gained his sight.
They asked them,
    "Is this your **son**, who you say was born **blind**?
How does he now **see**?"
His parents answered and said,
    "We **know** that this is our **son** and that he was born **blind**.
We do **not** know how he **sees** now,
    nor do we know who opened his eyes.
Ask **him**, he is of age;
    he can speak for **himself**."

Convey the man's statement about Jesus' identity ("He is a prophet") with confidence in your voice.

Place some suspicion and doubt in your voice as you ask, "Is this your son . . . ?" The dialogue between the Jewish authorities and the parents is oppositional. Let defensiveness be heard in your voice as your give the parents' answer ("We know that this is our son . . .").

we recognize as contrary to living in the light. Consider the ways in which you need to arise from the dead to know the light of Christ as you prepare for your proclamation of the word on the Fourth Sunday of Lent.

GOSPEL Today's Gospel, proclaimed on the Fourth Sunday of Lent, the Sunday on which the second scrutiny is celebrated, has long been associated with Baptism. The blind man who was sent by Jesus to wash in the pool of Siloam ("sent") went down into the pool and came up out of the pool able to see, just as the elect who will be baptized at the Easter Vigil go down into the baptismal font and come up seeing with the eyes of faith.

While John's story of the healing of the blind man does not detract from the physical healing that can occur through faith, its emphasis is on the spiritual healing that occurs when one believes in Jesus, the Light of the World. This is made clear through the final lines of the Gospel, which express disappointment in the Pharisees

as they remain mired in their arrogance, thinking they can see. Their sin becomes their blindness (verses 40 and 41).

As in John's account of the Samaritan woman at the well last Sunday, the heart of this Gospel lies in its Christological affirmations. The narrative progresses from Jesus' own identification of himself as "the light of the world" (verse 5) to the blind man's rather innocuous statement in his first description of his healing to his neighbors and others who had seen him

His parents said this because they were afraid
 of the Jews, for the Jews had already agreed
  that if anyone **acknowledged** him as the **Christ**,
 he would be **expelled** from the **synagogue**.
For this reason his parents said,
 "**He** is of age; question **him**."

So a **second** time they called the man who had been **blind**
 and said to him, "Give **God** the praise!
We know that this man is a **sinner**."
He replied,
 "If he is a **sinner**, I do not **know**.
One thing I **do** know is that I was **blind** and now I **see**."
So they said to him,
 "What did he **do** to you?
 How did he open your eyes?"
He answered them,
 "I told you **already** and you did not **listen**.
Why do you want to hear it **again**?
Do **you** want to become his disciples, too?"
They **ridiculed** him and said,
 "**You** are that man's disciple;
 we are disciples of **Moses**!
We know that God spoke to Moses,
 but we do **not** know where this one is from."
The man answered and said to them,
 "This is what is so **amazing**,
 that you do not know where he is from,
  yet he opened my eyes.
We **know** that God does not listen to **sinners**,
 but if one is **devout** and does his **will**, he **listens** to him.

The unreasonableness of the authorities grows in the section beginning with the words "So a second time." Express this in your voice as you read the dialogue between the man who had been blind and the Pharisees. The man's frustration also increases throughout their exchange.

blind, in which he referred to the person who healed him as "the man called Jesus" (verse 11).

 In the man born blind's second telling of his story to the Pharisees, he asserts that Jesus is a prophet, a man whose power comes from God. During the scene, the Pharisees are disturbed because Jesus performed the healing on a Sabbath. This fact, for some of the Pharisees, provides grounds for them to suggest that Jesus does not come from God. A division is created between the Pharisees, and even with the blind man's confession, the Gospel

tells us. They did not believe the miracle happened, which leads them to ask for the blind man's parents.

 Thus, for a third time the blind man must answer questions about what happened to him that he is now able to see. While his parents identify him as their son, they do not go so far to claim they know what transpired. They stop short of their own confession of faith, as the Gospel relates to us, because they were afraid of "the Jews." (This is a term used in the Gospel according to John to refer to the

Jewish leaders; it is not a general reference to all Jews, and in this Gospel it is likely a reference to the Pharisees.) In this scene, the ire of the man born blind is raised as he has to defend himself and the one who healed him once again. While "the Jews" perceive Jesus as a sinner, the blind man only testifies to his newfound sight. This leads to his being identified as Jesus' disciple in contrast to "the Jews," who refer to themselves as disciples of Moses, because they know that God was present to Moses. What they fail to realize is what the blind man knows and

It is **unheard** of that anyone ever opened the eyes
> of a person **born** blind.
If this man were not from **God**,
> he would not be able to do **anything**."
They answered and said to him,
> "You were born **totally** in sin,
> and are **you** trying to teach **us**?"
Then they threw him out.

When Jesus heard that they had thrown him out,
> he found him and said, "Do you **believe** in the Son of **Man**?"
He answered and said,
> "Who **is** he, sir, that I **may** believe in him?"
Jesus said to him,
> "You have **seen** him,
> and the one speaking with you is he."
He said,
> "I **do** believe, Lord," and he **worshiped** him.
Then Jesus said,
> "I came into this world for **judgment**,
> so that those who do **not** see **might** see,
> and those who **do** see might become **blind**."

Some of the Pharisees who were with him heard this
> and said to him, "Surely **we** are not also blind, **are** we?"
Jesus said to them,
> "If you **were** blind, you would have no **sin**;
> but now you are saying, 'We **see**,' so your sin **remains**."

[Shorter: John 9:1, 6–9, 13–17, 34–38]

The authorities' statement ("You were born totally in sin . . .") is in opposition to Jesus' statement ("Neither he nor his parents sinned") at the beginning of the reading. Express the authorities' point of view unhurriedly so that the assembly will have the chance to question their logic.

Proclaim the newly healed blind man's confession of faith ("I do believe, Lord") slowly and with conviction.

Pause slightly before the concluding verses ("Some of the Pharisees . . ."). There is still tension in this final exchange between the Pharisees and Jesus.

---

assumes in his response back to them: "This is what is so amazing that you do not know where he is from, yet he opened my eyes" (verse 30).

The Gospel ends with Jesus' reappearance both to the blind man and the Pharisees. In his dialogue with the blind man, Jesus refers to himself as the Son of Man. The blind man responds, "I do believe, Lord," a similar response to that given to the questions posed during the profession of faith at Baptism.

The blind man's "profession of faith" is the final Christological affirmation in this Gospel. Although others still did not believe, including his neighbors, his parents, and the Pharisees, he was convicted. For us, we are left with the hard truth that sometimes being faithful to our baptismal commitment will mean that others will question us. Yet through our worship of Jesus Christ, the one whose power comes from God, we are drawn into communion with God and with each other. Our sin no longer remains and "we see."

5TH SUNDAY OF LENT

Lectionary #35

READING I   Jeremiah 31:31–34

Jeremiah = jair-uh-MĪ-uh

This brief passage is Jeremiah's oracle of the new covenant the Lord will make with his people. Begin the proclamation with hope in your voice as you proclaim the words "The days are coming . . . ."

Israel = IZ-ree-ul

Judah = JOO-duh

Pause after the announcement of the new covenant and before the description of the covenant ("It will not be like the covenant . . ."). The remainder of the reading explains what the new covenant will be like.

Offer the line "I will place my law within them . . ." with a gentle, loving tone of voice.

In this season of repentance, proclaim this final line with confidence in what the Lord, for his part, will do to initiate and uphold the new covenant. To the confidence in your voice, add a little satisfaction, for the Lord will not only forgive the sins of the house of Israel and Judah (and ours as well!), but the Lord will also forget their sins.

A reading from the Book of the Prophet Jeremiah

The **days** are **coming**, says the LORD,
> when I will make a **new** covenant with the house of **Israel**
> and the house of **Judah**.
It will **not** be like the covenant I made with their **fathers**
> the day I **took** them by the **hand**
> to lead them forth from the land of **Egypt**;
> for they broke my **covenant**,
> and I had to show myself their **master**, says the LORD.
But **this is** the covenant that I will **make**
> with the house of Israel **after** those days, says the LORD.
I will **place** my law **within** them and **write** it upon their **hearts**;
> I will be their **God**, and **they** shall be my **people**.
No **longer** will they have need to teach their **friends** and **relatives**
> how to know the **LORD**.
All, from **least** to **greatest**, shall **know** me, says the LORD,
> for I will forgive their **evildoing** and remember their sin
>> **no more**.

READING I   Jeremiah lived as a prophet in Jerusalem during a tumultuous time. The Babylonians were approaching Judah, and the Assyrians and Egyptians were unable to hold them back. By frightening them with utter destruction, Jeremiah attempted to persuade the king and the people to rely solely on their covenant with the Lord. Jeremiah begged the king to surrender to the Babylonians, but this counsel went unheeded. Jerusalem and its Temple were destroyed, and the people were sent into exile.

While Jeremiah had a reputation of being a prophet of doom and gloom, he was also a man who staunchly believed in the Lord's love for his people. Despite Israel's infidelity to the Mosaic covenant, Jeremiah still proclaimed the Lord's faithfulness to his people. This was especially true during the last period of Jeremiah's life, which forms the context for today's passage.

Jeremiah believed that the Lord would change people. The Lord would accomplish this in a personal manner by writing his law on their hearts (verse 33). No longer would Jeremiah or others be respon-

sible for teaching and bringing people back to the Lord; the Lord will forgive them, and they will all know the Lord (verse 34).

Christians believe the new covenant of which the Lord speaks (verse 31) is fulfilled in the person of Jesus Christ. As the Word made flesh (John 1:1–14), God united himself personally with all of humanity. Through the Paschal Mystery, which is celebrated in every liturgy, and in a particular way during Holy Week, God in Jesus Christ unites people to life in him in a new covenant. Your proclamation of this reading

Use a mild tone of voice (staying away from a harsh or loud tone) as you offer the part of the reading that alludes to Jesus' prayer in Gethsemane (Mark 14:32–42).

Proclaim the last line of the reading after the semicolon ("and when he was made perfect . . .") with a stronger tone of voice and with hope. Jesus' obedience to his suffering on the cross led to his Resurrection and the gift of "eternal salvation" for those who choose to follow his example.

READING II   Hebrews 5:7–9

A reading from the Letter to the Hebrews

In the **days** when Christ **Jesus** was in the **flesh**,
    he offered **prayers** and **supplications** with loud **cries** and **tears**
    to the one who was able to **save** him from **death**,
    and he was **heard** because of his **reverence**.
Son though he **was**, he learned **obedience** from what he **suffered**;
    and when he was made **perfect**,
    he became the **source** of eternal salvation for **all** who
        obey him.

serves as a prelude to the celebration of the new covenant during Holy Week.

READING II As we draw closer to Holy Week, it is fitting that the Second Reading is this brief passage from Hebrews focusing on Christ's suffering and obedience. The letter to the Hebrews, a sermon written between 80–90 AD most likely to Christians enticed by Jewish cultic ideals by an unidentified author, portrays Jesus as the "high priest" of the new covenant.

Today's three verses are located in the section of Hebrews that describes Jesus' priesthood. Jesus is the quintessential high priest because he offered sacrifice not in an earthly temple, but in a heavenly one, and the sacrifice he offered was not the ritualistic animal sacrifice, but the sacrifice of his very self. In doing so, "he became the source of eternal salvation for all who obey him" (verse 9).

Jesus is a priest according to the order of Melchizedek (Hebrews 5:6), a priest in the Old Testament who was called by God and whose existence was without

beginning or end (Genesis 14:17–20; Psalm 110:4). Melchizedek's priesthood anticipated that of Jesus, the Son of God, who is the eternal high priest, fulfilling the Jewish priesthood rooted in Abraham.

While Hebrews emphasizes Jesus' full divinity and his superiority over all other beings, it also highlights the fullness of Jesus' humanity. His prayers and supplications (a common priestly activity), reminiscent of the agonizing prayer in the garden of Gethsemane (Mark 14:32–42), show the humanness of the beloved Son of God (verse 5). As a result of his obedience

GOSPEL   John 12:20–33

A reading from the holy Gospel according to John

Some **Greeks** who had come to **worship** at the Passover Feast
  came to **Philip**, who was from **Bethsaida** in **Galilee**,
  and asked him, "**Sir**, we would like to see **Jesus**."
Philip went and told **Andrew**;
  then **Andrew** and **Philip** went and told **Jesus**.
Jesus answered them,
  "The **hour** has come for the **Son** of Man to be **glorified**.
Amen, amen, I **say** to you,
  unless a grain of **wheat** falls to the ground and **dies**,
  it **remains** just a grain of **wheat**;
  but if it **dies**, it produces much **fruit.**
Whoever **loves** his life **loses** it,
  and whoever **hates** his life in this world
  will **preserve** it for **eternal** life.
Whoever **serves** me must **follow** me,
  and where **I** am, there also will my **servant** be.
The **Father** will honor whoever **serves** me.

"I am **troubled** now. Yet what should I say,
'Father, **save** me from this **hour**'?
But it was for **this** purpose that I **came** to this hour.
Father, **glorify** your **name**."

The opening verses ("Some Greeks . . . went and told Jesus") seemingly prepare the scene for the rest of the Gospel. Communicate them in a narrative tone of voice as if you are beginning a story.

Bethsaida = beth-SAY-ih-duh

Pause before the words "Jesus answered them." Pause again after each of Jesus' three teachings in this section: 1) "it produces much fruit," 2) "will preserve it for eternal life," and 3) "whoever serves me."

Pause after the series of three teachings as Jesus' words become more serious and solemn. Convey Jesus' fear and anxiety about his impending death with some angst in your voice.

---

to his suffering, Jesus was made perfect (verse 9) and consecrated as *the* eternal high priest.

Jesus himself did not seek out suffering; rather, he accepted it obediently. This example is what Christians are called to imitate. While we will never be perfectly obedient as Jesus was, our faith teaches us that, through the intercession of Christ Jesus the high priest, we are forgiven and saved. As faithful Christians we must learn obedience in new and deeper ways, growing in our relationship with God and others through the Church.

GOSPEL In today's Gospel, we find the Pharisees saying, "Look, the whole world has gone after him," as the crowds gathered around Jesus upon his entry into Jerusalem for Passover (verse 19). Among them were Greeks who asked to see Jesus (verse 20). Perhaps they were Greek-speaking Jews, or Greeks who were interested in Judaism. Recall that John was writing for a predominantly Greek audience, whose philosophical world was characterized by dualism: light/dark, flesh/spirit, earthly/heavenly. If part of John's purpose was to show that Jesus'

mission extended beyond the Jews to the Gentile world, then it would be logical for him to portray Gentiles (Greeks) inquiring to see Jesus.

It is unclear from the Gospel why the Greeks wanted to see Jesus and if their request was ever granted. The "them" to whom Jesus responds in verse 23 could include the Greeks or it could simply refer to Philip and Andrew. In either case, Jesus' words are a clear statement of his impending death and the "fruit" that that will come from it. The adage about the grain of wheat is likely a common proverb, a version of

Speak the words of the voice ("I have glorified it . . .") with authority, but not with such power that they lose the sense of being a response to Jesus' words.

Offer Jesus' words ("This voice did not come . . .") in a teacher-like tone of voice. "Now" in reference to the "time of judgment" points to Jesus' impending Crucifixion.

Pause before the concluding line ("He said this indicating . . ."). Distinguish this narrative line from the words of Jesus in your delivery.

Then a **voice** came from **heaven**,
   "I **have** glorified it and will **glorify** it again."
The crowd there **heard** it and said it was **thunder**;
   but **others** said, "An **angel** has spoken to him."
Jesus answered and said,
   "This voice did not come for **my** sake but for **yours**.
Now is the time of **judgment** on this world;
   now the **ruler** of this world will be driven **out**.
And when I am **lifted** up from the **earth**,
   I will draw **everyone** to myself."
He said this indicating the **kind** of death he would die.

which can also be found in 1 Corinthians 15:36. The saying about losing and preserving one's life also reiterates the point about new life coming through suffering. The third saying regarding servanthood is similar to Mark 8:34. Moreover, the language of the Father honoring those who serve Jesus, the Son of Man, will also be found later in the Gospel according to John in Jesus' farewell discourses (14:23; 16:27).

Jesus' words that follow the three moralizing statements are reminiscent of the scene in the garden of Gethsemane (Mark 14:34–36). Observe, though, that in

John's account Jesus speaks of glorifying the Father, whereas in Mark Jesus prays to the Father that the hour might pass by him if that is the Father's will. In Mark, Jesus appears more distraught, filled with more agony. In John, on the other hand, Jesus is in control, knowing that it is only through his Passion and death that the Father will be truly glorified. The language of glorification reveals Jesus' unity with the Father (John 10:30) and in the early centuries of the Church served to support claims for Jesus' full divinity.

For the evangelist John, Jesus' death is the fulfillment of his mission; it is only through death that Christ will be exalted and the Son of Man lifted up from the earth (verse 32). Through your proclamation of this Gospel the Sunday before Holy Week begins, invite your assembly to reflect on the ways in which the struggles and sufferings they face in life—both large and small—are united to those of Jesus. In their lives, then, they participate in the mission of Jesus, glorifying the Father and bringing others into communion with him.

5TH SUNDAY OF LENT, YEAR A

Lectionary #34

READING I   Ezekiel 37:12–14

Ezekiel = ee-ZEE-kee-ul

These three short verses are full of hope for the exiled people of Israel. Speak them with strength and confidence; they are the Lord's words, which offer the people a reason to be optimistic.

Pause slightly before the words "I will put my spirit . . . ." This is the climax of Ezekiel 37:1–14 and of the three verses in this passage. God will always be with the people of Israel and his promises will be fulfilled. Let reassurance be heard in your voice as you proclaim the Lord's certainty that his promise will be fulfilled.

A reading from the Book of the Prophet Ezekiel

Thus says the Lord **GOD**:
  O my **people**, I will open your **graves**
  and have you **rise** from them,
  and bring you **back** to the land of **Israel**.
Then you shall know that **I** am the **LORD**,
  when I **open** your graves and have you **rise** from them,
  O my **people**!
I will put my **spirit** in you that you may **live**,
  and I will **settle** you upon your **land**;
  thus you shall know that **I** am the LORD.
I have **promised**, and I will **do** it, says the LORD.

READING I The First Reading conveys an exciting message about the Lord's promise of new life, fitting for this Sunday on which the third scrutiny is celebrated. The Lord's promise that he will put his spirit (*ruah,* in Hebrew) in his people is the promise Christians see fulfilled in Christ.

The prophet Ezekiel wrote during difficult and tumultuous times. The people of Israel were in exile in Babylon. The kingdom of Judah was facing its final days of independence. Its rulers, steeped in their own political ambitions, wanted to overthrow the Babylonians. Ezekiel valiantly tried to refocus the kings on the Lord, believing that a kingdom of faithful people centered on God would be more successful than one governed by humans who sought to accomplish lofty goals apart from their real source of life—the Lord.

Today's reading is part of Ezekiel's prophecy resulting from a powerful vision he experienced (37:1–28). The vision began with dry bones scattered about in the center of the plain. These dry bones represented Israel after having been conquered by the Babylonians. Ezekiel prophesied that these bones would be brought to life by the Lord. Israel, who was dried up, withered, and without hope, would come to life again through the Spirit of the Lord.

While the language shifts from dry bones to "graves" in today's reading (this shift in language could be the result of an insertion in the text), but the word of the Lord spoken through Ezekiel carries a similar message. Israel will rise from the dead. The verse "when I open your graves and

In this reading, Paul compares "those who are in the flesh" with "those who are not in the flesh." The latter are "in the spirit." Practice this reading so that your proclamation is not singsong. There will be a natural tendency to have it come across that way because of the repetition of words and the contrasts Paul is describing.

Try pausing slightly after both occurrences of the word "dead" in the final sentence. The final sentence ("If the Spirit of the one . . .") is hopeful. Through the working of the Father, the Spirit of Christ continues to enliven believers today.

READING II   Romans 8:8–11

A reading from the Letter of Saint Paul to the Romans

Brothers and sisters:
Those who are in the **flesh** cannot **please** God.
But **you** are **not** in the **flesh**;
    on the **contrary**, **you** are in the **spirit**,
    if only the Spirit of **God dwells** in you.
Whoever does **not** have the Spirit of **Christ**
        does **not belong** to him.
But **if Christ** is in you,
    although the **body** is **dead** because of **sin**,
    the **spirit** is **alive** because of **righteousness**.
If the **Spirit** of the **one** who raised **Jesus** from the **dead**
        dwells in you,
    the **One** who raised **Christ** from the **dead**
    will give **life** to **your** mortal bodies **also**,
    through his **Spirit** dwelling in **you**.

GOSPEL   John 11:1–45

A reading from the holy Gospel according to John

Now a man was **ill**, **Lazarus** from **Bethany**,
    the village of **Mary** and her sister **Martha**.
Mary was the one who had **anointed** the Lord with perfumed **oil**
    and dried his **feet** with her **hair**;
    it was her **brother** Lazarus who was ill.

Lazarus = LAZ-uh-rus

Bethany = BETH-uh-nee

Communicate the opening verses ("Now a man was ill . . .") with attention to the names given.

have you rise from them . . ." serves as both a metaphorical reference to the new life Israel will experience through the Lord, and it is also an unmistakable reference to the Resurrection of the dead. It is not a reference to individuals rising from the dead, however (as in Jesus' individual Resurrection). The people of Israel at the time Ezekiel was prophesying believed only in a general Resurrection of the dead at the end of the world.

Through your proclamation of this passage, let the corporate image of the Resurrection—of breathing new life into a community of people that is dried up and hopeless—be heard as the Lord's promise to the assembly before you. Sometimes new life needs to be infused in communities that might be stuck, perhaps carrying out many of their tasks the same way from year to year because "we've always done it this way." Like the presider's celebration of the scrutiny, which is meant to be carried out in such a way "that the faithful in the assembly will also derive benefit" from it, your proclamation of the word can be beneficial to the community as a whole (RCIA, #145).

READING II This reading is built on the contrast between life in the flesh and life in the Spirit. Most of Romans 8 focuses on this contrast. But it is earlier in Paul's letter, where he develops his theology of the Baptism, that he gives hints as to what life according to the Spirit means. In Baptism, Christians are buried with Christ so that they, like Christ, will live in the newness of life (6:4). The old self—the sinful body—is done away with in Baptism so that Christians are now able to live for God in Christ Jesus (6:6, 11). Yet, for Paul, this does not mean that the body

Because Jesus' words here reveal
the purpose of Lazarus' illness, proclaim
them with confidence to demonstrate
that Jesus is in control of the situation
at hand.

Judea = joo-DEE-uh

The disciples did not understand the
meaning of Jesus' words ("Our friend
Lazarus is asleep"), so he needed to
make the direct statement ("Lazarus has
died"). Be straightforward and look up as
you communicate this to the assembly;
sometimes we do not understand Jesus'
words either.

So the sisters sent word to Jesus saying,
> "**Master**, the one you **love** is ill."

When Jesus heard this he said,
> "This illness is **not** to end in **death**,
> but is for the glory of **God**,
> that the Son of God may be **glorified** through it."

Now Jesus **loved** Martha and her **sister** and **Lazarus**.
So when he heard that he was **ill**,
> he remained for **two days** in the place where he was.

Then after this he said to his **disciples**,
> "Let us go back to **Judea**."

The disciples said to him,
> "**Rabbi**, the Jews were just trying to **stone** you,
> and you want to go **back** there?"

Jesus answered,
> "Are there not twelve hours in a **day**?
If one walks during the **day**, he does not **stumble**,
> because he sees the **light** of this world.
But if one walks at **night**, he **stumbles**,
> because the **light** is not **in** him."

He said this, and then told them,
> "Our friend Lazarus is **asleep**,
> but I am going to **awaken** him."

So the disciples said to him,
> "**Master**, if he is **asleep**, he will be **saved**."

But Jesus was talking about his **death**,
> while they thought that he meant ordinary **sleep**.

So then Jesus said to them **clearly**,
> "Lazarus has **died**.
And I am **glad** for you that I was not **there**,
> that you may **believe**.

is literally destroyed. Christians still have their human bodies, through which they carry out God's work. Now, however, the Spirit gives them life.

For Paul, showing how Christians participate in the death and Resurrection of Christ Jesus through Baptism was a step in presenting his theology that he needed to take before he spoke about life in the Spirit. Without Christ it would be impossible to talk about Christians living in the Spirit; sin would still have power over them. But now, because of Christ's death

and Resurrection, the baptized Christians are gifted with the Spirit dwelling in them. They are destined for a life that has as its goal pleasing God (8:8).

Notice that Paul uses the phrase "Spirit of God" and the "Spirit of Christ" interchangeably in the verse "if only the Spirit of God . . . the Spirit of Christ does not belong to him." While Paul did not have anywhere near a fully developed Trinitarian doctrine in his letters, these two references to the Spirit nevertheless affirm the interrelationship of God, Christ, and the Spirit. The Spirit has its origin in God, from

whom Christ came, but the Spirit is also Christ's because of Christ's Resurrection. This life-giving Spirit of Christ now dwells within Christians (verse 11).

As you prepare to proclaim this reading, take into consideration how close we are in proximity to Easter. The Resurrection message you will proclaim is a foretaste of the new life the elect will soon experience through Baptism. It also is a reminder to those of us already baptized that the Spirit of Christ is with us, energizing us, giving life to us as we seek to please God in all

Didymus = DID-ih-mus

Emphasize the "four days" that Lazarus has been in the tomb by pausing slightly after that statement and before the words "Now Bethany was near Jerusalem."

Martha's words to Jesus ("Lord, if you had been here . . .") are filled with her disappointment in the Lord. However, the words in the second sentence she speaks ("But even now I know that God . . .") are a powerful statement of faith in what God can do through Jesus. Express them as Martha's confident request in faith to Jesus.

Jesus' words ("I am the resurrection and the life") are central to the Gospel. Proclaim them slowly. Offer Jesus' question to Martha ("Do you believe this?") with a slight raising of your voice as you ask the question.

Let us go to him."
So **Thomas**, called Didymus, said to his fellow **disciples**,
    "Let us also go to **die** with him."

When Jesus **arrived**, he found that Lazarus
    had already been in the **tomb** for **four days**.
Now Bethany was near **Jerusalem**, only about two miles away.
And many of the Jews had come to Martha and Mary
    to **comfort** them about their **brother**.
When **Martha** heard that Jesus was coming,
    she went to **meet** him;
    but **Mary** sat at home.
Martha said to Jesus,
    "Lord, if you had **been** here,
    my brother would not have **died**.
But even now I **know** that **whatever** you ask of God,
    God will **give** you."
Jesus said to her,
    "Your brother will **rise**."
Martha said to him,
    "I **know** he will rise,
    in the **resurrection** on the last **day**."
Jesus told her,
    "I am the **resurrection** and the **life**;
    whoever believes in **me**, even if he **dies**, will **live**,
    and everyone who lives and believes in me will **never** die.
Do you **believe** this?"
She said to him, "**Yes**, Lord.
I have come to believe that you are the **Christ**, the Son of **God**,
    the one who is **coming** into the world."

that we do. We will celebrate this truth at Easter.

GOSPEL On the two previous Sundays, Jesus proclaimed himself to be "living water" and "the light of the world." John's narratives of the woman at the well and the man born blind were read in connection with the first two scrutinies, in order to make known that Jesus' "living water" quenches the thirst and gives sight to all those desiring to follow him. This Sunday the third and final scrutiny is celebrated after the proclamation of the Gospel of the raising of Lazarus, the last of the "great signs" in his work. In the Gospel Jesus announces that he is the "resurrection and the life." In the scrutiny, the elect experience new life that comes from being freed from the bondage of sin through faith in Jesus.

Jesus' power over death reigns supreme in this Gospel that serves as a prelude to his own death and Resurrection. Whereas in the other Gospels Jesus' cleansing of the Temple most directly resulted in the plot to condemn him, picking up its pace, in John's account Jesus' action bringing Lazarus back to life most immediately leads to an increase in hostility toward him, resulting in his suffering and death. Observe that in Jesus' conversation with his disciples, after he heard word from Martha and Mary that Lazarus was ill, the disciples attempt to dissuade him from going back to Judea because the Jews had tried to stone him when he had been there recently.

Pause before the words "When she had said this," as they mark a shift in the narrative to Mary's interaction with Jesus.

When she had said this,
    she went and called her sister Mary **secretly**, saying,
    "The **teacher** is here and is **asking** for you."
As soon as she **heard** this,
    she rose **quickly** and went to him.
For Jesus had not yet come into the **village**,
    but was still where Martha had **met** him.
So when the Jews who were with her in the house **comforting** her
    saw Mary get up quickly and go **out**,
    they **followed** her,
    presuming that she was going to the **tomb** to **weep** there.
When Mary came to where Jesus was and saw him,
    she **fell** at his feet and said to him,
    "Lord, if **you** had been here,
    my **brother** would not have **died**."

Lower your tone of voice as you deliver the lines of the narrative "When Jesus saw her weeping . . . . And Jesus wept," as they describe a lot of human emotion.

When Jesus saw her **weeping** and the Jews who had come
        with her weeping,
    he became **perturbed** and deeply **troubled**, and said,
    "Where have you **laid** him?"
They said to him, "Sir, come and **see**."
And Jesus **wept**.
So the Jews said, "See how he **loved** him."
But some of them said,
    "Could not the one who opened the eyes of the **blind** man
    have done something so that this man would not have **died**?"

So **Jesus**, perturbed **again**, came to the **tomb**.
It was a **cave**, and a **stone** lay across it.
Jesus said, "Take away the **stone**."
Martha, the dead man's **sister**, said to him,
    "Lord, by **now** there will be a **stench**;
    he has been **dead** for **four days**."

The detail of Lazarus being dead for "four days" is repeated. Emphasize it clearly again.

In the course of that same conversation, Jesus tells the disciples that Lazarus is asleep and he is going to awaken him, but the disciples do not understand his words. Jesus then clearly tells them that Lazarus has died. The listener—your assembly today—will know that these words not only refer to Lazarus' death, but to Jesus' approaching death as well. Thomas' statement ("Let us also go to die with him") at the end of the conversation between Jesus and his disciples makes this obvious. The reference to Bethany, where Lazarus was, being near Jerusalem

also is a link between this episode and Jesus' Passion and death that will take place in Jerusalem.

By the time Holy Week comes, the Christian community will have traveled through Lent with Jesus, and they too will once again go along with Jesus "to die." The elect, through the sacrament of Baptism, will die with Christ to their old selves. In the waters of Baptism, they will also rise with him to newness of life. And, at the end of our earthly journey, we will physically die with Jesus, but we will also be raised to life with him. For those

of us who are faithful, "life is changed, not ended. When the body of our earthly dwelling lies in death we gain an everlasting dwelling place in heaven" (see the Catechism, #1012).

Like the Gospel of the two preceding Sundays, this narrative also holds important Christological affirmations, the first of which comes from Jesus himself in his statement "I am the resurrection and the life." The second Martha speaks in her response to Jesus' question about whether she believes that he is the Resurrection and the life. She announces her belief in

Give Jesus' command ("Lazarus, come out!") in a strong and loud voice. Make sure to use your own voice to give this command, not a voice that sounds like one Jesus might have had.

Pause significantly before slowly reading the final verse ("Now many of the Jews . . .").

Jesus said to her,
　　"Did I not **tell** you that if you **believe**
　　you will see the glory of **God**?"
So they took away the **stone**.
And Jesus raised his eyes and said,
　　"**Father**, I **thank** you for **hearing** me.
I know that you **always** hear me;
　　but because of the **crowd** here I have said this,
　　that they may **believe** that you **sent** me."
And when he had said this,
　　he cried **out** in a loud **voice**,
　　"**Lazarus**, come **out**!"
The dead man came **out**,
　　tied hand and foot with **burial** bands,
　　and his **face** was wrapped in a **cloth**.
So Jesus said to them,
　　"**Untie** him and let him **go**."

Now **many** of the Jews who had come to **Mary**
　　and **seen** what he had done began to **believe** in him.

[Shorter: John 11:3–7, 17, 20–27, 33b–45]

Jesus as the Christ, the Son of God, the one coming into the world. Although her statements about Jesus do not directly relate to how he just identified himself, they do reflect Christological views that are important throughout the Gospel according to John. Indeed, in Jesus's exaltation on the cross and in glory, believers will see that the one who is the Christ, the Son of God, the one who descended and who ascended, is the one who is the Resurrection and the life. Through him, the possibility of Resurrection is extended to all who believe in him.

Thus, the Lazarus narrative you are tasked with proclaiming carries with it many layers of meaning. The time you spend in preparation, thinking about the ways it correlates with the third scrutiny, the season of Lent, and the approach of Holy Week will help make your proclamation more complete. Offer this Gospel to the assembly in a way that captures its drama, emphasizing the significant personal interactions between Jesus and the disciples, Martha, and Mary. In his love for them all, he is profoundly human. Through the raising of Lazarus, he shows his divine

power over death. Your proclamation can provide the assembly a means by which they can place themselves in the story. This will lead them to see how Jesus has been the "resurrection and the life" for them and how he will continue to give them new life.

PALM SUNDAY OF THE LORD'S PASSION

Lectionary #37

GOSPEL AT THE PROCESSION   Mark 11:1–10

A reading from the holy Gospel according to Mark

When **Jesus** and his **disciples** drew near to **Jerusalem**,
   to **Bethphage** and **Bethany** at the Mount of **Olives**,
   he sent **two** of his disciples and **said** to them,
   "Go into the village **opposite** you,
   and immediately on **entering** it,
   you will find a **colt** tethered on which no one has ever **sat**.
Untie it and **bring** it **here**.
If anyone should **say** to you,
   'Why are you **doing** this?' reply,
   'The **Master** has **need** of it
   and will send it **back** here at **once**.'"
So they went **off**
   and **found** a colt tethered at a **gate** outside on the **street**,
   and they **untied** it.
Some of the **bystanders** said to them,
   "What are you **doing**, untying the **colt**?"
They **answered** them just as Jesus had **told** them to,
   and they **permitted** them to **do** it.
So they **brought** the colt to Jesus
   and put their **cloaks** over it.
And he **sat** on it.

Bethphage = BETH-fayj

Bethany = BETH-uh-nee

Be confident when pronouncing the names in the opening line ("When Jesus and his disciples . . ."). Your confident tone here helps to continue the solemnity and dignity of the opening rites of today's liturgy.

Pause slightly before the narrative section begins with the words "So they went off." Use a different tone of voice, perhaps one with a little less strength, to report the events that followed Jesus' instructions.

PROCESSION GOSPEL At the beginning of the liturgy on Passion (Palm) Sunday, the entrance in Jerusalem is remembered and made present to us in the proclamation of an account of Jesus' triumphant entry into Jerusalem from one of the synoptic Gospels (Mark 11:1–10; Matthew 21:1–11; Luke 19:28–40; or the Gospel account from John may be proclaimed) and in the procession of the assembly with palm branches. In Year B, the Gospel account is from Mark. Later in the liturgy, Mark's account of the Passion will be proclaimed.

The narrative has a sense of mystery and secrecy, which is evident in the response the disciples are asked to give to anyone who inquires about why they need to untie a colt on which no one has ever sat. They justify their actions simply based on the authority of the Master. Whether the bystanders understood "the Master" to be the owner of the colt or Jesus is not clear. Perhaps the disciples are also unsure as to why Jesus would need a colt, but still they follow his instructions of regarding what to say to those who are curious about their actions.

That Mark has Jesus riding the colt for the last mile or so of his journey into Jerusalem shows how he sees Jesus as a fulfillment of Zechariah's prophecy of a humble savior-king riding on a colt. For Zechariah, the messiah will not be a conquering warrior, unlike the kings of Judah; through his meekness and the peace he brings (Zechariah 9:10) he will be recognized as the messiah. Yet in the Gospel according to Mark, the heart of Zechariah's

Many people spread their **cloaks** on the **road**,
    and **others** spread leafy **branches**
    that they had cut from the **fields**.
Those **preceding** him as well as those **following** kept crying **out**:
    "**Hosanna**!
        Blessed is he who **comes** in the name of the **Lord**!
        Blessed is the **kingdom** of our father **David** that is to **come**!
    Hosanna in the **highest**!"

Or:

GOSPEL AT THE PROCESSION   John 12:12–16

A reading from the holy Gospel according to John

When the great **crowd** that had come to the **feast** heard
    that **Jesus** was coming to **Jerusalem**,
    they took **palm** branches and went out to **meet** him,
        and cried **out**:
        "**Hosanna**!
        Blessed is he who **comes** in the name of the **Lord**,
            the king of **Israel**."

Jesus found an **ass** and **sat** upon it, as is **written**:
    *Fear no **more**, O daughter **Zion**;*
    *see, your king **comes**, seated upon an **ass's** colt.*
His disciples did not **understand** this at first,
    but when **Jesus** had been **glorified**
    they **remembered** that these things were **written** about him
    and that they had **done** this for him.

prophecy is lost on the crowds as they acclaim Jesus with shouts of joy. They expect Jesus to be a king who will replace the ruling Romans.

The mood created by the proclamation of this Gospel and the procession that follows it is one of solemnity and joyful exaltation. Yet while Christians acclaim Jesus as king, the mood in the liturgy of today quickly changes as we are reminded that Jesus is the Messiah in whose very person the kingdom of God is at hand, even in his suffering (Mark 1:15).

READING I This passage is a part of the third of four servant songs in Isaiah (42:1–4; 49:1–7; 50:4–11; 52:13–53:12). In the Christian tradition, Jesus is understood as the fulfillment of the prophecies of the suffering servant. That is why on Passion Sunday this Old Testament reading is paired with the proclamation of the Mark's Passion account.

In verses 4–9 of this servant song (of which verses 4–7 constitute the reading you proclaim), the servant speaks, seemingly resigned to the sufferings he experiences. The text seems to portray the

servant as one who is akin to a "disciple," speaking the word of the Lord to those who are weary and listening to the Lord to receive guidance each morning (verse 4). This follower of the Lord, in contrast to the people of Israel, is faithful despite those who mistreat and do harm to him (verse 6). The servant does not despair, even in the midst of his suffering, for he acknowledges the Lord as his help and protector in times of trial (verse 7).

Note the contrast between the servant in these verses from Isaiah and the suffering Son of God in Mark's account of

Lectionary #38

READING I Isaiah 50:4–7

Isaiah = ī-ZAY-uh

Practice this powerful reading aloud with someone else present so he or she can provide feedback. This will help your proclamation reflect that the Lord indeed has given you the gifts and skills necessary to proclaim his words. You will then be able to deliver the words "The Lord God has given me a well-trained tongue" with self-confidence and poise.

Pause before the section beginning with the words "I gave my back." Read these words with some sorrow.

Pause slightly again before the end of the passage. Change the tone in your voice to reflect hope and confidence in the Lord.

A reading from the Book of the Prophet Isaiah

The Lord **GOD** has **given** me
    a **well**-trained **tongue**,
that I might **know** how to **speak** to the **weary**
    a **word** that will **rouse** them.
Morning after **morning**
    he opens my **ear** that I may **hear**;
and I have not **rebelled**,
    have not turned **back**.
I **gave** my back to those who **beat** me,
    my **cheeks** to those who plucked my **beard**;
my **face** I did not **shield**
    from **buffets** and **spitting**.

The Lord **GOD** is my **help**,
    therefore I am not **disgraced**;
I have set my **face** like **flint**,
    knowing that I shall **not** be put to shame.

---

the Passion. The suffering servant in Isaiah does not rebel, does not turn back. And while Jesus does not refuse his suffering, according to the evangelist Mark, he seems to be a bit more reticent to accept it. On the cross, Mark has Jesus pleaded with God, asking, in the words of Psalm 22:19, "My God, my God, why have you forsaken me?"

READING II This reading is an early Christian hymn quoted by Paul to the Philippians. Its Christology is

profound and has shaped Christian understanding of Christ for centuries.

Paul established the Christian community at Philippi and felt deep affection for the Philippians (1:3–11; 7:8). His correspondence to them contained in Philippians, which is probably a composite of letters, reveals how the community was struggling with both internal dissension and external antagonists.

In the face of all these challenges, Paul offered much needed encouragement. From the verses just prior to this hymn, it is clear that Paul's purpose in quoting this

beautiful hymn to the Philippians is to show how their relations with one another are to mirror Christ's relationship with them (2:1–5). Christ Jesus, who emptied himself, taking the form of a slave, humbled himself and became obedient to the point of death (verses 7 and 8), is the one who serves as the model for their Christian life, a life they profess to live "in Christ." The comparison with the servant of the Lord in Isaiah 52:13—53:12 is also implicit in these verses.

The hymn's assertions that Christ Jesus was "in the form of God," meaning

Philippians = fih-LIP-ee-unz

Read this ancient hymn in a prayerful voice. This does not mean in a whisper, but rather with care and deliberateness.

Pause again before the hymn shifts to Christ Jesus' exultation by God in the words "Because of this, God greatly exalted him." In your proclamation of these words, build toward the confession of faith ("and every tongue confess . . ."). Keep your voice strong through the last phrase ("to the glory of God the Father").

READING II   Philippians 2:6–11

A reading from the Letter of Saint Paul to the Philippians

Christ **Jesus**, though he was in the **form** of **God**,
  did **not** regard **equality** with God
  something to be **grasped**.
Rather, he **emptied** himself,
  taking the form of a **slave**,
  coming in **human** likeness;
  and found **human** in **appearance**,
  he **humbled** himself,
  becoming **obedient** to the point of **death**,
  even death on a **cross**.
Because of this, God greatly **exalted** him
  and **bestowed** on him the **name**
  which is above **every** name,
  that at the name of **Jesus**
  every **knee** should **bend**,
  of those in **heaven** and on **earth** and **under** the earth,
  and every **tongue confess** that
  Jesus **Christ** is **Lord**,
  to the glory of **God** the **Father**.

his nature was that of God and he came in human likeness, are an early affirmation of Christ's preexistence, as well as his true divinity and true humanity. Christian belief sees in Christ's self-emptying his willingness to humble himself, obediently accepting death and experiencing it in the fullness of his humanity, while maintaining the fullness of his divinity.

At the end of the hymn, its theology transitions from the humility of the suffering Christ to his exaltation by God. The switch in the subject from Christ in verses 6–8 to God in verses 9–11 reflects this. The climax of the hymn is found in the confession that "Jesus Christ is Lord" (1 Corinthians 12:3 and Romans 10:9) and the doxology to the Father. Those in all three levels of the ancient universe (verse 10) are to offer this confession, as we offer it today in our worship and through our lives led in imitation of Christ Jesus.

PASSION | The proclamation of the Passion of the Lord begins without the customary greeting before a Gospel. Instead, the statement announcing "The Passion of our Lord Jesus Christ according to Mark" indicates the beginning of the Gospel. Its simplicity reflects the solemnity of the events that will be retold.

Every year a different synoptic narrative of the Passion is proclaimed on Passion Sunday (Matthew in Year A, Mark in Year B, and Luke in Year C). On Good Friday, the Passion is always taken from the Gospel according to John.

The evangelist Mark sees the Passion of Jesus as the highpoint of his ministry

PASSION   Mark 14:1—15:47

The Passion of our Lord Jesus Christ according to Mark

> The reading of the Passion begins with a simple and solemn introduction, unlike the usual announcement of the Sunday Gospel.

(1) The **Passover** and the Feast of Unleavened **Bread**
   were to take **place** in two days' **time**.
So the chief **priests** and the **scribes** were seeking a way
   to **arrest** him by **treachery** and put him to **death**.
They said, "**Not** during the **festival**,
   for fear that there may be a **riot** among the **people**."

> Pause before the section that begins with the words "When he was in Bethany." The scene has changed.
> Bethany = BETH-uh-nee

(2) When he was in **Bethany** reclining at **table**
   in the house of **Simon** the **leper**,
      a **woman** came with an alabaster **jar** of perfumed **oil**,
      costly genuine **spikenard**.
She **broke** the alabaster jar and **poured** it on his **head**.
There were **some** who were **indignant**.

> Let some annoyance be heard in your voice as you convey the objections of some of the people ("Why has there been this waste . . . ?").

"Why has there been this **waste** of perfumed **oil**?
It could have been **sold** for more than three **hundred** days' **wages**
   and the **money** given to the **poor**."
They were **infuriated** with her.

> Express Jesus' answer to those who complain "Let her alone . . ." with firmness in your voice. As you continue with Jesus' explanation of the kindness evident in the woman's action ("She has done a good thing . . ."), use a lighter tone of voice.

Jesus said, "Let her **alone**.
Why do you make **trouble** for her?
She has done a **good** thing for me.
The poor you will **always** have with you,
   and whenever you **wish** you can do **good** to them,
   but you will **not** always have **me**.

---

that began after his Baptism by John (1:9–11) and the Spirit driving him out into the desert, where he was tempted by Satan (1:12–13). While Mark's account of Jesus' ministry is brief and to the point, he uses what seems to be an inordinate amount of space on the Passion, almost a fifth of the entire Gospel! This has led to the description of his account as "a Passion narrative with a long introduction." Yet Mark knew what his purpose was. He wanted to show Jesus as the suffering servant who is the Son of God. Thus, Mark depicts Jesus as finding his glory by following the will of God to the cross.

Throughout the Gospel, Jesus alone seems to understand what is happening to him. The disciples are portrayed as never quite understanding Jesus' message, especially when he tells them he must suffer and die. The Passion narrative serves as a climax of Jesus' own isolation and the disciples' misunderstanding of his identity.

The proclamation of the Passion occurs in diverse ways in parish communities; however, the traditional manner of proclaiming the Passion is to have it sung or read in three parts. The *General Instruction to the Roman Missal* allows for the Passion of the Lord to be divided among multiple lectors (#109).

More specifically, the 1988 *Circular Letter Concerning the Preparation and Celebration of the Easter Feasts* from the Congregation for Divine Worship and Discipline of the Sacraments states that the Passion is to be proclaimed by three priests, deacons, or lay readers. When lay readers assist in the proclamation, the part of Christ is to be reserved to a priest (#33).

She has done what she **could**.
She has **anticipated** anointing my **body** for **burial**.
Amen, I **say** to you,
    wherever the **gospel** is **proclaimed** to the whole **world**,
    what she has **done** will be **told** in **memory** of her."

Iscariot = is-KAIR-ee-ut

Take your time proclaiming the line "Then Judas Iscariot . . ." at the beginning of the next scene.

(3) Then Judas **Iscariot**, one of the **Twelve**,
    went off to the chief **priests** to hand him **over** to them.
When they **heard** him they were **pleased**
      and promised to pay him **money**.
Then he looked for an **opportunity** to hand him **over**.

The reference to the "first day of Unleavened Bread" means that it was the fourteenth day of Nisan on the Jewish calendar. The Passover meal was eaten in the evening at the start of the fifteenth day of Nisan.

(4) On the first **day** of the Feast of Unleavened **Bread**,
    when they **sacrificed** the Passover **lamb**,
    his **disciples** said to him,
    "Where do you want us to **go**
    and **prepare** for you to eat the **Passover**?"
He **sent** two of his disciples and said to them,
    "Go into the **city** and a man will **meet** you,
    carrying a jar of **water**.
Follow him.
Wherever he **enters**, say to the **master** of the house,
    'The **Teacher** says, "Where is my **guest** room
    where I may eat the **Passover** with my **disciples**?"'
Then he will **show** you a large upper room **furnished** and **ready**.
Make the **preparations** for us **there**."
The disciples then went **off**, **entered** the city,
    and **found** it just as he had **told** them;
    and they prepared the **Passover**.

According to Jewish law, the Passover meal needed to be eaten within the boundaries of the city of Jerusalem (see Deuteronomy 16:7). This is why the disciples were sent to find a place where they, along with Jesus, could eat the Passover meal.

The Secretariat for Liturgy has provided a standard edition of the Passion in four parts that many parishes use. This edition gives the collective part of the observers, witnesses to the trial and death of Jesus, and "the crowd" to the assembly. However, the Bishops' Committee on the Liturgy cautions that pastoral sensitivity around the crowd's call to "Crucify him!" must prevail, thereby preventing any misunderstanding regarding the collective guilt of the Jewish people for the death of Jesus. In deciding whether to use the four-part

proclamation, due consideration is also to be given to whether or not it enhances the full participation of the assembly.

(1) Mark notes that the Passion is taking place during the Passover and the Feast of Unleavened Bread. Originally, the Passover, which commemorates the Israelites' deliverance from slavery, and the Feast of Unleavened Bread were two separate festivals (Exodus 12). Including the Feast of the Unleavened Bread in the context of the Passover gave it additional meaning. In the context of the Israelites' liberation, it served as an offering of thanks

and praise to God for all he had done and will do in the future.

Early on, the Passover was celebrated in homes, but after King Josiah limited sacrificial worship to the Temple in Jerusalem, Passover became a pilgrimage feast. Because Jerusalem swelled to about four times the size of its population, the chief priests and scribes were afraid to carry out their plot to put Jesus to death during the festival, lest a riot occur.

By placing Jesus' own sacrifice during these two festivals, Mark links the

Place some disappointment in your voice as you express Jesus' prediction that one who was his follower will turn against him found in the words "Amen, I say to you . . ." in an audible but lower tone of voice. Give the disciples' response ("Surely it is not I?") as a defensive response and one filled with much anxiety by placing some nervousness in your voice.

Speak the words of blessing Jesus offered at the Passover meal with reverence. They took on new meaning in the context of this particular Passover meal. The slowness and solemnity with which you deliver these words will give the assembly time to ponder their connection with our eucharistic celebration.

(5) When it was **evening**, he came with the **Twelve**.
And as they reclined at **table** and were **eating**, Jesus said,
 "**Amen**, I **say** to you, **one** of you will **betray** me,
 one who is **eating** with me."
They began to be **distressed** and to **say** to him, one by **one**,
 "**Surely** it is not **I**?"
He said to them,
 "One of the **Twelve**, the one who **dips** with me into
 the **dish**.
For the Son of **Man** indeed **goes**, as it is **written** of him,
 but **woe** to that man by **whom** the Son of **Man** is **betrayed**.
It would be **better** for that man if he had never been **born**."

(6) While they were **eating**,
 he took **bread**, said the **blessing**,
 broke it, and **gave** it to them, and said,
 "**Take** it; **this** is my **body**."
Then he took a **cup**, gave **thanks**, and **gave** it to them,
 and they all **drank** from it.
He said to them,
 "**This** is my **blood** of the **covenant**,
 which will be **shed** for **many**.
Amen, I **say** to you,
 I shall not drink **again** the fruit of the **vine**
 until the day when I drink it **new** in the kingdom of **God**."

meaning of Jesus' death with the liberation of the exiles. Jesus is the lamb who is innocently sacrificed so that his people might be free. Christians will memorialize this in the Eucharist, which has its roots in the Passover meal.

(2) This banquet was held in the house of Simon the leper, but if Simon's leprosy were infectious, he would not have been able to host a meal. In Jesus' time banquets were usually for men only. The woman who came to anoint Jesus must have had a lot of courage. The perfumed oil's worth was equal to almost a year's wages, implying

that her act was extremely important. In Jesus' time it was common for banquet hosts to anoint the heads of their guests as a gesture of welcome (Psalm 23; 5; Luke 7:46). Kings were also anointed, so Jesus' anointing on the head clearly symbolizes his messianic dignity.

Mark uses the woman's character as an obvious contrast to the priests and scribes, as well as Judas and Peter. Jesus' defense of the woman's actions attests that she is correct in recognizing who he is. Her faithfulness distinguishes her from those who chose not to follow Jesus to the

end—even the disciples abandoned Jesus and did not anoint his body for burial (16:1). Because of her actions, the woman will be remembered; her story will be told in the Gospel.

A final note on this section: Jesus' comment about "The poor you will always have with you" is often taken out of context. In defending the woman, Jesus is pointing out the necessity of what she has done, for he will not be present with them for much longer.

Jesus' words ("All of you will have your
faith shaken . . .") are an indictment
of his disciples who will fall away after
his death. In Jesus' words "But after
I have been raised up," the disciples—
and we today—are told that death
does not have the final word. (Jesus'
disciples—then and now—have
difficulty understanding this!)

Peter's response to Jesus ("Even though
all . . .") is self-righteous. In fact, Peter
will deny Jesus three times.

(7) **Then**, after singing a **hymn**,
  they went out to the Mount of **Olives**.

Then Jesus said to them,
  "**All** of you will have your **faith** shaken, for it is **written**:
    I will strike the **shepherd**,
    and the **sheep** *will be* **dispersed**.
But after I have been **raised up**,
  I shall go **before** you to **Galilee**."
Peter said to him,
  "Even though **all** should have their faith shaken,
  mine will **not** be."
Then Jesus said to him,
  "**Amen**, I **say** to you,
  this very **night** before the **cock** crows **twice**
  you will **deny** me three **times**."
But he **vehemently** replied,
  "Even though I should have to **die** with you,
  I will not **deny** you."
And they **all** spoke **similarly**.

(8) Then they came to a place named **Gethsemane**,
  and he said to his disciples,
  "Sit **here** while I **pray**."
He **took** with him **Peter**, **James**, and **John**,
  and began to be **troubled** and **distressed**.
Then he said to them, "My **soul** is **sorrowful** even to **death**.
Remain here and keep **watch**."

Gethsemane = geth-SEM-uh-nee

Gethsemane is an Aramaic name referring to a press for extracting oil from
olives. As tradition has it, Gethsemane
is located near the foot of the Mount
of Olives, so-called because it was used
for growing olives.

Address Jesus' instructions to his disciples ("Remain here and keep watch")
to the members of assembly by looking
up and making eye contact with
them. Let your voice be both respectful
and authoritative.

(3) Judas, one of the Twelve, like the
other disciples, had left everything to follow Jesus. In doing so, he became a member of Jesus' family (3:14–15). Mark does
not inform his reader why Judas suddenly
turned traitor. Whatever Judas' reason, his
actions led to Jesus' suffering and death.

(4) Jesus and his disciples were staying in Bethany, so they needed a place in
Jerusalem to eat the Passover meal. Jesus
seems to know where he and the disciples will be eating the meal. Whether or
not Jesus had made prearrangements is
unknown, but the fact that the disciples

simply did as they were told and everything worked out seems to indicate this.

The time frame developed in this passage also indicates that the Last Supper
meal was a Passover meal. The sacrifice
of the Passover lamb always took place on
the afternoon of the fourteenth day of
Nisan. Remember, the Jewish day goes
from sunset to sunset. Thus, the Passover
meal would be celebrated on Thursday, the
fifteenth day of Nisan, after sunset. The celebration of the institution of the Eucharist
on Holy Thursday reflects its origin within
the context of the Passover meal.

(5) Jesus' prediction of Judas' betrayal
comes as they were reclining at table to
eat the Passover meal. After the meal, Jesus
predicts Peter's denial. By placing both the
predictions around the meal, Mark forms
another contrast, this time between the
intimacy of a shared meal and betrayal.
While Jesus was no doubt saddened by the
knowledge that he would be betrayed by
those he considered members of his family,
his own obedience to God's will contrasts
with their lack of fidelity. Jesus' words
("For the Son of Man indeed goes, as it is
written of him") show that in his innocent

Use a slightly frustrated tone in your voice as you read Jesus' questions to Peter ("Simon, are you asleep . . . ?"). Increase from frustration to bitterness and annoyance in your tone of voice as Jesus finds the disciples asleep for the third time and asks, "Are you still sleeping . . . ?"

He **advanced** a little and fell to the **ground** and **prayed**
    that if it were **possible** the hour might **pass** by him;
    he said, "**Abba**, **Father**, all things are possible to **you**.
Take this cup **away** from me,
    but not what **I** will but what **you** will."
When he **returned** he found them **asleep**.
He said to **Peter**, "**Simon**, are you **asleep**?
Could you not keep **watch** for one **hour**?
Watch and **pray** that you may not undergo the **test**.
The **spirit** is **willing** but the **flesh** is **weak**."
Withdrawing **again**, he **prayed**, saying the same **thing**.
Then he returned once **more** and found them asleep,
    for they could not keep their **eyes** open
    and did not **know** what to **answer** him.
He returned a **third** time and said to them,
    "Are you still **sleeping** and taking your **rest**?
It is **enough**. The hour has **come**.
Behold, the Son of **Man** is to be handed **over** to **sinners**.
Get **up**, let us **go**.
See, my **betrayer** is at **hand**."

(9) **Then**, while he was still **speaking**,
    Judas, one of the **Twelve**, **arrived**,
    accompanied by a **crowd** with **swords** and **clubs**
    who had come from the chief **priests**,
    the **scribes**, and the **elders**.
His **betrayer** had arranged a **signal** with them, saying,
    "The man I shall **kiss** is the one;
    arrest him and lead him away **securely**."

State Judas' words ("The man I shall kiss is the one") in a deliberate and matter-of-fact tone of voice, because Judas knows exactly what he is doing and what will result from Jesus' arrest.

death is the fulfillment of God's plan for the suffering servant (Isaiah 52:13—53:12).

(6) The celebration of the Last Supper within the context of the Passover meal marks the transition to the new covenant in Jesus. His adaptation of the traditional words of blessing would have surprised his disciples. They probably were unsure of their meaning. Why would Jesus speak of a new covenant in reference to his own sacrifice?

Crucial to Mark's understanding of Jesus' death are Jesus' own words: "This is my blood of the covenant," recalling the ancient rite of sprinkling blood to seal a covenant with the Lord (Exodus 24:4–8). The disciples drinking from the cup is a sign of their participation in the new covenant, and presumably their faithfulness to it, although this will not be evident in Mark's narrative. Jesus' mention of his blood being shed "for many" shows that his death is not meant for just a few people, but "for all" as was the sacrifice of the servant in Isaiah 53:12. This new covenant in Jesus' body and blood is, for all time, universally available to those who believe in him. As Catholics, we memorialize this in the Eucharist.

(7) Hymns of thanksgiving traditionally were sung at the conclusion of the Passover meal. The transition between the thanksgiving hymns (usually Psalms 113–118) and Jesus' predictions that his disciples will abandon him marks a shift to an increasingly somber tone in the narrative. Jesus' predication that "all" of the disciples will have their faith shaken parallels his words that his blood will be shed "for many." Even though all will waver in their faith, he will gather them together again in

Deliver Jesus' reply to the violent action of the bystander ("Have you come out as against a robber . . . ?") in a strong but still somewhat reserved tone of voice. Jesus' protest to the events is relatively mild because he knows the scriptures need to be fulfilled.

Pause before and after the sentence "And they all left him and fled." It is one of the shortest sentences in the Gospel according to Mark. Even the young man in the following verse, who lingers after the disciples had fled, ends up fleeing.

Sanhedrin = san-HEE-drin

Relay the line "The chief priests and the entire Sanhedrin . . ." in a straightforward manner, looking up at the assembly.

He came and **immediately** went over to him and said,
"**Rabbi**." And he **kissed** him.
At this they laid **hands** on him and **arrested** him.
One of the **bystanders** drew his **sword**,
struck the high priest's **servant**, and cut off his **ear**.
Jesus said to them in **reply**,
"Have you come out as against a **robber**,
with **swords** and **clubs**, to seize me?
Day after **day** I was **with** you **teaching** in the **temple** area,
yet you did **not** arrest me;
but that the **Scriptures** may be **fulfilled**."
And they all **left** him and **fled**.
Now a **young man** followed him
wearing nothing but a linen **cloth** about his body.
They **seized** him,
but he left the cloth **behind** and ran off **naked**.

(10) They led Jesus away to the **high** priest,
and all the chief **priests** and the **elders** and the **scribes**
came **together**.
Peter followed him at a **distance** into the high priest's **courtyard**
and was seated with the **guards**, **warming** himself at the **fire**.
The chief **priests** and the entire **Sanhedrin**
kept trying to obtain **testimony** against Jesus
in order to put him to **death**, but they found **none**.

Galilee after his Resurrection. The significance of Galilee lies in the fact that the disciples return to Galilee, their home, after the Passover. Galilee is where the women are to tell Peter and the disciples that the risen Jesus is going (16:7). Even when we stray, the fact that God's will is fulfilled in Jesus' Resurrection is testimony that we will be gathered back together as a part of Jesus' community of disciples.

(8) Jesus and Peter, James, and John, the ones who were with him at the raising of Jairus' daughter (5:37) and the Transfiguration (9:2), move to Gethsemane,

where Jesus prays. All he asks of his disciples is to sit and keep watch, but Jesus finds them sleeping—not once, but three times. Even Peter, who had said he would die with Jesus if he had to (verse 31), was sleeping.

Mark's composition of this scene provides a balance between Jesus' complete obedience to the Father's will in his words "not what I will but what you will" and his humanity. Jesus' acknowledgment of his own sorrow and the evangelist's description of him as "troubled and distressed"

show that his ability to be completely obedient to God's will does not detract from the fullness of his humanity.

In the manner in which you proclaim this section, you have the opportunity again to highlight a contrast: this time between Jesus' own obedience and surrender to the will of the Father and the disciples' preference for sleep over following Jesus' instructions.

(9) Judas carries out his betrayal with a kiss, the traditional greeting offered to a teacher. In this scene, it is a repulsive act

Many gave **false** witness against him,
    but their **testimony** did not **agree**.
Some took the **stand** and testified **falsely** against him,
    alleging, "We heard him say,
    'I will **destroy** this **temple** made with **hands**
    and within three **days** I will build **another**
    not made with hands.'"
Even so their testimony did not **agree**.
(11) The **high** priest **rose** before the **assembly** and **questioned** Jesus,
    saying, "Have you no **answer**?
What are these men **testifying** against you?"
But he was **silent** and answered **nothing**.
Again the high priest asked him and said to him,
    "Are you the Christ, the son of the **Blessed** One?"
Then Jesus **answered**, "I **am**;
    and 'you will see the Son of Man
        seated at the right hand of the Power
        and coming with the clouds of heaven.'"
At **that** the high priest tore his **garments** and said,
    "What further **need** have we of **witnesses**?
You have **heard** the **blasphemy**.
What do you **think**?"
They all **condemned** him as deserving to **die**.
Some began to **spit** on him.
They **blindfolded** him and **struck** him and said to him,
    "**Prophesy**!"
And the **guards** greeted him with **blows**.

Make eye contact with the assembly as you deliver the line "even so their testimony . . ." with certainty in your tone of voice. You know the truth about who Jesus is, even though those who testified before the chief priests and the Sanhedrin did not.

Give Jesus' response after the high priest questions him a second time ("I am . . .") in a self-confident tone of voice, one filled with the power and authority Jesus knows he has because of his relationship with the Father.

Convey the high priest's retort ("What further need have we of witnesses . . . ?") with disgust in your tone of voice as blasphemy becomes the charge on which Jesus is found guilty.

prophesy = PROF-uh-sī

---

because it comes from an intimate companion of Jesus. The bonds of discipleship and friendship appear now to be broken.

Mark does not have Jesus respond to Judas' verbal greeting of "Rabbi" or to his kiss. Jesus' non-response demonstrates that he has willingly resigned himself to the Father's will. He will not put up a fight as the mob must have thought since they came with swords and clubs. His statement about teaching in the Temple day after day lets the mob and the readers of Mark know that what transpires is in fulfillment of the plan of God in accord with the scriptures.

Because all the disciples left Jesus and fled immediately after his words about the scriptures being fulfilled, perhaps they finally got the message about his death. As you proclaim this section, you might think about how you will portray the "young man" who followed Jesus. Did he mean to stay behind, to be faithful to Jesus until the authorities seized him, but got scared? Or was he just slower in fleeing than the others?

(10) In this scene, Mark presents a formal trial in front of the whole Sanhedrin.

According to Mosaic law, at least two witnesses were required (Deuteronomy 17:6; 19:5; Numbers 35:32). However, in this scene the chief priests and the Sanhedrin are having difficulty finding any. Mark purposefully crafts the presentation of this scene in this manner in order that Jesus' innocence might be obvious, thus making his comparison to the innocent suffering servant in Isaiah even more evident. There is no evidence on which to sentence Jesus to death!

While the statement of the witnesses who testified that Jesus said, "I will destroy

Use a narrative tone of voice for the lines that begin the next section ("While Peter was below . . .") so that the contrast with the agitation and momentum in the previous trial scene is clear. The focus of what follows in this section is Peter's three denials of Jesus. Each time you narrate a denial, take your time before proceeding to the next one. This will stress the significance of Peter's words in the face of his earlier self-righteous claim that he would not reject Jesus (14:29).

Nazarene = naz-uh-REEN

Galilean = gal-ih-LEE-un

The brief sentence "He broke down and wept" reveals that Peter recognizes his failure. Deliver it slowly and with regret.

Deliver Jesus' response to Pilate's first question ("You say so") in a slightly sarcastic tone of voice since it clearly identifies the title "king of the Jews" as Pilate's own words.

(12) While **Peter** was below in the **courtyard**,
   one of the high priest's **maids** came along.
Seeing Peter **warming** himself,
   she looked **intently** at him and said,
   "You **too** were with the **Nazarene, Jesus**."
But he **denied** it saying,
   "I neither **know** nor **understand** what you are **talking** about."
So he went **out** into the outer **court**.
Then the **cock** crowed.
The maid **saw** him and began **again** to say to the **bystanders**,
   "**This** man is **one** of them."
Once **again** he denied it.
A little **later** the bystanders said to Peter once **more**,
   "**Surely** you are **one** of them; for you **too** are a **Galilean**."
He began to **curse** and to **swear**,
   "I do not **know** this man about whom you are talking."
And **immediately** a **cock** crowed a **second** time.
Then Peter **remembered** the word that **Jesus** had **said** to him,
   "Before the **cock** crows **twice** you will **deny** me three **times**."
He broke **down** and **wept**.

(13) As soon as **morning** came,
   the chief **priests** with the **elders** and the **scribes**,
   that is, the whole **Sanhedrin**, held a **council**.
They **bound** Jesus, led him **away**, and handed him **over** to **Pilate**.
(14) Pilate **questioned** him,
   "**Are** you the **king** of the **Jews**?"
He said to him in **reply**, "**You** say so."
The chief **priests** accused him of **many** things.

this temple . . ." might sound familiar to you, but Jesus actually did not say this. What he did say was that the Temple would be destroyed, but not that *he* will destroy it (13:2). Their testimony implies a charge that Jesus is pretending to be a messiah who wants to overthrow the Jewish religious authorities.

(11) As the trial continues, the high priest, whom Mark does not name, but according to the other Gospel accounts was Caiaphas, interrogates Jesus, asking him to respond to the false testimony. The high priest questions Jesus a second time

because Jesus said nothing at first. In a rephrased question, the high priest asks whether Jesus is the Messiah, the Son of the Blessed One ("Blessed One" is surrogate for the divine name, which Jews did not pronounce). Jesus answers this time, and his answer is the only time in Mark that he proclaims himself to be the Messiah, the Son of God. His words show that his identity is related to the apocalyptic son of man of Daniel 7:13–14 and the king of Psalm 110:1 who will sit at the Lord's right hand with his enemies at his feet. Now

Jesus publicly acknowledges his identity in his own words.

His use of God's name ("I am") in reference to himself leads to the charge of blasphemy. Think of the relief the high priest must have felt with Jesus' "confession of guilt." No other witnesses were needed; Jesus, the innocent one, condemned himself with his own words. Then all agreed with the high priest's sentence of death and proceeded to mock him, striking him and beating him, providing another allusion to the suffering servant in Isaiah (50:6).

Narrate the line "Jesus gave him no further answer . . ." in a strong tone of voice to show that even in his silence, Jesus had authority, not Pilate.

Barabbas = buh-RAB-uhs

The name Barabbas means "son of Abba" or "son of the Father" in Aramaic.

Again Pilate questioned him,
"Have you no **answer**?
See how many things they **accuse** you of."
Jesus gave him no further **answer**, so that **Pilate** was **amazed**.

Now on the occasion of the **feast** he used to **release** to them
one **prisoner** whom they **requested**.
A man called **Barabbas** was then in prison
along with the **rebels** who had committed **murder** in
a **rebellion**.
The crowd came **forward** and began to **ask** him
to **do** for them as he was **accustomed**.
Pilate answered,
"Do you want me to **release** to you the **king** of the **Jews**?"
For he **knew** that it was out of **envy**
that the chief **priests** had handed him **over**.
But the chief priests **stirred** up the crowd
to have him release **Barabbas** for them **instead**.
Pilate **again** said to them in **reply**,
"Then what do you want me to **do**
with the man you call the **king** of the **Jews**?"
They shouted again, "**Crucify** him."
Pilate said to them, "**Why**? What **evil** has he done?"
They only shouted the **louder**, "**Crucify** him."
So Pilate, wishing to **satisfy** the crowd,
released **Barabbas** to them and, after he had Jesus **scourged**,
handed him **over** to be **crucified**.

The crowd's cry of "Crucify him" should resound loudly to differentiate it from the narrative. Remember, though, that you are not reenacting the events of the past, but simply trying to make present their meaning for today. Be careful not to over-dramatize this scene.

(12) The scene now switches to Peter's threefold denial predicted by Jesus. Peter had come to the high priest's courtyard with Jesus, but remained at a distance. At this point, Peter has not completely abandoned Jesus, but appears to be distancing himself from him. Though Peter does not seem to be under any duress when the maid remarks that she saw him with Jesus, he denies it. Then the maid begins to talk with the bystanders. When the maid questions him again, Peter denies that he is a disciple of Jesus. Peter's final rejection of Jesus comes when the bystanders identify him as "one of them" who knew and followed Jesus. Knowing that Jesus was sentenced to death was too much for Peter to handle. He too would need Jesus to give his life for him and rise from the dead in order to be reconciled with Jesus. Through the emotion contained in the very short sentence ("He broke down and wept"), we see that Peter understood this.

(13) In the morning, the Sanhedrin reconvenes and sends Jesus to Pilate. The Sanhedrin lacked the authority to carry out executions, leaving Pilate, the representative of the Roman government, to carry out their sentence.

(14) Pilate apparently knows of Jesus' innocence and the fraudulent motives of the chief priests. Envy is difficult to hide and Pilate picks it up right away, as can be seen in his initial question to Jesus: "Are you the king of the Jews?" Jesus' retort makes clear to Pilate that the chief priests have given him that title. Because Jesus does answer when Pilate asks him a second time, the charges are set. The trial before the Sanhedrin led to a religious

praetorium = prih-TOHR-ee-uhm

Pause before the words "They knelt before him in homage." The purpose of the entire scene has been mockery of Jesus, who had been proclaimed by Pilate and now the soldiers as the "King of the Jews." Lower your voice as you narrate the insincere homage and the movement toward Jesus' Crucifixion.

Cyrenian = si-REE-nee-un

Rufus = ROO-fus

Golgotha = GOL-guh-thuh

(15) The **soldiers** led him **away** inside the **palace**,
  that is, the **praetorium**, and **assembled** the whole **cohort**.
They **clothed** him in **purple** and,
  weaving a crown of **thorns**, **placed** it on him.
They began to **salute** him with, "**Hail**, King of the **Jews**!"
  and kept striking his **head** with a **reed** and **spitting** upon him.
They **knelt** before him in **homage**.
And when they had **mocked** him,
  they **stripped** him of the purple **cloak**,
  dressed him in his own **clothes**,
  and led him **out** to **crucify** him.

(16) They pressed into **service** a **passer**-by, **Simon**,
  a **Cyrenian**, who was coming in from the **country**,
  the father of **Alexander** and **Rufus**,
  to **carry** his cross.

They **brought** him to the place of **Golgotha**
  —which is translated Place of the **Skull**—.
They gave him **wine** drugged with **myrrh**,
  but he did not **take** it.
Then they **crucified** him and divided his **garments**
  by casting **lots** for them to see what each should **take**.
It was **nine o'clock** in the **morning** when they **crucified** him.
The **inscription** of the **charge** against him read,
  "The **King** of the **Jews**."

charge of blasphemy because Jesus applied the divine name to himself. The appearance before Pilate ends in a political charge based on Pilate's misuse of the title "king of the Jews."

Pilate, fearing the crowd, hands Jesus over to be crucified and releases Barabbas. Like the chief priests who go to Pilate to have Jesus executed, Pilate shirks his responsibility, leading people to believe that the crowd is responsible for Jesus' death, not him, the leader who knew Jesus was innocent. As a result, the one who

was guilty—Barabbas—becomes the first for whom Jesus gave his life.

(15) The irony and mockery intensify as Jesus is taken inside the palace where he is clothed in royal purple and crowned with thorns. The salutation "Hail, King of the Jews!" mimics the salute to the Roman emperor ("Hail, Caesar!"). Once the preparations were complete, Jesus was led outside of the city to die because crucifixions did not take place in Jerusalem.

(16) Mark mentions that Simon of Cyrene, a pilgrim who was probably there for Passover, was forced to help Jesus

carry his cross. While Simon does not help Jesus voluntarily, he does not refuse. His acceptance of his call to service differs from the insults and mockery given by three groups of people in this scene: the passersby, the chief priest and the scribes, and those crucified with Jesus. As the inscription on the cross reads, Jesus is condemned as the "The King of the Jews." In the end, this provides a political reason for his death, although he has been charged falsely.

The mockery of Jesus continues even while he is on the cross in the words of those passing by ("Aha! You who would destroy the temple . . .") and in the words of the chief priests and scribes ("He saved others . . ."). Deliver these words with a tone of ridicule in your voice.

Emphasize the other titles given to Jesus by the evangelist ("the Christ, the King of Israel").

With him they crucified two **revolutionaries**,
    one on his **right** and one on his **left**.
Those passing by **reviled** him,
    shaking their **heads** and saying,
    "Aha! **You** who would **destroy** the **temple**
    and **rebuild** it in three **days**,
    save yourself by coming **down** from the **cross**."
Likewise the chief **priests**, with the **scribes**,
    mocked him among themselves and said,
    "He saved **others**; he cannot save **himself**.
Let the **Christ**, the King of Israel,
    come **down** now from the **cross**
    that we may **see** and **believe**."
Those who were **crucified** with him **also** kept **abusing** him.

(17) At **noon darkness** came over the whole **land**
    until **three** in the **afternoon**.
And at three o'clock Jesus **cried out** in a loud **voice**,
    "Eloi, Eloi, lema sabachthani?"
    which is **translated**,
    "My **God**, my **God**, **why** have you **forsaken** me?"
Some of the **bystanders** who heard it said,
    "**Look**, he is calling **Elijah**."
One of them **ran**, soaked a **sponge** with **wine**, put it on a **reed**
    and gave it to him to **drink** saying,
    "**Wait**, let us see if **Elijah** comes to take him **down**."
Jesus gave a loud **cry** and breathed his **last**.

[Here all kneel and pause for a short time.]

Eloi, Eloi, lema sabachthani = el-oh-EE, el-oh-EE, luh-MAH-sah-bahk-TAH-nee
Let your voice cry out with these words of Jesus by increasing the volume somewhat. Lower your voice as you give the English translation.

Elijah = ee-LĪ-juh
Pause after the words of the bystander ("Wait, let us see if Elijah . . .").

Narrate the line "Jesus gave a loud cry . . ." slowly and in a matter-of-fact tone. The enormity of what took place will carry its own emotions for the assembly today.

(17) There are three time references in the entire Crucifixion scene. The first notes that it was nine o'clock in the morning when Jesus was crucified. Mark then makes the reader aware that between noon and three o'clock in the afternoon darkness came over the land. While the darkness could suggest that a natural event such as an eclipse of the sun occurred, it is more likely symbolic. In the Old Testament, darkness ushered in the Day of the Lord (Isaiah 13:9–10; Joel 2:10–11; Amos 8:9–10). Moreover, the dark cloud that appears

during the Exodus served as a sign of God's presence, providing a shield between the Israelites and the Egyptians (Exodus 14:19–20). The third mention of time occurs as Jesus cries out in Aramaic the words of Psalm 22:2. This is the first time that Jesus speaks since his response ("You say so") to Pilate's question whether he was the king of the Jews. It is the only time he speaks from the cross. Jesus' words seem to imply that even God has abandoned him. Yet the loud cry that is his last breath shows that God has not. Just as in Genesis 2:7, God breathed life into the nostrils of

man to give him life, here Jesus' last breath is the giving of his life back to God. In this sharing of life, Jesus fulfills his mission; God's work has been accomplished in him. His life has been given as a ransom for all (10:45); he has lost his life in order to save ours (8:35).

The veil of the sanctuary being torn in two and the Gentile centurion's confession of faith both show that Jesus' death on the cross truly brings life to all who believe. The presence of God is no longer reserved for the high priest, who alone could enter

The word *centurion* in Latin denotes a commander of a hundred troops and was a person who would oversee an execution. Proclaim his profession of faith with boldness.

Magdalene = MAG-duh-luhn

Joses = JOH-seez

Salome = suh-LOH-mee

Arimathea = air-ih-muh-THEE-uh.

Emphasize the courage it took for Joseph to ask Pilate for Jesus' body by taking your time in delivering the description of Joseph: "a distinguished member of the council."

Pause before the final verse ("Mary Magdalene and Mary . . ."). Mary Magdalene and Mary the mother of James, along with Salome, are also the first to go to the tomb, to find it empty, and to hear the news of the Resurrection (16:1–8).

The **veil** of the **sanctuary** was torn in **two** from top to **bottom**.
When the **centurion** who stood **facing** him
    saw how he breathed his **last** he said,
    "**Truly** this man **was** the Son of **God!**"
There were also **women** looking on from a **distance**.
Among them were Mary **Magdalene**,
    Mary the mother of the younger **James** and of **Joses**,
        and **Salome**.
These women had **followed** him when he was in **Galilee**
    and **ministered** to him.
There were also many **other** women
    who had come **up** with him to **Jerusalem**.

(18) When it was already **evening**,
    since it was the day of **preparation**,
    the day before the **sabbath**, **Joseph** of **Arimathea**,
    a distinguished member of the **council**,
    who was **himself** awaiting the **kingdom** of **God**,
    came and **courageously** went to **Pilate**
    and asked for the **body** of **Jesus**.
Pilate was **amazed** that he was already **dead**.
He summoned the **centurion**
    and asked him if **Jesus** had already **died**.
And when he **learned** of it from the centurion,
    he gave the **body** to **Joseph**.
Having bought a linen **cloth**, he took him **down**,
    wrapped him in the linen cloth,
    and **laid** him in a **tomb** that had been **hewn** out of the **rock**.
Then he rolled a **stone** against the **entrance** to the tomb.
Mary **Magdalene** and **Mary** the mother of **Joses**
    watched where he was **laid**.

[Shorter: Mark 15:1–39]

the Holy of Holies on the Day of Atonement. Now Gentile and Jew alike have access to an intimate relationship with God.

The voice from the heavens that identifies Jesus as his beloved Son at his Baptism is corroborated by the centurion. The innocent suffering servant, put to death on false grounds, is seen for who he really is: the Son of God. Thus, Mark's account comes full circle from the prologue, in which he identifies the Gospel as that of the Son of God (1:1).

(18) A new family has formed around Jesus, made up of some who were previously devoted to him and some who are newly united to him. The centurion, a Gentile, confesses belief in him, the women look on from a distance, and Joseph of Arimathea comes to claim his body. Perhaps Joseph, a member of the Sanhedrin, did so only to observe the law that said that a crucified body should not remain on the cross overnight, and he knew that burial had to take place before the Sabbath. The women are also present when the stone is placed across the tomb's entrance. These

same women will come to the tomb and find it empty. While the cross is central to the Marcan narrative, in the presence of the women at the tomb is a hint that there is more to the story. Jesus has given his life "for many," but the cross can never be separated from the Resurrection. Easter follows Holy Week!

HOLY THURSDAY: MASS OF THE LORD'S SUPPER

Lectionary #39

READING I   Exodus 12:1–8, 11–14

Exodus = EK-suh-dus

Speak the first line ("The Lord said to Moses . . .") with confidence; it identifies that the Lord speaks the instructions for celebrating the Passover meal.

A reading from the Book of Exodus

The LORD said to **Moses** and **Aaron** in the land of **Egypt**,
  "**This** month shall stand at the **head** of your **calendar**;
  you shall reckon it the **first** month of the year.
Tell the whole community of **Israel**:
  On the **tenth** of this month every one of your families
  must procure for itself a **lamb**, one **apiece** for each **household**.
If a family is too **small** for a **whole** lamb,
  it shall join the nearest **household** in procuring one
  and shall **share** in the lamb
  in proportion to the number of **persons** who **partake** of it.
The lamb must be a **year-old male** and without **blemish**.
You may **take** it from either the **sheep** or the **goats**.
You shall **keep** it until the **fourteenth** day of this month,
  and **then**, with the whole assembly of **Israel** present,
  it shall be **slaughtered** during the evening **twilight**.
They shall take some of its **blood**
  and apply it to the two **doorposts** and the **lintel**
  of every house in which they **partake** of the lamb.
That same night they shall **eat** its roasted **flesh**
  with unleavened **bread** and bitter **herbs**.

READING I The Easter Triduum of the Passion and Resurrection of Christ begins this evening with the Mass of the Lord's Supper, reaches its high point in the Easter Vigil, and ends with evening prayer on Easter Sunday (*General Norms for the Liturgical Year*, #18). This evening opens the remembrance and celebration of Christ's Passover from death to new life. The Passover ritual described in the First Reading focuses Christians on the origin of the image of Christ as the new Passover lamb "who takes away the sins of the world."

In its entirety, this reading consists of the words of the Lord spoken to Moses and Aaron. These words describe a Passover that is comprised of two rites, which were originally separate ceremonies: 1) the rite of herders to procure a lamb and sacrifice it, thereby appeasing the gods, as the herders journeyed from the moist winter fields to the dry summer pastures (Exodus 12:3–13). The rite often drew families together, especially in the case where one family could not afford a whole lamb by themselves (verse 3). 2) The rite of unleavened bread was performed by farmers and consisted of their eating unleavened bread for seven days. From the very first day of the observance, all leaven was cleansed from their houses. This custom of unleavened bread, then, served as a remembrance of the day that the Lord brought the Israelites out of Egypt (verses 14–20).

Note the First Reading ends only with the verse that acknowledges the memorial feast of the Passover; it does not include the ritual about unleavened bread, which became part of the Passover tradition related to the eucharistic feast. In the synoptic Gospels, Jesus' last meal was a

"**This** is how you are to **eat** it:
  with your **loins** girt, **sandals** on your **feet** and your **staff**
    in **hand**,
  you shall eat like those who are in **flight**.
It is the **Passover** of the LORD.
For on this **same** night I will go through **Egypt**,
  striking **down** every **firstborn** of the land, both **man** and **beast**,
  and executing **judgment** on all the gods of Egypt —-**I**, the LORD!
But the **blood** will mark the **houses** where **you** are.
Seeing the **blood**, I will **pass over** you;
  thus, when I strike the land of **Egypt**,
  no destructive blow will come upon **you**.

"**This** day shall be a memorial **feast** for you,
  which all your **generations** shall **celebrate**
  with **pilgrimage** to the LORD, as a perpetual **institution**."

Look up and make eye contact as you speak the line "It is the Passover of the Lord" with certainty. Pause slightly again before continuing.

Pause before the line "This day shall be a memorial feast for you." The last verse serves as a summary of the historical significance of the Passover and its continued significance in the lives of the Jewish people through the centuries.

Passover meal (Mark 14:22–25; Matthew 26:26–29; Luke 22:15–20). That Jesus celebrated the Passover meal as his last meal with his disciples placed the origins of his Passover deeply in the Jewish tradition of the Passover as memorial of the Israelites' deliverance from oppression. The blood of the lamb that protected the Israelites from the tenth and final plague that destroyed the first-born Egyptians is now associated with Christ's blood that was poured out on the cross, protecting Christians from their sins.

As Jews continue to celebrate the memorial feast of the Passover of the Lord, making it present in their lives through ritual and prayer, so they are able to participate today in the escape of their brothers and sisters in faith from Pharaoh's wrath. In and through the sharing of the Eucharist, we as Christians participate in Christ's Passover. We participate in the Lord's Passion and Resurrection until he comes again in glory. This is our memorial feast. It is one that is deeply rooted in the Jewish tradition, but one that is also made with Jesus on the cross.

READING II In his encyclical *Ecclesia de Eucharistia*, given on Holy Thursday 2003, Pope John Paul II wrote, "At every celebration of the Eucharist, we are spiritually brought back to the paschal Triduum: to the events of the evening of Holy Thursday, to the Last Supper and to what followed it. The institution of the Eucharist sacramentally anticipated the events which were about to take place, beginning with the agony in Gethsemane" (#3). Thus, the proclamation of the brief passage from Paul's first letter to the Corinthians makes the tradition of

Corinthians = kor-IN-thee-unz

A reading from the first Letter of Saint Paul to the Corinthians

Brothers and sisters:
I **received** from the Lord what I also **handed** on to you,
   that the Lord **Jesus**, on the **night** he was handed **over**,
   took **bread**, and, after he had given **thanks**,
   broke it and said, "**This** is my **body** that is for **you**.
Do this in **remembrance** of me."
In the **same** way also the **cup**, after **supper**, saying,
   "This **cup** is the new **covenant** in my **blood**.
Do this, as often as you **drink** it, in **remembrance** of me."
For as often as you **eat** this **bread** and **drink** the **cup**,
   you **proclaim** the **death** of the Lord until he **comes**.

Try not to "role-play" in your proclamation of the words of Jesus, written by Paul for the Corinthians and today spoken by you. These are similar words to those spoken by the presider during the eucharistic liturgy. Offer them in a solemn, prayerful tone of voice, but one that is modest, lacking in pretentiousness and priestly overtones.

Pause before proclaiming the final line ("For as often as you eat . . . you proclaim the death of the Lord until he comes") slowly, addressing it directly to those gathered for Mass of the Lord's Supper. This line connects the eucharistic meal with the Lord's sacrifice.

the Last Supper present to us during the Mass on Holy Thursday, a Mass that has as its focus the institution of the Eucharist.

Paul's account of the memorial feast of Jesus' body and blood is the earliest one we have. Whereas Mark's Gospel narrative of the Last Supper, the earliest of the three synoptic accounts, was written around 70 AD, Paul wrote his letter to the Corinthians around 53–54 AD, more than a decade earlier. In this account notice how Paul functions as a mediator of a tradition surrounding the meal the Lord celebrated;

Paul has "received from the Lord" what he passes on to the Corinthians (verse 23).

In the tradition Paul hands on, Jesus' self-giving—his sharing of his own body and blood in the meal—is emphasized. Paul uses Jesus' giving of himself as the basis for the case he makes to the Corinthians that they are to imitate Christ, and not eat or drink at the memorial meal if they are unworthy. For Paul this means that they need to pay attention especially to the weak among them whose consciences might be affected by immoral behavior or by people who might eat food that has been

sacrificed to idols. Moreover, the wealthy, who could afford a lavish meal, must participate in that meal prior to coming together to celebrate the common meal of Christians so as not to cause division in the community. Ultimately for Paul, when one comes to participate in the Eucharist, they must be selfless, like Christ (11:27–34).

Your proclamation of this reading creates a bridge between the Old Testament reading about the Jewish tradition of Passover and John's story about Jesus' example of service in the washing of his disciples' feet. It is the only time this evening

Use a narrative tone of voice for the lines
that set the stage for Jesus' action of
washing the feet of his disciples.

Judas = JOO-dus

Iscariot = is-KAIR-ee-ut

GOSPEL   John 13:1–15

A reading from the holy Gospel according to John

Before the feast of **Passover**, Jesus **knew** that his hour had **come**
    to pass from **this** world to the **Father**.
He **loved** his own in the world and he **loved** them to the **end**.
The **devil** had already induced **Judas**, son of Simon the **Iscariot**,
    to hand him **over**.
So, during **supper**,
    fully aware that the Father had put everything into his **power**
    and that he had come **from** God and was returning **to** God,
    he **rose** from supper and took off his outer **garments**.
He took a **towel** and tied it around his **waist**.
Then he poured **water** into a **basin**
    and began to **wash** the disciples' **feet**
    and **dry** them with the **towel** around his **waist**.
He came to Simon **Peter**, who said to him,
    "**Master**, are you going to wash **my** feet?"
Jesus answered and said to him,
    "What I am **doing**, you do not understand **now**,
    but you **will** understand **later**."
Peter said to him, "You will **never** wash my **feet**."

The narrative shifts from simple
description of the scene and Jesus'
action to recounting the dialogue
between Jesus and Peter. Ask Peter's
question with some confusion and
uncertainty in your tone of voice.
Remember to raise your voice slightly at
the end of the question. Deliver Peter's
opposition to Jesus' action evident in the
words "You will never wash my feet"
with determination. Speak Jesus' words
in response with conviction. Give Peter's
words in a relieved tone of voice as
his confusion has been resolved by
Jesus' answer. In an instructive tone,
deliver Jesus' lengthier response
to Peter.

when the assembly will hear an account of the institution of the Eucharist. Being aware of Paul's connection of the Eucharist with ethical behavior in the Corinthian community shows how Jesus' own service is carried on in Christian communities that celebrate the Eucharist. Thus, through your ministry the assembly this evening will be invited to "proclaim the death of the Lord until he comes" in the Eucharist and in their lives as a eucharistic people. (Note that these are also the words of Memorial Acclamation C: "When we eat this bread

and drink this cup, we proclaim your death, Lord Jesus, until you come in glory.")

GOSPEL | One of the synoptic accounts of the Last Supper is not proclaimed on Holy Thursday; John's narrative of Jesus washing his disciples' feet is. John's Last Supper narrative differs dramatically from that of the synoptics. The reader is left wondering when the supper took place and if it was a Passover meal. There is no account of the institution of the Eucharist in John, but there is the description of the foot washing.

In the opening verses of today's Gospel, the act of Jesus washing the feet of his disciples is described (verses 1–5). Foot washing, in a culture where sandals or bare feet were the norm, was a sign of hospitality (see Genesis 18:4; 1 Samuel 25:41; Luke 7:44). However, Peter's question to Jesus ("Master, are you going to wash my feet?") is necessary, since usually the master's slaves were the ones who washed the feet of their guests. Jesus' response focuses Peter and the other disciples on the meaning of his entrance into Jerusalem

Jesus answered him,
    "Unless I **wash** you, you will have no **inheritance** with me."
Simon Peter said to him,
    "**Master**, then not **only** my feet, but my **hands**
        and **head** as well."
Jesus said to him,
    "Whoever has **bathed** has no need except to have his **feet**
        washed, for he is clean all **over**;
    so **you** are clean, but not **all**."
For he knew who would **betray** him;
    for this reason, he said, "Not **all** of you are clean."

So when he had washed their **feet**
    and put his **garments** back on and reclined at **table** again,
    he said to them, "Do you **realize** what I have **done** for you?
You call me '**teacher**' and '**master**,' and rightly so, for indeed I **am**.
If **I**, therefore, the **master** and **teacher**, have washed **your** feet,
    you ought to wash one **another's** feet.
I have given you a **model** to follow,
    so that as **I** have done for **you**, **you** should **also** do."

Pause before the final section begins ("So when he had washed . . ."). Proclaim it, remembering that you, as well as those in the assembly, are Jesus' disciples who are called to follow his example of service. Take your time with these words so that when the foot washing takes place in the liturgy, the connection with John's narrative will be clear.

and Thomas' statement in the Lazarus narrative: "Let us also go to die with him" (11:16). Unless Jesus washes their feet, they will "have no inheritance" with him (13:8). The promise of the Resurrection will not be theirs.

The final verses of the narrative (verses 15–20) provide another explanation for Jesus' act of washing his disciples' feet: not only are the disciples to have their feet washed, but they are to imitate his action by washing the feet of others. No matter whether one is master, teacher, or disciple, those who bear witness to Jesus must emulate the service and hospitality shown by him. This second explanation applies to those of us who are disciples of Jesus now. The command (mandatum) of Jesus to wash each other's feet is symbolic of the service we as disciples offer to each other and those in need in the world. It is the basis for the ritual of foot washing that occurs after the homily in today's liturgy.

In the early Church, the call to wash feet was often connected with service to the poor and needy, the powerless in society. Monastic communities adopted foot washing as a sign of fellowship within their communities and with the poor. Saint Benedict's Rule includes a prescription for washing the feet of guests.

The proclamation of this Gospel on Holy Thursday connects the eucharistic meal with the tradition of hospitality and service. Jesus' ultimate service was his fulfillment of the Jewish Passover meal in his celebration of the Eucharist, the meal that we now celebrate as a memorial of his death and Resurrection (CCC, #1340). Our participation in the Eucharist today, then, also leads us to acts of service.

GOOD FRIDAY OF THE LORD'S PASSION

Lectionary #40

READING I   Isaiah 52:13—53:12

A reading from the Book of the Prophet Isaiah

Be aware that the speakers change a few times in this servant song from Isaiah. The Lord is speaking in the opening lines ("See, my servant shall prosper . . ."), announcing the exultation of his servant. Proclaim them with strength and confidence.

In the section beginning with the words "Who would believe what we have heard?" the people of Israel are speaking. Remember to raise your voice slightly at the end of the questions.

The suffering that the servant experienced is similar to many humans' experience—being "spurned and avoided" by people. Let the seriousness of the servant's rejection be heard in your voice.

Pause before beginning the section beginning with the words "Yet it was our infirmities that he bore." This is perhaps the most memorable section for Christians from this servant song. While there is sadness in these lines because of the infirmities the servant bore, there is also hope and light because the servant also carried our sufferings. Practice so that both sadness and hope can be heard in your voice.

See, my **servant** shall **prosper**,
   he shall be raised **high** and greatly **exalted**.
Even as many were **amazed** at him—
   so **marred** was his **look** beyond human **semblance**
   and his **appearance** beyond that of the sons of **man**—
so shall he **startle** many **nations**,
   because of him **kings** shall stand **speechless**;
for those who have **not** been told shall **see**,
   those who have **not** heard shall **ponder** it.

Who would **believe** what we have **heard**?
   To whom has the **arm** of the LORD been **revealed**?
He grew up like a **sapling** before him,
   like a **shoot** from the parched **earth**;
there was in him no **stately** bearing to make us **look** at him,
   nor **appearance** that would **attract** us to him.
He was **spurned** and **avoided** by people,
   a man of **suffering**, accustomed to **infirmity**,
one of those from whom people **hide** their **faces**,
   spurned, and we held him in no **esteem**.

Yet it was our **infirmities** that he **bore**,
   our **sufferings** that he **endured**,
while we thought of him as **stricken**,
   as one **smitten** by God and **afflicted**.

READING I   The liturgy of Good Friday, referred to in the Roman Missal as the "Celebration of the Lord's Passion," begins in silence. The opening prayer, offered without the usual invocation ("Let us pray"), brings the assembly out of the silence and focuses them on the salvific suffering of Jesus Christ.

The First Reading, taken from the fourth servant song of Isaiah, echoes a similar theme. The sacrificial suffering of the servant is expiatory; it makes up for human sins because the servant took on "our infirmities," "our sufferings," and "our offenses." Through the servant's suffering, the Lord promises that the sins of many will be taken away and pardon for their offenses will be given (53:12).

Much has been written about the identity of the servant in Isaiah's servant songs. The servant could represent all of Israel, Cyrus, a prophet, or perhaps deutero-Isaiah in the latter stages of his life, reflecting back on his experiences and the rejection he faced. Whatever the identity of the servant, in the historical context of this reading, two points stand out: 1) the servant is innocent and 2) messianic hopes rest in the servant. Christians apply both these ideas to Jesus Christ, thus avowing that "Jesus' redemptive death fulfills Isaiah's prophecy of the suffering Servant" (CCC, #601).

While the servant himself speaks in the middle section (53:1–11a), in the opening section (52:13–15) and the concluding section (53:11b–13) the Lord speaks. The

But he was **pierced** for our **offenses**,
    crushed for our **sins**;
upon **him** was the chastisement that makes us **whole**,
    by **his** stripes we were **healed**.
We had all gone astray like **sheep**,
    each following his own **way**;
but the LORD laid upon **him**
    the guilt of us **all**.

Though he was harshly **treated**, he submitted
    and opened not his **mouth**;
like a **lamb** led to the **slaughter**
    or a **sheep** before the **shearers**,
    he was **silent** and opened not his **mouth**.
Oppressed and **condemned**, he was taken **away**,
    and who would have thought any **more** of his **destiny**?
When he was cut **off** from the land of the **living**,
    and **smitten** for the **sin** of his **people**,
a **grave** was assigned him among the **wicked**
    and a burial place with **evildoers**,
though he had done no **wrong**
    nor spoken any **falsehood**.
But the LORD was pleased
    to crush him in **infirmity**.

If he gives his **life** as an offering for **sin**,
    he shall see his **descendants** in a long **life**,
    and the will of the LORD shall be **accomplished** through **him**.

Because of his **affliction**
    he shall see the **light** in **fullness** of days;

In the lines "Because of his affliction . . ." the Lord speaks again, affirming the people's words that the will of the Lord will be accomplished through the suffering of the servant. State the Lord's words with strength in your voice.

servant's words are more somber in tone, reflecting in poetic fashion the depths of his pain and anguish. In contrast, Lord's words attest to the redemptive nature of the suffering and therefore, the triumph of the servant over both his suffering and ours. In the end, the Lord will give the servant "his portion among the great."

The servant's triumph, too, fulfilled in Christ's Resurrection, is why the Church refers to the Friday on which we remember the Lord's Passion as *Good* Friday. It is also

why Good Friday must never be separated from Easter. Our faith must never be stripped down to despair and our churches so barren that sorrow seems to be the end of the story (see *The Liturgical Year, Study Text 9,* Bishops' Committee on the Liturgy, p. 51).

| READING II | The main theme of the letter to the Hebrews is the high priesthood of Jesus. In light of that theme, this reading, combining verses from two different chapters of the letter, teaches that 1) as our high priest Jesus is able to

identify with our weaknesses (4:14–16) and 2) when Christ was in the flesh—was on earth—he prayed to the Father who heard his prayer for salvation because of his obedience to the Father's will (5:7–9).

On the first point, the first verse in today's reading is the only place in Hebrews where the phrase "great high priest" is used to describe the Son of God. Other references are simply to the Son of God as "priest" or "high priest." The addition of "great" may signify Jesus' superiority over

through his **suffering**, my servant shall justify **many**,
   and their **guilt** he shall **bear**.
Therefore **I** will give him his **portion** among the **great**,
   and **he** shall divide the **spoils** with the **mighty**,
because he **surrendered** himself to **death**
   and was **counted** among the **wicked**;
and he shall take **away** the sins of **many**,
   and win **pardon** for their **offenses**.

READING II   Hebrews 4:14–16, 5:7–9

A reading from the Letter to the Hebrews

Brothers and sisters:
Since we have a great **high priest** who has passed
   through the **heavens**,
   Jesus, the Son of **God**,
   let us hold **fast** to our **confession**.
For we do **not** have a high priest
   who is unable to **sympathize** with our **weaknesses**,
   but one who has **similarly** been tested in **every** way,
   yet without **sin**.
So let us **confidently** approach the throne of **grace**
   to receive **mercy** and to find **grace** for timely **help**.

In the days when **Christ** was in the **flesh**,
   he offered **prayers** and **supplications** with loud **cries** and **tears**
   to the one who was able to **save** him from **death**,
   and he was **heard** because of his **reverence**.

Address the lines "Since we have a great high priest . . . grace for timely help" directly to the assembly by making eye contact with them as much as possible, without taking away from the smoothness of your proclamation.

Pause at the break before the new section begins with the words "In the days when Christ." This will help the assembly to hear that the subject switches to Christ in this section. Begin this section in a lower tone of voice in contrast to the confidence conveyed in the first section. Then build in strength and confidence through the last line "he became the source of eternal salvation . . . ."

the Jewish high priests. Jesus, the Son of God, is the "one high priest of the true sanctuary" now surpassing the high priests in the Levitical order who were in charge of the Temple worship and the only one allowed to enter the Holy of Holies, and of post-exilic times who were in charge of the Jewish state and performing religious rituals. During the Roman occupation, the high priests took on a life more according to the world, living in luxury and decadence—sometimes dismissing belief in immortality and/or life after death.

As our high priest, Jesus is truly human except for sin; he is the "perfect man" (*Gaudium et Spes*, #38) who entered history and who, through his priesthood, was able to draw everything and everyone to himself. Nevertheless, even he has been tested as seen in his temptation by Satan in the desert (Mark 1:12–15) read on the First Sunday of Lent.

The second section, reminiscent of the scene in the garden of Gethsemane, recounts Jesus' prayer to the Father. While

the Father did not take the cross away from Jesus, he heard Jesus' prayer: his exaltation followed his death on the cross. Thus, on this Good Friday we, as Christians, celebrate our belief that the cross does not have the last word. We acknowledge that our exalted high priest, Jesus, the Son of God "who prays for us is also the one who prays in us and the God who hears our prayer" (CCC, #2749). Consequently, we are not alone with the inevitable suffering naturally occurs as part of human life. Rather, we approach our suffering, that of

Son though he **was**, he learned **obedience** from what he **suffered**;
and when he was made **perfect**,
he became the source of eternal **salvation** for **all** who
obey him.

PASSION   John 18:1—19:42

The Passion of our Lord Jesus Christ according to John

(1) **Jesus** went out with his **disciples** across the Kidron **valley**
to where there was a **garden**,
into which he and his disciples **entered**.
Judas his **betrayer** also knew the place,
because Jesus had often met there with his disciples.
So **Judas** got a band of **soldiers** and **guards**
from the chief **priests** and the **Pharisees**
and went there with **lanterns**, **torches**, and **weapons**.
Jesus, knowing **everything** that was going to **happen** to him,
went out and said to them, "Whom are you **looking** for?"
They answered him, "Jesus the **Nazorean**."
He said to them, "**I AM**."
Judas his betrayer was also with them.
When he said to them, "**I AM**,"
they turned **away** and fell to the **ground**.
So he **again** asked them,
"Whom are you **looking** for?"
They said, "Jesus the **Nazorean**."
Jesus answered,
"I told you that **I AM**.

Kidron = KID-ruhn

Nazorean = Naz-uh-REE-un

Pause before you relay the many "I am" responses. It is probable that Jesus' "I am" statements here are connected to the divine name given in Exodus 3:13-14. State them with increasing firmness in your voice.

our neighbors and friends, and indeed of the entire world, united with the Son, and therefore confident as we seek God's mercy and help.

PASSION The Good Friday liturgy is divided into three parts: the Liturgy of the Word, the Veneration of the Cross, and the Communion Rite. For many, today we focus on the sorrow that surrounds Jesus' death on the cross; however, the cross that we venerate is a "tree

of life," which reminds us that through the cross comes new life. One of the antiphons that may be sung during the veneration of the cross makes exactly this point: "We worship you, Lord, we venerate your cross, we praise your resurrection. Through the cross you brought joy to the world" (see the Sacramentary).

In fourth-century Jerusalem, the observance of Good Friday lasted hours. From eight in the morning until noon, the faithful filed past a relic of the wood of the cross that was guarded by deacons. From noon until three in the afternoon, there

were readings, including psalms, epistles, and each of the four passion narratives. Imagine today's assemblies listening to four Passion readings! Today, one of the three Passion narratives from the synoptic Gospels is proclaimed each year on Palm (Passion) Sunday. The passion narrative from the Gospel according to John is reserved for Good Friday, perhaps because John understands Jesus' death as a glorious return to the Father—Jesus is exalted in his death. John's account leaves us with less sorrow and more gratitude for the

So if you are looking for **me**, let **these** men go."
This was to **fulfill** what he had said,
"I have not lost **any** of those you **gave** me."
(2) Then Simon **Peter**, who had a **sword**, drew it,
struck the high priest's **slave**, and cut off his right **ear**.
The slave's **name** was **Malchus**.
Jesus said to Peter,
"Put your **sword** into its **scabbard**.
Shall I not drink the **cup** that the Father **gave** me?"

So the band of **soldiers**, the **tribune**, and the Jewish **guards**
seized Jesus,
bound him, and brought him to **Annas** first.
He was the father-in-law of **Caiaphas**,
who was high priest that year.
It was **Caiaphas** who had counseled the Jews
that it was better that **one** man should die
rather than the **people**.

(3) Simon Peter and **another** disciple **followed** Jesus.
Now the **other** disciple was **known** to the high **priest**,
and he entered the **courtyard** of the high priest with **Jesus**.
But **Peter** stood at the gate **outside**.
So the **other** disciple, the **acquaintance** of the high priest,
went out and spoke to the **gatekeeper** and brought Peter **in**.
Then the **maid** who was the gatekeeper said to **Peter**,
"You are not one of this man's disciples, **are** you?"
He said, "I am **not**."
Now the slaves and the guards were standing
around a charcoal **fire**
that they had made, because it was **cold**,
and were **warming** themselves.
Peter was **also** standing there keeping warm.

Malchus = MAL-kus

Jesus' response to Peter ("Put your sword into its scabbard") shows that Jesus is in charge. Deliver the words as a command. Continue the authoritative tone of voice through the second half of Jesus' response, which shows that his authority comes from the Father.

Annas = ANN-us

Caiaphas = KĪ-uh-fus

Peter's denial of Jesus is straightforward and he is seemingly under little pressure when he gives it. State his words of denial ("I am not") forthrightly, thus marking the parallel with Jesus' "I am" statements earlier in the Passion.

---

newness that is begun through the cross. Perhaps this is why it is proclaimed on the day called *Good* Friday.

As noted in the commentary for Palm (Passion) Sunday, parishes have different ways of proclaiming the Passion. If you are in a parish that uses multiple readers, be sure to read the entire Passion so you understand your role within the context of the entire narrative. This will help your part to be connected to the entire narrative, making the entire proclamation flow

smoothly. Also, the reverence with which you approach the place from where you will proclaim your part, will convey to the assembly the solemnity of the narrative they are about to hear. Observe that, as on Palm (Passion) Sunday, the reading of the Passion begins without the customary greeting by the priest/deacon, but simply with the statement: "The Passion of our Lord Jesus Christ according to John." No additional words should be added.

(1) John's Passion narrative begins with the scene near the garden with Judas and the soldiers and guards who have come to arrest Jesus. However, John does not mention Jesus' agony in the garden, his prayer to the Father to take the cup of suffering away from him, or Judas' betrayal. Rather, John shows Jesus in total control of his fate. John has Jesus ask Judas and the soldiers twice for whom they are looking. When the respond, "Jesus the Nazorean," Jesus readily identifies himself as the one

You will want to decide in this section of the Passion (as in all the sections) how you will distinguish between the words the different characters speak and the narrative lines, so that it will be easier for the listeners to follow the progress of the events. One way to do this is to read the narrative lines in an unaffected manner, leaving more expression for the characters' lines.

Even after the temple guard struck Jesus (a detail probably taken from Mark 4:65), Jesus neither wavers in confidence nor becomes agitated. Simply maintain a steady confidence in your voice as you speak Jesus' words ("If I have spoken wrongly . . .").

Be deliberate and emphatic as you state Peter's second denial, spoken in the same words as the first ("I am not").

Make eye contact with the assembly as you deliver the line "Again Peter denied it" so that Peter's third rejection of Jesus is heard.

praetorium = prih-TOHR-ee-uhm

(4) The high priest **questioned** Jesus
    about his **disciples** and about his **doctrine**.
Jesus answered him,
    "I have spoken **publicly** to the world.
I have always taught in a **synagogue**
    or in the **temple** area where all the Jews **gather**,
    and in **secret** I have said **nothing**. Why ask **me**?
Ask those who **heard** me what I said to them.
They know what I said."
When he had said this,
    one of the temple guards standing there **struck** Jesus and said,
    "Is this the way you answer the high **priest**?"
Jesus answered him,
    "If I have spoken **wrongly**, **testify** to the wrong;
    but if I have spoken **rightly**, why do you **strike** me?"
Then **Annas** sent him bound to **Caiaphas** the high priest.

Now Simon **Peter** was standing there keeping warm.
And they said to him,
    "You are not one of his disciples, **are** you?"
He denied it and said,
    "I am **not**."
One of the **slaves** of the high priest,
    a **relative** of the one whose **ear** Peter had cut **off**, said,
    "Didn't I see you in the **garden** with him?"
Again Peter denied it.
And **immediately** the **cock crowed**.

(5) Then they brought Jesus from **Caiaphas** to the **praetorium**.
It was **morning**.
And they **themselves** did not enter the **praetorium**,
    in order not to be **defiled** so that they could eat the **Passover**.

by saying, "I am," a reference to the divine name. He does not ask to be delivered from the fate that he knows awaits him. His control of the situation extends to his order to release those disciples who were with him in fulfillment of his words that no one could take those who follow him out of his hand or his Father's (11:27–28). Through Jesus' own death, his disciples will be taken care, for through it will come eternal life.

The Christology that will be at the center of the entire Passion narrative is evident in the first scene: Jesus is the exalted Son of the Father, who reigns

supreme even on the cross. This reflects the statement Jesus made in John 10:18 in the good shepherd discourse that no one takes his life from him, but he lays it down of his own accord because he has the power to do so *and* the power to take it up.

(2) Once again, Jesus is in control as he commands Peter to return his sword to its scabbard. John's is the only account in which the names of those involved in the incident of cutting off the ear are provided. Also, only in John is there no reference to a formal meeting of the Sanhedrin.

Prior to the Passion narrative and immediately following the raising of Lazarus, the Sanhedrin does meet because some Jews had gone to the Pharisees and informed them of the signs Jesus was performing. At this session of the Sanhedrin, it becomes clear that the Jewish leaders are concerned about Jesus' growing popularity. Consequently, they are concerned that if they do nothing to stop Jesus, the Romans will take their land and nation. They decide that it is better for one man to die than for the whole nation to perish. From that point in John's account, the plot to kill Jesus

So **Pilate** came out to them and said,
    "What **charge** do you bring against this man?"
They answered and said to him,
    "If he were not a **criminal**,
    we would **not** have handed him over to you."
At **this**, Pilate said to them,
    "Take him **yourselves**, and judge him according to **your** law."
The Jews answered him,
    "We do not have the **right** to execute **anyone**,"
    in order that the word of Jesus might be **fulfilled**
    that he said indicating the kind of **death** he would die.
So **Pilate** went back into the **praetorium**
    and summoned **Jesus** and said to him,
    "Are **you** the King of the **Jews**?"
Jesus answered,
    "Do you say this on your **own**
    or have **others** told you **about** me?"
Pilate answered,
    "I am not a Jew, **am** I?
Your own **nation** and the chief **priests** handed you over to me.
What have you **done**?"
Jesus answered,
    "My **kingdom** does not belong to **this** world.
If my kingdom **did** belong to this world,
    my **attendants** would be **fighting**
    to keep me from being handed **over** to the **Jews**.
But as it **is**, my **kingdom** is not **here**."
So Pilate said to him,
    "Then you **are** a king?"
Jesus answered,
    "You **say** I am a king.

Pause slightly before the words "So Pilate went back into the praetorium."

Express Pilate's response ("I am not a Jew, am I?") with irony, even cynicism in your voice because it seems to be a play on Jesus' "I am" statements and Peter's "I am not" denial.

State the words "My kingdom does not belong to this world," which are not a denial of Jesus' kingship, but rather an affirmation of the different kind of king he is, with confidence: Jesus is in control and knows what his mission is.

picks up momentum (11:45–53). But in the face of Jesus, the one with power and control, those plotting against him stand little chance of succeeding. Even in death, Jesus will be triumphant.

(3) There is no prediction by Jesus of Peter's denial in John. At the time John was writing his account of the Gospel, the Johannine Christians were facing some persecution, though not a state-sponsored persecution. Some of the pressure from these persecutions could be reflected in John's description of Peter's denial, as John explicitly references the slaves and guards near Peter. Minimally, the pressure would make Peter's denial of someone he is close to more understandable. Notice also in John how Peter's threefold denial is split between two scenes with the high priest's questioning of Jesus placed in between.

(4) The interrogation of Jesus by Annas (the former high priest whom the Romans later deposed in favor of Caiaphas) suggests that Jesus is seen as a false prophet. Jesus' response, however, shows that he is in charge. He knows that what he taught publicly was the truth. The theme of testifying, which occurs often in John, appears again in Jesus' response to the Temple guard. The high priest does not seem to have sought out those who heard Jesus teach in order to gain their testimony as Jesus insisted, nor does it seem that the high priest is able to testify to any wrong that Jesus has committed. The inaction in seeking out other witnesses and the high priest's inability to testify to any wrong, contrasts with the testimony on behalf of Jesus that John the Baptist gave in the beginning of the Gospel. In the end, Jesus

For **this** I was born and for **this** I came into the world,
  to testify to the **truth**.
Everyone who **belongs** to the truth **listens** to my voice."
Pilate said to him, "What is **truth**?"

Pilate's question at the end of this section ("What is truth?") shows that he does not understand truth and, therefore, does not listen to Jesus. Try asking his question with a little sarcasm in your voice. It is not a genuine question.

(6) When he had said this,
  he **again** went out to the **Jews** and said to them,
  "I find no **guilt** in him.
But you have a **custom** that I release one **prisoner**
    to you at **Passover**.
Do you want me to release to you the King of the **Jews**?"
They cried out again,
  "Not **this** one but **Barabbas**!"
Now **Barabbas** was a **revolutionary**.

Barabbas = buh-RAB-us

(7) Then Pilate took Jesus and had him **scourged**.
And the **soldiers** wove a **crown** out of **thorns**
    and placed it on his **head**,
  and **clothed** him in a purple **cloak**,
  and they came to him and said,
  "**Hail**, King of the **Jews**!"
And they **struck** him repeatedly.
Once more Pilate went out and said to them,
  "**Look**, I am bringing him **out** to you,
  so that you may **know** that I find no **guilt** in him."
So Jesus came **out**,
  wearing the crown of **thorns** and the purple cloak.
And he said to them, "**Behold**, the man!"
When the chief **priests** and the **guards** saw him they cried out,
  "**Crucify** him, crucify him!"
Pilate said to them,
  "Take him **yourselves** and crucify him.

Because Pilate's words ("Behold, the man!") could be either an expression of disdain for Jesus or one of mockery, decide whether you want to deliver them with scorn or sarcasm in your voice.

knows that he needs no one to testify on his behalf, for his testimony can be verified by the Father, a claim that troubled the Pharisees earlier (8:12–20).

(5) The narrative shifts to the trial before Pilate, the Roman procurator. Between divisions 5, 6, and 7, Pilate goes back and forth seven times between "the Jews" outside the praetorium and Jesus inside, trying to decide whether to sentence Jesus to death or not. This trial scene is much more extensive in John than in the synoptics. "The Jews" see Jesus as a criminal. Since they had no authority to execute, they turned him over to Pilate. John's account is the only Gospel that provides the reader with this information.

Even Pilate's words as he questions Jesus convey a sense of the responsibility the Jewish leaders have for what will be Jesus' death. In response, Jesus speaks more than he does in any of the other gospels. His words are not so much a defense against what Pilate appears to think are the charges (Jesus proclaiming himself King of the Jews), but a confident explanation of the kingdom that is his. They are words that reflect his unique relationship with the Father.

Ironically, after Jesus speaks about his kingdom, the interrogation by Pilate ends with Jesus returning to his mission: he came into the world to testify to the truth (5:33; 8:40, 45, 46). But the truth was rejected by the Jews (8:44) and accepted by his disciples (14:6; 17:17, 19). Pilate stands in the middle, simply confused or perhaps ignorant, and asks, "What is truth?"

(6) Pilate, representative of Roman authority, does not think fondly of the Jewish leaders, perhaps because their

I find no **guilt** in him."
The Jews answered,
   "We have a **law**, and according to that law he ought to **die**,
    because he made himself the Son of **God**."
Now when **Pilate** heard this **statement**,
   he became even **more** afraid,
    and went back into the **praetorium** and said to Jesus,
   "**Where** are you **from**?"
Jesus did not answer him.
So Pilate said to him,
   "Do you not **speak** to me?
Do you not know that I have power to **release** you
   and I have power to **crucify** you?"
Jesus answered him,
   "You would have **no** power over me
   if it had not been **given** to you from **above**.
For this reason the one who handed me **over** to you
   has the **greater** sin."
Consequently, Pilate **tried** to release him; but the Jews cried **out**,
   "If you **release** him, you are **not** a Friend of **Caesar**.
Everyone who makes himself a king **opposes** Caesar."

When Pilate heard **these** words he brought Jesus out
   and **seated** him on the **judge's** bench
    in the place called **Stone Pavement**, in Hebrew, **Gabbatha**.
It was **preparation** day for **Passover**, and it was about **noon**.
And he said to the Jews,
   "**Behold**, your **king**!"
They cried out,
   "Take him **away**, take him **away**! **Crucify** him!"

Gabbatha = GAB-uh-thuh

Impart Pilate's pronouncement ("Behold, your king!") in a similar tone of voice to the one you chose for his earlier statement ("Behold, the man!"), because the two statements are parallel in structure. Increase the degree of intensity slightly in this second statement.

religious authority threatens his political authority and vice versa. Using the title "King of the Jews" in reference to Jesus when asking "the Jews" whether they want Jesus to be released, would be an affront to them. "The Jews" respond, calling for the release of Barabbas, an Aramaic name that means "son of the father." The Greek word used to identify Barabbas *(lēstēs)* can refer either to a robber or to a rebel fighting for a nationalistic cause. Whether a robber or a revolutionary, Barabbas stands in stark contrast to Jesus, who was neither a robber nor a revolutionary.

(7) Throughout the Gospel, John has used the term "the Jews" to apply to the Jewish leaders, and this is the case in the Passion narrative. At this point, Pilate has sent Jesus to be scourged and Jesus returns wearing symbols of royalty—a crown and purple clothing. The chief priests and guards call for his death, but Pilate tells them to crucify Jesus themselves, because he has not been able to find Jesus guilty of any crime. "The Jews" answer Pilate by confirming the guilt they have found in him.

For "the Jews," it is Jesus' claim to be the Son of God, to have a unique relationship with the Father, which provides the rationale for why he should die. Yet despite the guilt "the Jews" have found, Pilate tries to find a way to release Jesus, but both his declaration that Pilate has no power over him and "the Jews'" vindictive words, lead Pilate to bring him out to face "the Jews." Finally, Pilate forces "the Jews" to turn on one of their own, as they hand Jesus over to be crucified. Their disloyalty in this scene parallels their disbelief in Jesus, evident throughout John.

In asking the question "Shall I crucify your king?" Pilate is asking permission of the chief priests to hand Jesus over for crucifixion and trying to absolve himself of responsibility. He is "their" king, not Pilate's. Emphasize both "your" and "king."

Offer the summary line ("Then he handed him over . . .") with somberness and resignation in your voice. The mood of the Passion narrative shifts with this line.

Golgotha = GOL-guh-thuh

Pilate said to them,
    "Shall I crucify your **king**?"
The chief priests answered,
    "We **have** no king but **Caesar**."
Then he handed him **over** to them to be **crucified**.

(8) So they **took** Jesus, and, carrying the cross **himself**,
    he went out to what is called the Place of the **Skull**,
    in Hebrew, **Golgotha**.
There they **crucified** him, and with him two **others**,
    one on either **side**, with Jesus in the **middle**.
Pilate **also** had an **inscription** written and put on the cross.
It read,
    "**Jesus** the **Nazorean**, the **King** of the **Jews**."
Now many of the Jews **read** this inscription,
    because the place where Jesus was crucified was near the city;
    and it was written in **Hebrew**, **Latin**, and **Greek**.
So the chief priests of the Jews said to Pilate,
    "Do not write 'The **King** of the **Jews**,'
    but that he said, 'I am the King of the **Jews**.'"
Pilate answered,
    "What I have **written**, I have **written**."

When the soldiers had **crucified** Jesus,
    they took his **clothes** and **divided** them into four **shares**,
    a share for each **soldier**.
They also took his tunic, but the tunic was **seamless**,
    woven in **one** piece from the top down.
So they said to one another,
    "Let's not **tear** it, but cast **lots** for it to see whose it will be,"

Proclaim Pilate's retort to the chief priests ("What I have written, I have written") boldly.

This scene is the primary reason for falsely attributing Jesus' death to Jews in general. As a corrective to placing the blame for Jesus' death on all Jews, *Nostra Aetate* (NA), Vatican II's Declaration on the Relation of the Church to Non-Christian Religions, states: "Even though the Jewish authorities and those who followed their lead pressed for the death of Christ (cf. Jn 19:6), neither all Jews indiscriminately at that time, nor Jews today, can be charged with the crimes committed during his passion. It is true that the Church is the new people of God, yet the Jews should not be

spoken of as rejected or accursed as if this followed from holy Scripture" NA, #4).

(8) In John's account, Jesus carries the cross himself, without the help of Simon of Cyrene, showing that he is in complete control. The inscription Pilate had written on the cross is slightly different in each of the Gospels. In John, it reads "Jesus the Nazorean, the King of the Jews." The inscription, written in three languages, signifies that Jesus truly did come for the world; through the cross he will draw all people to himself in union with his Father. On many crucifixes the

letters INRI appear. They are the abbreviation for the Latin *Iesus Nazarenus Rex Iudaeorum*. Latin was the language used by the Roman administration.

A few other details are significant about this scene in John. First, where the synoptic Gospels place the women at a distance from the cross, John has them standing near it. Because of the syntax in the Greek, it is difficult to say whether there were two, three, or four women present. Regardless of how many women were present, Jesus' words to Mary stand out as significant. Through these words, Jesus unites

Pause slightly before "Standing by the cross of Jesus . . . ." The focus shifts from the soldiers to those who were close to Jesus during his lifetime and now are near him by the cross. This is also the only Gospel account that has the mother of Jesus at the cross. Communicate this section carefully, with reverence for the relationships expressed here.

Clopas = KLOH-pus

Jesus' words ("I thirst" and "It is finished") show that he is in control until the very end. Speak them with certainty.

Proclaim the line "And bowing his head, he handed over the spirit" not with despair in your voice, but rather with confidence, giving assurance that Jesus is in charge even at the moment of death.

in order that the passage of **Scripture** might be **fulfilled**
   that says:
    *They divided my **garments** among them,*
     *and for my **vesture** they cast **lots**.*
This is what the soldiers did.
Standing by the **cross** of Jesus were his **mother**
   and his mother's sister, **Mary** the wife of **Clopas**,
   and Mary of **Magdala**.
When Jesus saw his **mother** and the **disciple** there whom he **loved**
   he said to his mother, "**Woman**, behold, your **son**."
Then he said to the **disciple**,
   "Behold, your **mother**."
And from that hour the disciple took her into his **home**.

After **this**, aware that **everything** was now **finished**,
   in order that the **Scripture** might be **fulfilled**,
   Jesus said, "I **thirst**."
There was a **vessel** filled with common **wine**.
So they put a sponge **soaked** in wine on a sprig of **hyssop**
   and put it up to his **mouth**.
When Jesus had **taken** the wine, he said,
   "It is **finished**."
And bowing his **head**, he handed over the **spirit**.

[Here all kneel and pause for a short time.]

Now since it was **preparation** day,
   in order that the **bodies** might not remain
    on the cross on the **sabbath**,
   for the sabbath day of **that** week was a **solemn** one,
   the Jews asked Pilate that their **legs** be **broken**
   and that they be taken **down**.

Mary and the disciple whom he loved in a mother-son relationship. This places Mary in a special position for all of history. By her presence at Jesus' Crucifixion, she has become the woman to whom others seeking salvation can go. At the time Jesus passed on the spirit, Mary became "the new Eve ("mother of all the living"), the mother of the 'whole Christ' " (CCC, #726), and thus the mother of the Church.

Second, Jesus appears in command throughout his Crucifixion, even at the moment of death. Sorrow seems almost absent as Jesus speaks his final words: "It is finished." He gave his life freely; he was never in despair. In John, Jesus' death is his crowning moment, his time of exaltation. From the soldiers performing the two separate acts of dividing his garments and casting lots for his clothing (only in this Gospel are they separate acts), to Jesus' accepting the wine-soaked sponged, to Jesus' legs not being broken, to his side being pierced, everything is done in fulfillment of the scriptures, as if Jesus had orchestrated everything with his Father (John 10:30).

Third, the scene of the Crucifixion, death, and burial ends with the reappearance of Nicodemus, a Pharisee who had come to Jesus at night, having heard of the signs that he was performing (3:1–12; 7:50–51). In his initial appearance in the Gospel, Nicodemus asked Jesus how an old person could be born again and Jesus responded that a person must be born of

So the **soldiers** came and broke the legs of the **first**
    and then of the **other** one who was crucified with Jesus.
But when they came to **Jesus** and saw that he was already **dead**,
    they did not break **his** legs,
    but **one** soldier thrust his **lance** into his **side**,
    and **immediately blood** and **water** flowed out.
An **eyewitness** has testified, and his testimony is **true**;
    he **knows** that he is speaking the **truth**,
    so that you **also** may come to **believe**.
For this **happened** so that the Scripture passage might be **fulfilled**:
    *Not a **bone** of it will be **broken**.*
And again **another** passage says:
    *They will **look** upon him whom they have **pierced**.*

After **this**, Joseph of **Arimathea**,
    secretly a **disciple** of Jesus for fear of the Jews,
    asked **Pilate** if he could remove the **body** of Jesus.
And Pilate **permitted** it.
So he came and **took** his body.
Nicodemus, the one who had **first** come to him at **night**,
    also came bringing a mixture of **myrrh** and **aloes**
    weighing about one hundred **pounds**.
They took the **body** of Jesus
    and **bound** it with **burial** cloths along with the **spices**,
    according to the Jewish **burial** custom.
Now in the place where he had been **crucified** there was a **garden**,
    and in the garden a new **tomb**, in which no one
        had yet been **buried**.
So they laid Jesus **there** because of the Jewish **preparation** day;
    for the **tomb** was close **by**.

Pause before the words "An eyewitness has testified . . . ." Then proclaim these lines with conviction as Jesus' identity as the truth has been recognized.

Pause before the section beginning with the words "After this, Joseph of Arimathea . . . ."
Arimathea = air-ih-muh-THEE-uh
In Mark's Passion account, read on Palm Sunday, Joseph of Arimathea is identified as a member of the Sanhedrin.

Nicodemus = nik-oh-DEE-muhs

Let solemnity, reverence, and respect be heard in your voice as you provide the description of how Joseph and Nicodemus looked after the body of Jesus. Do not gloss over this section as if in a hurry to end a lengthy narrative.

---

water and the Spirit. Recall that in the middle of their dialogue, Nicodemus fades into the background, but Jesus proceeds to speak, saying that "God so loved the world that he gave his only Son, so that everyone who believes in him might not perish but might have eternal life" (3:16). It seems now that Nicodemus understands the answer to his question, the whole of which he might not have heard earlier in the Gospel. Nicodemus symbolizes that Jesus has fulfilled his mission to save the world (3:17) and to draw all people to himself once he has been lifted up (12:32). The extended General Intercessions on Good Friday reflect the desire of Jesus to draw all people to himself.

EASTER VIGIL

Lectionary #41

READING I   Genesis 1:1—2:2

Genesis = JEN-uh-sis

Emphasize the words "In the beginning" by proclaiming them with a deliberate pace, looking up at the assembly.

Pause before each new section that begins with the words "Then God said." Originally, each section might have been separate but later put together in the creation story of Genesis 1:1—2:2. Also, as you move from one section to the next, let intensity and excitement build in your voice. The pinnacle of the story is God's creation of man—male and female— in his image. When you come to the concluding line of each unit (for example, "Thus evening came . . . the first day"), change the tone of your voice to one that expresses contentment. God has accomplished a good day's work.

A reading from the Book of Genesis

In the **beginning**, when God created the **heavens** and the earth,
    the earth was a formless **wasteland**, and **darkness**
        covered the **abyss**,
    while a mighty **wind** swept over the waters.

Then God said,
    "Let there be **light**," and there **was** light.
God saw how **good** the light was.
God then **separated** the light from the **darkness**.
God called the light "**day**" and the darkness he called "**night**."
Thus **evening** came, and **morning** followed—the **first** day.

Then God said,
    "Let there be a **dome** in the middle of the waters,
    to separate **one** body of water from the **other**."
And so it **happened**:
    God made the dome,
    and it separated the water **above** the dome
        from the water **below** it.
God called the dome "the **sky**."
Evening came, and **morning** followed—the **second** day.

Then God said,
    "Let the water under the sky be **gathered** into a single **basin**,
    so that the **dry land** may appear."

READING I "Accept this Easter candle, a flame divided but undimmed, a pillar of fire that glows to the honor of God. Let it mingle with the lights of heaven and continue bravely burning to dispel the darkness of this night" (from the Exsultet).

On this night, when the image of darkness turning to light is central, the seven Old Testament readings begin with the story of Creation. Beginning at this point in salvation history is traditional at the Easter Vigil and in the instruction of catechumens

for Baptism. Many symbols and beliefs of our faith are rooted in this account of creation. Four in particular will be the focus of this commentary: 1) the image of light, 2) the creation of humanity in the image of God, and 3) the stewardship of the earth entrusted men and women, and 4) the worship of God on Sunday.

In this account, which appears as the first of two creation stories in Genesis even though it was written later than the second story (Genesis 2:4—3:24), God creates light first. Through a divine declaration, God was able to make light shine in

the darkness. Thus, we believe that God created *ex nihilo*, "out of nothing." Only the Word of God was necessary in order to accomplish the first act of creation, bringing light into the world (CCC, #298). And this light God created still shines; it is present in Christ, the light of the world (see John 9:5) and in those who live as his followers (1 John 1:5–7). The paschal candle, prominently placed and lit tonight and through the Easter season, is a symbol of the light of Christ.

And so it **happened**:
  the water **under** the sky was gathered into its **basin**,
  and the **dry land** appeared.
God called the **dry land** "the **earth**,"
  and the **basin** of the water he called "the **sea**."
God saw how **good** it was.
Then God said,
  "Let the earth bring forth **vegetation**:
  every kind of **plant** that bears **seed**
  and every kind of **fruit** tree on earth
  that bears **fruit** with its **seed** in it."
And so it **happened**:
  the earth brought forth **every** kind of plant that bears **seed**
  and **every** kind of fruit tree on **earth**
  that bears **fruit** with its **seed** in it.
God saw how **good** it was.
Evening came, and **morning** followed—the **third** day.

Then God said:
  "Let there be **lights** in the dome of the **sky**,
  to separate **day** from **night**.
Let them mark the fixed **times**, the **days** and the **years**,
  and serve as **luminaries** in the dome of the **sky**,
  to shed **light** upon the **earth**."
And so it **happened**:
  God made the two great **lights**,
  the **greater** one to govern the **day**,
  and the **lesser** one to govern the **night**;
  and he made the **stars**.
God **set** them in the dome of the sky,
  to shed light upon the earth,
  to govern the **day** and the **night**,
  and to separate the **light** from the **darkness**.

The eight units that begin "Then God said . . ." were probably originally separate, reflecting distinct creative acts. Beginning with the creation of light through the creation of man, this creation story attests that all of creation is good and that God created through his own word, the divine word. Thus, creation itself is distinguished from God, the Creator. While God made man in the divine image, still men and women are not God. Rather, as male and female they both share in the life of God. The common origin of the human race in God is the basis for the Catholic teaching on the human dignity and the reverence due all human persons who exist in both equality and difference (CCC, #369–370).

After the creation of humanity, male and female in the image of God, God offered them a blessing, asking them to procreate and giving them dominion over creation. While there is a sense of forceful control that is contained God's words to "subdue" the earth and "have dominion over" the living creatures, that God gave the world and all that is in it to men and women means that they have a responsibility to tend the world God created, treating all life and the environment with respects. They are to be stewards of creation, remembering always that it belongs to God (CCC, #373).

Finally, after God's work of creation of humanity and his blessing, observe that He notes that everything he had created is "very good," whereas after each individual act prior to the creation of humanity, he remarked that it was "good." Now God's work of creation is complete and He rests on the seventh day. That God refrains from work on this day is the foundation for the

God saw how **good** it was.
Evening came, and **morning** followed—the **fourth** day.

Then God said,
   "Let the water **teem** with an abundance of living **creatures**,
   and on the earth let **birds** fly beneath the dome of the **sky**."
And so it **happened**:
   God created the great **sea monsters**
   and all **kinds** of swimming creatures with which
      the water **teems**,
   and all **kinds** of winged birds.
God saw how **good** it was, and God **blessed** them, saying,
   "Be **fertile**, **multiply**, and **fill** the water of the **seas**;
   and let the **birds** multiply on the **earth**."
Evening came, and **morning** followed—the **fifth** day.

Then God said,
   "Let the earth bring forth all **kinds** of living **creatures**:
   cattle, **creeping** things, and wild **animals** of all **kinds**."
And so it **happened**:
   God made all **kinds** of wild **animals**, all **kinds** of **cattle**,
   and all kinds of **creeping** things of the earth.
God saw how **good** it was.
Then God said:
   "Let us make **man** in our **image**, after our **likeness**.
Let them have **dominion** over the **fish** of the sea,
   the **birds** of the air, and the **cattle**,
   and over **all** the wild **animals**
   and **all** the creatures that **crawl** on the **ground**."
God **created** man in his **image**;
   in the image of **God** he created him;
   male and **female** he created them.

Address the section about the creation of man—male and female—in the divine image by looking directly at the assembly. Proclaim this section with a joy that expresses the intimacy of the relationship between the Creator and those of us created in his image.

commandment to "keep holy the Sabbath" and the Church's precept regarding the Sunday obligation for the faithful to participate in the Mass (CCC, #2180).

In a world filled with evil, the proclamation of this reading provides hope: God created everything very good; God did not create evil. On this night when we celebrate the beauty of creation and our belief that the light of Christ has vanquished all darkness created by human sinfulness, this reading tells us the light of faith has been present from the very beginning and it will continue to be present, undimmed to the honor of God.

READING II This reading from Genesis of Abraham's sacrifice of his son Isaac was proclaimed on the Second Sunday of Lent this year, though verses 3–8, 9b, and 14 were left out. (See the previous commentary for more background.) On the Second Sunday of Lent, Abraham's role as our father in faith was emphasized, as was the idea of covenant. These themes again come to the fore at the Easter Vigil, as the Old Testament readings are a reflection of the Lord's ongoing covenant with his people, mediated through our ancestors in faith.

Verses 3–8, in the middle section of the reading, narrate the journey of Abraham and Isaac to the site where God had directed them to go, and the preparations for the sacrifice. Abraham's and Isaac's leaving house and home behind is similar to the disciples leaving their livelihoods and families behind to follow Jesus, heard in the Gospel on the Third Sunday in Ordinary Time (Mark 1:14–20).

153

APRIL 11–12, 2009 ■ EASTER VIGIL

God **blessed** them, saying:
  "Be **fertile** and **multiply**;
  fill the earth and **subdue** it.
Have **dominion** over the **fish** of the sea, the **birds** of the air,
  and **all** the living things that **move** on the **earth**."
God also said:
  "**See**, I give you every seed-bearing **plant** all over the **earth**
  and every **tree** that has seed-bearing **fruit** on it to be your **food**;
  and to all the **animals** of the land, all the **birds** of the air,
  and **all** the living creatures that crawl on the **ground**,
  I give all the green **plants** for **food**."
And so it **happened**.
God looked at **everything** he had made, and he found it
    very good.
Evening came, and **morning** followed—the **sixth** day.

Thus the **heavens** and the **earth** and all their array
    were **completed**.
Since on the **seventh** day God was **finished**
  with the work he had been **doing**,
  he **rested** on the **seventh** day from all the work
    he had **undertaken**.

[Shorter: Genesis 1:1, 26–31a]

READING II   Genesis 22:1–18

A reading from the Book of Genesis

God put **Abraham** to the **test**.
He called to him, "**Abraham**!"
"Here I **am**," he replied.

Pause after "And so it happened" and before "God looked at everything he had made." Offer the latter line very deliberately, as if you were looking around and admiring creation yourself. Previously, at the end of an act of creation, God recognizes what he has created as "good." Now, God sees all that He has created as *very good.* Emphasize this in your delivery.

**Genesis = JEN-uh-sis
For more suggestions on how to proclaim this reading, see the margin notes for the Second Sunday of Lent.
Abraham = AY-bruh-ham**

While Isaac is unaware of what is to transpire on the mountain, Abraham, without questioning, follows God's instructions. Abraham's response to Isaac's question about where the sheep is, that "God himself will provide the sheep," comes from the Hebrew *yir eh,* "see to." It indicates the God will take care of everything. Abraham trusted this, and in doing so clearly "let go and let God," believing that God would see to it that His ways would be followed.

Verse 14, which is included in the reading at the Easter Vigil, references the image of sight again. Here, Abraham names

the site of the sacrifice, "Yahweh-yireh," which literally means "The Lord will see." Abraham's naming of the site is followed by a restatement of the Lord's promises by his messenger. One of these promises is that "in the descendants of Abraham all the nations of the earth shall find blessing."

To this day, many Jews, Christians, and Muslims have been blessed because of Abraham's unqualified trust in the Lord when he was tested. For Christians, the promise of the blessing is fulfilled in Christ. The prayer after the reading at the Easter Vigil bears witness to this in its words:

"God and Father of all who believe in you, you promised Abraham that he would become the father of all nations, and through the death and resurrection of Christ you fulfill that promise: everywhere throughout the world you increase your chosen people."

READING III This reading begins after a few verses in Exodus that describe the Israelites complaining to Moses that he had brought them into the desert to die. At this point, they would prefer to go

Isaac = Ī-zik

Moriah = moh-RĪ-uh

Pause before the words "Early the next morning." This section describes the journey to the site of the sacrifice and the preparations for it.

Reverence the dialogue that takes place between Abraham and Isaac regarding "the sheep for the holocaust" by proclaiming these words in a serious tone of voice, one that indicates the gravity of the situation. Express Abraham's words ("God himself will provide") matter-of-factly, reassuring Isaac that everything will work out.

Then God said:
"Take your son **Isaac**, your only **one**, whom you **love**,
and go to the land of **Moriah**.
There you shall offer him up as a **holocaust**
on a **height** that I will point out to you."
Early the next **morning** Abraham saddled his **donkey**,
took with him his son **Isaac** and two of his servants as well,
and with the **wood** that he had cut for the **holocaust**,
set out for the **place** of which **God** had told him.

On the **third** day **Abraham** got sight of the **place** from afar.
Then he said to his **servants**:
"Both of you stay **here** with the donkey,
while the boy and I go on over **yonder**.
We will **worship** and then come **back** to you."
Thereupon Abraham took the **wood** for the **holocaust**
and **laid** it on his son Isaac's **shoulders**,
while he himself carried the **fire** and the **knife**.
As the two walked on **together**, Isaac spoke
to his father Abraham:
"**Father**!" Isaac said.
"Yes, son," he replied.
Isaac continued, "Here are the **fire** and the **wood**,
but **where** is the **sheep** for the **holocaust**?"
"**Son**," Abraham answered,
"God himself will provide the **sheep** for the **holocaust**."
Then the two continued going forward.

When they came to the **place** of which God had **told** him,
Abraham built an **altar** there and arranged the **wood** on it.
Next he tied up his son **Isaac**,
and put him on **top** of the wood on the **altar**.

back to Egypt and remain slaves of Pharaoh and the Egyptians. Moses' response to the Israelites falls within the framework of the religious traditions of the time, which saw the gods fighting on behalf of their people. God will fight for the Israelites, Moses tells his people. They simply need to refrain from panic and be confident that their God will prevail (verses 10–14).

In the opening line of this reading, the Lord asks Moses why he is pleading with the Lord. The Lord simply tells Moses to tell the Israelites that they must go forward and continue on their journey because the Lord will show the Egyptians that he is the Lord (verse 18). Through the protection offered by the angel of God and the cloud, the Israelites are shielded from the enemy. Through Moses' actions as a mediator of the Lord's power and presence, the Israelites are able to pass through the sea and likewise, through a similar action by Moses, water destroys the Egyptians.

The passage of the Israelites from approaching death by their enemy (and their own stubbornness in desiring to return to Israel!) to new life mirrors the passage of Christians from death to new life in the sacrament of Baptism. Back in the time of the early Church fathers (approximately the late first century through the fifth century), the waters of the Red Sea in this reading were seen as a *type* of Baptism. Early church writers often interpreted figures and events in the Old Testament as foreshadowing New Testament persons or occurrences that were then seen as the fulfillment of the Old Testament types.

Not only were the waters of the Red Sea symbolic of Christian Baptism, but

Then he reached out and took the knife to **slaughter** his son.
But the LORD's **messenger** called to him from **heaven**,
     "**Abraham, Abraham!**"
"Here I **am**," he answered.
"Do **not** lay your **hand** on the **boy**," said the **messenger**.
"Do **not** do the **least** thing to him.
I **know** now how **devoted** you are to God,
     since you did not **withhold** from me your own **beloved son**."
As Abraham looked about,
     he spied a **ram** caught by its **horns** in the **thicket**.
So he went and took the ram
     and offered it up as a **holocaust** in place of his **son**.
Abraham named the site Yahweh-yireh;
     hence people now say, "On the mountain the LORD will see."

Again the LORD's messenger called to Abraham from heaven
          and said:
     "I swear by myself, declares the **LORD**,
     that because you acted as you did
     in not **withholding** from me your beloved **son**,
     I will **bless** you **abundantly**
     and make your descendants as **countless**
     as the **stars** of the **sky** and the **sands** of the **seashore**;
     your **descendants** shall take possession
     of the gates of their **enemies**,
     and in your descendants all the **nations** of the earth
          shall find **blessing**—
     all this because you **obeyed** my **command**."

[Shorter: Genesis 22:1–2, 9a, 10–13, 15–18]

Speak the words of the Lord's messenger ("Do not lay your hand . . .") as a command, but one given with satisfaction because Abraham has been faithful to God.

Pause before the final section ("Again the Lord's messenger . . ."). Express the Lord's promise to Abraham with solemnity in your voice. God's blessing is extended over Jews, Christians, and Muslims today.

---

also the Song of Moses, which begins at the end of the reading (15:1–18), according to the Church father Tertullian, testifies to the presence of the Trinity in the salvation of the Israelites as the crossed through the waters. In his song of praise to the Lord for his triumph, Moses acknowledged the operation of the Father, the Son (the right hand of the father, verse 6), and the Holy Spirit (verses 8–10). According to Tertullian, in this song is a witness to "the unity of the Godhead, not an inequality of the Trinity" (*On the Duties of Clergy*, III.IV.20).

As the sacrament of Baptism and/or the renewal of our baptism are carried out this evening, this reading reminds us of the Trinitarian formula that is spoken as the waters of Baptism flow over the one receiving the sacrament. It also reminds us of the profession of faith we make each time we recite the Nicene Creed or respond to the questions of the profession of faith. Finally, in the way the early Church fathers interpreted the scriptures, we see the importance of recalling that our salvation is rooted in the salvation of the Israelites. Thus, the

Jewish and Christian faiths can never be completely cut off from each other.

READING IV | The next two readings come from the part of the book of Isaiah known written by deutero-Isaiah or second Isaiah (Is 40:1—55:13). Deutero-Isaiah is not a literal name for the author of these chapters, but rather is a way to reference an unknown author who wrote near the end of the Babylonian exile and the return of the Israelites to their

Exodus = EK-suh-dus

Ask the question "Why are you crying out to me?" that begins this reading with empathy in your tone of voice: God desires to understand the Israelites' consternation, but knows that they need not cower in fear for he will deliver them. Thus, Moses does not have a chance to respond to this question, but rather God continues with a set of commands for the Israelites and for Moses and a description of what God will do to the Egyptians. Deliver these lines with strength and reassurance in your voice.

Pause after God's words and before beginning the next section ("The angel of God . . ."). Lower your tone of voice to one that expresses the Lord's protection of the Israelites.

Pause again before the words "Then Moses stretched out his hand." Raise your voice as you tell the assembly how Moses followed the Lord's command to split the seas in two.

READING III Exodus 14:15—15:1

A reading from the Book of Exodus

The LORD said to Moses, "Why are you crying out to me?
Tell the **Israelites** to go **forward**.
And you, lift up your **staff** and, with hand **outstretched**
⟶ over the sea,
⟶ **split** the sea in **two**,
⟶ that the **Israelites** may pass through it on dry **land**.
But I will make the **Egyptians** so **obstinate**
⟶ that they will go in **after** them.
Then I will receive **glory** through **Pharaoh** and all his **army**,
⟶ his **chariots** and **charioteers**.
The **Egyptians** shall know that **I** am the LORD,
⟶ when I receive **glory** through **Pharaoh**
⟶ and his **chariots** and **charioteers**."

The **angel** of God, who had been **leading** Israel's camp,
⟶ now **moved** and went around **behind** them.
The column of **cloud** also, leaving the **front**,
⟶ took up its place **behind** them,
⟶ so that it came between the camp of the **Egyptians**
⟶ and that of **Israel**.
But the cloud now became **dark**, and thus the night **passed**
⟶ without the rival camps coming any closer **together**
⟶ all night **long**.
Then **Moses** stretched out his **hand** over the **sea**,
⟶ and the LORD **swept** the sea
⟶ with a strong east **wind** throughout the **night**
⟶ and so turned it into dry **land**.

homeland, centuries after the prophet Isaiah was active.

The prophecy of Isaiah in this reading begins with spousal imagery. The Lord, Israel's husband, is calling Israel back to him. At the end of Israel's period of captivity and exile, which lasted from 587–521 BC, the Lord now desires that Israel return home to Jerusalem. Jerusalem, throughout the exile, has been like a wife without children; with the return of the exiles to her, she will once again have many children. Thus, Israel's return to Jerusalem symbolizes her return to God.

Isaiah's prophecy acknowledges the Lord's wrath and momentary abandonment of his spouse because of her infidelity, which resulted in the exile. Yet now the Lord's tenderness and compassion is extended to her. God's enduring love will be a lasting testimony to his spousal union with Israel.

The prophecy then switches to a comparison between the end of the flood in the days of Noah and the end of the Israelites' exile. The captivity and exile of his people, seems to suggest that the Lord broke the promise he made to Noah after the flood.

If that is the case, then this passage is a restatement of that covenant in words that reflect the steadfastness of God's love for his spouse.

In the final section of this reading ("O afflicted one . . .") is an announcement of salvation. The prophecy describes the beauty and preciousness of the heavenly Jerusalem, the Lord's spouse, with references to her roadways and walls being made of precious and colorful gems. Her children will have the Lord for their teacher. Justice will reign in her city walls.

When the **water** was thus **divided**,
   the Israelites **marched** into the **midst** of the sea on dry **land**,
   with the water like a **wall** to their **right** and to their **left**.

The **Egyptians** followed in **pursuit**;
   all Pharaoh's **horses** and **chariots** and **charioteers**
      went after them
   right into the **midst** of the **sea**.
In the night watch just before dawn
   the LORD cast through the column of the fiery **cloud**
   upon the Egyptian force a **glance** that threw it into a **panic**;
   and he so **clogged** their chariot wheels
   that they could hardly **drive**.
With **that** the Egyptians sounded the **retreat** before Israel,
   because the LORD was fighting for them **against** the Egyptians.

Then the LORD told **Moses**, "Stretch out your **hand** over the **sea**,
   that the **water** may flow **back** upon the **Egyptians**,
   upon their **chariots** and their **charioteers**."
So Moses **stretched** out his hand over the **sea**,
   and at dawn the sea flowed **back** to its normal depth.
The Egyptians were fleeing **head on** toward the **sea**,
   when the LORD **hurled** them into its **midst**.
As the water flowed **back**,
   it covered the **chariots** and the **charioteers**
      of Pharaoh's whole **army**
   which had **followed** the Israelites into the **sea**.
Not a single **one** of them **escaped**.
But the **Israelites** had marched on dry **land**
   through the midst of the **sea**,
   with the water like a **wall** to their **right** and to their **left**.
Thus the LORD **saved Israel** on that day
   from the power of the **Egyptians**.

Pause slightly before the words "The Egyptians followed in pursuit." As you tell this part of the account, increase the intensity and drama in your voice. Many in the assembly will know what is coming next, but deliver the story as if they are hearing it for the first time.

Pause after noting the Egyptians' retreat and before the next section ("Then the Lord told Moses . . ."), which recounts the instructions the Lord gave to Moses and which Moses followed that led to the destruction of the Egyptians. Notice the phrase "chariots and charioteers" is repeated frequently. Read it in such a way that it is not glossed over, but rather paints the picture of the size of Pharaoh's army that the Lord was fighting.

Pause before the words "Thus the Lord saved Israel on that day." This is the most important line of the reading. It provides the reason this story is proclaimed on this night of the Church year. Take your time delivering this line, making sure to focus on the word "saved."

The heart of the application of this reading on the night of the Easter Vigil is in this offer of salvation. In the heavenly vision of the new Jerusalem, salvation is extended beyond the promises to Noah and beyond the Mosaic covenant. For Christians, we see gift of salvation fulfilled in Jesus. Thus, the spousal imagery in this reading, from New Testament times forward has been applied to Christ and the Church. Christ is the bridegroom, and the Church—the new, heavenly Jerusalem—is his spouse (Galatians 4:26–27; LG, #6; CCC, #757, 789).

As members of the Church on earth, we are like the exiled Israelites. We often journey away from the Lord, but through Christ, we are led back to God. In your proclamation of this reading, you take the place of the prophet, extending the Lord's words of compassion and mercy to all who have gathered this night. They have come back to the Lord after Lent, but still they are asked to continue their journey toward he new and heavenly Jerusalem, seeking that which is above.

READING V The theme of the fifth of the Old Testament readings during the Easter Vigil is our thirst and hunger for God. As human persons, we are religious beings, who seek to know God and to be in relationship with him. We can forget, overlook, and even sometimes reject the intimate bond we have with God (see CCC, #28–30; GS, #19). When this occurs, we need to be called back—and God does call us back. Sometimes, people need to be invited to respond to God for the first time. The Lord's words, announced by the

The lines "Then Moses and the Israelites sang . . ." lead to the canticle that the Israelites sang in praise of God for their rescue. Build momentum toward the canticle that will be sung as the Responsorial Psalm. Check with the music director to see whether the musicians will come in with the canticle as soon as the reading ends.

When Israel saw the **Egyptians** lying **dead** on the **seashore**
　　and beheld the great **power** that the LORD
　　had shown against the Egyptians,
　　they **feared** the LORD and **believed** in him
　　　　and in his servant **Moses**.

Then Moses and the Israelites sang this **song** to the LORD:
　　I will sing to the **LORD**, for he is gloriously **triumphant**;
　　horse and chariot he has **cast** into the **sea**.

READING IV　　Isaiah 54:5–14

Isaiah = ī-ZAY-uh

Convey the words of the first section ("The One who has become your husband is your Maker . . ."), which describe an intimate relationship between the Lord and his people, with warmth and tenderness.

A reading from the Book of the Prophet Isaiah

The One who has become your **husband** is your **Maker**;
　　his **name** is the LORD of **hosts**;
your **redeemer** is the **Holy** One of **Israel**,
　　called **God** of all the **earth**.
The LORD calls you **back**,
　　like a **wife** forsaken and grieved in spirit,
　　a **wife** married in **youth** and then cast **off**,
　　says your God.
For a brief moment I **abandoned** you,
　　but with great **tenderness** I will take you **back**.
In an outburst of **wrath**, for a **moment**
　　I hid my face from you;
　　but with enduring **love** I take **pity** on you,
　　says the LORD, your **redeemer**.

---

prophet Isaiah, inviting all, even the poor, to come to the water, to drink and eat well, show that the divine initiative is always at work, calling men and women to communion with God.

This passage was also read on the feast of the Baptism of the Lord, so you can turn to that commentary for more background. The reading comes from the part of Isaiah (chapters 40–55) composed by a different author than the first 39 chapters of Isaiah. This author, known as deutero-Isaiah or second Isaiah, wrote centuries after the prophet Isaiah was active, near

the end of the Babylonian exile and the exiles return to their homeland. Interestingly, many of the themes contained in chapter 40 are also found in chapter 55: the new exodus, the way, the call to eat and drink, the word of the Lord, the heavens and the earth, the call of Israel to repentance and the Lord's offer of mercy. These themes are played out in our journey to God as well, and in a particular way, they are evident on this night when the Church brings new members into her communion.

The sacraments quench the spiritual hunger and thirst of those who respond to

God's invitation to "come to the water" through the celebration of the Eucharist, the memorial meal of Christ's suffering and death. Each time we participate in the celebration of the Eucharist, we renew our commitment to the new covenant established in Jesus, a covenant that was itself the renewal of the Davidic covenant announced by the prophet. Yet we, like Israel, are called to forsake our evil ways and experience God's forgiveness and mercy. We are to come to the banquet meal with the right disposition and proper spirit—willingly, ready to listen to the Lord (verse 3).

This is for **me** like the days of **Noah**,
 when I swore that the **waters** of Noah
 should **never** again **deluge** the earth;
so I have sworn **not** to be angry with you,
 or to **rebuke** you.
Though the **mountains** leave their **place**
 and the **hills** be **shaken**,
my love shall **never** leave you
 nor my covenant of **peace** be shaken,
 says the LORD, who has mercy on you.
O **afflicted** one, **storm-battered** and **unconsoled**,
 I lay your **pavements** in **carnelians**,
 and your **foundations** in **sapphires**;
I will make your **battlements** of **rubies**,
 your **gates** of **carbuncles**,
 and all your **walls** of precious **stones**.
All your children shall be taught by the LORD,
 and great shall be the **peace** of your **children**.
In **justice** shall you be **established**,
 far from the fear of **oppression**,
 where destruction cannot **come** near you.

Pause before starting the section
"O afflicted one . . . ." Convey the beauty
of the new and heavenly Jerusalem, which
will adorned with precious, colorful
stones, by filling your voice with delight.

carnelians = kar-NEEL-yunz

carbuncles = KAR-bung-k*lz

Communicate the closing lines ("All your
children shall be taught . . .") in a voice
filled with strength and hope. God's justice
prevails, setting things aright in the world.
God will not leave his spouse or his
children behind.

READING V   Isaiah 55:1–11

A reading from the Book of the Prophet Isaiah

 Thus says the LORD:
All you who are **thirsty**,
 come to the **water**!

Isaiah = ī-ZAY-uh

See the margin notes for the feast of the
Baptism of the Lord, where this reading
also occurs.

   The beautiful images in the final verses of this chapter (10–13), of which only two are included in this evening's reading, form a magnificent conclusion to Isaiah 40—55. At the end of the chapters that spoke of Israel's need to repent and offered hope for the return of the exiles, the prophet confidently proclaims the word of the Lord, stating that his word will not return void; God's will *will* be accomplished. The two verses that follow on the end of the reading describe the joyful departure of the exiles, and the mountains and hills singing because of it. This is an everlasting sign of the greatness of the Lord.

   Having completed Lent, and now in the midst of the Triduum, the assembly—those already fully initiated and those about to celebrate the sacraments of initiation for the first time—return home to God this evening. Let the Church resound with joy, for the Lord's word does not return empty. Through their sharing in the eucharistic meal, they are also sent forth to be bearers of the Lord's invitation to come to the water to those they meet.

READING VI The book of the prophet Baruch is proclaimed only one other time in the three-year cycle of readings: on the Second Sunday of Advent in Year C. While traditionally attributed to Baruch, Jeremiah's scribe, Baruch is no longer believed to have written the work. The date of composition of the work also remains in question, but the book's content makes clear its connection with Israel's

The members of the assembly have responded to the Lord's invitation to "come to the water!" Offer these beautiful, descriptive words of invitation directly to them by making eye contact—looking up and at different places in the assembly—each time you speak the word "come."

Speak the word "listen" in a softer tone of voice. What follows ("I will renew with you . . .") recounts the Davidic covenant and the announcement of the new covenant Christians see fulfilled in Jesus.

Pause before the words "Seek the Lord." This section offers another invitation to the listeners to find the Lord. Deliver this invitation in a stronger tone of voice than the invitation to the meal.

You who have no money,
    come, receive grain and **eat**;
come, without **paying** and without **cost**,
    drink wine and **milk**!
Why spend your **money** for what is not **bread**,
    your **wages** for what fails to **satisfy**?
Heed me, and you shall eat **well**,
    you shall **delight** in rich **fare**.
Come to me **heedfully**,
    listen, that you may have **life**.
I will **renew** with you the **everlasting** covenant,
    the **benefits** assured to **David**.
As I made him a **witness** to the **peoples**,
    a **leader** and commander of **nations**,
so shall you summon a **nation** you knew **not**,
    and nations that knew you **not** shall **run** to you,
because of the LORD, your **God**,
    the **Holy** One of **Israel**, who has **glorified** you.

Seek the LORD while he may be found,
    call him while he is near.
Let the **scoundrel** forsake his **way**,
    and the **wicked** man his **thoughts**;
let him **turn** to the LORD for **mercy**;
    to our **God**, who is **generous** in **forgiving**.
For **my** thoughts are not **your** thoughts,
    nor are **your** ways **my** ways, says the LORD.
As high as the **heavens** are above the **earth**,
    so high are **my** ways above **your** ways
    and **my** thoughts above **your** thoughts.

exile in Babylon and their hope for a return to the Promised Land.

The book begins with the exiles' public confession of infidelity to the Lord and their prayer for deliverance in the face of their sin in which God's promises to Abraham and his clemency toward his servant Moses are recalled (1:15—3:8). The reading from Baruch at the Easter Vigil begins at this point in the book.

As a wisdom poem, related to a genre of writing known as "wisdom literature," which includes the books of Wisdom, Ecclesiastes, Sirach, and the eighth chapter of Proverbs, this reading speaks of Wisdom (*Sophia*, in Greek) personified. In representing Wisdom in relation to the Mosaic law (Deuteronomy 4:6; Psalm 19:8; 119:97–98; also Sirach 24:1–31; 39:1–11), the author connects Wisdom with the observance of the Lord's commandments. Obedience to the commandments will lead to the return of the exiles to their homeland.

There is a difference between the references to "prudence" and "wisdom" in the reading. Although "wisdom" is used to translate both the Greek words *sophia* and *phronesis*, these words have two distinct meanings. *Sophia* emphasizes the creative acts of wisdom and *phronesis* the practical aspects. For the Israelites in exile, both creativity and practicality are learned from Wisdom, the teacher of the law. She enables them to see how the Lord has been active in the world from the beginning and present with them throughout their ups and downs as his people. Wisdom also assists the exiles in making practical decisions in their own life situation.

Pause before beginning the final section
("For just as from the heavens . . .").
Notice it is one long sentence. Its meta-
phors require a lighter tone of voice
in order to convey the beauty of God's
promise contained in them.

For just as from the heavens
    the **rain** and **snow** come **down**
and do not **return** there
    till they have **watered** the **earth**,
    making it **fertile** and **fruitful**,
giving **seed** to the one who **sows**
    and **bread** to the one who **eats**,
so shall my **word** be
    that goes forth from my **mouth**;
my **word** shall not return to me **void**,
    but shall do my **will**,
    achieving the **end** for which I **sent** it.

READING VI   Baruch 3:9–15, 32—4:4

Baruch = buh-ROOK

Proclaim the lines "Hear, O Israel . . .
dwelt in enduring peace" as if you are
trying to get someone's attention in a
crowd of people.

A reading from the Book of the Prophet Baruch

Hear, O Israel, the **commandments** of **life**:
    listen, and know **prudence**!
How **is** it, Israel,
    that you are in the land of your foes,
    grown **old** in a foreign **land**,
defiled with the **dead**,
    accounted with those destined for the **netherworld**?
You have **forsaken** the fountain of **wisdom**!
    Had you **walked** in the way of **God**,
    you would have **dwelt** in enduring **peace**.

Near the end of the reading, the exiles are called to conversion; they are called to receive Wisdom and walk by her light. On the Easter Vigil night, the Church receives new members who have themselves accepted the call to conversion to the ways of Wisdom. In Baptism they came to the "fountain of wisdom" (verse 12), expressing their faith in God. The assembly has recently completed a Lenten season of penance, leading them to a deeper conversion to the Lord. Through the renewal of their baptismal promises, they will accept Wisdom once again, and be guided by her light as they continue toward a life of splendor in union with God, begun here on earth and completed in heaven.

READING VII At first glance, this passage from Ezekiel seems to characterize God as selfish. The Lord is going to act on behalf of the house of Israel because he is apparently concerned, not about Israel, but about his holy name. In their exile, the people of Israel spoke poorly of the Lord, leading others they met along the way to question the kind of Lord who claimed them as his people. The questioning is logical as is the very human response by the Israelites of profaning the Lord's name, for how can the Lord be respected and revered if he cannot care for his own people? It is similar to the response of children to parents who do not adequately watch over them or of a husband or wife who is rejected by their spouse.

Yet in the passage from Ezekiel, who prophesied during the first half of the Babylonian exile, it is really quite the opposite regarding the Lord's selfishness.

Beginning with the words "Learn where prudence is," shift your tone of voice from that of a herald crying out to that of an understanding teacher.

Proclaim the lines "the One who established the earth . . . stars at their post shine and rejoice"—which provide a synopsis of the creation story—with joy in your voice for the beauty of the Creator's work.

Pause before the words "Such is our God." State these words of affirmation with conviction and pride in your voice.

The words "Turn, O Jacob, and receive her . . ." call for the conversion of Israel—and ours as well—to Wisdom. Offer them in a serious, more reflective tone.

Learn where **prudence** is,
 where **strength**, where **understanding**;
that you may know **also**
 where are length of **days**, and **life**,
 where light of the **eyes**, and **peace**.
Who has found the place of **wisdom**,
 who has entered into her **treasuries**?

The One who knows **all** things knows **her**;
 he has **probed** her by his **knowledge**—
the One who established the earth for all **time**,
 and filled it with four-footed **beasts**;
 he who dismisses the **light**, and it **departs**,
 calls it, and it **obeys** him **trembling**;
before whom the **stars** at their posts
 shine and **rejoice**;
when he **calls** them, they answer, "**Here** we are!"
 shining with **joy** for their Maker.
Such is our **God**;
 no **other** is to be **compared** to him:
he has traced out the whole way of **understanding**,
 and has given her to **Jacob**, his **servant**,
 to **Israel**, his beloved **son**.

Since then she has appeared on **earth**,
 and moved among **people**.
She is the **book** of the precepts of **God**,
 the **law** that endures **forever**;
all who **cling** to her will **live**,
 but those will **die** who **forsake** her.
Turn, O Jacob, and **receive** her:
 walk by her **light** toward **splendor**.

Often seen as the climax of Ezekiel's theology, the reading is a straightforward affirmation of the divine initiative, of God seeking out his people, the side benefit of which is the glory of his name.

The house of Israel is not seeking to return to the Lord; rather, the Lord acts first. He will go among the nations gathering the people back; the Lord will sprinkle water on the people, cleansing them; the Lord will give the people a new heart and a new spirit; the Lord will bring them to the land of their fathers. In this reading, Ezekiel

speaks of nothing that the people can do to bring themselves back to the Lord, nor does he mention any commands the people should follow in order to be justified and put in right relationship with God. The spirit the Lord will put within them and make them live by his statutes (36:27).

After the house of Israel is cleansed, the new heart and new spirit the Lord gives them will help them to see their life from God's perspective. This new spirit is related to the spirit that enlivens the dry bones, which represent the whole house of Israel, to rise from their graves in the

next chapter of Ezekiel (37:1–14). The Lord will bring the exiles home to the land of their fathers, raising them up, but as the people of God, their new spirit means that they have the power to live as a people, not only as individuals. As a whole, they are united because they belong to God.

In Baptism, Christians respond to God's call to belong to his people; they are incorporated into Christ and formed into God's people (*Christian Initiation*, General Introduction, #1). Because God acts first in

Give not your **glory** to another,
your **privileges** to an alien **race**.
Blessed are we, O **Israel**;
for what pleases God is **known** to us!

A reading from the Book of the Prophet Ezekiel

The word of the LORD came to me, saying:
Son of **man**, when the house of **Israel** lived in their **land**,
they **defiled** it by their **conduct** and **deeds**.
Therefore I poured out my **fury** upon them
because of the **blood** that they poured out on the **ground**,
and because they **defiled** it with **idols**.
I **scattered** them among the **nations**,
dispersing them over foreign **lands**;
according to their **conduct** and **deeds** I **judged** them.
But when they **came** among the nations **wherever** they came,
they served to **profane** my holy **name**,
because it was said of them: "**These** are the people of the LORD,
yet they had to leave their **land**."
So I have **relented** because of my holy **name**
which the house of Israel **profaned**
among the nations where they **came**.
Therefore say to the house of **Israel**:
Thus says the Lord **GOD**:
Not for **your** sakes do I act, house of **Israel**,
but for the sake of my holy **name**,
which you **profaned** among the nations to which you came.

End the reading with the words "Blessed are we . . ." in a voice filled with gratitude: Israel and we know what pleases God.

Ezekiel = ee-ZEE-kee-ul

The reading changes in tone a number of times. In the section "Therefore I poured out my fury . . ." express the Lord's anger in your voice. Be careful not to over-dramatize.

In the second section, the focus shifts to the action of the people: profaning the name of the Lord. Deliver the words with disappointment in your voice. "These are the people of the Lord . . ." is an indictment of the sinfulness of the people.

Pause before the reading shifts again to the Lord's action beginning with the words "So I have relented." Express these words in a lower, gentler tone of voice. The Lord will still care for his people.

calling us to faith, there is nothing that we can do to earn our salvation. However, the new spirit that we receive by being part of God's people does mean that we have a responsibility to live not as isolated individuals, but as an entire people who belong to and worship God. Through the three sacraments of Christian initiation, we are brought closer to Christ and enabled to "carry out the mission of the entire people of God in the Church and in the world" (LG, #31; *Christian Initiation*, #2).

EPISTLE   The epistle for the Easter Vigil, from Paul's letter to the Romans, is the lengthiest discussion of baptism found in the Pauline letters. Proclaimed on a night when the Church keeps watch, awaiting Christ's Resurrection and celebrating it in the sacraments (GNLYC, #21), this reading connects Christ's death and Resurrection with the sacrament of Baptism.

In the context of Paul's letter to the Romans, this passage seems to respond to accusations of moral laxity against those

who follow the Gospel. Some say if justification comes through Christ, apart from the law, then why not persist in doing evil so that good might come of it (3:5–8)?

Paul's answer to the question of whether one can continue to sin, despite being saved by God through Christ, is twofold. First, through Baptism, Christians share in Christ's death. Our old self is crucified with him. For Paul this does not mean that our flesh or material self is done away with; rather, it means that although

Speak the Lord's promise ("I will prove the holiness of my great name . . .") with solemnity and dignity. Make eye contact with the assembly as much as possible in this section. The Lord's promise here extends to them today.

From "For I will take you away . . ." to the end of the reading, the passage details how the Lord will prove the holiness of his name. Address the words to the assembly. The words in this section climax with the final line: "you shall be my people, and I will be your God." Proclaim this reference to the Lord's covenant with Israel and with his Chosen People today, with sincerity and with the assurance that the Lord never forsakes his people.

I will prove the **holiness** of my great name,
    profaned among the **nations**,
  in whose midst you have **profaned** it.
Thus the nations shall **know** that I am the LORD,
    says the Lord GOD,
  when in their sight I **prove** my holiness through **you**.
For I will take you **away** from among the nations,
    gather you from all the foreign **lands**,
  and bring you **back** to your **own land**.
I will sprinkle clean **water** upon you
    to **cleanse** you from all your **impurities**,
  and from all your **idols** I will **cleanse** you.
I will give you a new **heart** and place a new **spirit** within you,
    taking from your **bodies** your **stony** hearts
  and giving you **natural** hearts.
I will put my **spirit** within you and make you live by my **statutes**,
    careful to observe my **decrees**.
You shall **live** in the land I gave your **fathers**;
  you shall be my **people**, and **I** will be your **God**.

---

our human tendency to sin will still be present, it will not predominate. The grace of God acting in us will prevail. Second, through Baptism Christians also share in Christ's Resurrection. By participating in Christ's resurrection, we are transformed and changed with Christ. While we will still commit sin, we will not be enslaved by it. Thus, we are "dead to sin" and alive for God in Christ Jesus.

Paul's use of the phrase "into Christ" *(eis Christon)* shows that baptism is not just about belief, but that Baptism is about

participation with Christ in his death and Resurrection. This passage might be from a baptismal sermon of Paul. If so, then the use of *eis Christon* might also point to immersion. Baptismal pools often had steps by which those who are to be baptized could descend into and ascend out of the pool. Today, many baptismal fonts are similar. The descending and ascending is an obvious symbol of dying and rising with Christ.

Proclaim this reading from Paul as the bold proclamation of Christ's triumph over death and sin that it is. Paul was a realist;

he was not exhorting those who follow Christ to sin boldly; rather, he knew that, in their attempts to live uprightly, they would sin again. Let your proclamation of Paul's letter give the assembly cause to rejoice as they hear of their intimate union with Christ in both his death and Resurrection.

GOSPEL We, along with the women in the Easter Vigil Gospel, have to respond "no" to the question "Were you there when they rolled the stone away?" posed in the traditional spiritual, *Were You*

Ask Paul's question directly to the members of the assembly by making eye contact with them.

Pause before the continuing with the words "For if we have grown into union with him." This section is more explanatory than the first, so try lowering the tone of your voice slightly as you deliver these words.

Pause again before the final section begins with the words "We know that Christ." Raise your voice again in confidence. Through Baptism, we are "living for God in Christ Jesus." This is our Easter faith. It is an enormous responsibility to be "living for God in Christ Jesus," but we know there can be no greater happiness. Let Easter joy fill your voice as you proclaim the words of this section.

EPISTLE   Romans 6:3–11

A reading from the Letter of Saint Paul to the Romans

Brothers and sisters:
Are you **unaware** that we who were **baptized** into Christ **Jesus**
    were **baptized** into his **death**?
We were indeed **buried** with him through baptism into **death**,
    so that, just as Christ was **raised** from the dead
    by the **glory** of the Father,
    we **too** might **live** in newness of **life**.

For if we have grown into **union** with him
        through a **death** like his,
    we shall also be **united** with him in the **resurrection**.
We know that our **old** self was **crucified** with him,
    so that our **sinful** body might be done **away** with,
    that we might no longer be in **slavery** to sin.
For a **dead** person has been **absolved** from sin.
If, then, we have **died** with Christ,
    we believe that we shall also **live** with him.
We know that **Christ**, raised from the **dead**, dies no **more**;
    death no longer has power over him.
As to his **death**, he died to sin **once** and for **all**;
    as to his **life**, he lives for **God**.
Consequently, you **too** must think of **yourselves**
        as being **dead** to sin
    and **living** for God in Christ **Jesus**.

There? The women in Mark's account of the empty tomb, the same ones who ministered to Jesus in Galilee and saw him die (15:40–41), at least two of whom were present for the burial in which the traditional anointing of the body was not performed (verse 47) decide to go to Jesus' tomb to perform the customary rituals.

Upon arriving at the tomb, the women find the stone already rolled away from the entrance—a good thing because they had not thought about how they would remove the stone prior to beginning their errand. Mark tells us that, upon entering the tomb,

the women saw a "young man" *(neaniskos)* clothed in white. In the Old Testament angels are depicted as looking like young men (Tobit 5:4–5; 2 Maccabees 3:26, 33). The book of Revelation contains references to heavenly beings wearing white robes (Revelation 7:9, 13–14).

Also significant is Mark's use of the Greek word *neaniskos* to portray the vision the women saw. Earlier, in 14:51–52, he uses the same word to describe the "young man" who ran away at the time of Jesus' arrest. Whether or not the same "young

man" is referred to in both passages, the contrast is powerful. The "young man" of Mark 14:51–21 abandons Jesus, and in tonight's passage from Mark he is the first to proclaim Jesus' Resurrection. His journey from skepticism and incredulity to faith is often our journey. On a night when we celebrate the "crowning truth of our faith," the Resurrection, our journey of faith and that of the catechumens who will soon be initiated into the faith reflects the "young man's" conversion (CCC, #638).

When all is said and done on this climactic night of the liturgical year—after

Salome = suh-LOH-mee

Convey the surprise (and perhaps fear) the women might have felt as they saw the stone had already been rolled back. From "When they looked up . . ." to the end of the Gospel, let a sense of excitement build in your voice.

With a sense of urgency and excitement, proclaim the lines "But go and tell his disciples and Peter . . ." directly to the members of the assembly, looking up and making eye contact. Through the words of the evangelist, you are calling them to spread their faith. The Easter message is not one we can keep to ourselves.

GOSPEL   Mark 16:1–7

A reading from the holy Gospel according to Mark

When the **sabbath** was **over**,
    Mary **Magdalene**, Mary, the mother of **James**, and **Salome**
    bought **spices** so that they might go and **anoint** him.
Very **early** when the sun had **risen**,
    on the **first** day of the **week**, they came to the **tomb**.
They were **saying** to one another,
    "Who will roll back the **stone** for us
    from the entrance to the **tomb**?"
When they looked **up**,
    they saw that the stone **had** been rolled back;
    it was very **large**.
On **entering** the tomb they saw a young **man**
    sitting on the **right** side, **clothed** in a white **robe**,
    and they were **utterly** amazed.
He said to them, "Do not be **amazed**!
You seek **Jesus** of **Nazareth**, the crucified.
He has been **raised**; he is not **here**.
Behold the **place** where they **laid** him.
But **go** and tell his **disciples** and **Peter**,
    'He is going **before** you to **Galilee**;
    there you will **see** him, as he **told** you.'"

lay ministers, clergy, and the assembly have had a chance to ponder their experiences of the Triduum—from all the intense preparations and hours of work involved in them—hopefully what will remain is the profound truth of the Resurrection. The Gospel passage from Mark leaves us with that truth tonight. Indeed, the oldest manuscripts of the Gospel according to Mark have it ending where this passage does. As in tonight's Gospel, they do not include verse 9, which tells us that the women were too afraid to go and tell the disciples

and Peter what they had experienced. Perhaps Mark intended to end his account with verse 8, in fulfillment of 14:28, because he assumed some knowledge of the appearances of the risen Christ. Alternatively, perhaps Mark ran into difficulty completing it.

Whatever the reason for the abruptness of the original ending to the Gospel, there is no need for an appearance story the night of the Easter Vigil. The proclamation that God has raised Jesus (passive, $\bar{e}gerth\bar{e}$) is enough. It is the answer to Jesus' plea from the cross (15:34). For those of us who professed Easter faith in

Baptism and now proclaim this faith each time we participate in the Eucharist, the message of Christ's Resurrection is the only response we need.

EASTER SUNDAY

Lectionary #42

READING I   Acts 10:34a, 37–43

Be clear in your announcement of this reading by not rushing through it. Hearing from the Acts of the Apostles will be a shift for the assembly; previously in the liturgical year they have heard the First Reading from the Old Testament.

A reading from the Acts of the Apostles

Peter proceeded to speak and said:
   "You **know** what has happened all over **Judea**,
   beginning in Galilee after the baptism
   that John **preached**,
   how God anointed **Jesus** of **Nazareth**
   with the Holy **Spirit** and **power**.
He went about doing **good**
   and **healing** all those **oppressed** by the **devil**,
   for God was with him.

Pause before the section beginning "We are witnesses." Note the shift in pronouns from "you" to "we." Understanding the assembly to be included in both pronouns will assist you as you deliver lines such as "We are witnesses."

We are **witnesses** of all that he **did**
   both in the country of the Jews and in Jerusalem.
They put him to **death** by hanging him on a **tree**.
This man God **raised** on the third **day** and granted
      that he be **visible**,
   not to **all** the people, but to **us**,
   the **witnesses** chosen by God in advance,
   who **ate** and **drank** with him after he rose from the **dead**.

Make eye contact with the assembly as you say, "He commissioned us." All people who have been witnesses to the Resurrection—then and now—are to go forth in mission, witnessing to the presence of the risen Lord in their lives. Proclaim with the enthusiasm of Easter faith.

He **commissioned** us to preach to the **people**
   and **testify** that he is the one appointed by God
   as **judge** of the **living** and the **dead**.
To him all the **prophets** bear **witness**,
   that **everyone** who **believes** in him
   will receive **forgiveness** of sins through his **name**."

READING I   The First Reading on Easter Sunday and throughout the Easter season is from the Acts of the Apostles. According to the Introduction to the Lectionary, this is the case because "the reading from the Apostle Paul concerns the living out of the paschal mystery in the Church" (#99). The Acts of the Apostles is the second in a two-volume work by the author known as Luke, who wrote around 85 AD. One of his main theological themes in both the Gospel and Acts is the extension of salvation to the Gentiles through the working of the Holy Spirit in those that were chosen by Jesus in his ministry—the apostles and witnesses. In particular, Peter and Paul play leading roles in carrying out the mission of Jesus to bring salvation to all.

The First Reading on Easter Sunday is taken from Peter's speech to the household of Cornelius. During his prayer one day, Cornelius, a God-fearing Gentile, had a vision of an angel who told him to call Peter to his household in Caesarea. Peter also had a vision in which a voice from heaven tells him that foods considered unclean in Jewish law are no longer to be thought of as such. Cornelius sends men to find Peter and bring him back. The entire scene ends with Peter's speech and the Baptism of Cornelius, and presumably also the relatives and friends who were present.

Peter's speech describes Jesus' ministry from its roots in the baptism that John preached through his commissioning of the apostles, testifying that he is "the one appointed by God" (10:42). His words reveal the importance of seeing the life, death, and Resurrection of Jesus as a unity.

At the conclusion of the speech, Peter mentions the reception of "forgiveness

Colossians = kuh-LOSH-unz

Look up at the assembly as you address them this Easter Sunday with "Brothers and sisters."

If you are able to do so with ease, memorize the last verse ("When Christ your life appears . . ."). Proclaim this verse with joy, as nothing on earth will be as great as life with Christ in glory!

READING II   Colossians 3:1–4

A reading from the Letter of Saint Paul to the Colossians

Brothers and sisters:
If then you were **raised** with **Christ**, seek what is **above**,
    where Christ is **seated** at the right hand of **God**.
Think of what is **above**, not of what is on **earth**.
For you have **died**, and your life is **hidden** with Christ in **God**.
When Christ your life **appears**,
    then you **too** will appear with him in **glory**.

Or:

READING II   1 Corinthians 5:6b–8

A reading from the first Letter of Saint Paul to the Corinthians

Brothers and sisters:
Do you not know that a little **yeast** leavens all the **dough**?
Clear **out** the **old** yeast,
    so that you may become a **fresh** batch of dough,
    inasmuch as you are **unleavened**.
For our paschal **lamb**, **Christ**, has been **sacrificed**.
Therefore, let us **celebrate** the feast,
    not with the **old** yeast, the yeast of **malice** and **wickedness**,
    but with the **unleavened** bread of **sincerity** and **truth**.

of sins through his name" (10:43). This is markedly different from what is known as the traditional Petrine kerygma, found in Peter's speech at Pentecost in Jerusalem, in which he calls everyone to "Repent and be baptized" (2:38). Whatever the reason for the omission of Peter's call to repentance, the fact that we as Christians experience the forgiveness of sins through our profession of faith serves as a culmination of our Lenten journey that began on Ash Wednesday.

READING II The author of Colossians could not be clearer about our Easter faith than he is in these three verses. Writing to a community of Christians in Colossae, the author (probably a disciple of Paul) aims to defend the foundational message of Christianity in the face of false teachers.

The false teachers employ "specious arguments" that can deceive (2:4) and espouse "an empty, seductive philosophy according to human tradition, according to the elemental powers of the world and not according to Christ" (2:8). The content of the false teaching suggests that it could be rooted in mystery religions, Gnosticism, or Jewish Christian syncretism. Many concepts of Gnosticism such as wisdom, knowledge, and the contrast between "what is above" and "what is on earth" are also found in the language of Colossians. Yet Colossians does not speak of emanations from God, a key Gnostic tenet. Lastly, the description of the opponents leads many to suggest they are Jewish Christian syncretists who have devised their own religion by picking and choosing elements of Judaism, Christianity, and the mystery religions.

GOSPEL John 20:1–9

A reading from the holy Gospel according to John

On the first day of the **week**,
  Mary of **Magdala** came to the **tomb** early in the **morning**,
  while it was still **dark**,
  and saw the **stone** removed from the **tomb**.
So she **ran** and went to Simon **Peter**
  and to the **other** disciple whom Jesus **loved**, and told them,
  "They have taken the **Lord** from the **tomb**,
  and we don't know where they **put** him."
So **Peter** and the **other** disciple went out and came to the **tomb**.
They **both** ran, but the **other** disciple ran **faster** than Peter
  and arrived at the tomb **first**;
  he bent **down** and saw the **burial** cloths there, but did
    not go in.
When Simon Peter arrived **after** him,
  he went **into** the tomb and saw the **burial** cloths there,
  and the cloth that had covered his **head**,
  not with the **burial** cloths but rolled **up** in a separate **place**.
Then the **other** disciple **also** went in,
  the one who had arrived at the tomb **first**,
  and he **saw** and **believed**.
For they did not yet **understand** the **Scripture**
  that he had to **rise** from the **dead**.

[The Gospel from the Easter Vigil (Mark 16:1–7, p. 152) may be read in place of this Gospel at any time of the day.]

The assembly knows what is coming in this Gospel, so place excitement in your voice from the beginning to draw them into the story of the Resurrection. Magdala = MAG-duh-la

Place in your voice some of Mary of Magdala's amazement, even shock, at finding the empty tomb as you tell of her running to tell Peter. Momentum is building in this reading. Quicken the pace of your proclamation a bit to reflect this; however, do not read so rapidly that it sounds like you are racing through the passage.

The Gospel only tells us that "the other disciple" "saw and believed." Be deliberate in your proclamation of this statement.

Regardless of the identity of the proponents of the false teaching, the argument the author of Colossians makes is that Christians must hold fast to the head of the body, the Church, who is Christ now "seated at the right hand of God" (3:1). In Christ, Christians were raised. Through him we are called to seek what is above. Our life on earth is meant to be a journey back to the Father, so that at the end of time, when Christ our life appears again in glory, we will appear with him (3:4).

Finally, for the author of Colossians, the Christian faith is not merely a belief in a particular message about Christ. The fact that an ethical section describing life in the body of Christ, the Church, follows upon these three summary verses of the faith shows that the Christian faith, the Easter faith, is to be seen in our relations with one another (3:5—4:5). We, as Christians, are to get rid of "anger, wrath, malice, slander, and abusive language" and put on "compassion, kindness, humility, meekness, and patience," and above all put on love, letting the peace of Christ rule in our

hearts (3:8, 12, 14–15). Proclaim this reading to lead the assembly to recommit to their Easter faith in both words and action.

GOSPEL **The proclamation of the Gospel on Easter Sunday morning is meant to exude joy. While assemblies are often filled with people who only attend church on Easter and Christmas, the proclamation of the Gospel ought to leave them wondering why Easter is so important in the life of Christians. The *General Norms for the Liturgical Year and***

Lectionary #46

AFTERNOON GOSPEL Luke 24:13—35

A reading from the holy Gospel according to Luke

That very day, the **first** day of the week,
  two of Jesus' disciples were going
  to a village seven miles from Jerusalem called **Emmaus**,
  and they were **conversing** about all the things
    that had **occurred**.
And it **happened** that while they were conversing and debating,
  Jesus **himself** drew near and **walked** with them,
  but their eyes were **prevented** from recognizing him.
He **asked** them,
  "What are you **discussing** as you walk along?"
They **stopped**, looking downcast.
One of them, named **Cleopas**, said to him in reply,
  "Are you the **only** visitor to Jerusalem
  who does not **know** of the **things**
  that have taken place there in these days?"
And he **replied** to them, "What **sort** of things?"
They said to him,
  "The **things** that happened to **Jesus** the **Nazarene**,
  who was a **prophet** mighty in **deed** and **word**
  before **God** and **all** the people,
  how our chief **priests** and **rulers both** handed him over
  to a sentence of **death** and **crucified** him.
But we were **hoping** that **he** would be the **one** to **redeem** Israel;
  and **besides** all this,
  it is **now** the **third day** since **this** took place.

Narrate the beginning of the Gospel ("That very day . . .") in a natural tone of voice because it simply recounts ordinary activities of daily life: walking and conversing.
 Emmaus = eh-MAY-uhs

Because the disciples do not recognize Jesus when he joins them, continue in with the same natural tone.

Cleopas = KLOH-pus
Emphasize the phrase "only visitor to Jerusalem." There might be someone in your assembly who also is not familiar with what has transpired.

Offer the summary ("The things about Jesus the Nazarene . . .") as if sharing important news.

Nazarene = naz-uh-REEN

the Calendar convey the sense of the significance of Easter this way: because Christ redeemed us through his death and Resurrection, the Easter Triduum is the culmination of the liturgical year and "the solemnity of Easter has the same kind of preeminence in the liturgical year that Sunday has in the week" (#18).

While all four Gospels have women visiting Jesus' tomb and finding it empty, the details in each narrative differ (Mark 16:1–8; Matthew 28:1–10; Luke 24:1–11). In all the accounts, the women's visit to the tomb occurs at dawn on the day after

the Sabbath. In John's narrative, Mary of Magdala appears to approach the tomb by herself (verse 1), but then the plural "we" is found in verse 2 when she ran to Peter and told them the Lord was taken from the tomb, implying others went with her.

Also, whereas the synoptics provide a lengthy description of the episode involving the women, John spends more time describing Peter and the beloved disciple—the one who was at Jesus' side at the Last Supper (13:23) and who was present at the cross (19:26–27)—at the empty tomb than he does the experience of Mary and the

women who might have been with her. In the verses read today from John, it is neither Mary of Magdala nor Peter who express belief in Jesus because of what has transpired. Rather, the "other disciple," who never left Jesus' side, came to the tomb, went in, saw it empty, and believed.

By emphasizing the faith of the other disciple, the proclamation of the Gospel can lead those in the assembly to ask whether they have experienced the Resurrection of Jesus. Can they see places in their lives where suffering has been turned into joy, where they have found empty tombs? On

Some **women** from our group, however, have **astounded** us:
  they were at the tomb **early** in the **morning**
  and did **not** find his **body**;
  they came **back** and reported
  that they had **indeed** seen a vision of **angels**
  who **announced** that he was **alive**.
Then some of those **with** us went to the tomb
  and found things **just** as the women had **described**,
  but **him** they did not **see**."
And he said to them, "Oh, how **foolish** you are!
How **slow** of **heart** to **believe** all that the prophets **spoke**!
Was it not **necessary** that the Christ should suffer **these things**
  and **enter** into his glory?"
Then beginning with **Moses** and all the **prophets**,
  he **interpreted** to them what referred to him
  in **all** the **Scriptures**.
As they **approached** the village to which they were **going**,
  he gave the impression that he was going on **farther**.
But they **urged** him, "**Stay** with us,
  for it is nearly **evening** and the day is almost **over**."
So he went in to **stay** with them.
And it **happened** that, while he was with them at **table**,
  he **took bread**, said the **blessing**,
  broke it, and **gave** it to them.
With **that** their **eyes** were **opened** and they **recognized** him,
  but he **vanished** from their **sight**.

Express Jesus' statement ("Oh, how foolish you are . . .") with some frustration.

Pause before beginning the table scene. This is the most significant part of the narrative; the connections with the eucharistic liturgy are obvious. Fill your voice with reverence as you communicate the words "while he was with them at table." Let excitement be in your voice as you tell of the disciples' recognition of the risen Christ in the breaking of the bread.

this solemnity that celebrates the central truth of our faith, we renew our baptismal commitment once again through either the creed or the renewal of our baptismal promises. Having gone down into the tomb with Jesus, we are invited to come out with him, in the joy of his Resurrection.

AFTERNOON GOSPEL This Gospel comes near the end of the Gospel according to Luke and is a beautiful narrative of a post-Resurrection appearance of Jesus to two

of his disciples. It is a story that contains elements that are characteristic of the Gospel according to Luke as a whole: journey, seeing, and hospitality. These uniquely Lucan elements color the interpretation of Jesus' breaking of bread with the disciples enlightening our understanding of the Eucharist today.

Today's Gospel begins with the disciples journeying to a village called Emmaus. While they were conversing with each other in the midst of their journey, they encounter a stranger. The disciples do not

recognize the person, but Luke tells his readers that the stranger is Jesus.

The theme of "seeing" or "sight" is evident from the beginning of this passage. It occurs again when we hear of the women's experience of a "vision of angels" at the tomb, others not seeing Jesus at the tomb, the eyes of the disciples being opened as Jesus broke bread with them, and the disciples' statement that the scriptures were opened to them on the road to Emmaus. Sometimes, like the disciples, we look to literally "see things," to find an

Then they said to each other,
> "**Were** not our **hearts burning** within us
> while he **spoke** to us on the way and **opened** the **Scriptures**
> to us?"

So they set out at **once** and **returned** to Jerusalem
> where they found gathered together
> the eleven and those **with them** who were saying,
> "The **Lord** has **truly** been **raised** and has **appeared** to **Simon**!"

Then the two **recounted**
> what had taken place on the **way**
> and how he was made **known** to them in the **breaking** of **bread**.

Pause before the concluding verse ("Then the two recounted . . ."). By having the two disciples tell others about their experience, the evangelist Luke teaches us that belief in the risen Christ is to be shared.

obvious sign of God's presence. The disciples probably did not recognize the stranger because they were looking for someone identical to Jesus. They were called through faith to look beyond physical appearances and to see where God is making our hearts burn within us (verse 32).

That Luke has the eyes of the disciples open after they ask the stranger to stay with them demonstrates the importance of hospitality in connection to belief. From Jesus' quotation of Isaiah in the synagogue (4:16–30) to the giving of the Beatitudes (6:20–23), Luke reveals the relationship between an ethic of hospitality and Jesus' life and ministry. This carries over to the lives of those who follow Jesus, as shown in today's Gospel. After the experience of the two disciples, they returned to Jerusalem and told the other disciples that the risen Lord had appeared to them.

In speaking about the liturgical celebration of the Eucharist, in which we partake of the one table of both the word of God and the body of the Lord, the Catechism references today's Gospel: "Is this not the same movement as the Paschal meal of the risen Jesus with his disciples? Walking with them he explained the Scriptures to them; sitting with them at table 'took bread, blessed and broke it, and gave it to them' " (#1347). Like the disciples, our eyes are opened in the sharing of the word and the breaking of the bread each Sunday. They are opened not because of what anyone else says, but because of the risen Lord's presence with us.

2ND SUNDAY OF EASTER DIVINE MERCY SUNDAY

Lectionary #44

READING I   Acts 4:32–35

A reading from the Acts of the Apostles

The **community** of **believers** was of one **heart** and **mind**,
    and **no** one claimed that any of his **possessions** was his **own**,
    but they had everything in **common**.
With great **power** the apostles bore **witness**
    to the **resurrection** of the Lord **Jesus**,
    and great **favor** was accorded them **all**.
There was no **needy** person among them,
    for those who owned **property** or **houses** would **sell** them,
    bring the **proceeds** of the sale,
    and put them at the feet of the **apostles**,
    and they were distributed to **each** according to **need**.

Emphasize the phrase "With great power."
It attests to the fact that the power of
the Resurrection of Jesus lived on in the
lives of the apostles as it lives on in the
members of the Church today.

The assembly might be surprised to hear
the last section, which begins with the
words "There was no needy person."
Deliver these words in a measured way
so that the assembly is able to think
about the connection between witnessing
to the Resurrection of Jesus Christ and
ensuring people's material needs are met.

READING I   During the Easter season, the First Reading, taken each year from the Acts of the Apostles, presents "the life, growth, and witness of the early Church" (Introduction to the Lectionary, #14). It is essential to recall that at the time Luke wrote Acts (c. 85), the second volume in his two-volume work (the Gospel being the first), there was no clear distinction between Judaism and Christianity. Thus, as Acts recounts the spread of the Gospel in Jerusalem, we often find Peter speaking in the Temple area or the Temple itself.

Today's passage is one of three summary statements in Acts that offer a description of life in the Jerusalem community (2:42–47; 4:32–35; 5:12–16). The first statement (2:42–47), which appears after Peter's speech in the Temple at Pentecost, emphasizes the importance of the teaching of the apostles, the communal life, the breaking of bread, and the prayers in the life of the community. The summary concludes that these actions led to the people praising God and celebrating, as

well as more people becoming a part of the community.

The second summary statement (4:32–35) that you will proclaim includes a similar reference to the distribution of goods and sharing of material possessions in the community. Goods and possessions were shared so that everything was held in common and no one was in need. From the beginning, this brotherly and sisterly concern for all of the faith community characterized believers. This reading from Acts, like the first summary statement, also points to the witness and power of the

Practice the first sentence ("Everyone who believes . . .") aloud before proclaiming it during the liturgy. This is a beautiful statement of the relationship with God in Jesus upon which our faith is based. You don't want to get tongue-tied with the repetition of the words "begotten" and "loves." Fill your voice with warmth and affection when you read these lines.

Build momentum and strength to the central point: "And the victory that conquers the world is our faith."

Proclaim the line "The Spirit is the one that testifies . . ." with certainty, making eye contact with the assembly.

READING II   1 John 5:1–6

A reading from the first Letter of Saint John

Beloved:

Everyone who **believes** that Jesus is the **Christ** is begotten
    by **God**,
  and everyone who loves the **Father**
    loves **also** the one **begotten** by him.
In this way we **know** that we love the **children** of God
    when we love **God** and obey his **commandments**.
For the love of God is **this**,
    that we **keep** his commandments.
And his commandments are not **burdensome**,
    for whoever is begotten by God **conquers** the world.
And the **victory** that conquers the world is our **faith**.
Who **indeed** is the **victor** over the world
    but the one who **believes** that Jesus is the Son of **God**?

This is the one who came through **water** and **blood**, Jesus **Christ**,
    not by water **alone**, but by **water** and **blood**.
The **Spirit** is the one that **testifies**,
    and the **Spirit** is **truth**.

---

apostles as characteristic of the early community of faith.

Lastly, the third summary statement (5:12–16) does not mention the distribution of goods in the community. Instead, its focus is on the signs and wonders done by the apostles. These signs, particularly the cure of the sick and the exorcism of unclean spirits, testify to the power of God working in the apostles.

Many of the tenets of our Catholic Church are based in the life of early church communities such as the ones at Jerusalem.

The roots of the Church's social doctrine and teaching on apostolic succession both stem from Acts. Your proclamation of this brief reading will help the assembly see the continuous presence of the risen one from the early Church through to the present.

READING II   In 2000, Pope John Paul II decreed that the Second Sunday of Easter should be known as "Divine Mercy Sunday." On this Sunday of the Easter season, the Church reflects on

the mystery of love that is at the heart of its faith and liturgy.

The first letter of John is an exhortation to Johannine Christians cautioning them not to follow the dissidents in their community. These dissidents claim to know who Jesus is, but they think that their knowledge of him is all that matters; ethical behavior, such as obeying the commandment of love, is not necessary. Following the progression of the reading, then, four main points become evident. First, Christian belief in Jesus implies that one is begotten by God. It places one in a relationship that

GOSPEL John 20:19–31

A reading from the holy Gospel according to John

On the **evening** of that **first** day of the **week**,
　　when the **doors** were locked, where the **disciples** were,
　　for fear of the **Jews**,
　　Jesus came and stood in their **midst**
　　and said to them, "**Peace** be with you."
When he had **said** this, he showed them his **hands** and his **side**.
The disciples **rejoiced** when they saw the Lord.
Jesus said to them **again**, "**Peace** be with you.
As the Father has sent **me**, so I send **you**."
And when he had said this, he **breathed** on them and said to them,
　　"**Receive** the Holy **Spirit**.
Whose **sins** you forgive are **forgiven** them,
　　and whose sins you **retain** are **retained**."

Thomas, called **Didymus**, one of the **Twelve**,
　　was not **with** them when Jesus came.
So the **other** disciples said to him, "We have **seen** the Lord."
But he said to them,
　　"Unless I see the mark of the **nails** in his **hands**
　　and put my **finger** into the **nailmarks**
　　and put my **hand** into his **side**, I will **not** believe."

Now a week **later** his disciples were **again** inside
　　and Thomas **was** with them.
Jesus came, although the **doors** were **locked**,
　　and **stood** in their **midst** and said, "**Peace** be with you."

Read the opening lines ("On the evening of that first day . . .") slowly to emphasize that what follows is an account of a post-Resurrection appearance of Jesus.

Jesus' words ("Peace be with you") are repeated three times in this Gospel. You might choose to deliver them in a slightly different manner each time. However you choose to deliver them, let warmth and affection be heard in your tone of voice. "Peace be with you" is not a simple friendly handshake greeting as we sometimes think when we share peace during the liturgy. It is a profound greeting. See the commentary below for a further explanation.

Pause before the Gospel shifts to the narrative about Thomas. Convey again the disciples' excitement about having seen the Lord evident in the words "We have seen the Lord." Express Thomas' skepticism with doubt in your voice.

Pause again as the Gospel moves ahead in time at the beginning of the next section ("Now a week later . . .").

is like a parent to a child. In a small way, our relationship with God mirrors the relationship of Jesus with the Father.

Second, love of God is connected to love of the children of God. Christians cannot simply say Jesus is the Son of God without reflecting the love the Father has for the Son, and that both have for them.

Third, the recognition that Christians are from God as the Son is, gives them a share in the victory that the Son won through his death and Resurrection. This

victory was the ultimate triumph of God's love over the power of evil in the world.

Fourth and finally, the victory of the Son of God came through both water and blood, through the Spirit present at Jesus' Baptism and through the cross that led to Christ's Resurrection and Ascension.

The spirit of the risen one is present today in the gifts of the sacraments of Baptism and Eucharist celebrated in the Church. Through these sacraments and the lives of those who follow God's commandment to love, the Spirit continues to work. This is evidence that the love of the risen

Christ continues to triumph over the powers of evil at work in humanity.

GOSPEL | In today's Gospel, John draws on the story of Jesus' post-Resurrection appearance to the disciples found in the Gospel according to Luke (24:36–49), but he adapts his source. There are three primary examples of this. First, the addition of the phrase "for fear of the Jews" continues the tension evident between Jesus and the Jewish leaders.

Jesus' action shows his willingness to lead Thomas to faith. Offer the words "Put your finger here and see my hands . . ." as an invitation.

Proclaim Thomas' response with exuberance. Do not shout the response into the microphone, but express it with genuine excitement as one whose relationship with a loved one has been rekindled at a deeper level.

Pause before the summary verses ("Now Jesus did many other signs . . ."). Emphasize the reason that bringing others to *believe* is the reason the evangelist John wrote them down.

Then he said to **Thomas**,
   "Put your finger **here** and **see** my hands,
   and bring your **hand** and put it into my **side**,
   and do not be **unbelieving**, but **believe**."
Thomas **answered** and said to him, "My **Lord** and my **God**!"
Jesus said to him, "Have you come to believe because you have
    seen me?
Blessed are those who have not seen and have **believed**."

Now Jesus did many **other** signs in the presence of his disciples
   that are **not** written in this **book**.
But these are written that you may come to **believe**
   that Jesus is the **Christ**, the Son of **God**,
    and that **through** this belief you may have **life** in his **name**.

Second, the repetition of Jesus' greeting signifies his gift of salvation given to all who are his disciples. Jesus' offer of peace to his disciples is more than calm and stillness. It includes all that the Hebrew term *shalom* does: communion with God, one's neighbor, and the earth. The peace that brings harmony and communion is found in the crucified and exalted one. We extend this peace to one another at the Rite of Peace. The sign of peace is the acknowledgment that our oneness as a Christian community is in the Lord.

Third, there is the separation of the story about Thomas and Jesus' second post-Resurrection appearance to his disciples from the first appearance of Jesus to the disciples. John's editing provides him the opportunity to use Thomas' words ("My Lord and my God") as a profound Christological confession with which to end the Gospel. In addition, John is able to make the point that even those who have not seen the risen one, and yet believe in him, are blessed—those gathered in the assembly.

The passage ends with a conclusion that understands Jesus' Resurrection as the last sign and summarizes the purpose of John's work—bringing people to believe in Jesus Christ as the Son of God so that they might live forever in union with him. Interestingly, there is another chapter to John, an epilogue, attributed to an editor who recounts the tradition of post-Resurrection appearances that have Peter as the primary witness, perhaps because of his central role early in the spread of the Gospel message.

3RD SUNDAY OF EASTER

Lectionary #47

READING I   Acts 3:13–15, 17–19

A reading from the Acts of the Apostles

Peter said to the **people**:
"The God of **Abraham**,
    the God of **Isaac**, and the God of **Jacob**,
    the God of our fathers, has **glorified** his servant **Jesus**,
    whom **you** handed over and **denied** in Pilate's **presence**
    when he had decided to **release** him.
You **denied** the Holy and **Righteous** One
    and asked that a **murderer** be released to you.
The author of **life** you put to **death**,
    but God **raised** him from the dead; of this we are **witnesses**.
Now I **know**, brothers,
    that you acted out of **ignorance**, just as your **leaders** did;
    but God has thus brought to **fulfillment**
    what he had announced **beforehand**
    through the mouth of all the **prophets**,
    that his **Christ** would **suffer**.
Repent, therefore, and be **converted**,
    that your **sins** may be wiped **away**."

Abraham = AY-bruh-ham

Isaac = Ī-zik

Jacob = JAY-kub

Pilate = PĪ-lut

Peter is offering the Easter message to a crowd of Jews. You do not want to be too accusatory in your tone as you put across his words ("You denied the Holy and Righteous One"). See the commentary for more explanation to assist your understanding of this part of the passage.

Although the assembly might be surprised to hear the call to repentance ("Repent, therefore . . .") in the Easter season, offer it as an invitation to continue to live in the new life of the Resurrection, rather than as the robust command it appears as in Advent.

READING I   The proclamation of the Acts of the Apostles during the Easter season is in accordance with an ancient tradition mentioned by Saint John Chrysostom (*Sermon IV on the Acts of the Apostles*, #5) and Saint Augustine in their writings (*Sermon*, #315). That we read from Acts, a book that narrates the story of the development of early Christianity, during the Easter season when we celebrate the Resurrection of Christ and his ongoing presence in believers, shows the centrality of the Paschal Mystery—Christ's suffering, death, and Resurrection—in the Christian faith. Without Christ having been raised from the dead, as Paul says, "faith is in vain" and sins remain (1 Corinthians 15:17).

Peter gives his speech, from which today's reading comes, after curing a crippled beggar who often sat outside the temple (13:12). Those present in the Temple seemed to assume that Peter and John, who was with him, healed the beggar through their own power. Peter, however, questions them and then proceeds with his speech aimed at testifying to the power of God at work in their midst.

Just as those present in the Temple failed to see that it was the power of God, not of Peter and John, that cured the beggar, so Peter goes on to point out how they were ignorant of the true identity of Holy and Righteous One. Along with their leaders, they failed to recognize that Jesus was the Messiah. Perhaps their ignorance stemmed from the fact that they did not expect a Messiah who was going to suffer and die. No matter the reason for their failure to recognize Christ, Peter speech calls them to conversion now (see Acts 2:38).

Address the endearing greeting ("My children") to the community before you in a caring tone of voice.

Pause before the second half of the reading starts ("The way we may be sure . . ."). Convey this section of the reading with certainty, making sure your voice does not waver.

The last verse ("But whoever keeps his word . . .") is more hopeful than the preceding verse. Express it in a lighter tone of voice that contrasts with the weightiness of the previous verse.

READING II 1 John 2:1–5a

A reading from the first Letter of Saint John

My **children**, I am **writing** this to you
    so that you may not commit **sin**.
But if anyone **does** sin, we have an **Advocate** with the Father,
    Jesus **Christ** the **righteous** one.
He is **expiation** for our **sins**,
    and not for **our** sins **only** but for those of the whole **world**.
The way we may be **sure** that we **know** him
    is to keep his **commandments**.
Those who say, "I **know** him," but do **not** keep
    his commandments
    are **liars**, and the **truth** is not **in** them.
But whoever **keeps** his word,
    the love of God is truly **perfected** in him.

In your presentation of Peter's words, you have the opportunity to bring others to faith. There are often visitors in the assembly who have not yet heard the message of Christianity, or perhaps have heard and have not yet believed. Offer Peter's kerygma to them and to the many that are Christians, but need to be reminded of their need to repent and be converted.

READING II There are a brief five chapters in the first letter of John, which is read semi-continuously during the Easter season. Some typically Johannine themes are found throughout the letter. In particular, chapter 1 of the first letter emphasizes the image of God as light. Then, chapter 2, the chapter from which today's reading is a part, carries the theme of light forward in its reference to Christ as the "true light" (verse 8).

For the author of 1 John, though, Christian belief in the true light is not sufficient. Rather, this belief must always be connected to ethical behavior, following God's commandment of love. To not follow this commandment is to commit sin, but to follow it is to be sure that we know him (2:3). In theological language, this means orthodoxy—"right belief"—and orthopraxis—"right living" go hand in hand. When the two are consistent in the life of a Christian, the result is perfect in through life in union with God (2:5).

Yet the reading for today is realistic. Despite the Christians desire not to sin, as humans, we sometimes fall short. But not to worry, for we have an Advocate, a Paraclete who intercedes on our behalf (see also John 14:16—17:26; 15:26; 16:7b–11, 13–15). In this reading, the Paraclete

And he said to them,
      "Thus it is **written** that the Christ would **suffer**
      and rise from the **dead** on the third day
      and that **repentance**, for the forgiveness of **sins**,
      would be **preached** in his name
      to all the **nations**, beginning from **Jerusalem**.
You are **witnesses** of these things."

Pause before the last line ("You are witnesses of these things"). Jesus was stating this to the disciples present. Your task is to state it to the members of the assembly. Do so by making eye contact with them. Practice emphasizing both "You" and "witnesses."

recounting what they had experienced on the road to Emmaus to the others. In the midst of their conversation, Jesus appears, offering peace. (For the similarities and differences between Luke's version of this appearance of Jesus and John's, see last Sunday's commentary.) Certainly, it is a normal human reaction to be started and terrified, as the disciples were, thinking that they saw a ghost. While Jesus lets them physically touch him, the Gospel does not tell us that the disciples recognized him until after he shares a meal with them

and speaks the words that help them understand the scriptures.

Through Jesus' words at the end of this Gospel, we learn the answer to the question that started this commentary. Christ's death and Resurrection, now present to us in the Eucharist, brought about the forgiveness of sins. In this, he fulfilled everything in the law of Moses, the prophets, and the psalms. The Church has long seen the forgiveness of sins as a fruit of receiving communion. While the "principal fruit" of receiving the Eucharist is a close union with Christ, this relationship with

Christ cannot be achieved without our sins being forgiven (CCC, #1391–1395). As Jesus' final words in today's Gospel sent the disciples forth in mission, so the Church's celebration of the Eucharist is also a sending forth of all who share in the body and blood of Christ. John Paul II acknowledged this: "Communion gives rise to mission, and mission is accomplished in communion" (*Christifidelis laici*, #32).

4TH SUNDAY OF EASTER

Lectionary #50

READING I   Acts: 4:8–12

Pause slightly after the announcement of the reading.

Look up as you begin Peter's speech ("Leaders of the people and elders . . .").

A reading from the Acts of the Apostles

Peter, filled with the Holy **Spirit**, said:
   "Leaders of the **people** and **elders**:
   If we are being **examined** today
   about a good **deed** done to a **cripple**,
   namely, by what **means** he was saved,
   then **all** of you and **all** the people of Israel should know
   that it was in the name of Jesus **Christ** the **Nazorean**
   whom you **crucified**, whom God **raised** from the **dead**;
   in **his** name this man stands before you **healed**.
He is *the stone **rejected** by you, the **builders**,*
   *which has become the **cornerstone**.*
There is **no** salvation through **anyone** else,
   nor is there **any** other name under heaven
   given to the human **race** by which we are to be **saved**."

Pause before and after the words from Psalm 118:22.

Proclaim the final verse ("There is no salvation . . .") with strength, power, and conviction in your tone of voice, as this verse makes clear the main theological point of the reading.

READING I This passage is part of Peter's speech before the Sanhedrin in defense of himself and his teaching. The speech was occasioned by the arrest of Peter and John by those who were upset at their teaching about the Resurrection of the dead occurring in Jesus (Acts 4:1–3). The speech begins with Peter's response to the question posed by the authorities, asking by what power they cured the crippled man who daily sat outside the Temple gate (3:1–10; 4:7). Peter's response comes in the form of a *kerygma*—a proclamation of faith that contains the primary elements of early Christian belief: proclamation in 1) Jesus Christ the Nazorean; 2) who was crucified; and 3) who was raised from the dead.

Peter gives his proclamation of faith before the authorities forthrightly, stating directly that salvation and healing *only* come through Jesus Christ (4:12). These words indicate that there is a sense of exclusivity to the salvation offered by Jesus Christ. This salvation cannot be found through other religions, other gods, or political powers. Both these strands—of exclusivity about salvation, as well as the belief that salvation is universally available to all—are found in the Catholic tradition; however, the fullness of salvation comes only through Jesus Christ (NA, #2).

READING II Throughout the entire Easter season the Second Reading proclaimed is from the first letter of John, a brief letter that exhorts Christians both to believe in Jesus Christ and to live among each other in love, thereby mirroring the love the Father gave us through Jesus.

Proclaim the words "See what love the Father has bestowed" in a blissful and content tone of voice.

Pause noticeably before the words "Beloved, we are God's children now" and proclaim them with optimism and confidence in your voice, as they speak of the present reality of God's love for us.

READING II   1 John 3:1–2

A reading from the first Letter of Saint John

Beloved:
See what **love** the Father has **bestowed** on us
    that we may be called the **children** of God.
Yet so we **are**.
The reason the **world** does not **know** us
    is that it did not know **him**.
Beloved, we **are** God's children **now**;
    what we **shall** be has not yet been **revealed**.
We **do** know that when it is revealed we shall be **like** him,
    for we shall **see** him as he **is**.

State the words "I am the good shepherd" directly to the assembly by looking up and making eye contact with them.

GOSPEL   John 10:11–18

A reading from the holy Gospel according to John

Jesus said:
    "I **am** the good shepherd.
A **good** shepherd lays down his **life** for the **sheep**.
A **hired** man, who is **not** a shepherd
    and whose sheep are not his **own**,
    sees a **wolf** coming and **leaves** the sheep and runs **away**,
    and the wolf **catches** and **scatters** them.
This is because he works for **pay** and has no **concern**
    for the sheep.

Today's reading focuses on the metaphor "children of God," used for the Christian community. In Baptism, the new Christian is designated a child of God and joins the community that includes all the sons and daughters of God. The metaphor "children of God" attests to the reality and intimacy of God's love for the members of this community.

As God's children, we know something of what God is like because of God's gift of his Son, Jesus. The Father loved us so much that he sent his Son so that we might know we are God's children *now.*

Yet, John tells us, in the future we do not know what we will be. All we know is that we will be like God. We will be able to see God's true identity and ours.

GOSPEL   The Fourth Sunday of Easter is often referred to as "Good Shepherd Sunday" because in each year in the three-year cycle of readings, a portion of John 10, Jesus' discourse on the good shepherd is proclaimed (John 10:1–10 in Year A, John 10:11–18 in Year B; and John 10:27–30 in Year C).

The good shepherd metaphor has its roots in the Old Testament (Genesis 49:24; Psalm 23). In particular, the book of the prophet Ezekiel contains passages that refer to corrupt leaders of Israel as bad shepherds and the Lord as the one who compassionately gathers his sheep, rescuing them from darkness and bringing them back to their homeland (Ezekiel 34:1–16).

While the Old Testament provides one context for understanding this Gospel passage, the healing of the man born blind, which immediately precedes the Good Shepherd discourse offers another (John

On the repetition of the words "I am the good shepherd," look up at the assembly and offer them in a reassuring tone of voice.

Strengthen your tone of voice slightly as you proclaim the concluding section of the Gospel that describes the power and authority Jesus has from the Father in the words "This is why the Father loves me."

I am the **good** shepherd,
    and I know **mine** and mine know **me**,
    just as the **Father** knows **me** and I know the **Father**;
    and I will lay down my **life** for the sheep.
I have **other** sheep that do **not** belong to this fold.
These **also** I must lead, and they will hear my **voice**,
    and there will be **one** flock, **one** shepherd.
This is why the Father **loves** me,
    because I lay down my **life** in order to take it **up** again.
No one **takes** it from me, but I lay it down on my **own**.
I have **power** to lay it **down**, and **power** to take it **up** again.
This **command** I have received from my **Father**."

9:1–41). This Gospel narrative was proclaimed on the Fourth Sunday of Lent, if your parish had any elect. In the narrative, a growing tension between the Pharisees and Jesus is obvious. Jesus' strong words to them at the end of the passage point out that their sin remains because of their arrogance (9:41).

In the brief parable included in today's Gospel, the hired man may reflect the Pharisees, as Jesus the Good Shepherd is seen in contrast to the sinful religious leaders who do not take care of their and fail to "see." While the hired man runs away from his sheep in the face of the danger posed by the wolf, Jesus remains close to his flock, even seeking out those that do not yet belong to his sheepfold—the Gentiles in Jesus' time (John 11:52) and those yet to be evangelized in our time.

Against those at the time of the writing of the Gospel (c. 100) who did not believe Jesus was truly human and lacked free will (the Docetists), John portrays a Jesus who, of his own accord, has the power to lay down and take up his own life, sacrificing his life for the unity of his flock.

We who receive Jesus in the Eucharist acknowledge the extent to which our Good Shepherd is willing to care for his flock. The Eucharist, then, is a sign of Jesus' abiding presence in the Church. Unlike the hired man who deserted his sheep, Jesus never abandons his sheep; through the Eucharist he is always present to those who hear his voice and receive him.

5TH SUNDAY OF EASTER

Lectionary #53

READING I   Acts 9:26–31

A reading from the Acts of the Apostles

When **Saul** arrived in **Jerusalem** he tried to **join** the disciples,
> but they were all **afraid** of him,
> not **believing** that he was a disciple.
Then **Barnabas** took charge of him and **brought** him
> to the apostles,
> and he **reported** to them how he had seen the **Lord**,
> and that he had **spoken** to him,
> and how in **Damascus** he had spoken out **boldly** in the name
> of **Jesus**.
He moved about freely with them in **Jerusalem**,
> and **spoke** out boldly in the name of the **Lord**.
He also spoke and debated with the **Hellenists**,
> but **they** tried to **kill** him.
And when the brothers **learned** of this,
> they took him down to **Caesarea**
> and sent him on his way to **Tarsus**.
The **church** throughout all Judea, Galilee, and Samaria was
> at **peace**.
It was being built **up** and walked in the fear of the **Lord**,
> and with the **consolation** of the Holy **Spirit** it grew in **numbers**.

Place some fear in your voice as you narrate the line "When Saul arrived in Jerusalem . . . ."

Barnabas = BAR-nuh-bus

Change the tone of your voice from fear to confidence, reflecting control, as you deliver the line "Then Barnabas took charge of him . . . ."

Damascus = duh-MAS-kus

Caesarea = see-zuh-REE-uh

Tarsus = TAR-sus

Pause before the words "The church throughout all Judea" to mark a transition in the reading. Convey these words in a lighter tone of voice, one that carries a sense of satisfaction for the growth of the Church and its peaceful state.

READING I   Today's passage begins with Saul meeting the other disciples in Jerusalem after his conversion. However, these disciples did not believe that Saul was actually a true disciple; perhaps they knew of his previous plots against followers of the Lord. Yet Barnabas, a leader in the Church of Jerusalem, defended Saul's integrity, noting how he had personally encountered Jesus and went on to proclaim his name.

In his lengthy defense, Barnabas also mentions that Saul experienced some difficulties with the Hellenists. In today's reading, "Hellenists" most likely refers to Greek-speaking Jews who were strictly loyal to the Mosaic law. Saul, a proponent of allowing Gentiles to be baptized and become Christian without observing Jewish laws such as those regarding circumcision, and dietary and ritual purity, would face much opposition from the Jewish traditionalists. Disagreements about the application of the Jewish law to converts would lead to the Council of Jerusalem (Acts 15:1–29; Galatians 2:1–10).

The conclusion of today's reading describes a Church that continued to grow and at the same time, despite the tension surrounding the issue of what was required of Gentile converts, was at peace. This early Church was centered on the testimony of its leaders in which they boldly proclaimed the Lord's name. While parishes and local churches are themselves not without tension today, still their mission is to proclaim courageously and with conviction the name of the risen one to a world, many of whose citizens are today's "Gentiles" and have not heard the Easter kerygma.

READING II   1 John 3:18–24

A reading from the first Letter of Saint John

Children, let us love not in **word** or **speech**
    but in **deed** and **truth**.
Now this is how we shall **know** that we belong to the **truth**
    and reassure our **hearts** before him
    in whatever our hearts **condemn**,
    for God is **greater** than our hearts and knows **everything**.
Beloved, if our hearts do not **condemn** us,
    we have **confidence** in God
    and **receive** from him **whatever** we ask,
    because we **keep his** commandments and **do** what pleases him.
And his commandment is **this**:
    we should **believe** in the name of his Son, Jesus **Christ**,
    and **love** one another just as he **commanded** us.
Those who **keep** his commandments remain in **him**, and **he**
      in **them**,
    and the way we **know** that he remains in us
    is from the **Spirit** he gave us.

Deliver the opening line ("Children, let us love not in word or speech . . .") as an instruction to the members of the assembly by looking up and making eye contact with them. If you can do so with ease, memorize the entire line; it is the main point of the reading.

Pause significantly after the words "And his commandment is this." Then proclaim the commandment "we should believe . . ." in a strong tone of voice, again making eye contact with the assembly. Pause after the commandment and before you convey the line "Those who keep his commandments . . ." in a warm and encouraging tone of voice.

READING II | The proclamation of the first letter of John continues today, skipping ahead a few verses from where the Second Reading left off last Sunday. Last Sunday the reading focused on how Christians are God's children *now* because of the love God gave them in Christ Jesus. While they do not know what the future holds, they eventually believe they will be like God, seeing God as he is.

But Christians live in the here and now. Accordingly, John writes that Christians—the children of God—are to love not only through the profession of their belief in Christ, but also through "deed and truth." In contrast to those Christians at the time who were suggesting all that was necessary was to profess their faith in Jesus, John throughout his letter continuously writes of the Christian obligation to love others.

In our contemporary idiom, John teaches in this passage that Christians cannot say one thing and mean another. John is realistic, though, recognizing that sometimes our hearts lead us to sin. In this case, we are to know that "God is greater than our hearts and knows everything"— God is a God of forgiveness (1 John 1:8— 2:2). Our sin, for a while, separates us from God, but so long as our hearts do not condemn us, God will not either.

Your proclamation of this reading to the assembly, whose members are the children of God, will help them to hear that they remain close to God by keeping his commandments. The Spirit of God, alive in them, will show them as true believers, separating them from the false believers whose speak their faith, but do not follow God's commandments.

State Jesus' words ("I am the true vine . . .") in a strong and clear tone of voice as they provide the theme for the Gospel.

Offer the second "I am" saying ("I am the vine, you are the branches") directly to the members of the assembly by making eye contact with them. Allow the statement to stand out by pausing after it.

Pause before the final section begins ("If you remain in me . . ."). Reflect in your tone of voice the comfort, encouragement, and hope found in these words.

GOSPEL   John 15:1–8

A reading from the holy Gospel according to John

Jesus said to his disciples:
   "**I** am the true **vine**, and my **Father** is the vine **grower**.
He takes away every **branch** in me that does not bear **fruit**,
   and every one that **does** he **prunes** so that it bears **more** fruit.
You are **already** pruned because of the **word** that I spoke to you.
Remain in me, as **I** remain in **you**.
Just as a branch cannot bear fruit on its **own**
   unless it remains on the **vine**,
   so neither can **you** unless you remain in **me**.
I am the **vine**, **you** are the **branches**.
Whoever remains in **me** and I in **him** will bear much **fruit**,
   because **without** me you can do **nothing**.
Anyone who does **not** remain in me
   will be thrown **out** like a **branch** and **wither**;
   people will **gather** them and throw them into a **fire**
   and they will be **burned**.
If you remain in **me** and my words remain in **you**,
   ask for **whatever** you want and it will be **done** for you.
By **this** is my Father **glorified**,
   that you **bear** much fruit and **become** my disciples."

GOSPEL   Today's passage comes from first half the lengthy discourse in which Jesus identifies himself as the True Vine and those who remain in him as the branches (John 15:1—16:4a).

Jesus identifies himself as the True Vine in today's Gospel by using an "I am" *(egō eimi)* statement. These statements are common in John. For example, Jesus says, "I am the bread of life" (6:35, 41, 48, 51); "I am the light of the world" (8:12; 9:5); "I am the gate for the sheep" (10:7, 9); "I am the

good shepherd" (10:11, 14); "I am the resurrection and the life" (11:25); and "I am the way and the truth and the life" (14:6).

In using the divine name "I am" without a symbol after it in describing his relationship with the Father (8:28) and in his teaching the Jews how he is to be understood in relation to Abraham (8:58), Jesus reveals his true identity as the one through whom salvation comes, the one equal to the Father, but who always remains in the Father (10:30). Images such as the vine, then, serve to show how Jesus brings about salvation to those who remain in him.

Your proclamation of this Gospel can assist the assembly in realizing Jesus is teaching that an individual person cannot and does not have to achieve salvation on his or her own. He or she will wither and die without Jesus and without the other branches, the other disciples in the Church. But by remaining in Jesus through the Church, new life is experienced. This gift of new life is why we celebrate Easter for 50 days.

6TH SUNDAY OF EASTER

Lectionary #56

READING I   Acts 10:25–26, 34–35, 44–48

A reading from the Acts of the Apostles

When Peter **entered**, Cornelius **met** him
   and, falling at his **feet**, paid him **homage**.
Peter, however, raised him **up**, saying,
   "Get **up**. I myself am **also** a human **being**."

Then Peter proceeded to **speak** and said,
   "In **truth**, I see that God shows **no partiality**.
Rather, in **every** nation whoever **fears** him and acts **uprightly**
   is **acceptable** to him."

While Peter was still **speaking** these things,
   the Holy **Spirit** fell upon **all** who were listening to the **word**.
The **circumcised** believers who had accompanied Peter
   were **astounded** that the gift of the Holy Spirit
   should have been **poured** out on the Gentiles **also**,
   for they could **hear** them speaking in **tongues** and
     glorifying **God**.
Then Peter **responded**,
   "Can anyone withhold the **water** for **baptizing** these people,
   who have received the Holy **Spirit** even as **we** have?"
He ordered them to be **baptized** in the name of Jesus **Christ**.

Cornelius = kor-NEEL-yus

Read the opening lines ("When Peter entered . . .") that set the stage for why Peter's words carry authority, deliberately and in a narrative tone of voice.

Proclaim Peter's words purposefully and with strength in your voice.

Pause after Peter's words and before the next section begins ("While Peter was still speaking . . .").

Address Peter's rhetorical question ("Can anyone withhold the water . . . ?") directly to the members of the assembly by making eye contact with them through the entire question. Then narrate the words "He ordered them . . ." with a strong, but not overpowering, tone of voice that communicates Peter's authority.

READING I   Today's reading contains two principles that have been an important part of the Church's understanding of the faith for centuries. First, the message that Peter delivers ("In truth, I see that God shows no partiality . . .") attests that God chooses everyone to believe in him. Through the mission of the Church, begun through Peter and the other apostles, God's call to be a part of his Chosen People is extended to Jews and Gentiles alike. As with the household of Cornelius, the Holy Spirit comes upon those who hear and respond to God's invitation.

The second principle is the gift of the Holy Spirit is present in all who hear and listen to the word of God. In this reading, it appears that the Holy Spirit has come down on the members of Cornelius' household even before they were baptized with water in the name of Jesus Christ. While the popular understanding among many Catholics may be that the Holy Spirit is given *first* when the sacrament of Confirmation is celebrated, the Church, in fact, believes that in the celebration of the sacrament of Baptism, the one baptized is "reborn in water and the Holy Spirit" (*Rite of Baptism for Children*, #2). And in Confirmation he or she will "receive the fullness of God's Spirit" (*Rite of Baptism for Children*, #68).

In the end, Luke's description of Peter's speech and the baptism of Cornelius' household bears witness to God's desire to work through all people, regardless of their background. Just as the welcoming of the Gentile converts into the early Christian

READING II   1 John 4:7–10

A reading from the first Letter of Saint John

Beloved, let us **love** one another,
  because **love** is of God;
  everyone who **loves** is **begotten** by God and **knows** God.
Whoever is **without** love does **not** know God, for God is **love**.
In this way the love of God was **revealed** to us:
  God sent his only **Son** into the world
  so that we might have **life** through him.
In **this** is love:
  not that **we** have loved **God**, but that **he** loved **us**
  and sent his **Son** as expiation for our **sins**.

Communicate the opening directive ("Beloved, let us love one another") in a compassionate, rather than a powerful, tone of voice; it is a directive, not a command.

Pause after stating in a confident tone of voice the words "In this is love." Look up at the assembly during the pause, making sure you have their attention. Then proceed to offer the words "not that we have loved God" with marvel and gratitude in your voice for God's initiative in loving us by sending his Son as an "expiation for our sins."

community caused some angst and quarrels among its members, so too today local parishes often struggle with welcoming those who are from a culture or economic background different from the majority. Yet, regardless of their background, those present to worship and participate in the life of the parish meet the criteria for belonging to household of God evident in this reading: hearing the word of God and acting uprightly before God.

READING II   For six Sundays now—and during the days of the week—the Church has been celebrating Easter. And, aside from Easter Sunday, the Second Reading has been taken from the first letter of John. To some, the short readings proclaimed from this letter might sound redundant as they echo a similar theme: "love one another, because love is of God," the first verse of today's reading.

John's first letter incorporates this theme through its language of love. The author is clear that God is the source of love; indeed, that God is love. We know that God is love because he sent his only Son into the world, and through his life, death, and Resurrection, God's love was revealed to us.

We are to follow God's initiative in loving us and reach out in loving others. Although we might get tired of hearing this theme over the course of the Easter season, our living God's love is closely tied to the Alleluias that we sing in praise of Christ's Resurrection. This is the case because it was in and through Christ's

GOSPEL   John 15:9–17

A reading from the holy Gospel according to John

Jesus said to his disciples:
"As the **Father** loves **me**, so **I** also love **you**.
Remain in my love.
If you **keep** my commandments, you will **remain** in my love,
    just as **I** have kept my **Father's** commandments
    and remain in **his** love.

"I have **told** you this so that my **joy** may be in you
    and **your** joy might be **complete**.
This is my commandment: love one **another** as I love **you**.
No one has greater love than **this**,
    to lay down one's **life** for one's **friends**.
You **are** my friends if you **do** what I **command** you.
I no longer call you **slaves**,
    because a slave does not **know** what his master is **doing**.
I have called you **friends**,
    because I have told you **everything** I have heard
        from my **Father**.
It was not **you** who chose **me**, but **I** who chose **you**
    and **appointed** you to go and bear **fruit** that will **remain**,
    so that **whatever** you ask the Father in **my** name he may
        give you.
This I command you: **love** one another."

Address the opening words ("Jesus said to his disciples") to the assembly, as they are Jesus' followers today.

Look up and make eye contact with the assembly as you deliver Jesus' commandment ("love one another as I love you") in a strong but loving tone of voice. Pause slightly again after the commandment and before continuing.

Look up and make eye contact with the assembly as you proclaim the final words of Jesus in this Gospel: "This I command you: love one another." Pause after the semicolon in this line and offer the command in a caring and gentle, but firm, tone of voice, looking around at various people in the assembly.

---

death and Resurrection that God's love became known.

As we celebrate this love in the Eucharist, we are reminded of our call to love one another as we have been loved by God in Christ. Your proclamation of this reading can lead others to see how their love of others is a joyful expression of their Easter faith in God, who is love.

| GOSPEL | In today's Gospel, the mutual love of the Father and the Son provides the basis for both

Jesus' love of his disciples, and the love Jesus commands the disciples to show for one another. In the Gospel according to John, Jesus loved his friends Lazarus, Mary, and Martha. But laying down his own life reflects the depth of love expected among his disciples. Those who follow his command to love accept the responsibility to follow his example if need be. In doing so, they become Jesus' friends, no longer being slaves, because they show they understand what the master is doing.

The Church understands Jesus' love for his own as the new commandment of

charity. Charity is virtue of faith by which "we love God above all things for his own sake, and our neighbor as ourselves for the love of God" (CCC, #1822–1824). Our life in Christ, lived out in our love for him and for others, shows that we are friends of Christ today, living in imitation of him in the world. The world today might—and does at times—reject Christian disciples and values. Yet we are compelled by Jesus' example to continue loving one another. Through the Spirit, Jesus' love abides with us as we carry out this mission.

ASCENSION OF THE LORD

Lectionary #58

READING I   Acts 1:1–11

A reading from the beginning of the Acts of the Apostles

In the **first** book, Theophilus,
    I dealt with all that Jesus **did** and **taught**
    until the day he was taken **up**,
    after giving **instructions** through the Holy **Spirit**
    to the **apostles** whom he had **chosen**.
He presented himself **alive** to them
    by many **proofs** after he had **suffered**,
    appearing to them during forty **days**
    and **speaking** about the kingdom of God.
While **meeting** with them,
    he **enjoined** them not to depart from **Jerusalem**,
    but to wait for "the promise of the **Father**
    about which you have heard me **speak**;
    for **John** baptized with **water**,
    but in a few **days** you will be baptized with the Holy **Spirit**."

When they had gathered **together** they **asked** him,
    "Lord, are you at this time going to **restore**
        the kingdom to **Israel**?"
He answered them, "It is not for **you** to know the **times**
        or **seasons**
    that the Father has **established** by his own **authority**.

Theophilus = thee-OF-uh-lus

Deliver the words beginning the second section ("While meeting with them . . .") in a measured pace, knowing that these words start the description of the Ascension.

Remember to raise your voice slightly at the end of the apostles' question ("Lord, are you at this time . . . ?").

Pause before speaking Jesus' response ("It is not for you to know . . .") with authority in your voice. Though Jesus' response is not the response for which the apostles are looking, be careful not to let your tone of voice suggest he is reprimanding them.

If the Ascension of the Lord is celebrated next Sunday, today's readings are used in place of those for the Seventh Sunday of Easter.

READING I   Today's First Reading is the account of Jesus' Ascension from the Acts of the Apostles, Luke's second volume, his Gospel being the first book he wrote. Both works he addresses to "Theophilus," a Greek word that comes from *theo* ("God") and *philus* ("one who loves"), and thus means "one who loves God." Theophilus could be either a proper name for a person or a general reference to those who love God. The Gospel according to Luke also contains an account of the Ascension (Luke 24:50–53), but between the two accounts there are some differences.

First, the Ascension in Luke concludes the entire narrative, ending his description of the time of Jesus. In Acts, the Ascension comes at the very beginning of the book. Since this book focuses on the time of the early Church, the Ascension serves as the event that inaugurates a new age—the age of the Church.

Second, in the Gospel, Luke places the Ascension on Easter Sunday night, thus closely associating the Resurrection and Ascension so that both events appear as part of one movement of Jesus' glorification. In Acts, Luke gives a historical account of the Ascension, noting a 40-day period prior to the Ascension during which Jesus appeared to the disciples.

Third, the Gospel does not reference the sending of the Spirit upon the disciples. Rather, it merely ends with the disciples paying homage to Jesus, returning to Jerusalem filled with joy, and praising God

But you will receive **power** when the Holy **Spirit** comes upon you,
    and you will be my **witnesses** in **Jerusalem**,
        throughout **Judea** and **Samaria**,
    and to the ends of the **earth**."
When he had **said** this, as they were **looking on**,
    he was lifted **up**, and a **cloud** took him from their **sight**.
While they were looking **intently** at the **sky** as he was **going**,
    suddenly two **men** dressed in white **garments**
        stood **beside** them.
They said, "Men of **Galilee**,
    why are you **standing** there looking at the **sky**?
This **Jesus** who has been taken **up** from you into **heaven**
    will **return** in the same way as you have **seen** him
        going into heaven."

READING II   Ephesians 1:17–23

A reading from the Letter of Saint Paul to the Ephesians

Brothers and sisters:
May the **God** of our Lord Jesus **Christ**, the Father of **glory**,
    give you a Spirit of **wisdom** and **revelation**
        resulting in **knowledge** of him.
May the **eyes** of your **hearts** be **enlightened**,
    that you may **know** what is the **hope** that belongs to his **call**,
    what are the riches of **glory**
    in his **inheritance** among the **holy** ones,
    and what is the surpassing **greatness** of his **power**
    for us who **believe**,
        in accord with the **exercise** of his great **might**,

---

in the Temple. On the other hand, in Acts, Luke has Jesus tell the disciples that they will receive power when the Holy Spirit comes upon them. The coming of the Holy Spirit will enable the disciples to proclaim Jesus beginning in Jerusalem—the place where the salvation of the Lord is accomplished in the two-volume Lucan narrative. Then, the disciples will proceed to witness to Jesus "to the ends of the earth." This outline for the proclamation of salvation corresponds to the outline of Acts, in

which the Church's mission begins with Peter and other apostles speaking in and around the synagogue in Jerusalem. The latter half of Acts, then, tells of the extension of the Christian mission beyond the Jews to the Gentiles.

The narrative account of the Ascension in Acts concludes with a statement about the *parousia*, Jesus' second coming at the end of time. This prediction is made by two men dressed in white, reminiscent of the two men in dazzling garments who were present to the women who entered the empty tomb (Luke 24:4–7).

In one way or another, this First Reading references the major solemnities that the Church celebrates during the Easter season: Easter itself, Ascension, and Pentecost. In doing so, it directs those of us who are tasked with proclaiming the Easter faith today "to the ends of the earth," to the hope that is the source of encouragement for us in this mission: the hope in the second coming of Jesus—and the hope that one day we will be united with him.

which he worked in **Christ**,
raising him from the **dead**
and **seating** him at his **right** hand in the **heavens**,
far above every **principality**, **authority**, **power**, and **dominion**,
and **every** name that is **named**
not only in **this** age but also in the one to **come**.
And he put **all** things beneath his **feet**
and gave him as **head** over **all** things to the **church**,
which is his **body**,
the **fullness** of the one who fills **all** things in every **way**.

Or:

READING II   Ephesians 4:1–13

Ephesians = ee-FEE-zhunz

Emphasize that the reading is in Paul's
voice by stating the "I" in a strong tone of
voice and then lowering your voice for
the parenthetical remark ("a prisoner for
the Lord . . .").

Pause after "bond of peace." Then build
gradually in intensity in your voice
as you state the sevenfold description
of Christian unity in the words "one
body and one Spirit . . ." and move toward
the doxology ("one God and Father of
all . . .").

A reading from the Letter of Saint Paul to the Ephesians

Brothers and sisters,
I, a **prisoner** for the Lord,
    urge you to **live** in a manner **worthy** of the **call**
        you have received,
    with all **humility** and **gentleness**, with **patience**,
    bearing with one another through **love**,
    striving to preserve the **unity** of the spirit
    through the bond of **peace**:
    one **body** and one **Spirit**,
    as you were also **called** to the one **hope** of your call;
    one **Lord**, one **faith**, one **baptism**;
    one **God** and Father of **all**,
    who is **over** all and **through** all and **in** all.

READING II The letter of Paul to the Ephesians was not written for a particular Christian community, but rather was addressed to the larger Church in the area of Asia Minor. Its ecclesiology, or understanding of the Church, is more universal in scope than that of the undisputed Pauline letters. In today's reading on the solemnity of the Ascension, we hear Paul's appeal to Christians for unity in the Church. This unity is seven-fold (one body and one Spirit) and Trinitarian: one Spirit, one Lord, and one God. Moreover, this unity in the faith also serves as the foundation for

Paul to discuss the diversity that exists in the Church. (The first half of today's reading will also be proclaimed on the Seventeenth Sunday in Ordinary Time. Please see that commentary for more background.)

Using a quotation from Psalm 68:18, which refers to Moses ascending Mount Sinai to receive the law and bring it back down to the Israelites, Paul describes Christ descending to earth in the Incarnation and ascending above all the heavens. Through Christ's Ascension he bestows many and diverse gifts on the Church.

In contrast to 1 Corinthians 12:28 and Romans 12:6–8, which provide lists of charisms bestowed on individuals by the Spirit, this passage from Ephesians has Christ bestowing the gifts on the Church. The gifts themselves depict individuals' roles in the Church. Thus, they refer more to how the Church is structured than how the Spirit works in the hearts of individuals. While there are different roles for people to carry out in the Church, Paul makes clear that the apostles, prophets, evangelists, and pastors and teachers (a single group, meaning that to shepherd as

Isolate the quote from Psalm 68:18
("He ascended on high . . .") by pausing
noticeably after "it says" and at the end
of the citation.

Address the concluding section to your
assembly by making eye contact with the
people sitting in various places in the
church as you narrate the different gifts
resulting from the Ascension of Christ
described in the words "And he gave
some as apostles . . . ."

But **grace** was given to **each** of us
 according to the measure of **Christ's** gift.
Therefore, it says:
 *He ascended on **high** and took prisoners **captive**;*
 *he gave **gifts** to men.*
What does "he **ascended**" mean except that he also **descended**
 into the **lower** regions of the **earth**?
The one who **descended** is also the one who **ascended**
 far above all the **heavens**,
 that he might **fill** all things.

And he gave some as **apostles**, others as **prophets**,
 others as **evangelists**, others as **pastors** and **teachers**,
 to **equip** the holy ones for the work of **ministry**,
 for building up the body of **Christ**,
 until we all attain to the unity of **faith**
 and **knowledge** of the Son of God, to mature manhood,
 to the extent of the full **stature** of Christ.

[Shorter: Ephesians 4:1–7, 11–13]

---

a pastor involves teaching) are all to be of service to the holy ones—the faithful—so that they also might serve the building up of Christ's body, working toward the unity outlined in the first half of the reading.

The two beliefs that the Spirit showers charisms on individuals in the Church and that Christ is the source of ministries in the Church, do not stand in contradiction to one another; if they did, this would place the Holy Spirit and Christ in conflict, dividing them. Even liturgically, the Church wants to witness to the unity of Christ and the Spirit. In order to show "the close relationship between the gift of the Holy Spirit and the resurrection and ascension of the Lord," the octave of Pentecost was suppressed, and the weekdays after the Ascension until the Saturday before Pentecost inclusive are viewed as a preparation for the coming of the Holy Spirit (*Commentary on the GNLYC*, p. 64; GNLYC, #26).

GOSPEL | Since the Council of Trent (1545–1563), the Church has accepted as canonical the longer ending of Mark (Mark 16:9–20), which is part of today's Gospel. Most scholars believe that this longer ending was not written by the same author as the rest of Mark, and was appended at a later date, perhaps by the early second century. Overall, it is consistent with the post-resurrection appearances of Jesus narrated in Luke 24 and John 20. As a whole, the longer ending connects Jesus' Resurrection to his Ascension, and to the disciples' mission in the world.

Jesus' words to his disciples ("Go into the whole world . . .") show that the

Deliver Jesus' command to his disciples ("Go into the whole world . . .") in a strong tone of voice. Pause before and after the command to make it stand out. Lower you tone of voice in the words that follow the command "Whoever believes and is baptized . . . ."

Express the sign that the believers will "lay hands on the sick" in a compassionate but firm tone of voice.

Pause before narrating Mark's brief and straightforward account of the Ascension ("So then the Lord Jesus . . .").

GOSPEL Mark 16:15–20

A reading from the holy Gospel according to Mark

Jesus said to his disciples:
  "Go into the **whole world**
    and proclaim the **gospel** to every **creature**.
Whoever **believes** and is **baptized** will be **saved**;
    whoever does **not** believe will be **condemned**.
These **signs** will accompany those who **believe**:
    in my **name** they will drive out **demons**,
      they will speak new **languages**.
They will pick up **serpents** with their **hands**,
    and if they drink any **deadly** thing, it will not **harm** them.
They will lay hands on the **sick**, and they will **recover**."

So **then** the Lord **Jesus**, after he **spoke** to them,
    was taken up into **heaven**
      and took his **seat** at the right hand of **God**.
But they went **forth** and preached **everywhere**,
    while the Lord **worked** with them
      and **confirmed** the word through accompanying **signs**.

Good News was meant to be proclaimed to Gentiles and Jews alike. Everyone is to be invited to hear and respond to the Resurrection Gospel. When people respond in faith to the Good News, they are to be baptized and incorporated into the community of believers.

The signs that accompany people who believe—exorcising demons, curing the sick, speaking in new languages—are similar to those signs that revealed Jesus' power and authority in Mark and are consistent with the Lucan tradition in the Acts of the Apostles. Belief in Jesus, therefore, is not without effect. The effects mentioned in the Gospel are possible because the risen Jesus remains with his followers in their ministry.

This Gospel passage is also one of the scriptural references for article 6 in the creed: "He ascended into heaven and is seated at the right hand of the Father." Our belief in the Ascension is not only a belief about what happened to Jesus, but it is also a message of hope for us as we continue Jesus' mission on earth. "Jesus Christ, the head of the Church, precedes us into the Father's glorious kingdom so that we, the members of his Body, may live in the hope of one day being with him forever" (CCC, #666). Through the proclamation of this Gospel, those in the assembly can see how they can bring their hope in the risen-ascended one to others who do no yet believe.

7TH SUNDAY OF EASTER

Lower your tone of voice slightly on the parenthetical statement ("there was a group . . .").

Communicate Peter's words concerning Judas ("My brothers, the Scripture had to be fulfilled . . .") in a matter-of-fact tone of voice. While surely Peter is disappointed, his purpose now is to move on with the choice of another person to witness to Jesus' Resurrection.

Pause before and after stating clearly the citation from Psalm 109:8 ("May another take his office").

Lectionary #60

READING I   Acts 1:15–17, 20a, 20c–26

A reading from the Acts of the Apostles

Peter stood up in the **midst** of the brothers
   —there was a **group** of about one hundred and twenty persons
   in the one **place**—.
He said, "My brothers,
   the **Scripture** had to be **fulfilled**
   which the Holy **Spirit** spoke **beforehand**
   through the mouth of **David**, concerning **Judas**,
   who was the **guide** for those who arrested **Jesus**.
He was **numbered** among us
   and was **allotted** a share in this **ministry**.

"For it is written in the Book of **Psalms**:
   *May **another** take his **office**.*

"Therefore, it is **necessary** that one of the men
   who **accompanied** us the whole time
   the Lord Jesus **came** and **went** among us,

If the Ascension of the Lord is celebrated today, please see pages 190–194 for the appropriate readings.

READING I   Next Sunday the Easter season concludes with the celebration of Pentecost, the solemnity on which we celebrate the descent of the Spirit on the apostles that gave birth to the Church. So it is fitting that today's passage from Acts is the choosing of a successor to Judas, a successor needed in order to maintain the symbolism of the Twelve, a number that stood for the 12 tribes of Israel.

Two aspects of this reading are of particular interest: 1) the process by which Matthias was chosen and 2) the continuity between Jesus, the apostles, and the Church—then and now. First, from the reading we learn that the choice of Matthias did not come through an election. Nor does the casting of lots, an Old Testament tradition (Leviticus 16:7–10), point to any type of gambling as the means for choosing a successor. Instead, the choice of Matthias comes through discernment, a method focused on prayer, asking the Lord for guidance.

Second, Peter's message detailed the criteria for which the selection of nominees. The new apostle would have to have 1) known Jesus from the time of his Baptism through his Resurrection and Ascension and 2) followed along in the company of the other apostles. In these conditions are the roots of the Church's teachings regarding apostolic succession. The bishops themselves, then, take the place of the apostles as pastors and teachers so that "whoever listens to them is listening to Christ" (LG, #20; CCC, #862).

Barsabbas = bar-SAH-bus

Justus = JUS-tus

Matthias = muh-THĪ-us

Offer the prayer of discernment ("You, Lord, who know the hearts of all . . .") in a lower tone of voice and one that expresses humility, for those choosing Judas' replacement are asking for the Lord's guidance.

beginning from the baptism of **John**
until the day on which he was taken **up** from us,
become with us a **witness** to his **resurrection**."
So they proposed **two**, **Judas** called **Barsabbas**,
who was **also** known as **Justus**, and **Matthias**.
Then they **prayed**,
"**You**, Lord, who know the hearts of **all**,
show which one of these two you have **chosen**
to take the **place** in this apostolic ministry
from which **Judas** turned away to go to his **own** place."
Then they gave **lots** to them, and the lot fell upon **Matthias**,
and he was **counted** with the eleven **apostles**.

The unique role accorded to the bishops, however, is held together with the conviction that the whole Church is apostolic. This means that the Church follows in the footsteps of her origins—Jesus Christ—by 1) remaining in communion through the Pope and bishops with Christ Jesus and 2) being sent out into the world to proclaim with joy the Easter faith.

READING II | On this Seventh Sunday of Easter, we begin the final week of the Easter season, which leads us to Pentecost. Today's passage includes two other themes that are prominent in John as well as the three letters of John, though the same person did not write the Gospel and the letters.

First, John's statement that "no one has ever seen God" needs to be interpreted in light of last Sunday's passage, in which he writes that the love of God was revealed to us by God sending his only Son into the world (1 John 4:9). Taking these two statements together, we can see it is only Jesus who reveals the Father.

Second, in this brief reading John explains that the presence of the Spirit in a person who believes confirms that he or she is one with God. The Spirit of God, however, does not reside in false prophets—those who fail to acknowledge that Jesus Christ came in the flesh, that is, was truly human, and truly suffered, dying on the cross. In fact, the spirit that does

READING II   1 John 4:11–16

A reading from the first Letter of Saint John

Beloved, if God so loved **us**,
  we **also** must love one **another**.
No one has ever **seen** God.
Yet, if we **love** one another, God **remains** in us,
  and his **love** is brought to **perfection** in us.

This is how we **know** that we remain in **him** and **he** in **us**,
  that he has given us of his **Spirit**.
Moreover, we have **seen** and **testify**
  that the **Father** sent his **Son** as **savior** of the world.
Whoever **acknowledges** that Jesus is the Son of **God**,
  God remains in **him** and he in **God**.
We have come to **know** and to **believe** in the love God **has** for us.

God is **love**, and whoever remains in **love**
  remains in **God** and God in **him**.

Address the assembly as "Beloved" by looking up and making eye contact with them. Be clear as you communicate the instruction to them ("we also must love one another"). You want them to take notice that they heard an almost identical phrase at the beginning of last week's Second Reading.

Take your time proclaiming the last verse ("God is love . . .") by pausing after the comma and reading the verse as if there are commas after "whoever remains in love," and again after "remains in God," thus helping the assembly to make the connection between God's love, our love of others, and our closeness to God. Use an encouraging, supportive tone of voice for these words.

reside in those who do not acknowledge Jesus as the Son of God is the spirit of the antichrist.

Third, while the children of God who believe in and act on God's love remain in God, belonging to him, those who do not believe the Father sent his Son as Savior of the world and love each other accordingly, belong not to God, but to the world. Those who believe and love as children of God, receive the gift of eternal life offered through Jesus, the Christ. This truth the author of the epistle testifies to at the end of his letter (1 John 5:13) and it is the reason we celebrate not just Easter Sunday, but the Fifty Days of the Easter season.

GOSPEL   On the Seventh Sunday of Easter, the Gospel switches from the Last Supper discourses of Jesus proclaimed on the Fourth, Fifth, and Sixth Sundays of Easter to Jesus' high priestly prayer he offers for his disciples before the events of his Passion begin (John 17:1–26). The prayer itself can be divided into three segments: 1) Jesus' prayer for his own glorification (verses 1–5), 2) Jesus' prayer for his disciples as he sends them into the world (verses 6–19), and 3) Jesus' prayer that his disciples and those they will bring to believe in him will be one. Today's Gospel comes from the middle segment of Jesus' prayer.

The solemnity and importance of the prayer is seen from the beginning of this Gospel passage as Jesus prayed, "Holy Father," an address that could indicate the

GOSPEL   Luke 24:35—48

A reading from the holy Gospel according to Luke

The two disciples **recounted** what had taken place on the **way**,
   and how **Jesus** was made **known** to them
   in the breaking of **bread**.

While they were still **speaking** about this,
   he stood in their **midst** and said to them,
   "**Peace** be with you."
But they were **startled** and **terrified**
   and thought that they were seeing a **ghost**.
Then he said to them, "Why are you **troubled**?
And why do **questions** arise in your **hearts**?
Look at my **hands** and my **feet**, that it is I **myself**.
Touch me and **see**, because a **ghost** does not have **flesh** and **bones**
   as you can see I have."
And as he **said** this,
   he **showed** them his **hands** and his **feet**.
While they were still **incredulous** for joy and were **amazed**,
   he asked them, "Have you **anything** here to **eat**?"
They gave him a piece of baked **fish**;
   he **took** it and **ate** it in front of them.

He said to them,
   "These are my **words** that I **spoke** to you while I was still
      with you,
   that everything **written** about me in the law of **Moses**
   and in the **prophets** and **psalms** must be **fulfilled**."
Then he **opened** their minds to understand the **Scriptures**.

Proclaim the introductory sentence ("The two disciples . . .") deliberately in order to help lead the assembly to make the connection with the Eucharist they will celebrate.

We heard the words "Peace be with you" three times in last Sunday's Gospel (John 20:19-31). Speak the Lord's greeting of peace in a warm, hospitable tone of voice.

Proceed with care in delivering the words "They gave him . . . ."

Proclaim the risen Lord's teaching ("These are my words that I spoke . . .") in a confident tone of voice, aware of your own faith that Jesus is the fulfillment of the law and the prophets.

(*Paraklētos*, in Greek) is Jesus Christ, who through his Crucifixion offered himself for our sins, and indeed the sins of the whole world. The *Agnus Dei* in the eucharistic liturgy reflects this belief.

The original setting for this reading was probably an initiation ritual that entailed a public confession of sinfulness prior to being welcomed into the Christian community. This, along with the celebration of a baptismal rite, would have symbolized a person's transition from living in darkness to living in the light. During the Easter season, we celebrate our life in the light. We do so not only through our profession of faith, but also by our "right living." Proclaim this reading as one that extols the assembly keep God's commandments, and offers the hope of forgiveness for their failure to do so.

GOSPEL | The *General Norms for the Liturgical Year and Calendar* state that "The fifty days from Easter Sunday to Pentecost are celebrated in joyful exultation as one feast day, or better as one 'great Sunday'" (#22). So why do the readings on the Third Sunday of Easter focus on sin, repentance, and forgiveness?

Today's Gospel, which comes at the end of Luke, follows the Emmaus story (which was the afternoon Gospel on Easter Sunday). We learn at the end of that story that Peter was one of the disciples who recognized Jesus in the breaking of the bread. The Lord's appearance to Peter was an act of forgiveness and Peter's acknowledgment that his heart was burning within him, a sign of repentance.

The passage for today picks up with the disciples, having returned to Jerusalem,

While the entire Gospel is Jesus' prayer for his disciples, you are not literally re-enacting that prayer today, so you do not want to lift your eyes up to heaven (or to the ceiling of the church) as you proclaim the Gospel. Rather, simply offer Jesus' prayer ("Holy Father, keep them in your name . . .") in a sincere, caring tone of voice, mindful that this is Jesus' prayer for us today as well.

Pace your proclamation of Jesus' words ("I speak this in the world . . .") so as not to get tongue-tied with the number of occurrences of the word "world." A rushed proclamation will hinder the assembly's comprehension of these lines and distract from your expression of Jesus' concern for his disciples.

Increase the intensity in your voice as Jesus asks the Father to "Consecrate them in the truth" as he consecrates himself for them.

GOSPEL   John 17:11b–19

A reading from the holy Gospel according to John

Lifting up his eyes to **heaven**, Jesus **prayed**, saying:
     "Holy **Father**, keep them in your **name** that you have **given** me,
     so that **they** may be one just as **we** are one.
When I was **with** them I **protected** them in your name that you
          gave me,
     and I **guarded** them, and **none** of them was **lost**
     except the son of **destruction**,
     in order that the **Scripture** might be **fulfilled**.
But **now** I am **coming** to you.
I **speak** this in the world
     so that they may share my joy **completely**.
I gave them your **word**, and the world **hated** them,
     because **they** do not belong to the world
     any more than **I** belong to the world.
I do not ask that you take them **out** of the world
     but that you **keep** them from the **evil** one.
They do not belong to the world
     any more than **I** belong to the world.
Consecrate them in the **truth**. Your **word** is truth.
As **you** sent **me** into the world,
     so I sent **them** into the world.
And I **consecrate** myself for them,
     so that they **also** may be **consecrated** in **truth**."

prayer was used in liturgical assemblies in the Johannine community. His prayer for unity in the opening line recalls the interconnectedness between the Father and the Son, and the Son and his disciples he spoke about using the metaphor of the vine and the branches (John 15:1—16:4a).

Jesus' prayer also emphasizes the difference between the world and the disciples. While the disciples, like Jesus, are "in the world," they are not "of the world." They, having heard the word of the Father through Jesus, now belong to the Father as Jesus does. But the world has not received

the truth of the Father's word. In fact, it has been hostile to the Word became flesh.

Knowing the difficulties the disciples will face in the world, and how the world will attempt to allure them away from belonging to the Father, Jesus prays that through his death (his consecration of himself), the disciples might remain firm in the truth. With this prayer, Jesus sends his disciples forth in the world.

The weight of the prayer, coupled with its poetry, makes its proclamation a challenge. Because you are proclaiming Jesus' words, you have the opportunity to

offer the Gospel as Jesus' prayer and yours for the assembly gathered to worship. At the end of the eucharistic celebration, they will be sent forth into the world to bring others to faith in Jesus. Sometimes they will face hostility from the world as the disciples did. Still, this prayer gives hope as it lifts up the unity already present between the Father and the Son as an image for the unity that will exist when, together with the disciples, the world will also be one with the Father.

PENTECOST: VIGIL

Lectionary #62

READING I   Genesis 11:1–9

A reading from the Book of Genesis

The whole **world** spoke the same **language**, using the
    same **words**.
While the people were **migrating** in the east,
   they came upon a **valley** in the land of **Shinar** and **settled** there.
They said to one another,
    "**Come**, let us mold **bricks** and harden them with **fire**."
They used bricks for **stone**, and bitumen for **mortar**.
Then they said, "**Come**, let us build ourselves a **city**
   and a **tower** with its **top** in the **sky**,
   and so make a **name** for ourselves;
    otherwise we shall be **scattered** all over the **earth**."

The LORD came down to **see** the city and the tower
   that the people had built.
Then the LORD said: "If now, while they are **one** people,
   all speaking the same **language**,
   they have started to do **this**,
   nothing will **later** stop them from doing
    whatever they presume to do.
Let us then go **down** there and **confuse** their language,
   so that one will not **understand** what another says."
Thus the LORD **scattered** them from there all over the **earth**,
   and they stopped building the city.

Pause after the announcement of the reading and after the opening line since it sets the stage for the events of the rest of the reading.
Shinar = SHEE-nar

bitumen = bih-TOO-m*n
Bitumen was an asphalt or tar used as cement or mortar in Asia Minor.

Place some excitement, even arrogance, in your tone of voice as you communicate the people's plans to build a tower ("Come let us mold bricks" and "Come, let us build ourselves a city").

Express the Lord's words ("If now, while they are one people . . .") with some disappointment and resignation in your tone of voice: the Lord realizes their humanness and that he will need to take control of the situation.

READING I The Genesis narrative of the tower of Babel is familiar to many; however, because there is no mention of the Spirit in the reading, a logical question is, why is this story proclaimed at the Vigil Mass of Pentecost? Yet, paired with the Gospel of Jesus' promise of the Spirit to those who believe, an understanding of the Spirit begins to emerge that reflects the Spirit's mission in the world.

The passage from Genesis begins by presenting the whole world united through the speaking of a common language. The people, against God's intention to have

them return to their homelands (Genesis 9:19; 10:15, 20, 25, 31, 32), chose to migrate to the city of Babel (10:1). Once there, their pride continued to manifest itself as they freely chose to build a tower that reached to the heavens. Their motivation was arrogance, their attitude egotistical as they strove to outdo God, making a name for themselves, rather than glorifying the Lord's name. The people's "perverse ambition to forge its own unity" (CCC, #57) illustrated the capital sin of pride at its height (CCC, #1866).

In the second half of the narrative, the Lord responds to the people's achievements, seemingly punishing them by scattering them across the world. The people are now divided and speak many languages. Unity among the people will now only occur through a restored relationship with the Lord.

The Second Reading and the Gospel passage both present hope for a new kind of unity through the Spirit. And, in the account of Pentecost from Acts 2:1–11, which is proclaimed during the Pentecost Mass during the day, the people from the

Babel = BAB-*l

That is why it was called **Babel**,
because **there** the LORD confused the **speech** of all the **world**.
It was from that place that he **scattered** them all over the **earth**.

Or:

READING I   Exodus 19:3–8a, 16–20b

A reading from the Book of Exodus

Jacob = JAY-kub

Moses went up the mountain to **God**.
Then the LORD **called** to him and said,
    "**Thus** shall you say to the house of **Jacob**;
    tell the Israelites:
    You have **seen** for yourselves how I **treated** the Egyptians
    and how I **bore** you up on **eagle** wings
    and **brought** you here to **myself**.
Therefore, if you hearken to my **voice** and keep my **covenant**,
    you shall be my special **possession**,
    dearer to me than all **other** people,
    though **all** the earth is **mine**.
You shall be to me a kingdom of **priests**, a holy **nation**.
That is what you must tell the **Israelites**."
So Moses **went** and summoned the **elders** of the people.
When he set before them
    all that the LORD had **ordered** him to tell them,
    the people all answered **together**,
    "Everything the LORD has **said**, we will **do**."

East and West are united through the outpouring of the Spirit, not in a common verbal language, but in the one Gospel of Jesus Christ.

Saint Augustine, in the fourth century, was the first to speak of the Holy Spirit as the bond of love, the bond of communion between the Father and Son. Through the Incarnation of the Son and the sending of the Spirit, this bond has been extended to humanity, indeed all of creation. In contrast, then, to the unity that the people themselves tried to create by building themselves a city and a tower of great

heights in Babel, the Spirit brings about the *true* and lasting communion between God and humanity.

READING II The Introduction to the Lectionary states that the reading from Paul to the Romans for the Vigil Mass of Pentecost "shows the actual working of the Holy Spirit in the Church" (#102). In this passage, Paul is addressing believers who have been led by the Spirit of God and as a result are now called "children of God" (Romans 8:14). These "children of God" are the Jewish and Gentile

members of the house churches in Rome, the capital city of the empire at the time of Paul's writing of Romans, about 58 or 59 AD. Today, our assemblies gathered together to celebrate the Spirit working within individuals members and the Church as a whole are the children of God.

As children of God, we have the "firstfruits of the Spirit." In the Old Testament, the offering of the firstfruits of the harvest to the Lord signified the consecration of the whole harvest yet to come to God (Leviticus 23:15–21). Paul's use of this metaphor in

On the morning of the third day
  there were peals of thunder and lightning,
  and a heavy cloud over the mountain,
  and a very loud trumpet blast,
  so that all the people in the camp trembled.
But Moses led the people out of the camp to meet God,
  and they stationed themselves at the foot of the mountain.
Mount Sinai was all wrapped in smoke,
  for the LORD came down upon it in fire.
The smoke rose from it as though from a furnace,
  and the whole mountain trembled violently.
The trumpet blast grew louder and louder,
   while Moses was speaking,
  and God answering him with thunder.

When the LORD came down to the top of Mount Sinai,
  he summoned Moses to the top of the mountain.

Or:

READING I   Ezekiel 37:1–14

Ezekiel = ee-ZEE-kee-ul

A reading from the Book of the Prophet Ezekiel

The hand of the LORD came upon me,
  and he led me out in the spirit of the LORD
  and set me in the center of the plain,
  which was now filled with bones.
He made me walk among the bones in every direction
  so that I saw how many they were on the surface of the plain.

---

relation to the Spirit allows him to say that the Spirit enables the children of God to look forward in hope to glory that awaits them at the time when they will be glorified with Christ (8:17, 19). What they and we experience through our life in relation to God in the Church is but a foretaste, the "firstfruits" of the communion with him yet to come.

Empowered by the Spirit, our role is to live in the hope by which we were saved. Despite the fact that we groan in our attempts to patiently endure the imperfections of our fellow brothers and sisters—

despite the fact that creation groans because at times we fail to be good stewards of it—through our Baptism as children of God we are tasked with proclaiming to the world our hope that the best is yet to come! This we do not do as individuals but in the communion of the Church, which is itself in communion with God—Father, Son, and Holy Spirit.

GOSPEL   While Pentecost, for Christians, marks the closing of the Easter season, the close of the

feast referred to in the opening line of the Gospel is Jewish Feast of Tabernacles (Tents, Booths). In the Jewish calendar, this was an eight-day pilgrimage feast during which Jews went up to Jerusalem to celebrate the harvest. In Exodus, it is understood as the feast of ingathering at the end of the year, a feast of celebrating that the harvest has come home (Exodus 23:16; Deuteronomy 16:13–15). For seven days of the feast, water was brought as an offering from the pool of Siloam, the same pool where the blind man was told to go and wash (John 9:7) On the eighth day,

prophesy = PROF-uh-sī

sinews = SIN-yooz

How **dry** they were!
He asked me:
    Son of **man**, can these bones come to **life**?
I answered, "Lord GOD, you **alone** know that."
Then he said to me:
    Prophesy over these bones, and **say** to them:
    Dry **bones**, hear the word of the LORD!
Thus says the Lord GOD to these **bones**:
    See! I will bring spirit into you, that you may come to **life**.
I will put **sinews** upon you, make **flesh** grow over you,
    cover you with **skin**, and put **spirit** in you
    so that you may come to **life** and know that **I** am the LORD.
I, **Ezekiel**, prophesied as I had been **told**,
    and even as I was **prophesying** I heard a **noise**;
    it was a **rattling** as the bones came together, **bone** joining **bone**.
I saw the **sinews** and the **flesh** come upon them,
    and the skin **cover** them, but there was no **spirit** in them.
Then the LORD said to me:
    Prophesy to the **spirit**, **prophesy**, son of man,
    and say to the spirit: Thus says the Lord GOD:
    From the four winds **come**, O spirit,
    and **breathe** into these **slain** that they may come to **life**.
I **prophesied** as he told me, and the spirit **came** into them;
    they came **alive** and stood **upright**, a vast **army**.
Then he said to me:
    Son of **man**, these **bones** are the whole house of **Israel**.
They have been saying,
    "Our bones are **dried up**,
    our **hope** is lost, and we are cut **off**."

---

there was a "holy convocation" (Leviticus 23:33–6) marked by rituals performed around the altar by priests with water from the pool of Siloam. This is most likely the setting for Jesus' words in today's Gospel.

The source of the scripture passage ("Rivers of living water . . .") that Jesus quotes cannot be identified with any certainty. Yet connections with Psalms 105:40–41 and 78:15–16, which speak of the rock in the desert being split by the

Lord and then flowing with water, and texts from Ezekiel 47:1–12 and Zechariah 14:8, which refer to streams of water flowing out from the Temple, are reasonable. Regardless of the source of Jesus' quotation and whether the rivers of living water flow from him or the believer (the text is ambiguous), his use of this scripture coupled with John's explanation of it, point to a reinterpretation of the Feast of Tabernacles in relation to Jesus as the true source of living water (John 4:10–15) through his promise to send the Spirit.

This shows that the Spirit cannot be understood apart from Jesus. The Spirit is the Spirit of Christ. Moreover, one could expand on the meaning of the passage in relation to Pentecost and say that the Spirit that was given to the disciples is the same Spirit that has flowed within the church and in the hearts of all who believe for centuries. This gift of the Spirit, alive and well in the Church throughout the world is cause to celebrate on the Vigil of Pentecost.

prophesy = PROF-uh-sī

Therefore, **prophesy** and say to them:
  Thus says the Lord **GOD**:
  O my **people**, I will open your **graves**
  and have you **rise** from them,
  and bring you **back** to the land of **Israel**.
Then you shall **know** that I am the **LORD**,
  when I **open** your graves and have you **rise** from them,
  O my **people**!
I will put my **spirit** in you that you may **live**,
  and I will **settle** you upon your **land**;
  thus you shall know that **I** am the **LORD**.
I have **promised**, and I will **do** it, says the LORD.

Or:

READING I   Joel 3:1–5

A reading from the Book of the Prophet Joel

Thus says the **LORD**:
I will pour out my **spirit** upon all **flesh**.
Your sons and **daughters** shall **prophesy**,
  your **old** men shall dream **dreams**,
  your **young** men shall see **visions**;
even upon the **servants** and the **handmaids**,
  in those days, I will pour out my **spirit**.
And I will work **wonders** in the **heavens** and on the **earth**,
  blood, **fire**, and columns of **smoke**;

the **sun** will be turned to **darkness**,
  and the **moon** to **blood**,
at the **coming** of the day of the L̜ord,
  the **great** and **terrible** day.
Then everyone shall be **rescued**
  who **calls** on the name of the L̜ord;
for on Mount **Zion** there shall be a **remnant**,
  as the L̜ord has said,
and in Jerusalem **survivors**
  whom the L̜ord shall **call**.

READING II   Romans 8:22–27

A reading from the Letter of Saint Paul to the Romans

Proclaim the first section of the reading ("We know that all creation . . .") with longing in your voice.

Brothers and sisters:
We know that all **creation** is **groaning** in **labor** pains
    even until **now**;
  and not only **that**, but we **ourselves**,
  who have the **firstfruits** of the Spirit,
  we **also** groan within ourselves
    as we wait for **adoption**, the redemption of our **bodies**.
For in **hope** we were **saved**.
Now **hope** that **sees** is **not** hope.
For who **hopes** for what one **sees**?
But if we hope for what we do **not** see, we wait with **endurance**.

Pause before the next section begins ("For in hope . . ."). Use a lighter tone of voice to convey the hope that comes from our salvation through faith in Jesus Christ. Practice this section aloud so you are able to proclaim the repetition of the forms of the words "hope" and "see" without stumbling.

Pause before proclaiming the final
section ("In the same way, the
Spirit . . .") with hope and
encouragement in your voice.

In the **same** way, the Spirit **too** comes to the **aid** of our **weakness**;
for we do not know **how** to pray as we **ought**,
but the Spirit **himself** intercedes with inexpressible **groanings**.
And the one who searches **hearts**
knows what is the **intention** of the **Spirit**,
because he **intercedes** for the **holy** ones
according to God's **will**.

GOSPEL John 7:37–39

A reading from the holy Gospel according to John

Exclaim Jesus' invitation to "Let anyone
who thirsts come to me and drink" with
vigor and strength in your tone of voice
as you look directly at the assembly.

On the **last** and **greatest** day of the feast,
Jesus stood up and **exclaimed**,
"Let anyone who **thirsts** come to me and **drink**.
As Scripture says:
*Rivers of living **water** will flow from **within** him*
who believes in me."

Take your time in narrating these final
explanatory lines, pausing slightly
at the commas and longer at the periods.
Use a slightly lower tone of voice than
you used for Jesus' exclamation above,
projecting as if you were simply reading
a narrative aloud.

He said this in reference to the **Spirit**
that those who came to **believe** in him were to **receive**.
There **was**, of course, no Spirit **yet**,
because **Jesus** had not yet been **glorified**.

PENTECOST: DAY

Lectionary #63

READING I   Acts 2:1–11

A reading from the Acts of the Apostles

When the time for **Pentecost** was fulfilled,
 they were all in one place **together**.
And **suddenly** there came from the sky
 a **noise** like a strong driving **wind**,
 and it filled the entire house in which they were.
Then there appeared to them **tongues** as of **fire**,
 which **parted** and came to rest on **each** one of them.
And they were all **filled** with the Holy **Spirit**
 and began to **speak** in different **tongues**,
 as the **Spirit** enabled them to **proclaim**.

Now there were devout **Jews** from every nation under heaven
 staying in Jerusalem.
At this **sound**, they gathered in a large **crowd**,
 but they were **confused**
 because **each** one heard them **speaking** in his own **language**.
They were **astounded**, and in **amazement** they asked,
 "Are **not** all these people who are speaking **Galileans**?
Then how does **each** of us hear them in his native **language**?
We are Parthians, Medes, and Elamites,
 inhabitants of Mesopotamia, Judea and Cappadocia,

Beginning with the words "And suddenly," build momentum in your proclamation through the words "as the Spirit enabled . . ." by incrementally increasing the energy in your voice as you are telling of a dramatic event.

Pause before the words "Now there were devout Jews . . . ." Lower your tone of voice back down to a narrative tone as you read this line.

Practice out loud the names that follow to allow for smooth proclamation on Pentecost. Do not rush through the list; taking your time and clearly enunciating each name will help the assembly to understand the universal reach of God's saving work through Christ in the Spirit.

Galileans = gal-ih-LEE-unz
Parthians = PAR-thee-unz
Medes = meedz
Elamites = EE-luh-mīts
Mesopotamia = mes-uh-poh-TAY-mee-uh
Judea = joo-DEE-uh
Cappadocia = kap-uh-DOH-shuh

READING I The account in the Acts of the Apostles of the great event of the coming of the Holy Spirit upon those gathered together in Jerusalem is the First Reading proclaimed on Pentecost in all three years of the Lectionary cycle. The Introduction to the Lectionary states that this is "in accord with received usage," meaning that throughout the history of the Church this reading is one that has been proclaimed on Pentecost (#102). Liturgical scholars have provided evidence for this as well, noting that early on this reading from Acts, which has as its theme beginnings of "the messianic community inaugurated by the gift of the tongues of all nations," provided one tradition for understanding Pentecost "that achieved particular importance as the mission of the Church spread into all lands" (Thomas Talley, *The Origins of the Liturgical Year*, p. 66).

"Pentecost" itself is the Greek name, meaning "the fiftieth day," which is given to the Jewish Feast of Weeks. In the Jewish calendar Pentecost was celebrated on the fiftieth day after Passover, bringing to a close the season of harvest begun with the Feast of Unleavened Bread. By the first century AD, Pentecost also became the commemoration of the Lord's covenants with Moses, Abraham, and Noah. At this time, as is clear from those crowds of pilgrims who journeyed from the far reaches of both the East and the West in today's reading, Jerusalem was the focal point of the celebration.

The name "Pentecost" eventually came to be applied to the feast in the Church that celebrates the event of the Spirit filling the hearts of the disciples and enabling them

Pontus = PON-tus
Phrygia = FRIJ-ee-uh
Pamphilia = pam-FIL-ee-uh
Egypt = EE-jipt
Libya = LIB-ee-uh
Cyrene = sī-REE-nee
Cretans = KREE-tuns
Arabs = AIR-ubs
Proclaim the concluding line of the reading ("yet we hear them speaking") in a measured pace, not rushing through it, and with marvel and excitement in your voice.

Pontus and Asia, Phrygia and Pamphylia,
Egypt and the districts of Libya near Cyrene,
as well as travelers from Rome,
both Jews and converts to Judaism, Cretans and Arabs,
yet we hear them speaking in our own **tongues**
of the mighty acts of **God**."

READING II   1 Corinthians 12:3b–7, 12–13

A reading from the first Letter of Saint Paul to the Corinthians

Brothers and sisters:
No one can say, "Jesus is Lord," **except** by the Holy **Spirit**.

There are different **kinds** of spiritual **gifts** but the same **Spirit**;
    there are different **forms** of **service** but the same **Lord**;
    there are different **workings** but the same **God**
    who produces **all** of them in **everyone**.
To each **individual** the manifestation of the Spirit
    is given for some **benefit**.

As a **body** is one though it has many **parts**,
    and all the **parts** of the body, though **many**, are one **body**,
    so also **Christ**.
For in one **Spirit** we were all **baptized** into one **body**,
    whether **Jews** or **Greeks**, **slaves** or **free** persons,
    and we were **all** given to drink of one **Spirit**.

Or:

"to proclaim" as recounted in this passage from Acts. Although Luke only tells us that they were able "to proclaim," we can presume that their proclamation included the Good News of the mightiest act of God—the Resurrection of Jesus Christ—and the new life that comes from that act for all who believe!

The disciples speaking in "different tongues" has been variously interpreted by biblical scholars as both a manifestation of ecstatic, charismatic prayer and communication in many languages. In either case, Luke's emphasis in this historical account of the Pentecost event is on the universality and catholicity of the Church and the proclamation of the word in an intelligible fashion. With the outpouring of the Holy Spirit, "the age of the Church" has dawned (CCC, #1076). Through the working of the Spirit in the Church, the ministry and mission of Jesus continues to this day.

To visualize the extent of the universal scope of the presence of the Spirit in the church, and understand from where the many people in the reading came, you might want to find a Bible that has both maps of the Greco-Roman world in New Testament times and their modern-day counterparts.

READING II The reading from Galatians is proclaimed on Pentecost because it "bring[s] out the effect of the action of the Spirit in the life of the Church" (Introduction to the Lectionary, #102). In fact, this reading from Galatians catalogs both the consequences of living according to the flesh and the fruits of the Spirit, contrasting them with each other.

State the opening command ("live by the Spirit") with strength in your voice, making eye contact with the assembly as you do so.

Deliver the list of vices ("immorality, impurity, lust . . .") at a moderate pace and articulating each "work of the flesh" clearly in a firm tone of voice.

Put a tone of firmness in your delivery of Paul's counsel ("I warn you").

Contrast your communication of the virtues that come from the Spirit ("love, joy, peace . . .") with your delivery of the vices by using a lighter, more compassionate tone of voice for the virtues.

Look up at the assembly as you proclaim the conditional statement ("If we live in the Spirit . . ."). Proclaim these words in a supportive tone of voice that is rooted in your own conviction of the Spirit's presence in the Christian community.

READING II   Galatians 5:16–25

A reading from the Letter of Saint Paul to the Galatians

Brothers and sisters, **live** by the **Spirit**
    and you will certainly not **gratify** the desire of the **flesh**.
For the **flesh** has desires **against** the Spirit,
    and the **Spirit** against the **flesh**;
    these are **opposed** to each other,
        so that you may **not** do what you **want**.
But if you are guided by the **Spirit**, you are not under the **law**.
Now the works of the flesh are **obvious**:
    immorality, impurity, lust, idolatry,
    sorcery, hatreds, rivalry, jealousy,
    outbursts of fury, acts of selfishness,
    dissensions, factions, occasions of envy,
    drinking bouts, orgies, and the like.
I **warn** you, as I warned you **before**,
    that those who **do** such things will not **inherit**
        the kingdom of **God**.
In **contrast**, the fruit of the **Spirit** is love, joy, peace,
    patience, kindness, generosity,
    faithfulness, gentleness, self-control.
Against **such** there **is** no law.
Now those who belong to Christ **Jesus** have **crucified** their flesh
    with its **passions** and **desires**.
If we **live** in the Spirit, let us also **follow** the Spirit.

Paul addressed this letter to the Galatians, converts of his from paganism (Galatians 4:8–9), around the year 54 or 55 AD. The Galatians, who had accepted the Gospel he preached, were being challenged by other missionaries who preached a different Gospel and perverted the Gospel of Christ (1:7). These missionaries, probably Judaizers, sought to add observances of Jewish laws and rituals such as circumcision to the practice of Christianity by the Gentile converts. Paul, however, believed following of the Mosaic law was unnecessary for new Christians, since Christ fulfilled the law by accomplishing redemption for all through the cross.

But Paul did not argue that Christians could behave in a manner of their choosing, such that their ethical behavior was unbridled and seemingly left uncolored by any norms. Galatians 5 and 6, from which today's reading comes, make up Paul's exhortation to Christian living. He gives this exhortation or strong plea toward living a life in the Spirit and against the flesh (sarx) to the Galatians and against the libertines. The libertines, others who taught contrary to Paul, were trying to influence the fledgling Christians that, since Christ saved them already, there is no need for any standards of conduct.

For Paul, those who have been baptized in Christ have died with him and thus died to the flesh. In Baptism, they have also become sons and daughters of God through the Spirit. The Spirit compels them to live in a new way. While the works of the flesh are the sinful vices ("immorality, impurity . . ."), the fruits of the Spirit are

Use a lighter tone of voice on the subordinate clauses that precede the main clause ("he will testify to me") of the first sentence.

Notice the series of "he will" statements describing what the Spirit will do. Emphasize in your proclamation what the Spirit will do: "guide," "speak," "declare," "glorify," and "take from," rather than emphasizing the "he will" in each statement to prevent the sense of redundancy in your proclamation.

Pause before slowly proclaiming the final verse ("Everything that the Father has . . .").

GOSPEL   John 15:26–27; 16:12–15

A reading from the holy Gospel according to John

Jesus said to his disciples:
  "When the **Advocate** comes whom I will **send** you
    from the **Father**,
  the Spirit of truth that proceeds from the Father,
  he will **testify** to me.
And you **also** testify,
  because you have **been** with me from the **beginning**.

"I have **much** more to tell you, but you cannot **bear** it now.
But when **he** comes, the Spirit of **truth**,
  he will guide you to **all** truth.
He will **not** speak on his **own**,
  but he will speak what he **hears**,
  and will **declare** to you the things that are **coming**.
He will **glorify** me,
  because he will take from what is **mine** and **declare** it to you.
Everything that the Father **has** is mine;
  for this reason I **told** you that he will take from what is **mine**
  and declare it to **you**."

Or:

---

the virtues of "love, joy . . . ." In Paul's catalog of vices sand virtues, the works of the flesh are significantly more numerous than the fruits of the Spirit. But Paul notes that there is no law prohibiting the manifestation of these fruits. The manifestation of the fruits of the Spirit occurs when Christians act in their daily lives in a manner consistent with the working of the Holy Spirit.

As Christians today, we endeavor not to be modern-day Judaizers or libertines. And while we realize we may not be perfect, we do believe that "The *fruits* of the

Spirit are perfections that the Holy Spirit forms in us as the first fruits of eternal glory" (CCC, #1832).

GOSPEL   During the Easter season, the Gospels have focused on the person of Jesus, the second person of the Trinity, with the Gospels of the first three Sundays recounting appearances of the risen Christ and the fourth through seventh Sundays excerpting from Jesus' teaching on himself as the Good Shepherd, and his Last Supper discourse and prayer. On Pentecost, a feast many people associate

only with the Holy Spirit, the third person of the Trinity, one might expect the Spirit to be the center of attention in the Gospel. Yet today's Gospel reflects the intimate relationship that exists between Jesus and the Spirit—as well as the Father.

All three persons of the Trinity are distinct in their own right; nevertheless, the Trinity is a communion of persons interconnected in mutual relationship. Thus, the Easter season cannot be seen solely as the season of the Son, Jesus, the risen Christ, nor can Pentecost be seen as only a day when the Holy Spirit is celebrated.

GOSPEL John 20:19–23

A reading from the holy Gospel according to John

On the evening of that **first** day of the week,
    when the doors were **locked**, where the **disciples** were,
    for fear of the **Jews**,
    Jesus **came** and **stood** in their midst
    and said to them, "**Peace** be with you."
When he had **said** this, he showed them his **hands** and his **side**.
The disciples **rejoiced** when they saw the Lord.
Jesus said to them **again**, "**Peace** be with you.
As the **Father** has sent **me**, so **I** send **you**."
And when he had **said** this, he **breathed** on them
    and said to them,
    "**Receive** the Holy **Spirit**.
Whose sins you **forgive** are **forgiven** them,
    and whose sins you **retain** are **retained**."

As the passage from John shows, the Advocate—the Spirit—will be sent by Jesus from the Father. The Spirit is the Spirit of truth who has his origin in the Father and who will witness to Jesus. This means that the Spirit was present with the Father from the beginning of time, as the Word was with God in the beginning (John 1:1). As a gift of Jesus from the Father, the Spirit comes to Jesus' disciples so that they might proclaim the truth of salvation they have come to know through Jesus.

Notice the repetition of Jesus' description of the mission of the Spirit: the Spirit will take from Jesus the truth about who he is ("what the Father has") and "declare" (*anangellein*) it to the disciples. The verb *anangellein* was often used in apocalyptic literature of the time to designate the revelation coming at the end times. Its use in this passage in relation to the Spirit's declaration of "the things that are coming" could suggest a reference to Jesus' second coming. Exclusive of that, what it does point to is that the disciples will share fully in the truth which belongs to the Father and Jesus because the Spirit will communicate this to them.

Through the gifts of the Spirit, then, any chasm that might be thought to exist between the divine communion of persons and human persons is forever closed. The Spirit—always in relation to the Father and Son—is present with us now as then with the disciples. The Spirit helps us—like Jesus' disciples—to remain close to him, the desire he expressed in his discourse about the vine and the branches (John 15:1—16:4a). As members of the Church, the Spirit guides us as we participate in the Spirit's ongoing mission to declare the truth of God's love to the world.

MOST HOLY TRINITY

Lectionary #165

Deuteronomy = d<u>oo</u>-ter-AH-nuh-mee

READING I Deuteronomy 4:32–34, 39–40

A reading from the Book of Deuteronomy

Moses said to the people:
  "**Ask** now of the days of **old**, **before** your time,
  ever since God **created** man upon the earth;
  ask from **one** end of the sky to the **other**:
  Did **anything** so **great** ever **happen** before?
Was it ever **heard** of?
Did a people ever hear the voice of God
  speaking from the midst of **fire**, as **you** did, and **live**?
Or did any **god** venture to go and take a **nation** for **himself**
  from the midst of **another** nation,
  by **testings**, by signs and **wonders**, by **war**,
  with strong **hand** and outstretched **arm**, and by great **terrors**,
  all of which the LORD, your **God**,
  did for you in **Egypt** before your very **eyes**?
This is why you must now **know**,
  and **fix** in your heart, that the LORD is God
  in the heavens **above** and on earth **below**,
  and that there is no **other**.
You must keep his **statutes** and **commandments** that I **enjoin**
    on you today,
  that **you** and your **children after** you may **prosper**,
  and that you may have long **life** on the land
  which the LORD, your God, is **giving** you forever."

The four questions Moses asks are all rhetorical in nature, but remember to raise your voice slightly at the end of each one. Also, pause slightly after each question and heighten the intensity in your voice as each question focuses the assembly more and more on the marvels God has done.

State Moses' words in this section in a convincing tone of voice reflective of your own confidence and faith in God.

Deliver the final commands ("You must keep his statutes . . .") in a firm but hopeful tone of voice, making as much eye contact with the assembly as possible.

READING I — As Christians, we understand our God to be triune—three in one—Father, Son, and Holy Spirit. The doctrine of the Trinity developed first out of the scriptures and the communal prayer of the Church. Then, through numerous Trinitarian controversies, the doctrine was formulated at the Councils of Nicea (325) and Constantinople (381), and is now professed in the recitation of the creed.

The First Reading from Deuteronomy is an address from Moses that gives evidence of the uniqueness of God's relationship to his people, one that no other god can ever have. Through God's work of creation, God's greatness is evident. Through the revelation of God in the fire and the victory he won for Israel in its escape from Egypt (Deuteronomy 7:19; 29:2), God's might and power show forth.

The Christian God—Father, Son, and Holy Spirit—is the same one God who chose the Israelite people to be his own, cared for them (and us) even before creation, and preserved them from the Egyptians. This God is the one who is "in the heavens above and on the earth below," who led his people to prosperity through the law, who saved his people through the mission of his Son's Incarnation and the Paschal Mystery, and continues to care for his people through the sending of the Spirit. Thus, Catholics believe that the Christian God has and will always be triune—three in one. For this, may God be praised today!

READING II — Paul's letter to the Romans, written between 56 and 58 AD, is thought of by many as the letter most central to understanding his thoughts about the developing Christian faith.

Romans = ROH-munz

Proclaim the first line of the reading in a straightforward manner, with the confidence that you believe this is true.

Do not shout "Abba, Father!" so as to over-dramatize the address; rather, convey the warmth and intimacy of this address by proclaiming the words slowly, in a warm but strong tone of voice, reflecting a longing to be close to the Father.

A reading from the Letter of Saint Paul to the Romans

Brothers and sisters:
Those who are led by the **Spirit** of God are **sons** of God.
For you did not receive a spirit of **slavery** to fall back into **fear**,
    but you received a Spirit of **adoption**,
    through whom we cry, "**Abba, Father!**"
The Spirit **himself** bears witness with **our** spirit
    that we are **children** of God,
    and if **children**, then **heirs**,
    heirs of God and **joint** heirs with **Christ**,
    if only we **suffer** with him
    so that we may also be **glorified** with him.

The passage from Romans proclaimed today is found in the eighth chapter of the letter, a chapter that focuses on the relationship between life in the Spirit and life in the flesh. For Paul, life according to the flesh means falling victim to sin and living in a sinful body (Romans 8:6). In contrast, life in the Spirit means that we are "dead to sin" and living for God in Christ Jesus (8:11).

Through Baptism, Christians participate in both the death and Resurrection of Christ (8:3–4). As a result, we enjoy a new relationship with God. We are his adopted sons and daughters. The Spirit of God is the one who makes this possible, creating the bond of communion between God and us. In a sense, then, through Baptism and the working of the Spirit, we are taken into God's family, the divine communion of persons—Father, Son, and Holy Spirit—to be one with God forever. That is what Paul means when he refers to those who are led by the Spirit as "heirs of God and joint heirs with Christ" (8:17).

Saint Augustine, writing in the late fourth and early fifth centuries, reflected on the Trinity in terms of the triad of the lover, the beloved, and the bond of love. While the Spirit is sometimes neglected in our life of faith, Paul, as evidenced in today's reading, and Augustine in his image of the Spirit as the bond of love, show that the Spirit is just as an important a "person" in the Trinity as the Father and the Son. It is the Spirit who unites the three persons of the Trinity together, and holds us together with them allowing us to share in the joy of their life—keeping us in relationship with God and our brothers and sisters in faith.

GOSPEL Matthew 28:16–20

A reading from the holy Gospel according to Matthew

The eleven disciples went to **Galilee**,
    to the **mountain** to which Jesus had **ordered** them.
When they all **saw** him, they **worshiped**, but they **doubted**.
Then Jesus **approached** and said to them,
    "All power in **heaven** and on **earth** has been **given** to me.
Go, therefore, and make **disciples** of all **nations**,
    baptizing them in the name of the **Father**,
    and of the **Son**, and of the Holy **Spirit**,
    teaching them to **observe** all that I have **commanded** you.
And **behold**, I am **with** you **always**, until the end of the **age**."

Proclaim Jesus' commission of the disciples ("All power in heaven and earth . . .") and continue through to the end of the Gospel in a confident, unwavering tone of voice. Direct his command ("Go, therefore, and make disciples . . .") to the members of the assembly by making eye contact with them.

GOSPEL This brief passage comes at the end of Matthew. Known as the "Great Commission," it tells of the risen Jesus sending the 11 disciples (not 12, because Judas is no longer with them) forth to all the nations and charging them with the task of forming more people as his followers.

One of the unique features of today's Gospel is the time sequence contained in it. Past, present, and future are all referenced. First, Jesus notes that power has been given to him, a power that comes from his Father (past). Second, during his encounter with the disciples, Jesus commissions them to make disciples of all nations and baptize them in the name of the Father, and of the Son, and of the Holy Spirit (present). Third, Jesus assures the disciples that he will be with them until the end of time (future).

While not written using sophisticated theological terminology, these verses from Matthew show us the abiding presence of God as Trinity. The triune God has been present from the beginning of creation, is now, and will be forever, as we pray: "Glory be to the Father . . . ."

Finally, we might have doubts about our experience of God, as the 11 disciples doubted the risen Jesus. Yet we, like the disciples, are commissioned to spread our Christian faith, leading others to profess their faith in God—Father, Son, and Holy Spirit and be baptized into the communion of faith, the Church.

MOST HOLY BODY AND BLOOD OF CHRIST

Lectionary #168

READING I   Exodus 24:3–8

Exodus = EK-suh-dus

A reading from the Book of Exodus

Proclaim the people's response to the words of the Lord conveyed by Moses ("We will do everything") in a strong voice filled with conviction.

Pause before continuing the narrative ("Moses then wrote down . . .") with a solemn tone of voice as you are now describing a formal covenant ritual.

When Moses came to the people
  and related all the **words** and **ordinances** of the LORD,
  they all **answered** with one **voice**,
  "We will do **everything** that the LORD has **told** us."
Moses then wrote **down** all the words of the LORD and,
  rising **early** the next **day**,
  he **erected** at the foot of the mountain an **altar**
  and twelve **pillars** for the twelve **tribes** of Israel.
Then, having sent certain young men of the Israelites
  to offer **holocausts** and sacrifice young **bulls**
  as **peace** offerings to the LORD,
  Moses took half of the **blood** and put it in large **bowls**;
  the **other** half he splashed on the **altar**.
Taking the book of the **covenant**, he read it **aloud** to the people,
  who answered, "**All** that the LORD has **said**, we will
      heed and **do**."

Emphasize the repetition of the people's response ("All that the Lord has said . . .") by heightening the degree of conviction in your voice slightly from the tone of voice you used at the beginning of the reading.

Then he took the **blood** and **sprinkled** it on the people, saying,
  "This is the blood of the **covenant**
  that the LORD has **made** with you
  in **accordance** with all these **words** of his."

READING I — The solemn ritual movement in this reading discloses the importance of the events that are narrated. Exodus 24 as a whole describes two different episodes in which the covenant given to Moses at Sinai is approved by the people. First, in Exodus 24:1–2; 9–11, Moses, Aaron, Nadab, Abihu, and 70 of the elders of Israel went up the mountain to the Lord. They gazed upon him, and even after doing so, were able to feast, eating and drinking the sacrificial meal in God's sight.

Exodus 24:3–8, which is today's reading, describes Moses coming to the people, presenting them the words and ordinances of the Lord. The people accept the covenant, saying, "We will do everything." The ritual then proceeds in clear steps: 1) Moses wrote down the Lord's words, 2) built an altar, 3) sanctified the altar with the blood of the young bulls, 4) proclaimed the word of the Lord to the people, 5) the people responded, and 6) their commitment to the covenant was sealed by Moses sprinkling them with the blood of the covenant.

What both rituals in Exodus 24 have in common is that the Lord never leaves his people. With respect to the first ritual, the common belief at the time was that if a person gazed upon God, this would bring immediate death. Yet those who saw God were able to continue the ritual, a sign that in and through the sacrificial meal, God was present with them.

In the second ritual, Moses splashing the altar with blood and sprinkling the people with the same blood shows

A reading from the Letter to the Hebrews

Brothers and sisters:
When **Christ** came as **high** priest
    of the good things that have come to **be**,
    passing **through** the **greater** and more **perfect** tabernacle
    not made by **hands**, that is, not belonging to **this** creation,
    he entered **once** for **all** into the **sanctuary**,
    not with the blood of **goats** and **calves**
    but with his **own** blood, thus obtaining **eternal** redemption.
For if the blood of **goats** and bulls
    and the sprinkling of a **heifer's ashes**
    can sanctify those who are **defiled**
    so that their flesh is **cleansed**,
    how much **more** will the blood of **Christ**,
    who through the eternal Spirit **offered** himself **unblemished**
        to God,
    cleanse our **consciences** from dead **works**
    to **worship** the living **God**.

For this reason **he** is mediator of a **new** covenant:
    since a **death** has taken place for deliverance
    from **transgressions** under the **first** covenant,
    those who are **called** may **receive** the promised
        eternal inheritance.

The emphasis on the first lengthy sentence should fall on the two phrases: "When Christ came as high priest" and "he entered once for all into the sanctuary." Lowering your tone of voice on the other phrases in this sentence and pausing at the commas will assist you in your proclamation of the main thought contained in these two phrases.

Pause before the words "For if the blood of goats . . . ." Begin this section in a moderate tone of voice and increase in intensity as you speak the words "how much more will the blood of Christ . . . ."

Proclaim "For this reason he is mediator of a new covenant" in a declarative tone of voice, making eye contact with the assembly and pausing at the semicolon before delivering the reason.

that God shares the covenant with the Israelites, despite the fact that often they will be unfaithful.

On this solemnity we commemorate both Christ's body and blood, the gifts that brought the Mosaic covenant to fulfillment. The word of God proclaimed in this reading, as well as other texts such as the Responsorial Psalm, make clear that this feast is celebrated with respect to both Christ's precious body and blood (see *Commentary on the GNLYC*, USCCB, p. 70).

READING II The letter to the Hebrews was written in the eighties by an unknown author to Christians who understood the worth of Jewish law and ritual practices. The author, understanding this also, developed one of the main themes of Hebrews, that of the high priesthood of Jesus, in light of the Jewish concept of the sacrificial priesthood. This theme is elaborated on in Hebrews 5:11—6:20, the section from which today's Second Reading is taken. (The letter to the Hebrews is proclaimed on the Twenty-seventh through the Thirty-third Sundays in Ordinary Time

this year. See those commentaries for more background.)

The high priest, whose functions are described in Exodus 28, was head of the Levitical priesthood. He alone could enter the Holy of Holies, the innermost part of the Temple, to offer a sacrifice once a year on the Day of Atonement. Christians believe that Christ's own high priesthood was foreshadowed through this priesthood. Through the sacrificial offering of his own body and blood, Christ entered not into the Holy of Holies, but into the new sanctuary of heaven

GOSPEL Mark 14:12–16, 22–26

A reading from the holy Gospel according to Mark

Make sure your proclamation of the opening clause ("On the first day . . .") is clearly enunciated.

On the **first** day of the **Feast** of Unleavened **Bread**,
   when they sacrificed the **Passover** lamb,
   Jesus' **disciples** said to him,
   "Where do you want us to **go**
   and **prepare** for you to eat the **Passover**?"
He **sent** two of his disciples and said to them,
   "Go into the **city** and a man will **meet** you,
   carrying a jar of **water**.
Follow him.

Deliver Jesus' lengthy and detailed instructions ("Go into the city . . . . Make the preparations for us there") in an instructive, but not overly commanding, tone of voice.

Wherever he **enters**, say to the **master** of the house,
   'The **Teacher** says, "Where is my **guest** room
   where I may eat the **Passover** with my **disciples**?"'
Then he will show you a large upper **room** furnished and ready.
Make the **preparations** for us **there**."
The disciples then went **off**, **entered** the city,
   and **found** it just as he had **told** them;
   and they prepared the **Passover**.

As you speak the words of Jesus ("Take it; this is my body . . . . This is my blood . . ."), try to differentiate in your tone of voice between the way these familiar words are prayed in the Eucharistic Prayer and how you proclaim them now as part of today's Gospel, perhaps by using a more declarative tone here.

While they were **eating**,
   he took **bread**, said the **blessing**,
   broke it, **gave** it to them, and said,
   "**Take** it; this is my **body**."
Then he took a **cup**, gave **thanks**, and **gave** it to them,
   and they all **drank** from it.

and became the mediator of a new covenant. Thus, the Catholic Church teaches that the "sacrifice of Christ is unique; it completes and surpasses all other sacrifices" (CCC, #614). There is no need now for other sacrificial offerings.

While each celebration of the Eucharist memorializes Christ's sacrifice, today the Church draws attention to the meaning of Christ's sacrifice and its relationship to the eucharistic sacrifice. The reading from Hebrews makes clear that Christ's sacrifice, "which he was to accomplish once for all on the cross would be re-presented,

its memory perpetuated until the end of the world, and its salutary power be applied to the forgiveness of the sins we daily commit," is made present each time the Church celebrates the Eucharist (see CCC, #1362–1372).

GOSPEL | The Gospel for the solemnity of the Most Holy Body and Blood of Christ comes from Mark's account of the Passion. (Mark's Passion narrative was proclaimed on Palm Sunday;

see that commentary for background.) In Mark's Passion narrative, the description of the preparation and celebration of the Passover meal follows immediately after the scene depicting Judas' willingness to betray Jesus. And after the meal, Mark offers Jesus' prediction of Peter's threefold denial. As a whole, the disciples in Mark's account are depicted as lacking in understanding and fidelity to Jesus.

Jesus' actions as he was celebrating the Passover meal with his disciples show how through his suffering, death, and Resurrection, he is the "new Passover

He said to them,
 "This is my **blood** of the **covenant**,
 which will be **shed** for **many**.
Amen, I **say** to you,
 I shall not drink **again** the fruit of the **vine**
 until the day when I drink it **new** in the kingdom of **God**."
Then, after singing a **hymn**,
 they went out to the Mount of **Olives**.

lamb." Through his blood, he is the mediator of a new covenant, a covenant in which his blood was shed for the sins of all. Every time the Church gathers to celebrate the Eucharist, we remember and make present Jesus' sacrifice and the new meaning he gave to the Passover and the covenant (CCC, #1362–1367).

The memorial meal of the Eucharist that Jesus instituted at the Passover meal is also a sacrifice of the Church (see Matthew 26:17 29 and Luke 22:7–20). As Jesus gathered his disciples around him

for the original celebration, so the Church, through the bishop whose name is mentioned in the Eucharistic Prayer, is united in its celebration of the Eucharist. Thus, the Eucharist can also be seen as the sacrifice of the Church. In this prayer the members of the Church, the body of Christ, join their lives, their praise, sufferings, prayers, and work to those of Christ (CCC, #1368).

Through the Eucharist, then, men and women of the Church are nourished to live as the body of Christ in the world, drawing others into communion with Christ in the Church, despite the fact that sometimes

we, like the disciples in the Gospel according to Mark, are not faithful to Jesus. Saint Augustine, in a sermon to the newly baptized, expresses the mission that flows from participation in the Eucharist in these words: "Through bread and wine, the Lord gives us His body and blood. If you receive them well, you are that which you receive; you become what you receive; you become what you eat. That is the call of God to us" (*Sermon* CCXXVII, PL, #38, 1099).

12TH SUNDAY IN ORDINARY TIME

Lectionary #95

READING I   Job 38:1, 8–11

A reading from the Book of Job

The Lord addressed **Job** out of the **storm** and said:
   Who **shut** within doors the **sea**,
      when it burst **forth** from the **womb**;
   when I made the clouds its **garment**
      and thick **darkness** its **swaddling** bands?
   When I set **limits** for it
      and **fastened** the bar of its **door**,
   and **said**: **Thus** far shall you come but no **farther**,
      and **here** shall your proud waves be **stilled**!

Job = johb

Proclaim the announcement of the Lord's words ("The Lord addressed Job . . .") in a moderate speaking voice. Proclaim the rest of the reading in a confident, self-assured, and authoritative tone of voice.

READING I   The book of Job, most likely written after the exile (sixth to fifth century BC) narrates Job's struggle with the suffering that has befallen him, an innocent man. Today's brief First Reading is part of the Lord's speech to Job, which is found in chapters 38 and 39, and most of chapter 40.

Throughout the Lord's speech, as exemplified in the small portion of it proclaimed today, it is the Lord's power and omnipotence that serve as an answer to Job's questions about his fate in life. The Lord has the power to still the waves of the sea as He has the power to calm the storms of life. Realizing the Lord's power, we, like Job, can return to a deeper faith, and a sense of our own humble role in the course of life.

READING II   On the Twelfth Sunday in Ordinary Time, the Lectionary cycle of readings continues the semi-continuous journey, begun on the Seventh Sunday of Ordinary Time, through Paul's second letter to the Corinthians. This reading will continue for three more Sundays (see the commentary for the Seventh Sunday of Ordinary Time for more background).

In today's reading, the love of Christ, shown by his death and Resurrection for the sake of others, is what impels Paul to undertake his ministry. Paul—and you through the proclamation of Paul's teaching—impels others to imitate this love of Christ in their relations to one another.

The "old things" of the law of the old covenant have "passed away" and everything in Christ has begun a "new creation." Paul was not as concerned about new

READING II   2 Corinthians 5:14–17

Corinthians = kor-IN-thee-unz

Speak the address ("Brothers and sisters") in an affectionate tone of voice, making eye contact with the members of the assembly.

A reading from the second Letter of Saint Paul to the Corinthians

Brothers and sisters:
The **love** of Christ **impels** us,
  once we have **come** to the **conviction** that **one** died for **all**;
  therefore, all have died.
He **indeed** died for all,
  so that those who **live** might no longer live for **themselves**
  but for **him** who for **their** sake **died** and was **raised**.

Pause before the new section beings ("Consequently . . .").

Consequently, from now on we regard **no** one according to
     the **flesh**;
  even if we once knew **Christ** according to the **flesh**,
  yet **now** we know him so no **longer**.
So **whoever** is in Christ is a **new** creation:
  the **old** things have passed **away**;
  behold, new things have **come**.

Portray the certainty of Paul's belief with an unwavering and optimistic tone in your voice as you proclaim the words "So whoever is in Christ . . . ."

Christians following every detail of the Jewish law in order to become a part of the Christian community as he was that new Christians participate in Baptism and Eucharist, and love one another in imitation of Christ's love.

The new covenant in Christ and his Spirit, which Christians embrace in the celebration of the sacrament of Baptism, now guides their life. As baptized Christians, we, like Paul, are sent to proclaim the newness of Jesus to others, allowing the love of Christ to impel us in this mission.

GOSPEL Today's Gospel from Mark narrates Jesus' calming of the storm. The opening lines set the stage for the display of Jesus' power. He is not alone; rather, the disciples accompany him. Mark also provides the interesting detail that the boat with the disciples and Jesus was not the only boat that would experience the violent seas—"other boats were with him" (verse 36). Mark neither specifies who occupies these other boats, nor does he mention them again in this gospel. Presumably it is other disciples, perhaps some known and some unknown,

who wanted to be close to Jesus. By not drawing attention to the other boats, Mark keeps the attention on Jesus. Yet, even though they are in the background, the others are not forgotten. Rather, they are a subtle reminder of people's growing interest in the person of Jesus.

As the storm on the sea arises, the disciples wake Jesus up. Their question to him reflects concern for their safety. They are worried about drowning. Jesus' rebuke of the wind and commands to the sea are a display of his authority. He does not call on

GOSPEL   Mark 4:35–41

A reading from the holy Gospel according to Mark

On that day, as **evening** drew on, Jesus said to his **disciples**:
   "Let us cross to the other **side**."
Leaving the crowd, they took **Jesus** with them in the **boat**
   just as he was.
And **other** boats were with him.
A violent **squall** came up and **waves** were breaking over the **boat**,
   so that it was **already** filling up.
Jesus was in the stern, **asleep** on a **cushion**.
They **woke** him and said to him,
   "**Teacher**, do you not **care** that we are **perishing**?"
He **woke** up,
   rebuked the wind, and said to the **sea**, "**Quiet**! Be **still**!"
The wind **ceased** and there was great **calm**.
Then he asked them, "**Why** are you **terrified**?
Do you **not** yet have **faith**?"
They were filled with great **awe** and said to one another,
   "Who then **is** this whom even **wind** and **sea** obey?"

Pause after the line "And other boats were with him."

Ask the disciples' question in a slightly indignant tone of voice.

Deliver Jesus' rebuke of the wind and the sea in an authoritative, loud tone of voice, but don't shout.

In a softer voice, narrate the line "The wind ceased . . . ."

Ask Jesus' questions to his disciples with curiosity and concern, not mockery or disappointment, remembering to raise the tone of your voice somewhat at the end of each question. When you pose the disciples' question, look up at the assembly and use a strong tone of voice. You and those in the assembly know the answer to this question!

God, the Father, to assist him in carrying out the miracle; he accomplishes it on his own. This demonstration of power coincides with the Lord's power seen in the first reading from Job. Here, too, the Lord stills the proud waves (Job 38:11).

After the calming of the storm, Jesus questions the disciples about their fear and the state of their faith. Mark records no verbal response of the disciples directly to Jesus. Instead, he tells of their awe, a common reaction to the witnessing of divine power, and the question they ask each other. The normalcy of the question is striking, as surely they believed in the power of the Lord, but they no doubt had not witnessed this power manifested through a person as of yet. The disciples have given up everything to follow Jesus, but their question bespeaks their anxiety about their lack of knowledge of the one they have chosen to follow. In a sense, the members of the assembly are the disciples. The journey through the weeks of Ordinary Time will assist them in discovering more of whom this person is who calmed the storm and in whom they profess faith.

13TH SUNDAY IN ORDINARY TIME

Lectionary #98

READING I	Wisdom 1:13–15, 2:23–24

A reading from the Book of Wisdom

God did not make **death**,
    nor does he **rejoice** in the **destruction** of the **living**.
For he fashioned all things that they might have being;
    and the **creatures** of the world are **wholesome**,
and there is not a **destructive** drug among them
    nor any domain of the **netherworld** on earth,
    for justice is **undying**.
For God **formed** man to be **imperishable**;
    the **image** of his own nature he **made** him.
But by the envy of the **devil**, **death** entered the world,
    and they who **belong** to his company **experience** it.

Use a serious tone of voice as you begin this reading.

Lighten your tone as you convey the goodness of God's creation ("For he fashioned all things . . .").

Change back to a more serious, heavier tone of voice as you conclude with the reading's verse about death and the envy of the devil.

READING I This brief First Reading from the book of Wisdom comes from the section that offers praises to Wisdom for the reward of immortality, which those who seek her on earth experience upon their death (1:1—6:21) and for her role in the creation of the world (6:22—11:1). Specifically, the four verses of today's reading provide us with a theological understanding of the relationship between creation and death that recalls the creation accounts in Genesis 1 and 2.

Because God created all things that they might have life and being, purposefully breathing the breath of his own life into man (Genesis 2:7), the creatures of the world are "wholesome." In the words of Genesis, God's creation is good, and the creation of man and woman in the divine image is "very good" (Genesis 1:31). Created in the image of the one who gave them life, then, nothing that could cause destruction can be found among them. Thus, from their creation God and humankind were in communion with each other.

Yet this reading tells us that through the devil, death came into the world. Death can be understood both in a spiritual sense and a physical sense. In the former, it is a separation from communion with God. In the latter, it is simply an end to our earthly life. The Church, in both instances, teaches that death is a consequence of sin (Genesis 2:17; CCC, #1008). God did not desire us to experience death; he created us to be "imperishable," to live always and forever united with him in the deepest of communion.

As you proclaim the opening line in a confident and optimistic tone of voice, look up at the assembly.

Lower your tone of voice slightly as you speak of the "gracious act of our Lord Jesus Christ."

Pause before the words "Not that others should have relief."

Pause slightly after the words "As it is written" to allow the quote to stand out. Then proclaim the quotation from Exodus 16:18 slowly and deliberately in order to emphasize the paradox.

READING II   2 Corinthians 8:7, 9, 13–15

A reading from the second Letter of Saint Paul to the Corinthians

Brothers and sisters:
As you excel in **every** respect, in **faith**, **discourse**,
    knowledge, all **earnestness**, and in the **love** we have for **you**,
    may you excel in **this** gracious act **also**.

For you know the gracious **act** of our Lord Jesus **Christ**,
    that though he was **rich**, for your sake he became **poor**,
    so that by his **poverty** you might **become** rich.
Not that **others** should have relief while you are **burdened**,
    but that as a matter of equality
    your abundance at the present time should supply **their**
        needs,
    so that **their** abundance may also supply **your** needs,
    that there may be **equality**.
As it is **written**:
    *Whoever had **much** did not have **more**,*
        *and whoever had **little** did not have **less**.*

In the face of sin and evil, though, God's justice is undying. Through God's justice, embodied in the person of Christ, immortality and communion with God are forever restored as gifts to the human person. "The obedience of Jesus has transformed the curse of death into a blessing" (Romans 5:19–21; CCC, #1009). Our challenge, even though in our humanity we bear the mark of original sin, is to live the virtues of God's justice and righteousness to the best of our abilities. When we do so our experience of communion with our brothers and sisters in faith and in the world will, however incomplete, also be an experience of communion with God.

READING II   "This gracious act" in which Paul is encouraging the Corinthians to excel at the beginning of the passage is the collection they will take up for the Jerusalem Church, an early Christian community in need. In this reading, he develops two arguments—one practical and one theological—for why the Corinthians are to come to the aid of their sister community at Jerusalem.

First, "this gracious act" of economic stewardship to which Paul is calling the Corinthians, was exemplified by the collection already taken up by the Macedonians (2 Corinthians 8:1–6). The Macedonians, through the grace of God working in them, gave joyfully and charitably out of their own resources. By using the example of the Macedonians, Paul positions himself as a good salesman, trying to persuade the Corinthians on the basis of the goodness of what others have already accomplished. The Corinthians would not want the Macedonians to "one up" them.

GOSPEL   Mark 5:21–43

A reading from the holy Gospel according to Mark

When Jesus had crossed again in the boat
    to the other side,
    a large **crowd** gathered around him, and he stayed close
      to the **sea.**
One of the **synagogue** officials, named **Jairus,** came **forward.**
Seeing him he **fell** at his feet and pleaded **earnestly** with him,
      saying,
    "My **daughter** is at the point of **death.**
Please, **come** lay your hands on her
    that she may get **well** and **live.**"
He went off with him,
    and a large crowd **followed** him and pressed **upon** him.

There was a **woman** afflicted with **hemorrhages** for twelve **years.**
She had suffered **greatly** at the hands of many **doctors**
    and had spent all that she had.
Yet she was not **helped** but only grew **worse.**
She had heard about Jesus and came up **behind** him in the crowd
    and **touched** his **cloak.**
She said, "If I but touch his **clothes,** I shall be **cured.**"
Immediately her flow of blood **dried up.**
She felt in her **body** that she was **healed** of her **affliction.**
Jesus, aware at **once** that **power** had gone **out** from him,
    turned **around** in the crowd and **asked,** "**Who** has touched
      my **clothes?**"

Jairus = JĪ-rus

Express Jairus' words ("My daughter . . .") with pleading in your voice. Pause after these words as the Gospel transitions to the story of the woman with a hemorrhage.

hemorrhage = HEM-er-rij

Proclaim the woman's words ("If I but touch . . .") with eagerness.

Ask Jesus' question ("Who has touched my clothes?") in an inquisitive but authoritative tone of voice.

Second, Paul develops the theological foundation for giving. Christian communities are to give out of their abundance because the "gracious act" of the Lord Jesus Christ provides the example par excellence of charity. The one who was rich became poor: the one who was God, became human, so that we, too, might be taken up into communion with God.

In this reading Paul is not suggesting that by giving we become poor; rather, he is developing a principle of equality. A community's surplus wealth is meant to be equitably distributed so that no community remains in need. Jerusalem is the community in need now, but the Corinthians very well could be in need later. Thus, at this point, the Corinthians are to respond as Christ would, by providing for the Jerusalem Church.

The Catholic Church has a long history of sharing economic resources with those in need. In North America, Catholic relief agencies facilitate the response of parishes throughout the United States and Canada in times of crisis and with respect to poverty on all levels—locally, nationally, and internationally—especially through the Catholic Campaign for Human Development. Often Catholic parishes support a local chapter of Saint Vincent de Paul and have a Human Concerns Committee that addresses the needs of those in their particular area. These practical efforts are founded on the theology Paul develops in this reading, the writings of Church fathers, as well as the long-standing tradition of Catholic social doctrine, dating back to Pope Leo XIII's *Rerum novarum* ("On the

Narrate the woman's approach of Jesus ("The woman, realizing . . .") with some nervousness in your voice.

Express Jesus' words to the woman ("Daughter, your faith . . .") in a compassionate, gentle, and peaceful tone of voice.

Pause before the narrative returns to the story of Jairus' daughter in the words "While he was still speaking."

But his disciples said to Jesus,
    "You see how the crowd is **pressing** upon you,
    and yet you ask, 'Who **touched** me?'"
And he looked around to see who had done it.
The **woman**, realizing what had happened to her,
    approached in **fear** and **trembling**.
She fell **down** before Jesus and told him the whole **truth**.
He said to her, "**Daughter**, your **faith** has saved you.
Go in **peace** and be **cured** of your **affliction**."

While he was still speaking,
    people from the synagogue official's house arrived and said,
    "Your **daughter** has **died**; why trouble the **teacher** any longer?"
Disregarding the message that was reported,
    Jesus said to the synagogue **official**,
    "**Do** not be **afraid**; just have **faith**."
He did not allow **anyone** to accompany him inside
    except **Peter**, **James**, and **John**, the brother of **James**.
When they arrived at the house of the synagogue official,
    he caught sight of a **commotion**,
    people **weeping** and wailing **loudly**.
So he went in and said to them,
    "**Why** this commotion and **weeping**?

State Jesus' words "The child is not dead but asleep" in a firm tone of voice filled with conviction.

The child is not **dead** but **asleep**."
And they **ridiculed** him.
Then he put them all out.

Condition of Working Classes") promulgated in 1891 (see also CCC, #2419–2449).

GOSPEL In Mark's account, today's passage follows upon two other miracle stories: Jesus' calming of the storm at sea (4:35–41), which was proclaimed last Sunday, and the healing of a man possessed by a demon (5:1–20). Next Sunday, we will hear that after Jesus performed these miracles, he traveled to his native town of Nazareth, where he was rejected by those who heard him preach in the synagogue (6:1–6).

Today's Gospel narrative is an interesting literary composition. The evangelist Mark has included two healing stories in one passage. He begins the Gospel with Jairus appealing to Jesus to lay his hands on his daughter so she will get well. At his request, Jesus goes off with Jairus, presumably going to visit his daughter, and upon seeing her, offer her physical and spiritual healing (Mark 8:35; 10:26; 13:13). Yet in the midst of Jesus' journey, Mark inserts another story. Jesus encounters a woman who has been afflicted with a severe hemorrhage for 12 years and greatly

desires to be healed. In effect, the story of Jairus' daughter forms the back and front covers to a book whose contents is the story of the woman with a hemorrhage.

By conflating these two stories, Mark has made sure that these stories are understood as a unit. To do so, he has provided three connections between them for the reader. First, the number of years the woman has suffered with a hemorrhage—12—is the same number of years as the age of Jairus' daughter. Second, in seeking healing from Jesus, the woman with a hemorrhage approaches Jesus and believes

He took along the child's **father** and **mother**
    and those who were **with** him
    and **entered** the room where the **child** was.
He took the child by the **hand** and said to her, *"Talitha koum,"*
    which means, **"Little girl**, I say to you, **arise**!"
The **girl**, a child of **twelve**, arose **immediately** and
    walked **around**.
At that they were **utterly** astounded.
He gave strict orders that **no** one should **know** this
    and said that she should be given something to **eat**.

[Shorter: Mark 5:21–24, 35b–43]

Convey Jesus' actions and words in the section "He took the child by the hand . . ." with the same compassionate tone of voice used previously to express Jesus' words to the woman cured of a hemorrhage ("Daughter, your faith . . .").

Talitha koum = TAH-lee-thah KOOM

Pause briefly before the final verse.

that she only needs to touch Jesus' clothes in order to be cured. As the Gospel returns to the story of Jairus' daughter, Jesus approaches the child and takes her by the hand, also touching her, and commanding her to arise. Third, after the woman with a hemorrhage was cured, she approached Jesus to speak with him. In their conversation, Jesus addressed her with the relational term "daughter." This provides a link with the first story, as it is Jairus' daughter who was ill and later died, thus presenting Jesus with an even greater miracle to perform.

The beautiful stories of healing in this Gospel reading relate in many ways to the Church's sacrament of the Anointing of the Sick, a sacrament that involves an anointing for the forgiveness of sins and strengthening in the time of grave illness or approaching death. Through the sacrament, the Church carries on Jesus' mission to heal the sick and proclaims in a particular way that Jesus is "God who saves" as the meaning of his name suggests. The use of touch in today's reading corresponds to the laying on of hands in the sacrament of the Anointing of the Sick.

Moreover, in faith a sick person comes to the sacrament of the Anointing of the Sick, in which Christ is present through the Church's minister, and God's presence is known through other believers who are present to pray with the recipient of the sacrament. In faith Jairus approached Jesus, as did the woman with a hemorrhage. Your proclamation of the Gospel can help the assembly to know that, in times of need, they too only need to step forward in faith. The simplicity and hope of Jesus' words to Jairus ("Do not be afraid, just have faith") reflect this truth.

14TH SUNDAY IN ORDINARY TIME

Lectionary #101

READING I   Ezekiel 2:2–5

Ezekiel = ee-ZEE-kee-ul

Narrate the dramatic scene that begins the reading with excitement and energy in your voice.

Make eye contact with the assembly and direct the personal words of the Lord to Ezekiel ("Son of man, I am sending you . . .") to them as the Lord calls them to face those in the world who are "obstinate of heart."

Deliver the parenthetical remark "for they are a rebellious house" in a slightly lighter tone of voice than the main clause of the sentence ("And whether they heed . . .").

A reading from the Book of the Prophet Ezekiel

As the LORD **spoke** to me, the spirit **entered** into me
    and set me on my **feet**,
    and I heard the one who was speaking say to me:
    Son of **man**, I am **sending** you to the **Israelites**,
    rebels who have **rebelled** against me;
    they and their ancestors have **revolted** against me
      to this very **day**.
Hard of face and **obstinate** of **heart**
    are **they** to whom I am sending you.
But you shall say to them: Thus says the LORD **God**!
And whether they **heed** or **resist**—
     for they are a **rebellious** house—
    they shall **know** that a **prophet** has been **among** them.

READING I   Today's First Reading comes from the early chapters of the prophetic book that narrate Ezekiel's prophetic call (Ezekiel 1:1—3:27). The basis for Ezekiel's call is the Spirit of the Lord entering into him. This life force or breath *(ruah)* compels Ezekiel on his way as a prophet, giving him the strength and courage to face the Israelites, whom the Lord warns will be obstinate in response to Ezekiel's message. In fact, this reading coincides with today's Gospel of Jesus' own prophetic teaching not being accepted among his own household and kin.

Occasionally, your role as a proclaimer of the word might not be without difficulty. Your ability to fulfill your service as a lector, boldly proclaiming the word of the Lord, witnesses to others that the Spirit is within you as it was within Ezekiel.

READING II   This reading from the second letter to the Corinthians attests to the fact that, like many human beings, Paul was at least slightly worried his ego might get out of hand leading him to appear arrogant. Whether or not this is the case, we will never know. Certainly it takes a certain amount of pride and self-confidence to be a leader of any kind.

To understand this reading in its proper context, however, two points need to be made. First, at different points in 2 Corinthians, the reader is made aware that Paul is struggling with some other apostles who are competing for attention from the Corinthians, claiming superiority for their teaching and revelations. Some even had letters of recommendation (11:4). Therefore, Paul's desire that he "not become too elated" might reflect his own wish not to

READING II   2 Corinthians 12:7–10

A reading from the second Letter of Saint Paul to the Corinthians

Brothers and sisters:
That I, **Paul**, might not become too **elated**,
    because of the **abundance** of the **revelations**,
        a thorn in the **flesh** was **given** to me, an angel of **Satan**,
        to **beat** me, to keep me from being too **elated**.
Three **times** I begged the Lord about this, that it might **leave** me,
    but he said to me, "My **grace** is **sufficient** for you,
        for **power** is made perfect in **weakness**."
I will rather boast most **gladly** of my **weaknesses**,
    in order that the power of **Christ** may **dwell** with me.
Therefore, I am **content** with weaknesses, insults,
    hardships, persecutions and constraints,
        for the sake of **Christ**;
    for when I am **weak**, then I am **strong**.

Corinthians = kor-IN-thee-unz

Deliver the opening lines of the epistle as if you were giving an admission about your own weakness by speaking in a poignant and humble tone of voice.

Proclaim the Lord's words to Paul ("My grace is sufficient . . .") slowly, looking up at the assembly, and with kindness and concern in your voice.

Deliver Paul's final words ("for when I am weak . . .") with strength but not arrogance in your voice, again making eye contact with the assembly.

---

become like those whom he considers to be "false apostles."

Second, Paul clearly understands the "thorn in the flesh," which he was given to tone down any rising ego, to be caused by Satan. In the Old Testament thorns were symbols of enemies (Numbers 33:55). And earlier in 2 Corinthians, Paul refers to Satan in relation to the persecutions he is experiencing regarding his apostolic authority (11:14–15).

The centerpiece of today's passage, the words that Paul heard from the Lord ("My grace is sufficient . . ."), can thus be understood within the context of Paul's internal and external struggles. The Lord's words draw Paul and us back to the source and heart of his and our vocation: the grace of God.

Theologically, the Lord's words to Paul "power is made perfect in weakness" and Paul's reflection on those words expressing his contentment with "weaknesses, insults . . ." do not imply that Christians are to seek weakness, insults, and so on. Rather, Paul's line of reasoning is that when weakness and challenges come one's way, the Lord's grace will be enough to get one through.

| GOSPEL | Today's Gospel of Jesus' rejection by his own people begins where last Sunday's left off. In Mark, this event comes after four miracle stories, whereas in Luke it occurs at the beginning of Jesus' public ministry, and in Matthew it follows a series of parables Jesus uses to describe the kingdom of heaven (Matthew 13;53–58; Luke 4:16–30). Evidently, Mark chose to place this scene |

Observe the four questions in this Gospel and notice that an exclamatory statement ("What mighty deeds . . .") is placed in between them. Distinguish between the questions and the exclamatory statement by raising the tone of your voice slightly as you approach the end of the questions and delivering the exclamatory statement with excitement and amazement in your tone of voice, keeping the tone consistent through the end of the statement.

Joses = JOH-seez

Judas = JOO-dus

Simon = SI-mun

Use a strong tone of voice in your proclamation of the words "A prophet is not without honor . . . ." Despite the fact that Jesus is probably disappointed at the reception he received, he is resigned to it and speaks these words with authority.

Communicate shock in your tone of voice as you say, "He was amazed at their lack of faith," looking up and making eye contact, panning around the assembly.

GOSPEL   Mark 6:1–6

A reading from the holy Gospel according to Mark

Jesus **departed** from there and came to his native **place**,
     accompanied by his **disciples**.
When the **sabbath** came he began to **teach** in the **synagogue**,
     and many who **heard** him were **astonished**.
They said, "Where did this man **get** all this?
What kind of **wisdom** has been given him?
What mighty **deeds** are wrought by his **hands**!
Is he not the **carpenter**, the son of **Mary**,
     and the brother of **James** and **Joses** and **Judas** and **Simon**?
And are not his **sisters** here **with** us?"
And they took **offense** at him.
Jesus said to them,
     "A **prophet** is not without **honor** except in his native **place**
     and among his own **kin** and in his own **house**."
So he was **not** able to perform any mighty **deed** there,
     apart from curing a few **sick** people by laying his **hands**
          on them.
He was **amazed** at their lack of **faith**.

here in order to connect Jesus' mighty deeds, which were only a prelude to his Resurrection, with his rejection.

Those in the synagogue not only had difficulty understanding Jesus' teaching, but they also knew something of the "mighty deeds" that he had performed and this too troubled them. Since their prior experience of Jesus was as a child, they struggled, wondering how this man could be the same person who was "the son of Mary, and the brother of James." The four

questions posed by those who were listening to Jesus, then, are legitimate.

However, in their attempt to understand Jesus' identity, they realize Jesus was proclaiming something new, something they could not accept. Jesus' own words ("A prophet is not . . ."), similar to proverbs that were common during his time, solidifies his position of authority. In Jesus, the kingdom of God is at hand (Mark 1:15).

As a result, like the prophet Ezekiel in today's First Reading, Jesus faced rejection from his own. Obstinacy on their part,

however, did not take anything away from Jesus. A prophet, whom believers recognize as the Son of God, still had been in their midst in the synagogue.

15TH SUNDAY IN ORDINARY TIME

Lectionary #104

READING I   Amos 7:12–15

Amos = AY-m*s

Amaziah = am-uh-ZĪ-uh

Bethel = BETH-*l

Declare Amaziah's words to Amos in an authoritative tone of voice, one that cannot wait for Amos to leave town.

prophesy = PROF-uh-sī

Speak Amos' words ("I was no prophet . . ."), which continue to the end of the reading, with simple confidence, not defensiveness, in your tone of voice. Amos knows he is only following the Lord's instructions, as he should.

A reading from the Book of the Prophet Amos

Amaziah, priest of **Bethel**, said to **Amos**,
   "**Off** with you, **visionary**, **flee** to the land of **Judah**!
There earn your bread by **prophesying**,
   but never **again** prophesy in **Bethel**;
   for it is the king's **sanctuary** and a royal **temple**."
Amos **answered** Amaziah, "I was no **prophet**,
   nor have I belonged to a **company** of prophets;
   I was a **shepherd** and a dresser of **sycamores**.
The LORD took me from following the flock, and said to me,
   Go, **prophesy** to my people **Israel**."

READING I   The prophet Amos is one of the 12 minor prophets. He prophesied in the northern kingdom at a time when Israel was experiencing military, political, and economic success. Yet the threat of destruction by Assyria was continuously present. Amos is often remembered as a prophet of social justice, for he conspired against the kings and those who would claim more power and wealth than what was due them, including those of the professional class of prophets.

In today's brief passage, Amaziah, a priest of Bethel, a town just north of the border between the northern and southern kingdoms, commands Amos to return to Judah, the southern land from which he came. Amaziah's words seem to indicate that he thinks Amos belongs to the professional class of prophets who prophesy for a living and not on the basis of a personal call from the Lord. Amos' response, however, flatly denies any connection to the prophetic class. Instead, Amos states that his previous occupation was that of a shepherd and pruner of sycamore trees. While he was engaged in that ordinary work, the Lord personally called him to prophesy to the people of Israel.

This reading, along with the Gospel of the commissioning of the Twelve Apostles, both attest to the fact that following the Lord's call will not always be easy. We will be rejected by those who know us— our neighbors and friends—as well as by the strangers we encounter as we lead our lives as the Lord's disciples. Yet because it is the Lord who calls and invites us to this life, we know that the Lord is present with us as we cooperate in carrying out his work.

READING II Ephesians 1:3–14

A reading from the Letter of Saint Paul to the Ephesians

Blessed be the God and **Father** of our Lord Jesus **Christ**,
   who has **blessed** us in Christ
   with every spiritual blessing in the **heavens**,
   as he **chose** us in him, before the foundation of the **world**,
   to be **holy** and without **blemish** before him.
In **love** he destined us for **adoption** to himself
     through Jesus **Christ**,
   in accord with the **favor** of his **will**,
   for the **praise** of the glory of his **grace**
   that he **granted** us in the **beloved**.
In him we have **redemption** by his blood,
   the **forgiveness** of **transgressions**,
   in accord with the **riches** of his grace that he **lavished** upon us.
In all **wisdom** and **insight**, he has made **known** to us
   the mystery of his **will** in accord with his **favor**
   that he set **forth** in him as a **plan** for the fullness of **times**,
   to sum up **all** things in **Christ**, in **heaven** and on **earth**.

READING II Today is the first of seven Sundays in a row on which the Second Reading comes from the letter of Paul to the Ephesians. This letter was written at the end of the first century by a disciple of Paul who wanted to expand on the meaning of Paul's thought for the grow-ing Christian community. Thus, the letter is not addressed to a particular community of Christians as are those letters actually written by Paul, but to the worldwide Church. Its ecclesiology is more universal in scope, noting the expansiveness of the Church in God's heavenly plan of salvation.

Today's reading comes from the very beginning of Ephesians. Its verses can be understood as a great hymn of blessing. This blessing falls between the traditional greeting included in the letter (1:1–2) and an offering of thanksgiving (1:15–23). The opening formula of the blessing is reminis-cent of the *berakah* (a Jewish prayer of blessing) common in the Old Testament and in early Christian prayers.

The blessing shifts from opening verses that specifically address God who is the Father of Jesus Christ, to Christ as the sub-ject. Through Christ, "the beloved"—those who have been baptized—have redemp-tion. To them also the divine plan *(oikono-mia)* of salvation has been made known.

The final section of the blessing (verses 11–14), which is similar to Colossians 1:13–14, turns to the Holy Spirit. Those who have heard the "gospel of salvation" and believed in Christ are sealed with the Holy Spirit. This Spirit begins to lead all toward communion with God through Christ Jesus.

Make eye contact with the assembly on the line "In him we were also chosen . . . ." Be mindful of the parenthetical phrases ("destined in accord," "who accomplishes," and "we who first hoped") in lengthy, complex sentences such as "In him we were also chosen . . . ." Make sure to lighten your voice in the proclamation of these phrases.

In him we were also **chosen**,
    destined in accord with the **purpose** of the One
    who **accomplishes** all things according to the **intention**
        of his will,
    so that we might exist for the praise of his **glory**,
    we who **first** hoped in **Christ**.
In him you **also**, who have heard the word of **truth**,
    the gospel of your **salvation**, and have **believed** in him,
    were **sealed** with the promised Holy **Spirit**,
    which is the first **installment** of our **inheritance**
        toward **redemption** as God's **possession**, to the praise
        of his **glory**.

[Shorter: Ephesians 1:3–10]

GOSPEL   Mark 6:7–13

A reading from the holy Gospel according to Mark

Jesus summoned the **Twelve** and began to send them out
        two by **two**
    and gave them **authority** over unclean **spirits**.
He instructed them to take **nothing** for the journey
    but a **walking** stick—
    no food, no sack, no money in their belts.
They were, however, to wear **sandals**
    but **not** a second **tunic**.
He said to them,
    "Wherever you enter a house, **stay** there until you **leave**.

The evangelist Mark does not often include many details in his narratives, so communicate what the disciples are and are not to take with them on their journey ("walking stick . . .") slowly and with great care, clearly enunciating each item.

To understand the context of this blessing, it will be important for you to read through the thanksgiving that follows it (1:15–23). In this thanksgiving, the ecclesiological emphasis (the role of the Church) in all of Ephesians is made known. As previously noted, the Father's divine plan of salvation, which is accomplished through Christ in the Spirit, is mentioned in the blessing (1:9–10). Ephesians 1:22–23 describes the fulfillment of this communion for the "fullness of time" *(plērōma)* as taking place in the church, Christ's body, with Christ as its head.

GOSPEL   This Gospel deals with the mission of the 12 disciples who were appointed in Mark 3:14–15. It continues where last Sunday's Gospel left off in the Marcan narrative, although the second half of the sixth verse, which offers a transition between Jesus' teaching in the synagogue and his going out into the surrounding villages to continue his teaching, is dropped. This transitional half of the verse is important because it makes a connection between Jesus' own ministry and that of his disciples. Because they are sent by Jesus to act with his authority, they are known as apostles (in Greek, *apostolos,* meaning "one who is sent").

Like Jesus, the apostles are to go out preaching and teaching the Good News. They too, like Jesus and the prophet Amos in today's First Reading and Ezekiel from last Sunday, will face rejection. Welcome will not always be given to them on their journey. Yet they are to keep going.

To keep going on their missionary journey, although they have taken nothing

Pause again before narrating the description of the ministry the Twelve Apostles performed in the final section ("The Twelve drove out . . .") in a positive, encouraging tone of voice. The Twelve Apostles followed in Jesus' footsteps and accomplished a lot.

Whatever place does not **welcome** you or **listen** to you,
   leave there and shake the **dust** off your **feet**
   in testimony **against** them."
So they went **off** and preached **repentance**.
The Twelve drove out many **demons**,
   and they anointed with **oil** many who were **sick**
     and **cured** them.

with them except for the bare essentials— a walking stick, one tunic, and the pair of sandals they wear—involves a strong belief in their message and the person who sent them. Because Jesus is the one who sends them forth to follow in his footsteps, preaching repentance and driving out demons, surely these apostles will ultimately be successful. And the end of this Gospel passage, which occurs less the halfway through Mark, already tells the reader of their success.

In our time, there are many peoples in the world, both in developing and developed countries that are in need of hearing apostles who will preach and teach the word of God. Some places will welcome the Gospel message; others will not, but the ministry of the apostles carries on through the Church which herself is apostolic. All members of the Church share in her mission to teach and spread the Good News, yet they do so in various ways and

according to their state in life. Every activity, however, that seeks to grow the kingdom of God through the world is considered an apostolate (CCC, #863–864; AA, #2–4).

16TH SUNDAY IN ORDINARY TIME

Lectionary #107

READING I   Jeremiah 23:1–6

Jeremiah = jayr-uh-MĪ-uh

Speak the words "Woe to the shepherds . . ." in a stern tone of voice that is fitting for the Lord's warning.

A reading from the Book of the Prophet Jeremiah

Woe to the shepherds
   who **mislead** and **scatter** the flock of my **pasture**,
   says the LORD.
Therefore, thus says the LORD, the God of **Israel**,
   against the shepherds who shepherd my **people**:
   You have **scattered** my sheep and **driven** them away.
You have not **cared** for them,
   but **I** will take care to **punish** your evil deeds.
I **myself** will gather the **remnant** of my flock
   from all the lands to which I have **driven** them
   and bring them back to their **meadow**;
   there they shall **increase** and **multiply**.
I will appoint shepherds for them who will **shepherd** them
   so that they need no **longer** fear and **tremble**;
   and none shall be **missing**, says the LORD.

Pause before communicating the Lord's words regarding what he will do to respond to the needs of his flock ("I myself will gather . . .")in a caring tone of voice, one befitting a true shepherd.

Pause again before the final section begins ("Behold, the days are coming . . ."). Proclaim these words with hope in your tone of voice.

Behold, the days are **coming**, says the LORD,
   when I will raise up a **righteous** shoot to **David**;
as king he shall **reign** and govern **wisely**,
   he shall do what is **just** and **right** in the land.
In his days **Judah** shall be **saved**,
   Israel shall dwell in **security**.
This is the **name** they give him:
   "The LORD our **justice**."

Proclaim the name Israel will give their king ("The Lord our justice") with certainty and conviction, looking at the assembly who knows this is the kind of king Jesus is.

READING I — **Today's reading from the book of Jeremiah, which contrasts the Lord as the true shepherd with the shepherds who mislead his people, corresponds to the Gospel account from Mark, which portrays Jesus as the Good Shepherd who teaches the crowd who longs to hear his words.**

Often referred to as a prophet of doom and gloom, Jeremiah's first oracle in this reading substantiates that view as it begins directly with the Lord's words of warning.

The Lord's words spoken through Jeremiah indict the kings of Judah, the bad shepherds, who are at work among the people.

Although there is not an individual oracle about Zedekiah, as there was previously about his predecessors, Zedekiah is still charged by the prophet. While Jeremiah has tried to counsel King Zedekiah, he failed to listen.

This second poetic oracle on the "shoot of David" offers hope to the Lord's people, but warning to those in power. The Hebrew word for "shoot," referred to the messiah who would save both Israel and

Judah by reigning with justice (see Isaiah 11:1; Zechariah 3:8; 6:12). Through him, the Davidic dynasty would be restored because he would act uprightly, shepherding his people, if not politically, then ethically and religiously, leading them back to God.

Christians believe this royal messiah came in the person of the Savior and Good Shepherd Jesus Christ. Your strong and hopeful proclamation of the end of this reading can lead the assembly to recognize the fulfillment of this passage in Jesus.

Ephesians = ee-FEE-zhunz

Proclaim the opening line in a warm, affectionate tone of voice, making eye contact with the members of the assembly who themselves have been brought near by the blood of Christ.

Deliver the lengthy sentence "For he is our peace . . ." with gratitude in your tone of voice for the unity Christ has created.

Proclaim the line "He came and preached peace," which repeats—although in somewhat different words—the idea of the opening sentence, in a slightly stronger tone of voice than you used at the beginning.

READING II   Ephesians 2:13–18

A reading from the Letter of Saint Paul to the Ephesians

Brothers and sisters:
In Christ **Jesus** you who once were far **off**
　have become **near** by the blood of **Christ**.

For he is our **peace**, he who made both one
　and broke down the **dividing** wall of **enmity**, through his flesh,
　abolishing the law with its **commandments** and **legal** claims,
　that he might create in himself **one new** person in place
　　of the **two**,
　thus establishing **peace**,
　and might reconcile **both** with God,
　in one **body**, through the **cross**,
　putting that **enmity** to death by it.
He came and preached **peace** to you who were far **off**
　and **peace** to those who were **near**,
　for through him we **both** have access in one **Spirit**
　　to the **Father**.

READING II In today's Second Reading, the "dividing wall of enmity" of which Paul speaks, is the division that existed between Gentiles and Jews, a division that Christ healed through his own flesh. Verses 11 and 12 of the second chapter of Ephesians, which come immediately before this passage begins, remind the Gentiles that at one time they lacked Israel's hope for a messiah, were strangers to the covenant God promised, and were without hope in God and the world.

In Christ, the Mosaic law was fulfilled; it was abolished and no longer necessary for salvation. Through him and the cross he endured, a single community was formed in his body. This one body is the one universal Church. In the Church, there are no longer strangers and sojourners, but "fellow citizens" in union with all the holy ones. Together, all are part of the "household of God" founded on the apostles and prophets. The household of God, the one body has none other than Christ Jesus as the cornerstone.

Factionalism still exists in our day within the Church. As Catholics, we profess the oneness of the Church every time we recite the creed. Your proclamation of this reading can serve as a reminder of the peace Christ brought among peoples.

GOSPEL Today's brief Gospel begins by recounting the mission the disciples were sent out on in last Sunday's Gospel. In this Gospel (verse 30)

GOSPEL Mark 6:30–34

A reading from the holy Gospel according to Mark

The **apostles** gathered together with **Jesus**
    and reported **all** they had **done** and **taught**.
He said to them,
    "Come away by yourselves to a **deserted** place and **rest**
      a while."
People were coming and going in great numbers,
    and they had **no** opportunity even to **eat**.
So they went off in the boat by **themselves** to a deserted **place**.
People **saw** them leaving and **many** came to **know** about it.
They **hastened** there on foot from all the towns
    and **arrived** at the place **before** them.

When he **disembarked** and saw the vast **crowd**,
    his **heart** was moved with **pity** for them,
    for they were like **sheep** without a **shepherd**;
    and he began to **teach** them many things.

Offer Jesus' invitation to the apostles ("Come away by yourselves . . .") in a hospitable, caring tone of voice.

Place a little energy, even stress, in your voice as you describe the hectic scene ("People were coming . . .").

Pause before the words "When he disembarked . . . ." Release the stress from your voice as you tell how Jesus took care of the crowd like a caring shepherd ("his heart was moved . . .") in an empathetic tone of voice.

---

and in Mark 3:14, the term "apostles" is used to described the Twelve who are sent forth by Jesus to preach, expel demons, and cure the sick. However, it is only after Pentecost that the title for the Twelve-less-Judas is used in the technical sense of those sent forth to carry on the mission of their leader who is no longer with them. While Mark does not describe much of what happened, we know by his words that the Twelve have been successful.

Even at Jesus' invitation for them to take some time to rest, still there is a great crowd of people who wants to hear what Jesus and the apostles have to say. Like tired ministers and church workers, Jesus and the apostles attempt to go off to a deserted place. Yet there were those who so desperately wanted to hear what they were teaching that they found a faster way to find them, and were at their new location even before they arrived. Instead of being frustrated and angry because the

vast crowd was present at the "deserted place," Jesus opened himself one more time, finding a way to continue to teach them, and thus showing himself as a faithful shepherd to the crowd.

17TH SUNDAY IN ORDINARY TIME

Lectionary #110

READING I 2 Kings 4:42–44

A reading from the second Book of Kings

A man came from Baal-shalishah bringing to **Elisha**, the man
    of **God**,
  twenty **barley** loaves made from the **firstfruits**,
  and fresh **grain** in the **ear**.
Elisha said, "**Give** it to the people to **eat**."
But his servant **objected**,
  "How can I set this before a **hundred** people?"
Elisha insisted, "**Give** it to the people to **eat**."
For thus says the LORD,
  'They shall **eat** and there shall be some left **over**.'"
And when they had **eaten**, there **was** some left over,
  as the LORD had **said**.

Baal-shalishah = BAH-ahl shahl-ih-SHAH
Elisha = ee-LĪ-shuh

Emphasize the fact that it was "*twenty
barley loaves*" so the logic of the
question of Elisha's servant makes sense
to the assembly.

Ask the servant's question ("How can I
set this . . . ?") with opposition and
doubt in your voice, clearly emphasizing
the number of people. Deliver Elisha's
response to the question ("Give it
to . . .") in a forceful, insistent manner.
Conclude by delivering the Lord's words
that are spoken by Elisha ("They shall
eat . . .") in a confident tone of voice that
fittingly describes that the Lord takes
care of his people.

READING I The second book of Kings
(2:9–18) tells us that Elisha
succeeded Elijah as a prophet in Israel
after the Lord takes Elijah up to heaven.
Today's narrative shows one example of
the wonder-working power that Elisha
inherited from Elijah, who received it from
the Lord.

The miracle story proclaimed today is
thought to have provided the framework
for the stories in the New Testament that
deal with the multiplication of loaves and
fish so that thousands might be fed (Mark
6:34–44; 8:1–10; Matthew 14:31–34;
15:32–39; Luke 9:10–17; John 6:1–15). The
parallel between the reading from 2 Kings
and the beloved story of the multiplication
of the loaves and fish, which is today's
Gospel, is obvious. In both instances, the
wonder of the miracles lies in God's abundant love and care for his people. God provides for his people so much so that there
is even some left over for when they get
hungry again or for other's who might come
by who are hungry.

READING II This passage is taken
from a section of Ephesians
that is a "moral exhortation" (Ephesians
4:1—6:20). In this section, the author gives
ethical instructions for living the Christian
life. The authority behind these instructions is clear as the author invokes the

READING II   Ephesians 4:1–6

Ephesians = ee-FEE-zhunz

A reading from the Letter of Saint Paul to the Ephesians

Brothers and sisters:
I, a **prisoner** for the Lord,
    urge you to live in a manner **worthy** of the call
        you have received,
    with all **humility** and **gentleness**, with **patience**,
    bearing with one another through **love**,
    striving to preserve the **unity** of the spirit through the **bond**
        of **peace**:
    one body and **one** Spirit,
    as you were also **called** to the one **hope** of your call;
    one **Lord**, one **faith**, one **baptism**;
    one **God** and **Father** of **all**,
    who is **over** all and **through** all and **in** all.

Let your tone of voice reflect "humility," "gentleness," "patience," and "love" as you speak those words.

Pause slightly before the proclamation of the sevenfold unity in faith ("one body and one Spirit . . ."). Increase the power and confidence in your tone of voice as you build toward the fourfold climax ("one God and Father of all . . .").

---

image of Paul, a prisoner of the Lord, at the beginning of the section (4:1).

Specifically, the instructions given in today's reading take the form of a list of virtues that reflect what it means to live in unity with Christ and with others in Christ's body, the Church. This list of virtues is similar to that found in Colossians 3:12–15.

The sevenfold statement of unity that concludes the reading reflects the bond

that hold Christians together. In the post-apostolic period, Christians were attempting to define their way of life in contrast to polytheistic pagan society that challenged their belief in the unity of the one Spirit, one Lord, and one God. As the early Christian communities grew and the Church needed more organization, it was this sevenfold unity of belief that held Christians together as one. This unity was made visible in and through the apostolic institution of the Church (CCC, #172–3; LG, #4).

The Church today faces many challenges both externally and internally. Your proclamation of this reading can serve as a reminder to the assembly to live the virtues of Christian life with a goal of maintaining and preserving unity in the Church through the one God, who is Father, Son, and Holy Spirit.

GOSPEL   John 6:1–15

A reading from the holy Gospel according to John

Proclaim the narrative lines that open the
Gospel deliberately, setting the scene
for the beloved story of the miracle of the
loaves and fish that follows.

Jesus went across the Sea of **Galilee**.
A large **crowd** followed him,
      because they saw the **signs** he was performing on the **sick**.
Jesus went up on the **mountain**,
      and there he sat **down** with his **disciples**.
The Jewish feast of **Passover** was near.
When Jesus raised his **eyes**
      and saw that a large **crowd** was coming to him,
      he said to **Philip**,
      "Where can we buy enough **food** for them to eat?"
He said this to test him,
      because he himself **knew** what he was going to do.
Philip **answered** him,
      "Two hundred days' **wages** worth of food would not
            be enough
      for **each** of them to have a **little**."
One of his disciples,
      Andrew, the brother of Simon **Peter**, said to him,
      "There is a **boy** here who has five **barley** loaves and two **fish**;
      but what good are **these** for so many?"
Jesus said, "Have the people **recline**."
Now there was a great deal of **grass** in that place.
So the men **reclined**, about five **thousand** in number.

Ask Jesus' question to Philip ("Where
can we buy . . . ?") with concern in your
tone of voice, reflecting Jesus' desire to
feed the crowd.

Give Philip's answer to Jesus ("Two
hundred days' wages . . .") with a sense
that Philip understands Jesus' desire
to feed the multitude as unrealistic by
placing a bit of disbelief in your tone
of voice.

Deliver Jesus' command ("Have the
people recline") with authority in your
voice. Jesus clearly knows now what
he is going to do to feed the crowd.

GOSPEL   Today we begin a five-week pause from the proclamation of the Gospel according to Mark as we hear proclaimed a series of passages from the Bread of Life discourse in John. Each liturgical Year B, after the Sixteenth Sunday, five readings are incorporated from John 6. According to the Introduction to the Lectionary, "this is the natural place for these readings because the multiplication of the loaves from the Gospel of John takes the place of the same account in Mark" (#105).

Today's passage comes from the beginning of the Bread of Life discourse (John 6:1–71), so-called because it presents Jesus' teaching that he is the Bread of Life, the food that will forever sustain those who believe in him. The narrative proclaimed today serves as a prelude to this teaching that we will hear proclaimed next Sunday.

The detail John provides regarding the close proximity of the Passover to the multiplication miracle helps the reader understand that Jesus reinterprets this Jewish feast in light of his actions. John's presentation of Jesus in this light is a common occurrence in chapters 5 through 10 of his Gospel. As the eminent scripture scholar Raymond Brown, SS, explains, through his actions of healing on an "unnamed feast" of the Jews that occurs on a Sabbath, Jesus reinterprets this as a day of life rather than a day simply of rest (5:1–47). The Jewish Fest of Tabernacles is understood anew in relation to Jesus'

Pause before describing the sharing of the food ("Then Jesus took the loaves . . ."). Narrate these lines reverently.

Pause again before the words "When they had . . . ." Build in wonder and awe as you recount the scale of the miracle and the people's confession of faith ("This is truly the Prophet . . .").

Then Jesus took the **loaves**, gave **thanks**,
and **distributed** them to those who were **reclining**,
and also as much of the **fish** as they **wanted**.
When they had had their **fill**, he said to his **disciples**,
"Gather the **fragments** left over,
so that **nothing** will be wasted."
So they collected them,
and filled twelve wicker **baskets** with fragments
from the five **barley** loaves
that had been **more** than they could **eat**.
When the people **saw** the sign he had done, they said,
"This is **truly** the **Prophet**, the one who is to come
into the **world**."

Pause again before giving the concluding statement ("Since Jesus knew . . .").

Since Jesus **knew** that they were going to come and carry him **off**
to make him **king**,
he **withdrew** again to the mountain **alone**.

---

claim to be "the light of the world" (7:1—10:21). And, with Jesus, the Jewish Feast of Dedication (Hanukkah) is now to be seen in light of faith in him as the one whom the Father consecrated and sent into the world (10:22–42) (Raymond Brown, SS, *Introduction to the New Testament,* pp. 344–349).

In today's Gospel, Jesus reinterprets the Passover with a eucharistic theme. Jesus does not do away with the feast of the old covenant, but through the miracle of the multiplication of the loaves and fish, gives it a new meaning relationship to the

Eucharist. According to the Catechism, "the miracles of the multiplication of the loaves, when the Lord says the blessing, breaks and distributes the loaves through his disciples to feed the multitude, prefigure the superabundance of this unique bread of his Eucharist" (#1335; parallels for the Gospel passage: Mark 6:30–53; 8:1–10; Matthew 14:13–34; 15:32–39; Luke 9:10–17).

Because the Gospel according to John does not have a Last Supper narrative as the synoptic Gospels do, the multiplication miracle and the entire Bread of Life discourse is where the evangelist develops

the core of his eucharistic theology, with the Greek verb *eucharistein* ("gave thanks") being used in the description of Jesus' actions (6:11). At the end of today's passage, John notes how Jesus withdrew from the crowd who was going to make him king. For Jesus, the heart of the Eucharist is not any political kingship, but achieving the will of his Father, the one who sent him into the world. The Father's will is the will those of us who participate in the Eucharist today are nourished to follow also.

18TH SUNDAY IN ORDINARY TIME

Lectionary #113

READING I   Exodus 16:2–4, 12–15

A reading from the Book of Exodus

The whole Israelite **community grumbled** against **Moses**
and **Aaron**.
The Israelites **said** to them,
"Would that we had **died** at the LORD'S hand in the land
of **Egypt**,
as we sat by our **fleshpots** and ate our fill of **bread**!
But **you** had to lead us into this **desert**
to make the whole **community** die of **famine**!"

Then the LORD said to **Moses**,
"I will now rain down **bread** from **heaven** for you.
Each **day** the people are to go out and **gather** their daily **portion**;
thus will I **test** them,
to see whether they **follow** my instructions or **not**.

"I have **heard** the grumbling of the Israelites.
Tell them: In the evening **twilight** you shall eat **flesh**,
and in the **morning** you shall have your fill of **bread**,
so that you may **know** that **I**, the LORD, am your **God**."

In the **evening quail** came up and covered the **camp**.
In the **morning** a **dew** lay all about the camp,
and when the dew **evaporated**, there on the surface of the desert
were fine **flakes** like **hoarfrost** on the ground.

Convey the Israelites' complaint to Moses and Aaron ("Would that we had died . . .") in a strong tone of voice filled bitterness. Use an accusatory tone as they blame Moses and Aaron in the words "But you had to lead . . . ." Make eye contact with the assembly as you proclaim these words.

The Lord's words in the following two sections tell what he will do to take care of the Israelites. Convey them in a straightforward manner, using a tone of voice that carries no sense that the Lord is upset with the Israelites since the reading does not tell us the Lord is annoyed at all.

Pause before the section beginning "In the evening quail . . . ." The narrative shifts here to the fulfillment of God's promise.

READING I   The book of Exodus is the second book of the Torah or Pentateuch, the first five books of the Old Testament. Exodus tells the story of the Israelites beginning where Genesis ended. It narrates the history of the Israelites in Egypt, their departure ("exodus") from Egypt, their journey to Sinai, the covenant the Lord made with them at the holy mountain, and their building of a dwelling complete with a meeting tent, a place for the Ark of the Covenant, and altars for worship. In all, it is a narrative that recounts the history of the Chosen People centered on the theme of God's fidelity and commitment to them.

As evident in today's reading, God's faithfulness is contrasted with the Israelites' discontent. Taken from the section of Exodus that describes the Israelites' journey to Sinai and Canaan, this reading presents the second of three tests the Israelites faced. In the first test at Marah, the Israelites were given bitter water to quench their thirst from traveling in the desert. They complained to Moses and he appealed to the Lord who provided fresh water (15:22–27). In this second test, the Israelites complained again to Moses and Aaron, although their complaint is obviously against the Lord (see verses 5–11, which are not included in the reading). The Lord again responds to the Israelites' grumbling by providing manna for them to eat. Finally, in the third test, there was no water for the Israelites to drink. Once again, they argued with Moses and pleaded with him to provide water. Moses addressed the Lord on their behalf and water miraculously flowed from a rock after Moses followed the Lord's commands (17:1–7). (See

While the Israelites ask the question "What is this?" because they simply do not know what the manna is, give Moses' reply ("This is the bread . . .") in a serious and reverent tone of voice because it conveys the deeper meaning of the Lord providing for his people.

On **seeing** it, the Israelites **asked** one another, "What is **this**?"
  for they did not **know** what it was.
But Moses **told** them,
  "This is the **bread** that the LORD has given you to **eat**."

READING II Ephesians 4:17, 20–24

Ephesians = ee-FEE-zhunz

A reading from the Letter of Saint Paul to the Ephesians

Brothers and sisters:
I **declare** and **testify** in the **Lord**
  that you must no **longer** live as the **Gentiles** do,
  in the **futility** of their **minds**;
  that is **not** how you learned **Christ**,
  assuming that you have **heard** of him and were **taught** in him,
  as **truth** is in **Jesus**,
  that you should put **away** the **old** self of your **former** way of life,
  corrupted through deceitful **desires**,
  and be **renewed** in the spirit of your **minds**,
  and put on the **new** self,
  created in **God's** way in **righteousness** and holiness of **truth**.

This reading is one lengthy sentence. To assist you in your proclamation, practice pausing after the semicolon after the words "in the futility of their minds" as if it were a period. Then state the line "that is not how you learned Christ" as a declarative sentence in itself. Also, pause after the words "as truth is in Jesus" before continuing with the main thoughts of putting "away the old self" and being "renewed in the spirit."

---

the commentary for the Third Sunday of Lent, Year A, for background.)

The miracle of the bread from heaven is referenced in today's Gospel from John. In this Gospel, Jesus clarifies to his disciples that Moses did not provide the bread from heaven, but rather Jesus' Father gave this bread. At the disciples' own request for the bread of life, then, Jesus identifies himself as such, saying, "I am the bread of life."

While we, like the Israelites, are not always faithful to God in following the instructions and commands he gives us

(Exodus 16:20, 27), still God continues to offer us the miracle of life that comes through believing in him and his Son, the bread of life. As the Lord always quenched the Israelites' thirst and satisfied their hunger in the desert, so too Jesus quenches the thirst of those who believe in him and satisfies those who come to him in the struggles and hungers of their daily life through the Eucharist.

READING II This brief passage is best understood in the context

of the verses that immediately precede it in Ephesians 4. Last Sunday, the reading from Ephesians focused on the sevenfold unity of Christians in one body, one Spirit, one hope, one Lord, one faith, one Baptism, and one God who is Father of all (Ephesians 4:4–6). Following these verses, the author of Ephesians discusses the diversity of gifts that exist within the Church (4:7–12).

In Paul's first letter to the Corinthians, he had to preach the necessity of the different gifts because some gifts were considered more important than others. Writing later in the first century and with a

GOSPEL John 6:24–35

A reading from the holy Gospel according to John

When the crowd **saw** that neither **Jesus** nor his **disciples**
   were there,
  they **themselves** got into boats
  and came to **Capernaum looking** for Jesus.
And when they **found** him across the **sea** they said to him,
  "**Rabbi**, when did you get **here**?"
Jesus **answered** them and said,
  "**Amen**, amen, I **say** to you,
  you are **looking** for me **not** because you saw **signs**
  but because you ate the **loaves** and were **filled**.
Do not work for food that **perishes**
  but for the food that **endures** for eternal **life**,
  which the Son of **Man** will **give** you.
For on **him** the Father, **God**, has set his **seal**."
So they said to him,
  "What can we **do** to accomplish the works of God?"
Jesus answered and said to them,
  "**This** is the work of God, that you **believe** in the one he **sent**."
So they said to him,
  "What **sign** can you do, that we may **see** and **believe** in you?
What can you **do**?
Our **ancestors** ate **manna** in the **desert**, as it is written:
  *He gave them bread from **heaven** to eat.*"

Eagerness and enthusiasm on the part of the crowd abound in this Gospel, beginning with the opening narrative lines ("When the crowd saw . . .").

Deliver Jesus' response to the crowd's question ("Amen, amen, I say to you . . .") in a patient, teacher-like tone of voice that is simply explaining an instruction, which, if they follow, will lead to eternal life.

Reflect the crowd's enthusiasm and their zeal to move forward to receive the food of eternal life in your tone of voice as you ask the question "What can we do . . . ?")

Convey the sincerity in the crowd's question ("What sign can you do . . . ?") by using a serious tone of voice, but one that does not lose their eagerness to believe.

---

broader scope, the author of Ephesians does not face the same situation. His intention is to show how through the use of the diverse gifts the Church grows into Christ, its head, attaining the full stature of Christ by ascending to him (4:13–15). The whole body, then, with its diverse parts working together will bring the Church to fulfillment in Christ.

Today's passage, then, forms the conclusion to Ephesians 4. It shows how new life in Christ in the Church contrasts with the life of the Gentiles, describing how Christian behavior will build up the body of

Christ. In the discussion of the "old self" and "new self," the author of Ephesians employs the Greek word *anthrōpos* ("man" or "human"), so as to make a connection with the "mature manhood" of verse 13, the perfect maturity everyone develops in Christ (Colossians 1:28). The use of this terminology, and not the term *sōma* as used in Corinthians, allows the author to stress the growth and movement of the individual Christian and the Church to fullness with Christ in the heavenly plan of salvation (CCC, #2045).

GOSPEL   Prior to this passage in the Gospel according to John are two miracle stories: the multiplication of the loaves and fish, which was proclaimed last Sunday (6:1–15), and Jesus' walking on water (6:16–21). These miracles stories are preludes to Jesus' teaching contained in the Bread of Life discourse, a discourse that elaborates many of our fundamental beliefs about Jesus, the Eucharist, and eternal life.

Often in the discourse the crowds are found asking questions of Jesus or among themselves in an effort to understand what

Be patient in your delivering of Jesus' response to the crowd's request for a sign ("Amen, amen . . ."), as it explains the deeper meaning of the manna their ancestors ate in the desert as recounted in today's First Reading.

Use a strong, confident tone of voice to state the crowd's request ("Sir, give us . . .").

Proclaim Jesus' words ("I am the bread of life . . .") with reassurance in your tone of voice that reflects the truth that the crowd has made the right decision of faith in asking for the bread that Jesus offers.

So Jesus said to them,
  "Amen, amen, I **say** to you,
  it was not **Moses** who gave the bread from heaven;
  my **Father** gives you the **true** bread from heaven.
For the bread of **God** is that which comes down from heaven
  and gives **life** to the **world**."

So they said to him,
  "Sir, **give** us this bread **always**."
Jesus said to them,
  "**I** am the bread of life;
  whoever comes to **me** will never **hunger**,
    and whoever **believes** in me will never **thirst**."

Jesus is teaching. In today's Gospel, the crowds posed three questions to Jesus—the last question including a follow-up question to emphasize the point of the first question: 1) "When did you get here?" 2) "What can we do to accomplish the works of God?" and 3) "What sign can you do, that we may see and believe in you? What can you do?"

Jesus answers each question as a good teacher would. He addresses the concern in the question and responds to it with the correct teaching that prods and pushes the crowd, directing them toward a new insight. His responses never stifle the dialogue with the crowd.

In Jesus' responses to the questions posed today, the crowd learns: 1) the Son of Man whom the Father has sent will provide the imperishable food for which they should work; 2) there is nothing they need to do except believe in order to receive this food, for it comes to them through God's initiative—it cannot be earned; and 3) Jesus is the new Moses, the one through whom the Father gives the true bread of heaven.

At the conclusion of this Gospel, the crowds respond eagerly to Jesus' teaching expressing their desire for the bread about which he has spoken. Sometimes participation in the Eucharist can become so routine, its meaning is lost, even though the sacrament does not lose its efficacy. Your proclamation of this Gospel can assist the assembly to reflect on the level of their desire for the eucharistic bread and renew their commitment to Jesus the Bread of Life.

19TH SUNDAY IN ORDINARY TIME

Lectionary #116

READING I   1 Kings 19:4–8

A reading from the first Book of Kings

Elijah = ee-LĪ-juh

Express Elijah's appeal to the Lord ("This is enough, O Lord!") with a sense of exhaustion and pleading in your tone of voice.

Pause before continuing after Elijah's demand ("He lay down . . .").

Elijah went a day's **journey** into the **desert**,
    until he came to a **broom** tree and sat **beneath** it.
He prayed for **death** saying:
    "This is **enough**, O LORD!
Take my **life**, for I am no better than my **fathers**."
He lay **down** and fell **asleep** under the **broom** tree,
    but then an **angel** touched him and **ordered** him
        to get **up** and **eat**.
Elijah **looked** and there at his **head** was a **hearth** cake
    and a jug of **water**.
After he ate and drank, he lay **down** again,
    but the angel of the LORD came back a **second** time,
    touched him, and **ordered**,
    "Get up and eat, else the **journey** will be too **long** for you!"
He got **up**, **ate**, and **drank**;
    then **strengthened** by that food,
    he walked forty **days** and forty **nights** to the mountain
        of God, **Horeb**.

Communicate the order the angel of the Lord speaks to Elijah the second time the angel appears ("Get up and eat . . .") with compassion. This will distinguish the angel's spoken words from the simple description of the order in the angel's first appearance.

Horeb = HOH-reb

READING I The context of this reading is Elijah the prophet fearing for his life at the hands of Ahab, king of Israel. Ahab thought of Elijah as a "disturber of Israel" who called Israel to follow the commands of the Lord instead of those of Baal, the god his wife, Jezebel, had chosen to promote in Israel (1 Kings 18:17). Upon hearing that Elijah had put the prophets of Baal to death, Jezebel sent a messenger to Elijah telling him that he would experience the same fate (1 Kings 19:1–2).

Today's First Reading picks up the narrative at this point with Elijah beginning his pilgrimage to Horeb, the sacred place that was the mountain of Moses' divine experiences (Exodus 3—4; 33:18—34:8). Elijah leaves behind all that he knew, including companionship and food, two ordinary human needs, as he embarks on journey.

Elijah's only words in this reading are words of deep frustration. He has performed admirably in his prophetic vocation and he does not understand why his life would now be at risk. Ultimately, Elijah is

saying he is "fed up" with the Lord. While the shade of the broom tree offers him time to reflect and relax, that the angel of the Lord appears twice ordering him to eat and drink, shows us that there is little time for Elijah engage in self-pity. He must continue to do the Lord's work! But he does not do so without nourishment, without sacred food provided by the Lord.

When Elijah came to the holy mountain, the Lord is seemingly surprised at Elijah's presence there, asking, "Why are

Ephesians = ee-FEE-zhunz

Communicate the list of vices ("All bitterness . . .") in a firm tone of voice, enunciating each one clearly. Lighten your tone of voice as you proclaim the virtues ("And be kind . . .").

Pause before the concluding section ("So be imitators of God . . ."). Let the tone of your voice be strongest on the imperative ("So be imitators of God").

READING II   Ephesians 4:30—5:2

A reading from the Letter of Saint Paul to the Ephesians

Brothers and sisters:
Do not **grieve** the Holy Spirit of **God**,
    with which you were **sealed** for the day of **redemption**.
All bitterness, fury, anger, shouting, and reviling
    must be **removed** from you, along with all **malice**.
And be **kind** to one another, **compassionate**,
    forgiving one another as God has forgiven **you** in **Christ**.

So be imitators of **God**, as beloved **children**, and live in **love**,
    as Christ loved **us** and handed himself over for **us**
    as a sacrificial **offering** to God for a fragrant **aroma**.

you here, Elijah?" Elijah responded with a lengthy complaint, detailing his frustration. He has worked long and hard and obviously to no avail, as the Israelites are after his life (19:10). The sequence of the Lord's question and Elijah's complaint are repeated in 19:13–15. Finally, the saga concludes as the Lord resolves Elijah's dilemma by having him anoint two new kings (Hazael and Jehu) and a new prophet, Elisha, who

will help Elijah fulfill his mission to stop the Israelites from worshipping Baal and return them to the Lord (19:15–16).

Everyone at some point and time in his or her life feels as if he or she is doing the best that he or she can, but still not succeeding. Your proclamation of this reading can help those in the assembly to relate their frustration with that of Elijah's. It can also provide hope for them: the Lord always provides for his prophets, for those who are living and proclaiming his word.

READING II   Our Christian life has ethical implications! This cannot be stated more straightforwardly than it is in today's brief passage from Paul's letter to the Ephesians.

Taken from the section of Ephesians that deals primarily with Christian and non-Christian behavior (4:17—5:20), today's reading begins with an imperative not to disappoint the Holy Spirit. Disappointing or grieving the Spirit, with whom one was

Fill your voice with some tension as you proclaim the opening exchange between the Jews and Jesus ("The Jews murmured . . .").

Communicate Jesus' words in response to the questions of the Jews in a self-assured manner. Jesus knows who he is and is sure of his relationship with the Father.

GOSPEL   John 6:41–51

A reading from the holy Gospel according to John

The Jews **murmured** about Jesus because he said,
    "**I** am the bread that came **down** from **heaven**,"
and they said,
    "Is this not **Jesus**, the son of **Joseph**?
Do we not **know** his **father** and **mother**?
Then how can he say,
    'I have come down from **heaven**'?"
Jesus answered and said to them,
    "Stop **murmuring** among yourselves.
No one can come to me unless the Father who sent me **draw** him,
    and I will **raise** him on the last **day**.
It is written in the **prophets**:
    *They shall all be taught by **God**.*
Everyone who **listens** to my Father and **learns** from him **comes**
        to me.

---

sealed at the conclusion of the baptismal rite, would mean acting on the list of vices. The opposite conduct, living the virtues of kindness, compassion, and forgiveness (note the reversal of the forgiveness formula from the "Our Father" of Matthew 6:12 and Luke 11:4), testifies to a life lived in the Spirit in imitation of Christ. The latter is the life to which Christians are called through their Baptism.

Ultimately, Christian ethical conduct cannot be separated from one's relationship with God. Because the body of Christ

is one and held together in the unity of the Spirit, to cause harm or injury—spiritual, psychological, or physical—to a fellow human being is equivalent to harming the Spirit. Thus, as the imperative in the final verse of the reading commands us, we are to "be imitators of God," living in love as Christ loved us.

| GOSPEL | Today's Gospel begins with the Jews murmuring about |

Jesus in an attempt to understand who he really is. As we heard in last Sunday's

Gospel, Jesus claimed, "I am the bread of life," the "true bread from heaven." This assertion Jesus made clearly unsettled the Jews. Their murmuring is reminiscent of the Israelites' grumbling against Moses when they were in the desert and could not find water to drink (Exodus 15:24), and against both Moses and Aaron when they were hungry and the Lord responded by raining down manna from heaven (Exodus 16:2, 7, 12).

Just as the Lord responded to the Israelites' grumbling by providing water

Pause before beginning the final section ("I am the bread of life . . .") in a positive tone of voice that contrasts with the confrontational tone used at the beginning of the Gospel.

Not that anyone has **seen** the Father
  except the one who is from God;
  he has seen the **Father**.
Amen, amen, I **say** to you,
  whoever **believes** has eternal **life**.
I am the bread of **life**.
Your **ancestors** ate the **manna** in the **desert**, but they **died**;
  this is the bread that comes down from **heaven**
  so that one may eat it and **not** die.
I am the **living** bread that came **down** from heaven;
  whoever **eats** this bread will live **forever**;
  and the **bread** that I will **give** is my **flesh** for the life
    of the **world**."

and food for them in the desert, Jesus seemingly overhears the murmuring of the Jews and then quells it by revealing more of his identity to them. He does not deny that he is the son of Joseph and Mary, but through his statements, the Jews do learn that the Father in heaven and Jesus stand in a unique relationship to one another. The Father draws people to Jesus, the Bread of Life, and Jesus, because he has seen the Father, reveals the Father to those who believe in him, the one whom the Father has sent.

On these five Sundays of Ordinary Time when passages from the Gospel according to John from the Bread of Life discourse are proclaimed, often one of the songs the assembly may sing is Taizé's "Eat This Bread," part of the refrain of which is taken from the concluding verse of this Gospel ("I am the living bread . . ."). Because John's account does not have a Last Supper narrative, some scholars consider this verse to be the Johannine eucharistic formula instead of "Take it; this is my body. . . ." Rather than highlighting his sacrifice for the sins of all, Jesus' words in

John focus on the gift of eternal life that comes from him because he himself has come from the Father. This gift also shows how Jesus himself provides the life-giving bread that sustains spiritually and not just physically as the manna given to the Israelites in the desert did. Because of the gift of this sacred bread, murmuring about Jesus is no longer necessary.

ASSUMPTION OF THE BLESSED VIRGIN MARY: VIGIL

Lectionary #621

READING I   1 Chronicles 15:3–4, 15–16; 16:1–2

Chronicles = KRAH-nih-k*ls

In your proclamation of this reading, emphasize David's actions ("David assembled," "David also called together," "David commanded," and so on) and the actions of the Levites.

Aaron = AIR-un
Levites = LEE-vīts

lyres = līrz

Narrate the conclusion of the ritual recounted in the reading ("When David had finished . . .") and David's blessing of the people, using a reverent, sincere tone of voice.

A reading from the first Book of Chronicles

David assembled all **Israel** in **Jerusalem** to bring the **ark**
of the LORD
to the place that he had **prepared** for it.
David **also** called together the sons of **Aaron** and the **Levites**.

The **Levites** bore the ark of God on their **shoulders** with **poles**,
as **Moses** had **ordained** according to the word of the LORD.

David commanded the **chiefs** of the **Levites**
to appoint their **kinsmen** as **chanters**,
to play on musical **instruments**, **harps**, **lyres**, and **cymbals**,
to make a loud **sound** of **rejoicing**.

They **brought** in the ark of God and set it within the **tent**
which David had **pitched** for it.
Then they offered up burnt **offerings** and **peace** offerings to God.
When David had **finished** offering up the burnt offerings
and peace offerings,
he **blessed** the people in the **name** of the LORD.

READING I Initially, it may not be clear why this reading is proclaimed on the Vigil of the Assumption, but reflection on the importance of the Ark of the Covenant reveals its appropriateness. The Israelite people believed the Ark of the Covenant, an ornate, rectangular box that they carried with them from the time of the Exodus until the building of the Temple, represented God's presence with them. Some traditions suggest that the ark contained the written word of the law (1 Kings 8:9). Whatever was held within the ark, it

was so holy that only an authorized person could come in contact with it. Once the Temple of Solomon was built, the ark was placed in the Holy of Holies, a site only the High Priest could enter. Prior to Solomon's reign, the ark would be kept safe in a tent or tabernacle set up at each location where the Israelites remained for a while.

In the scriptures, a clear parallel can be seen between Mary and the Ark of the Covenant. The story of David bringing the original Ark of the Covenant into Jerusalem in 2 Samuel 6:4–16 is similar to the Mary's visitation of Elizabeth in Luke 1:39–56, a

narrative proclaimed tomorrow for the solemnity of the Assumption. For example, as David journeys to Jerusalem within the ark, Mary too, pregnant with Jesus, journeys to Elizabeth. Thus, on the basis of scripture, the tradition of the Church has understood Mary as the Ark of the Covenant, the bearer of God's presence. The Litany of Loretto, most likely composed in the sixteenth century, contains many titles for the Blessed Virgin, including "Mary, Ark of the Covenant."

READING II   1 Corinthians 15:54b–57

A reading from the first Letter of Saint Paul to the Corinthians

Brothers and sisters:
When that which is **mortal** clothes itself with **immortality**,
    then the **word** that is **written** shall come **about**:

> *Death is swallowed up in **victory**.*
> ***Where**, O death, is your **victory**?*
> ***Where**, O death, is your **sting**?*

The sting of **death** is sin,
    and the **power** of sin is the **law**.
But thanks be to **God** who gives **us** the victory
    through our **Lord** Jesus **Christ**.

Corinthians = kor-IN-thee-unz

Pause slightly before and after the lines referencing Isaiah 25:8 and Hosea 13:14 ("Death is swallowed up . . ."). Remember to raise your voice slightly as you near the end of the questions.

Proclaim the concluding verse ("But thanks be to God . . .") in an exsultant tone of voice, filled with gratitude.

READING II This short passage from Paul's first letter to the Corinthians is part of his response to questions raised in verse 35 about the nature of the risen body and how the dead are actually restored to life. Drawing on Isaiah 25:8 and Hosea 13:14, Paul makes his point that death does not last; rather, God, through Jesus Christ, gives victory over death. Thus, the sting of death—sin—no longer has power over us.

One of the reasons this reading is proclaimed at the Vigil Mass for the solemnity of the Blessed Virgin Mary is to show the connection between Mary's Assumption and Christ's Resurrection. Pope Pius XII defined the dogma of Mary's Assumption in the Apostolic Constitution *Munificentissimus Deus,* "The Most Bountiful God," on November 1, 1950. This dogma states that Mary, "preserved free from all stain of original sin, when the course of her earthly life was finished, was taken up body and soul into heavenly glory, and exalted by the Lord as Queen over all things, so that she might be the more fully conformed to her Son, the Lord of lords and conqueror of sin and death" (LG, #59; CCC, #966).

Just as Saint Paul was teaching the Corinthian community that through Christ's Resurrection they will become a transformed body, bearing the image of the risen body of Christ, so too "the Assumption of the Blessed Virgin is a singular participation in her Son's Resurrection and an anticipation of the resurrection of other Christians" (CCC, #966). Through her Assumption, then, Mary's participation in Christ's Resurrection exemplifies the transformation that awaits all Christians at the end of our earthly life.

State the opening announcement ("A reading from . . .") clearly, in a strong tone of voice. Pause after the announcement, gaining the assembly's attention for the very brief Gospel that follows.

Pause slightly at the comma after the words "he replied." Proclaim Jesus' reply ("Rather, blessed . . .") directly to the members of the assembly, inviting them to follow Mary's example of hearing the word of God, by making eye contact with them.

GOSPEL   Luke 11:27–28

A reading from the holy Gospel according to Luke

While **Jesus** was **speaking**,
  a **woman** from the **crowd called** out and said to him,
  "Blessed is the womb that **carried** you
  and the **breasts** at which you **nursed**."
He replied,
  "**Rather, blessed** are those
  who **hear** the word of God and **observe** it."

GOSPEL | The two verses that compose the Gospel reading on the Vigil of the solemnity of the Assumption are found in the section of Luke that narrates the journey of Jesus and his disciples to Jerusalem (9:51—19:27). Immediately prior to these verses, Jesus casts out a demon (11:14), speaks about Satan (verses 18–19), and teaches about the effects of unclean spirits (verses 24–26). In the midst of his teaching, an unidentified woman in the crowd interrupts Jesus, raising her voice to say, "Blessed is the womb . . . ."

Jesus' response is not necessarily meant as a rebuke or denial of her words. Instead his teaching is appropriately understood as completing the woman's words. As relates to Mary, the woman's statement praises and honors Mary for her role as his mother. Jesus' statement makes it clear that Mary is also blessed because she heard the word of God and responded obediently to it.

Because we all will not physically carry Jesus in the womb, Mary stands as a model of holiness for us; her hearing of the word stands in stark contrast to the evil disobedience of the demons and unclean spirits. Through her obedience she has shown she is with Jesus, not against him; she gathers others with Jesus to be one with God (verses 22–23), thus making her the Mother of God and the Mother of the Church (CCC, #963; see also LG, VIII).

ASSUMPTION OF THE BLESSED VIRGIN MARY: DAY

Lectionary #622

READING I   Revelation 11:19a; 12:1–6a, 10ab

A reading from the Book of Revelation

God's **temple** in heaven was **opened**,
> and the ark of his **covenant** could be seen in the temple.

A great sign appeared in the **sky**, a **woman** clothed with the **sun**,
> with the **moon** under her **feet**,
> and on her **head** a crown of twelve **stars**.
She was with **child** and wailed aloud in **pain** as she **labored**
> to give **birth**.
Then **another** sign appeared in the sky;
> it was a huge red **dragon**, with **seven** heads and ten **horns**,
> and on its heads were seven **diadems**.
Its **tail** swept away a third of the **stars** in the sky
> and hurled them down to the **earth**.
Then the dragon **stood** before the woman about to give **birth**,
> to **devour** her child when she gave birth.
She gave **birth** to a son, a **male** child,
> **destined** to rule all the **nations** with an iron rod.

Be clear in your announcement of the reading from "the Book of Revelation," not Revelations.

Let beauty and wonder be heard in your tone of voice as you narrate the words "A great sign appeared . . . ."

Pause before the dragon is introduced into the vision ("Then the dragon stood . . ."). While these lines are dramatic and dreadful, it is best to hold back on the drama in your tone of voice, lest you take away from the meaning of the reading for the solemnity.

READING I   The book of Revelation was probably written between 92 and 96 AD at the end of the reign of Emperor Domitian. Through a vision given by Christ to a man named John, the apocalypticism in Revelation expresses the belief that, near the end of the first century, the world is corrupt and therefore will be destroyed. In the end, the righteous will be led to life in union with God. In the face of persecution by Roman leaders, the vision contained in Revelation buoyed the early Christians to stand up for their faith, for in doing so they would be rescued—if not in this life, then in the next.

Apocalyptic literature is usually replete with symbolism, as is the case with today's First Reading, but this symbolism is not to be taken literally. For example, in the first section of the reading, the Catholic tradition has historically interpreted the "woman clothed with the sun" as Mary and the child the woman bears as Jesus. Yet the woman also symbolizes the heavenly Israel, the bringing together of God's Chosen People in the Old Testament with the new Israel, the Church, of the New Testament.

In the second section of the reading, the sign of the "huge red dragon" represents the power of the devil and the many forces of evil in the world that oppose the goodness of God and God's people, the Church. At the time of the writing of Revelation, the

Fill your voice with trust and faith as you narrate how the child and the woman were united with God in their respective ways ("Her child was caught . . . . The woman herself . . .").

Proclaim boldly the entire verse "Now have salvation . . ." without letting up at all in the strength of your voice.

Her child was **caught** up to **God** and his **throne**.
The woman **herself** fled into the **desert**
   where she had a place **prepared** by God.

Then I heard a loud **voice** in heaven say:
   "**Now** have **salvation** and power come,
      and the **kingdom** of our **God**
      and the **authority** of his **Anointed** One."

READING II   1 Corinthians 15:20–27

Corinthians = kor-IN-thee-unz

A reading from the first Letter of Saint Paul to the Corinthians

Use a serious tone of voice as you present Paul's teaching about the Resurrection of the dead ("Christ has been raised . . .").

Pause before the words "For just as in Adam . . . ." On the next phrase ("so too in Christ . . ."), shift to a more hopeful tone of voice.

Brothers and sisters:
Christ has been **raised** from the **dead**,
   the **firstfruits** of those who have fallen **asleep**.
For since **death** came through man,
   the **resurrection** of the dead came **also** through man.
For just as in **Adam** all **die**,
   so **too** in **Christ** shall all be brought to **life**,
   but each one in proper **order**:
   Christ the **firstfruits**;
   then, at his **coming**, those who **belong** to Christ;

dragon most likely symbolized the Roman leaders who were putting down the nascent Church (see Revelation 12:13–18).

   Finally, the third section of the reading shows that the child to whom the woman gives birth is protected by God and taken to his throne, a reference to the fact that Christ reigns forever with God through ~~~ Resurrection and Ascension. The ~~~ too resides in a special place in ~~~ where God is present and is ~~~ by him.

Because we understand the woman to symbolize Mary, who is the Mother of the Church, this vision also signifies that the Church will last throughout all time, a fundamental conviction about the Church that has been held since the earliest days of the Christian community. The permanence of the Church is referred to as the Church's indefectibility and is rooted in the indestructibility of her most fundamental belief that Jesus, the Son of God and the son of Mary, is Lord for all time.

READING II   Like the Second Reading for the Assumption Vigil, the Second Reading for the Assumption Mass during the Day comes from the fifteenth chapter of Paul's first letter to the Corinthians. The focus of chapter 15 is Paul's teaching about the Resurrection of Christ and what it means for our Resurrection.

   Paul develops his theology of Resurrection around two main points in today's Second Reading. First, the agricultural image of the "firstfruits," which Paul

then comes the **end**,
> when he hands **over** the Kingdom to his God and **Father**,
> when he has **destroyed** every **sovereignty**
> and every **authority** and **power**.

For he must **reign** until he has put all his **enemies** under his feet.
The **last** enemy to be destroyed is **death**,
> for "he subjected **everything** under his **feet**."

Build in intensity in your proclamation of Paul's argument from the words "then, at his coming" until "The last enemy to be destroyed . . . ."

GOSPEL   Luke 1:39–56

A reading from the holy Gospel according to Luke

Mary set out
> and traveled to the **hill** country in **haste**
> to a town of **Judah**,
> where she entered the house of **Zechariah**
> and greeted **Elizabeth**.

When Elizabeth heard Mary's **greeting**,
> the infant **leaped** in her womb,
> and **Elizabeth**, filled with the Holy **Spirit**,
> cried out in a loud voice and **said**,
> "**Blessed** are you among **women**,
> and **blessed** is the fruit of your **womb**.

As you narrate the opening lines, convey the sense of urgency in Mary's journey by placing some excitement and anticipation in your tone of voice.

Zechariah = zek-uh-RĪ-uh

Proclaim Elizabeth's words acknowledging Mary's identity that are familiar to us from the Hail Mary ("Blessed are you . . .") as the acclamation they are by filling your voice with praise.

---

uses to understand the risen Christ, refers to the part of the harvest that is offered in thanksgiving to God in anticipation of the whole harvest that will come. By speaking of Christ's Resurrection as the "firstfruits," Paul is able make a connection Christ's Resurrection and that of Christians. The "first" Resurrection anticipates the Resurrection of Christians at the end of time.

Second, Paul develops an Adam/Christ typology through which Christ is identified as a human being like Adam. Paul argued that since death (sin) came through Adam, then life must also come through a person like Adam—Christ. Thus, since we all have inherited the human condition of sinfulness from Adam, so at the second coming of Christ—the risen one who has destroyed sin—we too will be raised.

But why proclaim this reading on the solemnity of the Assumption? Through Mary's Assumption, she participated in a unique way in her Son's Resurrection, and in doing so she anticipated our Resurrection (CCC, #966). From the Annunciation through the cross, Mary's role as Mother of God never ceased. Because of her closeness to Christ and to us, she is able to intercede for all Christians as we look forward to the gift of eternal salvation. Thus, the Church

Pause after Elizabeth's acclamation of Mary and before her question ("And how does this happen . . . ?"

Return again to the tone of praise—though somewhat more reserved than the tone used for the initial acclamation—as Elizabeth's words to Mary conclude with another acclamation ("Blessed are you who believed . . .").

Proclaim the canticle of Mary ("My soul proclaims . . .") with joy in your voice as you are praising God through your proclamation of these words and calling the assembly to do the same.

And how does this happen to **me**,
    that the mother of my Lord should come to me?
For at the moment the sound of your **greeting** reached my **ears**,
    the **infant** in my womb **leaped** for joy.
Blessed are you who believed
    that what was **spoken** to you by the Lord
    would be **fulfilled**."

And Mary said:

"My **soul** proclaims the **greatness** of the Lord;
    my spirit **rejoices** in God my **Savior**
    for he has looked with favor on his lowly **servant**.
From this day all **generations** will call me **blessed**:
    the **Almighty** has done great **things** for me
    and **holy** is his **Name**.
    He has **mercy** on those who **fear** him
    in every generation.

gives her the titles of Advocate, Helper, Benefactress, and Mediatrix (CCC, #969; LG, #62).

GOSPEL On the solemnity of the Immaculate Conception, December 8, and the Fourth Sunday of Advent of this liturgical year, the Gospel proclaimed was the announcement of the birth of Jesus and Mary's fiat (Luke 1:26–28). Today, on the solemnity of the Assumption, the Gospel is the beloved narrative of the Visitation and Mary's canticle of praise to the Lord, which, in Luke, follows immediately after the Annunciation.

In today's Gospel, Elizabeth praises Mary twice in her words of response to her greeting. First, Elizabeth's words ("Blessed are you among women, and blessed is the fruit of your womb") draw attention to Mary's election from among all other women to be the mother of the Lord. These words are a statement of faith regarding the child Mary is carrying in her womb. They are also reminiscent of Jael's and Judith's liberation of their people in Judges 5:24 and Judith 13:18, respectively, and as such serve to show how Mary will contribute to the freedom of believers by giving birth to the Savior, Jesus Christ. Together with the angel Gabriel's words, "Hail, full of grace! The Lord is with you" (Luke 1:28), they form the basis for the first half of the traditional prayer, the Hail Mary.

He has shown the **strength** of his **arm**,
    and has **scattered** the proud in their **conceit**.
He has cast down the **mighty** from their **thrones**,
    and has **lifted up** the **lowly**.
He has filled the **hungry** with **good** things,
    and the **rich** he has sent away **empty**.
He has come to the **help** of his servant **Israel**
    for he has **remembered** his promise of **mercy**,
    the promise he made to our **fathers**,
    to **Abraham** and his children for **ever**."

Mary **remained** with her about **three months**
    and then returned to her **home**.

Pause after the canticle ends and before offering the concluding summary ("Mary remained . . .") slowly, in a reserved tone of voice.

Second, at the conclusion of her response to Mary, Elizabeth praises Mary with the words "Blessed are you who believed that what was spoken to you by the Lord would be fulfilled." Elizabeth's words set Mary apart as a model believer whose obedience to the Lord's word we are to emulate.

The Gospel concludes with Mary's hymn of praise to God, placed by Luke at this point in his narrative to show how Mary's experience of the Lord's presence in her life, while unique, is extended by God to all. Notice how the first stanza of the Magnificat is Mary's praise of God for what God has done specifically for her (1:46–50). The second stanza generalizes Mary's experiences and speaks of God's presence to all people, and in a particular way to the lowly, the hungry, and his servant Israel (1:51–55).

Mary's praise of God, which follows her being praised by Elizabeth, shows us our praise and veneration of Mary is ultimately meant to draw us to a deeper praise and worship of God. As the popular devotional phrase attests, our faith goes "to Jesus through Mary." Mary's Assumption has placed her forever as our mother in the order of grace, allowing her to intercede on our behalf, leading us closer to Jesus and union with the Father. Her role as Mother of God and Mother of the Church in no way diminishes the unique mediation of Christ, but rather it shows its power (LG, #60). Thus, any celebration of Mary is first a celebration of her Son, Jesus Christ.

20TH SUNDAY IN ORDINARY TIME

Lectionary #119

READING I Proverbs 9:1–6

A reading from the Book of Proverbs

> **Wisdom** has built her **house**,
>   she has set up her seven **columns**;
> she has **dressed** her meat, **mixed** her wine,
>   **yes**, she has spread her **table**.
> She has sent out her **maidens**; she calls
>   from the **heights** out over the **city**:
> "Let **whoever** is **simple** turn in **here**";
>   to the one who lacks **understanding**, she says,
> "**Come**, eat of my **food**,
>   and drink of the **wine** I have **mixed**!
> Forsake **foolishness** that you may **live**;
>   **advance** in the way of **understanding**."

Fill your voice with certainty as you describe the actions of Wisdom in the first part of the reading ("Wisdom has built her house . . ."), almost as if you have witnessed firsthand Wisdom doing them.

Speak Wisdom's words ("Let whoever is simple . . .") in a warm and inviting tone of voice directly to the assembly by looking up and making eye contact with them. For each of the three invitations, you might want to try looking at different sections of the assembly.

READING I Today's reading comes from the end of the prologue to the book of Proverbs (Proverbs 1—9). In the prologue, encouragement is offered particularly to the young and the simple, those who might be inexperienced or immature (1:4; 9:4), to follow Wisdom, portrayed as a woman who has set a beautiful table and then invites those in need of understanding to dine with her.

As you prepare to proclaim this reading, it would be helpful for you to study the entire poem of 9:1–18. This poem contains three sections: 1) the one that composes today's reading (verses 1–6); 2) verses 7–12, which are six individual proverbs that break up the poem; and 3) verses 13–18, in which "Folly" is depicted, like Wisdom, as a woman who invites the simple and those who lack understanding to a banquet. Folly's banquet, though, consists of stolen water and bread gotten secretly (verse 17). The guests at her feast reside in the depths of the nether world (verse 18).

Christians understand the fulfillment of Wisdom's banquet to be the eucharistic feast at which we share in Christ's own body and blood. Through this memorial meal we believe that our days are multiplied and the years of our life increased (verse 11), since, as we hear in today's Gospel, Jesus is "the living bread that came down from heaven; whoever eats this bread will live forever" (John 6:51).

READING II Many of the verses in Ephesians that come between the end of last Sunday's Second Reading and the beginning of this Sunday's epistle are proclaimed on the Fourth Sunday of Lent in Year A because they deal with

Ephesians = ee-FEE-zhunz

Give Paul's directives ("Watch carefully . . .") with a concerned tone of voice, showing your care for those gathered with you to worship.

The next two sentences ("Therefore, do not . . ." and "And do not get drunk . . .") both begin with a negative command and then offer a positive interpretation of the command. Use a firmer tone of voice to state the negative command and a kinder, more encouraging tone for the positive interpretation.

A reading from the Letter of Saint Paul to the Ephesians

Brothers and sisters:
Watch **carefully** how you **live**,
    not as **foolish** persons but as **wise**,
    making the **most** of the opportunity,
    because the days are **evil**.
Therefore, do not continue in **ignorance**,
    but try to **understand** what is the will of the **Lord**.
And do not get drunk on **wine**, in which lies **debauchery**,
    but be filled with the **Spirit**,
    addressing one another in **psalms** and **hymns** and
        spiritual **songs**,
    singing and **playing** to the Lord in your **hearts**,
    giving thanks **always** and for **everything**
    in the name of our Lord **Jesus** Christ to God the **Father**.

the theme of living as children of light in the Lord.

Today's five verses offer more specific ways for Christians to live in the light. They also continue the theme of Ephesians 4:17—5:20, which covers Christian and non-Christian conduct. In general, Christians, as God's children, are to be "imitators of God," living in love as Christ loved them (5:1).

The author expresses forthrightly the contrast between the ethical behavior of Christians and non-Christians. Christians are to live as "wise" persons do, not as "foolish persons". (Note the connection

to the contrast between "Wisdom" and "Folly" in the commentary for the First Reading). Through their Baptism, they are no longer people of darkness, but are people of the light (5:8). Their daily, ordinary actions must reflect this. When they do, the joy that flows from them is as palpable as that in the musical images in the concluding section of the epistle.

Notice in the final two sections of today's reading the contrast between the negative behaviors and the Spirit-filled behaviors. While the author is not reducing Christianity to ethical behavior—meaning

that the Christian faith is *only* a set of ethical norms to live by—he is affirming that there are certain ethical requirements to believing in Jesus Christ. Indeed, through the Spirit's assistance in living a moral life, Christians draw nearer to Jesus who leads them to the Father. The Catechism expresses this teaching in these words: "When we believe in Jesus Christ, partake of his mysteries, and keep his commandments, the Savior himself comes to love, in us, his Father and his brethren, our Father and our brethren. His person becomes,

Take your time with Jesus' opening statement ("I am the living bread . . .") so that the assembly will once again realize that this Gospel, like the ones of the previous three Sundays, will present Jesus' teaching about his identity as the Bread of Life.

Pause after the opening statement and before the words "The Jews quarreled . . . ." As in last Sunday's Gospel, place some tension in your voice as you ask the Jews' question ("How can this man . . . ?"). Proclaim Jesus' lengthy response ("Amen, amen . . .") with reverence and solemnity for it contains core beliefs about the Eucharist.

GOSPEL John 6:51–58

A reading from the holy Gospel according to John

Jesus said to the **crowds**:
  "I am the **living** bread that came down from **heaven**;
  whoever **eats** this bread will live **forever**;
  and the bread that I will give
  is my **flesh** for the life of the **world**."

The Jews **quarreled** among themselves, saying,
  "How can this man give us his **flesh** to eat?"
Jesus said to them,
  "Amen, amen, I **say** to you,
  unless you **eat** the flesh of the Son of **Man** and **drink** his **blood**,
  you **do** not have life **within** you.
Whoever **eats** my flesh and **drinks** my blood
  has **eternal** life,
  and I will **raise** him on the last **day**.

through the Spirit, the living and interior rule of our activity" (#2074).

GOSPEL Does the first verse of today's Gospel sound familiar? If it does, that is because it was the concluding verse of last Sunday's Gospel! The Gospel passage at hand, while perhaps a later addition to the Bread of Life discourse, continues the development of John's eucharistic theology in two ways: 1) by emphasizing the sacrificial nature of the Eucharistic meal and 2) by identifying the

Eucharist as the locus of communion in the Christian community.

As in the previous Gospels proclaimed on the Eighteenth and Nineteenth Sundays in Ordinary Time, the dialog between Jesus and the crowd is set in motion with a question. Jesus overhears the Jews arguing among themselves, and asking a question ("How can this man . . . ?") that shows they understand Jesus' teaching literally, and thus are struggling to make sense of it. After this question, the rest of the narrative is solely the words Jesus

offered explaining what it means to eat of his flesh and drink of his blood.

First, the Jews do not understand that Jesus will sacrifice his body and blood on the cross. This is precisely the point that Jesus is attempting to make to them. Eternal life will only come through Jesus' doing the will of the Father who sent him. That Jesus descended from the Father is the first step in the Father's will. Second, Jesus remained in the world for a time, teaching about the Father, his unique relationship to the Father, and how all people are invited to share in the communion he

Pause after the words "and still died."
Then make eye contact with the assembly
as you confidently proclaim the words
"whoever eats this bread . . . ."

For my **flesh** is true **food**,
    and my **blood** is true **drink**.
Whoever eats my **flesh** and drinks my **blood**
    remains in me and I in **him**.
Just as the living Father sent **me**
    and I have life **because** of the Father,
    so also the one who **feeds** on me
    will have life **because** of me.
This is the bread that came down from **heaven**.
Unlike your **ancestors** who ate and still died,
    whoever eats **this** bread will live **forever**."

has with the Father by eating and drinking of the meal that gives eternal life. Third, through Jesus' sacrifice on the cross and his Resurrection, he returns in glory to the Father and thus is able to give others the gift of eternal life. Through this movement, then, the Eucharist is forever linked to Jesus' sacrifice. Eucharist is a meal that remembers and makes present sacramentally Jesus' gift of himself in the events of his life, death, and Resurrection.

The second way in which the Johannine theology of the Eucharist is extended in today's Gospel is by uniting our participation in the Eucharist with our relationship to Jesus and the community of believers. Jesus' words ("Whoever eats my flesh and drinks my blood remains in me and I in him") inform us that through the Eucharist the bond between Jesus, the believer, and the entire community of disciples is maintained and strengthened. In times of persecution and disunity in the developing Christian community, it was participation in the Eucharist that determined whether or not one was in communion with the Church and thus remained connected with Jesus.

So it is today. The Eucharist is the sign of unity; it is the sacrament of those who are in full communion with the Church (CCC, #1395) and who, through the Eucharist, are drawn into a deeper communion with the Father. Thus, we pray for the one body of the Church, marred by divisions, that "the time of complete unity among all who believe in him may return," leaving no one cut off from the vine (CCC, #1398; John 15:1–9).

21ST SUNDAY IN ORDINARY TIME

Lectionary #122

Shechem = SHEK-um

Use a narrative tone of voice for the opening lines ("Joshua gathered together . . ."), which set the scene.

Deliver Joshua's address to the people ("If it does not please you . . .") in a strong, challenging, and direct tone of voice, making eye contact with the members of the assembly as if you are putting forward the challenge to them today.

Amorites = AM-er-its

Pause before and after boldly proclaiming Joshua's conviction ("As for me and my household . . .").

In conveying the people's response to Joshua ("Far be it from us . . ."), use a strong and firm tone throughout. Try pausing slightly after the word "Therefore" in the final line to stress the people's conclusion ("we also will serve . . ."). Use a declarative tone for this statement.

READING I   Joshua 24:1–2a, 15–17, 18b

A reading from the Book of Joshua

Joshua gathered together all the tribes of **Israel** at **Shechem**,
    summoning their **elders**, their **leaders**,
    their **judges**, and their **officers**.
When they stood in ranks before **God**,
    Joshua **addressed** all the people:
    "If it does not **please** you to serve the LORD,
    decide today whom you will **serve**,
    the gods your **fathers** served beyond the **River**
    or the gods of the **Amorites** in whose **country** you are
        now **dwelling**.
As for **me** and my **household**, we will serve the LORD."

But the people answered,
    "Far be it from **us** to forsake the LORD
    for the service of **other** gods.
For it was the LORD, our **God**,
    who brought **us** and our **fathers** up out of the land of **Egypt**,
    out of a state of **slavery**.
He performed those great **miracles** before our very **eyes**
    and **protected** us along our entire **journey**
    and among the **peoples** through whom we **passed**.
Therefore we **also** will serve the LORD, for he is our **God**."

READING I The Lord appointed Joshua to be Moses' successor to at the end of the book of Deuteronomy (31:7–8; 14–15, 23). Through Joshua, God's promise of land is fulfilled as the Israelites take possession of the land of Canaan (see Genesis 12:1–3).

Today's reading comes from the conclusion of Joshua in which he gathers the tribes of Israel together at Shechem for a renewal of their covenant with the Lord. Joshua reminds the Israelites of their responsibility to follow the Mosaic law. But he is forthright with them, giving them a choice whether or not they will serve the Lord. The choice Joshua gives them is similar to the choice between life or death Moses gave them in Deuteronomy 30:19 and the one Elijah presents them with in 1 Kings 18:21 between the Lord and Baal. The choice Joshua presents further coincides with that which Jesus gives to Simon Peter in today's Gospel after many of Jesus' disciples had already returned to their former way of life.

Through your proclamation of the Lord's word in this reading, the choice Joshua offers the Israelites is made present to the assembly before you. Your service as a lector today can facilitate a renewal among those in the assembly to say as the Israelites did: "As for me and my household we will serve the Lord."

READING II Today's Second Reading begins where last Sunday's left off. It continues the discussion of Christian conduct by elaborating how the relationship of Christ and the Church is an image for the spousal relationship of husband and wife.

READING II   Ephesians 5:21–32

A reading from the Letter of Saint Paul to the Ephesians

Brothers and sisters:
Be **subordinate** to one another out of **reverence** for **Christ**.
Wives should be subordinate to their **husbands** as to the **Lord**.
For the husband is **head** of his wife
    just as **Christ** is head of the **church**,
    he **himself** the savior of the **body**.
As the **church** is subordinate to **Christ**,.
    so **wives** should be subordinate to their **husbands**
        in **everything**.
Husbands, love your **wives**,
    even as **Christ** loved the **church**
    and handed himself **over** for her to **sanctify** her,
    cleansing her by the bath of **water** with the **word**,
    that he might present to himself the church in **splendor**,
    without **spot** or **wrinkle** or **any** such thing,
    that she might be **holy** and without **blemish**.
So **also** husbands should love their **wives** as their own **bodies**.
He who loves his **wife** loves **himself**.
For no one hates his own **flesh**
    but rather **nourishes** and **cherishes** it,
    even as **Christ** does the **church**,
    because we are **members** of his **body**.
*For this reason a **man** shall leave his **father** and his **mother***
    *and be **joined** to his **wife**,*
    *and the **two** shall become one **flesh**.*
This is a great **mystery**,
    but I speak in reference to **Christ** and the **church**.

[Shorter: Ephesians 5:2a, 25–32]

Ephesians = ee-FEE-zhunz

Be clear in your pronouncement of the line "Be subordinate to one another." Make eye contact with the members of the assembly to help them understand the mutuality suggested in this sentence.

Pause before and after the quotation from Genesis 2:24 ("For this reason a man . . .") to set it off.

The final verse ("This is a great mystery . . .") is a summary. Proclaim it slowly and with reverence.

The verses that form the passage you proclaim are part of what is known as a "household code" (Ephesians 5:21—6:9). In all, three "household codes" are found in the New Testament—the one in Ephesians is similar to Colossians 3:18—4:1 and 1 Peter 2:18—2:7. These codes were common in Greco-Roman literature of the late first century.

In the code presented in today's reading, the relationships among members of the Christian household are shown to be hierarchically ordered by Christ. This means that the way that husbands and wives treat one another mirrors the manner in which they love the Lord. Moreover, the love between husband and wife is a reflection, however imperfect, of the love Christ, the bridegroom, has for the church, his bride.

The love of husband for his wife, expressed for Catholics sacramentally in the sacrament of Marriage, is to be as deep and profound as the love he has for his own body. As he nurtures and provides for himself, so too is he to nourish his wife. In this regard, Christ provides an example for the husband, for Christ continues to feed the church through the Eucharist.

While to some this reading might seem antiquated because of the subordinate relationships described in it, still much is to be gained by reflecting on the love and care that is expected of members of the Christian household. As the Church grew near the end of the first century, more organization and structure became necessary. The societal structure of the time was that which the Church had available to it to draw upon in modeling its own structure. Yet the Church did not simply

GOSPEL   John 6:60–69

A reading from the holy Gospel according to John

Many of Jesus' **disciples** who were **listening** said,
  "This **saying** is **hard**; who can **accept** it?"
Since Jesus **knew** that his disciples were **murmuring** about this,
  he said to them, "Does this **shock** you?
What if you were to see the Son of Man **ascending**
  to where he was **before**?
It is the **spirit** that gives life,
  while the **flesh** is of no **avail**.
The words I have **spoken** to you are **Spirit** and **life**.
But there are **some** of you who do not **believe**."
Jesus **knew** from the **beginning** the ones who would not **believe**
  and the one who would **betray** him.
And he said,
  "For this **reason** I have told you that **no** one can **come** to me
  unless it is **granted** him by my **Father**."

As a **result** of this,
  many of his disciples **returned** to their former way of life
  and no longer **accompanied** him.
Jesus then said to the **Twelve**, "Do you **also** want to leave?"
Simon **Peter** answered him, "**Master**, to **whom** shall we go?
You have the **words** of eternal **life**.
We have come to **believe**
  and are convinced that **you** are the **Holy** One of **God**."

adapt that structure exactly; rather, it conditioned the structure with the love of Christ, creating higher expectations for relationships among its members than in pagan society. In the end, it was in and through Christian love—not the overturning of the social fabric—that the Church witnessed to a new reality in Christ.

GOSPEL This Gospel comes at the end of the Bread of Life discourse and begins with murmuring among

Jesus' disciples. The saying that the disciples purport is "hard" and thus is not easy to accept is "unless you eat the flesh of the Son of Man and drink his blood, you do not have life within you" (6:53).

Jesus himself knew that some of his disciples would have difficulty accepting the saying. Peter, however, speaking for the Twelve, professes faith in Jesus as the one who has the "words of eternal life." Peter's words at the conclusion of the discourse serve as the Johannine form of Peter's confession. They also signify the

requirements for remaining within the eucharistic communion of faith.

Those of us who have professed our faith in Jesus and celebrate it in the Eucharist each week, know the ups and downs that come with being a disciple; we have probably even seen our share of fellow disciples return to their former way of life, leaving the communion of the Church. Yet, like Peter, we are convinced that Jesus, whom we receive in the Eucharist, is "the Holy One of God."

22ND SUNDAY IN ORDINARY TIME

Lectionary #125

READING I   Deuteronomy 4:1–2, 6–8

Deuteronomy = d<u>oo</u>-ter-AH-nuh-mee

Deliver Moses' words to Israel ("Now, Israel . . .") with an authoritative tone in your voice and make eye contact with the members of the assembly as they are part of the Church, the new Israel.

Pause before the words "In your observance." Emphasize that the commandments are not to be altered by adding a slight pause after the phrase "you shall not add to what I command you" and before "nor subtract from it."

Pause before the section that begins "Observe them carefully . . ." and lighten your authoritative tone of voice slightly as you proclaim these words.

Pose the rhetorical questions at the conclusion of the reading ("For what great nation is there . . . ?") in a persuasive and confident tone of voice.

A reading from the Book of Deuteronomy

Moses said to the **people**:
   "Now, Israel, **hear** the statutes and decrees
   which I am **teaching** you to **observe**,
   that you may **live**, and may enter in and take **possession**
      of the land
   which the LORD, the God of your **fathers**, is **giving** you.
In your **observance** of the commandments of the LORD,
      your **God**,
   which I **enjoin** upon you,
   you shall not **add** to what I command you nor **subtract** from it.
Observe them **carefully**,
   for thus will you give **evidence**
   of your **wisdom** and **intelligence** to the **nations**,
   who will **hear** of all these statutes and say,
   'This great **nation** is truly a **wise** and **intelligent** people.'
For what great nation **is** there
   that has gods so **close** to it as the LORD, our God, is to **us**
   whenever we **call** upon him?
Or what great nation has **statutes** and **decrees**
   that are as **just** as this whole **law**
   which I am setting **before** you **today**?"

READING I Today's First Reading begins with an opening phrase, "Now, Israel, hear" *(shema)*, commonly used in Deuteronomy to introduce a liturgical address (5:1; 6:1, 3, 4; 9:7). In this reading, Moses, like Jesus in today's Gospel, is portrayed as a teacher as he delivers the address. This portrayal of Moses occurs elsewhere in Deuteronomy as well (1:5; 4:5; 5:31; 6:1). Whereas Moses speaks of a strict observance of the Lord's commandments, in the Gospel Jesus distinguishes between God's commandment and human tradition, pointing out the importance of what is inside the heart of a person.

The teacher, Moses, instructs the Israelites of the importance of the Lord's commandment that they must follow in order to enter into the Promised Land. If they Israelites choose to obey the Lord's statutes and decrees, not changing them at all, then other nations will know of the Israelites' "wisdom and intelligence."

By following the acknowledgment of Israel's wisdom and intelligence with the rhetorical questions ("For what great nation . . ."), the author of Deuteronomy makes the point that God is in relationship with his people through the law. The law that regulated the life of the Israelites was meant to be of service to their relationships with one another and with their God.

Because the Mosaic discourses in Deuteronomy are written in the first person and often in the present tense as in today's reading, you have the opportunity to deliver Moses' words as if he were addressing the assembly before you. This assists them in hearing that the law is also the foundation of their relationship with the Lord as it was for the Israelites.

READING II   James 1:17–18, 21b–22, 27

A reading from the Letter of Saint James

Dearest brothers and sisters:
All **good** giving and every perfect **gift** is from **above**,
  coming down from the Father of **lights**,
  with whom there is no **alteration** or **shadow** caused by **change**.
He willed to give us **birth** by the word of **truth**
  that we may be a kind of **firstfruits** of his **creatures**.

Humbly **welcome** the word that has been **planted** in you
  and is able to save your **souls**.

Be **doers** of the word and not **hearers** only, **deluding** yourselves.

Religion that is **pure** and **undefiled** before God and the Father
    is **this**:
  to care for **orphans** and **widows** in their affliction
  and to keep oneself **unstained** by the world.

READING II For the next five Sundays, the Second Reading comes from the letter of James. Along with the 1–3 John, 1 and 2 Peter, and Jude, the letter of James is considered one of the "catholic" epistles, which means that its intention and scope are universal. Its author desired to impact not just a particular local community, as was the case with the authentic Pauline letters, but rather the Church at large near the end of the first century. From the introductory verse of the letter, we know that the author addressed it to "the twelve tribes in dispersion" (1:1).

In other words, it was written to Christians living outside Palestine.

In this reading, James begins by pointing out the goodness of all the gifts that come from the Father. The Father purposefully gave us life so that we in turn might be the "firstfruits" of his creatures. "Firstfruits" is an agricultural image that refers to the initial part of the harvest that was traditionally offered in thanksgiving to God in anticipation of the entire harvest yet to come. As "firstfruits," our offer of thanksgiving to the Father for his gifts

anticipates the beauty and gift of our brothers and sisters who will be with us in faith in the future. God's first act of creation came through the command of his word. Now in a sense, through Jesus, God's Word made flesh, alive in us today, James is telling us that God's creation continues in and through us.

At the end of the reading, James provides an application of how Christians are to be "doers of the word." Concern for those the forgotten among us—the orphans and widows—is to be an essential part of the practice of religion. For Catholics, the

GOSPEL   Mark 7:1–8, 14–15, 21–23

A reading from the holy Gospel according to Mark

When the **Pharisees** with some **scribes** who had
        come from **Jerusalem**
gathered around **Jesus**,
    they **observed** that some of his **disciples** ate their meals
    with **unclean**, that is, **unwashed**, **hands**.
—For the **Pharisees** and, in fact, **all** Jews,
    do not **eat** without **carefully** washing their **hands**,
    keeping the **tradition** of the **elders**.
And on coming from the **marketplace**
    they do not eat without **purifying** themselves.
And there are many **other** things that they have
        traditionally observed,
    the **purification** of cups and jugs and kettles and beds.—
So the Pharisees and scribes **questioned** him,
    "Why do **your** disciples **not** follow the tradition of the **elders**
    but **instead** eat a meal with **unclean** hands?"
He responded,
    "Well did **Isaiah** prophesy about you **hypocrites**, as it is writ-
        ten:
    This people honors me with their **lips**,
        but their **hearts** are far from me;
    in **vain** do they worship me,
        teaching as doctrines **human** precepts.
You disregard God's **commandment** but cling to
        human tradition."

Take your time with the lines "When the Pharisees with some scribes . . ." because they set the scene for what follows. However, since the lines that "set the scene" are lengthy, be careful not to read too slowly so as to lose the assembly's attention.

Pause slightly before the words "So the Pharisees," which mark the transition of the narrative to a dialogue between the Pharisees and Jesus.

In Jesus' response to the Pharisees' question ("Well did Isaiah prophesy . . ."), distinguish between Jesus' words and the quotation from Isaiah ("This people honors . . .") by pausing before and after the quotation.

Corporal Works of Mercy—especially feeding the hungry, sheltering the homeless, clothing the naked, visiting the sick and imprisoned, and burying the dead— have been traditional and primary ways to put their faith into practice (CCC, #2447).

GOSPEL   Today is the first Sunday since the Sixteenth Sunday in Ordinary Time that we will hear the Gospel according to Mark proclaimed. This account of the controversy between Jesus and the Pharisees about ritual purity

serves as the climax to the section in Mark in which Jesus' power and authority are revealed through the feeding of the 5,000 (6:35–44), his walking on the water (6:45–52), and his healing of the sick in many villages and towns (6:53–56).

A similar pattern occurs in the previous section of the Gospel according to Mark, where Jesus' calming of the storm (4:35–41), his healing a man possessed by a demon (5:1–20), his healing the woman with a hemorrhage, and his raising of Jairus' daughter (5:21–43) are followed by Jesus' rejection by his own people as he

was teaching in the synagogue (6:1–6a). In the section that comes after today's Gospel (7:24—8:21), Mark repeats the pattern again, this time concluding with a controversy between Jesus and the Pharisees, in which the Pharisees ask for a sign to prove Jesus' identity.

One of Mark's points in using this literary structure is to show that Jesus is doing something new and new is always difficult to accept. Both in the miracles he performs and in his relativization of the

**Pause before the words "He summoned,"
as Jesus now brings the crowd into the
scene. Give his instructions to the crowd
("Hear me . . .") in a firm tone of voice.**

**Pause before concluding with Jesus'
words ("From within people . . .").
Although they are discouraging—even
depressing—words, deliver them in an
instructive tone of voice. Jesus desires
that people realize where evil comes from
so that they can change their hearts and
live according to God's commands.**

He summoned the crowd **again** and said to them,
    "**Hear** me, **all** of you, and **understand**.
Nothing that enters one from **outside** can **defile** that person;
    but the things that come out from **within** are what **defile**.

"From **within** people, from their **hearts**,
    come evil thoughts, unchastity, theft, murder,
    adultery, greed, malice, deceit,
    licentiousness, envy, blasphemy, arrogance, folly.
All **these** evils come from **within** and they **defile**."

Jewish purity ritual and laws in today's
Gospel, Jesus demonstrates that belief in
him and the proclamation of the kingdom
of God present already in his very person
are what really matter. While the reader is
aware of this from the beginning of Mark's
account (1:15), the disciples and the
Pharisees are not. They continually misunderstand or refuse to understand what
Jesus is about.

In today's Gospel, Jesus teaches that
hypocrites (*hypokritēs,* in Greek)—literally,
those whose faces are hidden behind

masks—are truly those who attempt to
hide behind the Old Testament law. The
Pharisees sought to apply the ritual and
purity laws of the Old Testament, which
only priests had to observe, to all of the
Israelites, thus forming them as a priestly
people. However, their attempt to do so
resulted in Jesus' quotation of Isaiah 29:13,
criticizing them for only paying lip service
to him and not having their heart in right
relationship with him.

While it appears in this passage that
Jesus does jettison the Old Testament
laws of ritual purity, the main point is not *if*

or *how many* of these laws he has abandoned, but rather that he is calling people to a new relationship with him, based
on what is in their hearts. Human traditions that can lead to the defilement of
people and their relationship with God,
Jesus now sets in their proper place—in
service to God's commandment—the Great
Commandment, love of God, neighbor, and
self (Mark 12:28–34).

23RD SUNDAY IN ORDINARY TIME

Lectionary #128

READING I   Isaiah 35:4–7a

Isaiah = ī-ZAY-uh

A reading from the Book of the Prophet Isaiah

Thus says the LORD:
   Say to those whose hearts are **frightened**:
     Be **strong**, fear **not**!
Here is your **God**,
   he comes with **vindication**;
with divine **recompense**
   he comes to **save** you.
Then will the **eyes** of the blind be **opened**,
   the **ears** of the deaf be **cleared**;
then will the lame **leap** like a **stag**,
   then the **tongue** of the mute will **sing**.
Streams will burst forth in the **desert**,
   and **rivers** in the **steppe**.
The **burning** sands will become **pools**,
   and the **thirsty** ground, springs of **water**.

Deliver the imperative ("Be strong") in a powerful and firm tone of voice. Then lower your tone of voice slightly as you convey the command to "fear not" with a sense of hope and reassurance.

As you proclaim the particular events and images that witness to the salvation offered by God's coming, build in rejoicing from the words "Then will the eyes of the blind" through to the end of the reading. Do not lose any strength and confidence in your tone of voice as you complete the reading with "and the thirsty ground . . . ."

READING I Today's reading from the prophet Isaiah begins with a command to those who are wracked with fear of Edom, which was across the Dead Sea to the southeast, not to be afraid. The reading continues with God's promise to bring salvation and concludes with a poetic portrait of what this salvation will look like.

Notice that Isaiah 35:10 is similar to Isaiah 51:11, which describes the return of the Israelites from exile. The ending of the salvation oracle with verse 10 might have been a later editorial addition in order to

indicate that the salvation God brings includes the coming of God's Chosen People home to him.

While this reading sounds like an Advent reading, your proclamation of it during Ordinary Time can assist the assembly in hearing that God comes to us, not only during a particular liturgical season or on a particular holy day, but also throughout the year. Through Jesus and in the Holy Spirit, the Father saves, bringing freedom from our enemies and impediments as God saves Judah from Edom and as Jesus heals

the deaf man with a speech impediment in today's Gospel.

READING II Today's passage begins with the command that directs Christians to avoid discrimination and favoritism. The reading then offers the hypothetical example in which a rich person is shown more attention than a poor person by a Christian assembly at the time. By using this example, James illustrates that wealth and economic status are neither determinative of who belongs to

A reading from the Letter of Saint James

My brothers and sisters, show no **partiality**
    as you adhere to the **faith** in our glorious Lord Jesus **Christ**.
For if a man with **gold** rings and fine **clothes**
    comes into your **assembly**,
    and a **poor** person in **shabby** clothes **also** comes in,
    and you pay **attention** to the one wearing the **fine** clothes
    and say, "Sit **here**, please,"
    while you say to the **poor** one, "Stand **there**," or
      "Sit at my **feet**,"
    have you not made **distinctions** among yourselves
    and become **judges** with evil **designs**?

Listen, my beloved brothers and sisters.
Did not God **choose** those who are **poor** in the world
    to be **rich** in faith and **heirs** of the kingdom
    that he **promised** to those who **love** him?

Deliver the directive ("show no partiality") in an emphatic tone of voice that leaves the members of the assembly questioning their own actions.

In recounting the example about the rich person and the poor person, pick up the pace of your delivery slightly to continue the momentum toward the end of the rhetorical question (". . . with evil designs?").

Pause before the final section begins ("Listen . . ."). Pose the final question ("Did not God choose . . . ?") in a gentler, more understanding tone of voice than you used for the opening of the reading ("show no partiality").

---

the Christian community nor status within the community.

    James' theological intent in this passage becomes clear in the concluding section: "Listen, my beloved . . . ." The rhetorical question, to which the Christian assembly being addressed already knows the answer, serves to emphasize that it is *God* who chooses the poor to be with him in his kingdom. The question does not deny the wealthy entrance into the kingdom, but rather puts forth that life with God in his kingdom is determined by love of God. And

love of God includes showing no partiality to our neighbor, rich or poor.

    While the hypothetical example in this reading is especially pertinent to ministers of hospitality and ushers in our Christian assemblies today, James is addressing the entire assembly as he presents this example. In your role as a lector, you will have the opportunity to put this reading into practice as you greet people before and after the liturgy.

GOSPEL Today's Gospel begins with Jesus leaving the district of Tyre and traveling by way of Sidon to the district of Decapolis where a deaf man with a speech impediment (*mogilalos;* the same word is used in the Septuagint in Isaiah 35:6, part of today's First Reading) was brought to him. Decapolis itself was principally a Gentile area, thus making it very plausible that the deaf man was a Gentile. If this were the case, then the closeness of the connection that Jesus

GOSPEL   Mark 7:31–37

A reading from the holy Gospel according to Mark

Again Jesus left the district of **Tyre**
  and went by way of **Sidon** to the Sea of **Galilee**,
  into the district of the **Decapolis**.
And people brought to him a **deaf** man who had a
    speech impediment
  and **begged** him to lay his **hand** on him.
He took him **off** by himself **away** from the crowd.
He put his **finger** into the man's **ears**
  and, **spitting**, touched his **tongue**;
  then he looked up to heaven and **groaned**, and said to him,
  "Ephphatha!"—that is, "Be **opened**!"—
And **immediately** the man's ears were **opened**,
  his **speech** impediment was **removed**,
  and he spoke **plainly**.
He ordered them not to tell **anyone**.
But the **more** he ordered them not to,
  the **more** they proclaimed it.
They were exceedingly **astonished** and they said,
  "He has done **all** things **well**.
He makes the **deaf hear** and the **mute speak**."

Tyre = tīr
Sidon = SĪ-dun
Galilee = GAL-ih-lee
Decapolis = dih-KAP-uh-lis

Clearly accentuate every detail of the story of the healing of the deaf man from the people's action of begging Jesus to "lay his hand on him" through to Jesus groaning by taking your time with this part of the narrative, pausing at the given punctuation.

Ephphatha = EF-fah-thah

Do not shout Jesus' words to the deaf man ("Ephphatha!"). Rather, simply offer them in a calm tone of voice, similar to the one you would use during the Baptismal Rite for the Ephphetha or Prayer over Ears and Mouth that comes from this Gospel story.

Put some excitement in your tone of voice as you proclaim the people's words ("He has done . . .").

makes with him by taking him away from the crowd and carrying out the ritual of touching his ears and tongue shows that the salvation of the kingdom of God available through Jesus is personally available for Jew and Gentile alike.

The healing received from Jesus by the deaf man who could not speak plainly was so complete that his ears were opened and the speech impediment was no longer present. Presumably, the man went back to the crowd after being healed, although this

is not stated in the Gospel. However, the Gospel does tell us that Jesus ordered "them"—the crowd—not to tell anyone about what transpired. Yet the miracle of healing that occurred was so amazing the crowd disobeyed Jesus' command and consciously chose to go out and proclaim the Good News.

The words Mark puts on the lips of the crowd attesting to the presence of the kingdom of God in Jesus ("He makes the deaf . . .") come from Isaiah 35:5–6, part of the salvation oracle proclaimed in today's

First Reading. These words show the salvation promised by God in the Old Testament is fulfilled in the person of Jesus.

Your proclamation of this Gospel can serve as a reminder to the assembly to go out and proclaim the kingdom of God already—but not yet—available to those who have faith. Through their Baptism, believers have seen for themselves their own ears opened and mouth set free to hear and witness to the kingdom.

24TH SUNDAY IN ORDINARY TIME

Lectionary #131

READING I   Isaiah 50:4c–9a

Isaiah = ī-ZAY-uh

Deliver the words of the servant accepting the divine calling ("The Lord God opens my ear . . .") in a peaceful and calm tone of voice.

A reading from the Book of the Prophet Isaiah

The Lord **GOD** opens my **ear** that I may **hear**;
and I **have** not rebelled,
    have not turned back.
I gave my **back** to those who **beat** me,
    my **cheeks** to those who **plucked** my beard;
my **face** I did not **shield**
    from **buffets** and **spitting**.

Pause before the new section, which describes the help the Lord gives to the servant ("The Lord God is my help . . ."). Proclaim these words with a sense of relief and hope in your tone of voice.

The Lord **GOD** is my **help**,
    therefore I am not **disgraced**;
I have **set** my face like **flint**,
    knowing that I shall **not** be put to **shame**.
He is **near** who upholds my **right**;
    if **anyone** wishes to **oppose** me,
    let us appear **together**.
Who disputes my right?
    Let **that** man confront me.
See, the Lord **GOD** is my **help**;
    who will prove me wrong?

Pause before the final line ("See, the Lord God . . .") and ask the question with strength and confidence. The servant knows no one can discount the Lord.

READING I   The selection from the third servant song that serves as today's First Reading begins with the servant accepting the Lord's call to follow him. Even in the face of suffering, the servant has not refused to remain faithful to the Lord. While the identity of the servant of the Lord is not known, what *is* known is that the servant stands as an example of fidelity to the Lord. Despite the suffering that comes the way of the servant, the servant trusts that the Lord will always be by his or her side.

The servant of the Lord in today's passage stands in stark contrast to the unfaithful Israelites who seek to return to the Lord. At the conclusion of the servant song, the Lord chastises the Israelites for not following the servant and in doing so gives support to the servant, acknowledging his or her faithfulness to the Lord. Paired with today's Gospel reading in which Jesus teaches that whoever comes after him must "deny himself, take up his cross, and follow me," this reading connects the servant of the Lord with both Jesus, who exemplifies the suffering servant, and his

disciples, who also are faithful servants when they accept Jesus' call to follow him with all that it entails.

READING II   The two questions at the beginning of this reading will catch the assembly's attention. Even occasional churchgoers who are a part of the assembly will know the relationship between faith and works is at the heart of different understandings of salvation.

In response to the opening questions whether faith without works can save,

READING II   James 2:14–18

A reading from the Letter of Saint James

What **good** is it, my brothers and sisters,
    if someone says he has **faith** but does not have **works**?
Can that faith **save** him?
If a brother or sister has **nothing** to wear
    and has no **food** for the day,
    and one of you says to them,
    "**Go** in peace, **keep** warm, and **eat** well,"
    but you do not give them the **necessities** of the **body**,
    what **good** is it?
So **also** faith of **itself**,
    if it does not have **works**, is **dead**.

Indeed someone might **say**,
    "**You** have faith and **I** have works."
Demonstrate your faith to me **without** works,
    and **I** will demonstrate my faith to you **from** my works.

Ask the opening question ("What good is it . . . ?") deliberately, emphasizing the words "faith" and "works" by pausing slightly before and after "faith" and significantly after "works," thus allowing the assembly to hear the question, which sets the stage for the main point of the reading.

Look up and make eye contact with the assembly as you proclaim the line "if it does not have works, is dead" in firm tone of voice, reiterating the main point of the reading.

Deliver the entirety of the final line ("Demonstrate your faith . . .") with conviction, not letting down in the tone or volume of your voice on the second half of the sentence. It is equally important for James' argument.

James provides the hypothetical example of a person approaching you in need of clothing and food and you simply responding to them by sending them on their way, wishing them well. You meet neither their material nor physical needs. Your kind sentiments are James' metaphor for faith. The person's needs show the good works that need to be carried out.

However, since the kind sentiments were not rooted in actions, they were an incomplete response to the situation. This James explains in the conclusion of the reading. His reply to the objection ("Indeed someone might say . . .") to the connection between faith and works he developed in the hypothetical example makes the case that the two cannot be separated.

GOSPEL   Today's Gospel begins with Jesus desiring to know who the people he has been teaching think he is. In response, the disciples offer the same suggestions that are found in Mark 6:14–16, where the evangelist describes speculations about Jesus' identity and recounts that Herod Antipas said it is John the Baptist who has been raised up. Jesus, however, desires to know more than just what others are saying about him. When he asks the question "But who do . . . ?" a second time, he personalizes it, asking the disciples directly for their opinion. In response, Peter steps forward, offering a statement of faith identifying Jesus as the Messiah, the Christ.

The Gospel proceeds with Jesus neither confirming nor denying Peter's confession. Jesus' warning not to tell anyone about him, however, minimally qualifies as an implicit corroboration of his messianic

GOSPEL   Mark 8:27–35

A reading from the holy Gospel according to Mark

Jesus and his **disciples** set out
   for the villages of **Caesarea Philippi**.
Along the way he asked his **disciples**,
   "**Who** do people say that I **am**?"
They said in reply,
   "John the **Baptist**, others **Elijah**,
   still others one of the **prophets**."
And he asked them,
   "But who do **you** say that I am?"
Peter said to him in **reply**,
   "You are the **Christ**."
Then he warned them not to tell **anyone** about him.

He began to **teach** them
   that the Son of **Man** must suffer **greatly**
   and be **rejected** by the **elders**, the **chief** priests, and the **scribes**,
   and be **killed**, and rise after three **days**.
He spoke this openly.
Then Peter took him **aside** and began to **rebuke** him.
At this he turned around and, **looking** at his disciples,
   rebuked Peter and said, "Get **behind** me, **Satan**.
You are thinking not as **God** does, but as human **beings** do."

He summoned the crowd with his disciples and **said** to them,
   "**Whoever** wishes to come after me must **deny** himself,
   take up his cross, and **follow** me.
For whoever wishes to **save** his life will **lose** it,
   but whoever **loses** his life for **my** sake
   and that of the **gospel** will **save** it."

Caesarea = see-zuh-REE-uh
Philippi = fih-LIP-ī

Ask the first question ("Who do people say that I am?"), which is in the third person, in a conversational tone of voice, as if you were, like Jesus, just discussing this with those around you.

Ask the second question, which is similar to the first, except in the second person, and which Jesus addresses personally to his disciples, directly to the members of the assembly by looking up, making eye contact with them, thereby personalizing the question also to them.

Deliver Jesus' rebuke of Peter ("Get behind me, Satan!") in a powerful tone of voice that conveys Jesus' aversion to Peter's own rebuke. Make sure to maintain this powerful tone throughout Jesus' entire rebuke.

---

identity. After this warning, the Gospel passage shifts as Jesus' begins to teach about his identity and the requirements of discipleship.

The first prediction of the Passion marks the beginning of the first of three instructions on Christology and discipleship explaining Jesus' identity as the messianic Son of Man who must suffer, die, and rise. Jesus, like the suffering servant of Isaiah, does not seek out his suffering; rather, it is inevitable because of his person, teaching, and actions.

Although Peter confesses Jesus' identity correctly earlier in this passage, now he fails to understand its meaning, staunchly disputing Jesus' prediction of his Passion, death, and Resurrection. Peter also struggles in the Marcan Passion narrative where at first he declares that even though others will have their faith shaken, his will not be (14:29), and then later denies knowing Jesus three times (14:66–72).

At the conclusion of today's Gospel, Jesus shows the disciples that following the Son of Man will not only entail changing their messianic expectations, but also

changing their human ways of thinking about discipleship. Just as the Messiah must suffer, die, and rise, so too those who follow him must also take up their cross, accepting suffering when it comes their way, in order to save their life.

Thus, from this point forward in the Gospel according to Mark the readers and your assembly know the extent of what is expected of them if they choose to follow Jesus, though they, like Peter, may not like all of what they hear. They also know the reward that comes with fidelity to Christ.

25TH SUNDAY IN ORDINARY TIME

Lectionary #134

READING I   Wisdom 2:12, 17–20

A reading from the Book of Wisdom

The **wicked** say:
   Let us beset the **just** one, because he is **obnoxious** to us;
      he sets himself **against** our doings,
   reproaches us for **transgressions** of the law
      and **charges** us with violations of our **training**.
   Let us **see** whether his words be **true**;
      let us find **out** what will happen to him.
   For if the **just** one be the son of **God**, God will **defend** him
      and **deliver** him from the hand of his **foes**.
   With **revilement** and **torture** let us put the **just** one to the **test**
      that we may have **proof** of his **gentleness**
      and **try** his **patience**.
   Let us **condemn** him to a shameful **death**;
      for according to his own **words**, God will take **care** of him.

Let some evil and malice be heard in your tone of voice as you speak the words of this entire reading ("Let us beset the just one . . ."), as the wicked ones are plotting against him.

Proclaim the first half of the final line ("Let us condemn him . . .") with disappointment in your voice, for as Christians we know this was the death Jesus faced. Then offer the second half of the line ("for according to his own words . . .") with self-assurance, because, despite the mockery in these words, God does take care of the just one.

READING I   In today's passage, the wicked connive and plot against "the just one," who, according to them, has disrupted the way in which they carry out their actions. The just one has chastised the wicked for disobeying the law of Moses in which they have been formed. Yet the wicked do not want to take responsibility for their own misdeeds.

   To find out whether the just one's reproach of them is reasonable, the wicked conspire to see if God will come to the aid of the just one if they condemn him to death. In their plot are similarities both to the innocent suffering servant of Isaiah 52:13—53:12, which is proclaimed on Good Friday, as well as to the crucifixion scene in Matthew, during which the chief priests, scribes, and elders mocked Jesus with the words "He trusted in God; let him deliver him now if he wants him. For he said, 'I am the Son of God'" (Matthew 27:43).

   Although the author of Wisdom was not thinking of Jesus when he wrote this passage, the Christian tradition has long interpreted Old Testament passages in light of the New Testament. Thus, the Christian tradition sees in the wicked's condemnation of the just one a parallel with Jesus' own innocent suffering and death. In the end, Jesus' Resurrection holds forth the gift of new life that the followers of Wisdom will experience.

READING II   In today's reading, James exhorts Christians to change their disposition of jealousy and selfishness. Within the Christian community of the time it seems difficulties or conflicts between

With your tone of voice, underline the contrast between "jealousy" and "selfish ambition" and "wisdom from above" that is "pure, then peaceable, gentle" by stating the first in a strong and critical tone of voice, and the latter in a softer, lighter tone.

Deliver the list of indictments ("You covet . . .") in a direct, somewhat accusatory tone of voice. Do not, however, increase the intensity as you go through the list. That James has provided a list of accusations speaks for itself. Do not exaggerate the faults of his community and yours in your proclamation.

READING II   James 3:16—4:3

A reading from the Letter of Saint James

Beloved:
Where **jealousy** and selfish **ambition** exist,
    there is **disorder** and every foul **practice**.
But the wisdom from **above** is first of all **pure**,
    then **peaceable**, **gentle**, **compliant**,
    full of **mercy** and good **fruits**,
    without **inconstancy** or **insincerity**.
And the fruit of **righteousness** is sown in **peace**
    for those who **cultivate** peace.

Where do the **wars**
    and where do the **conflicts** among you **come** from?
Is it not from your **passions**
    that make war within your **members**?
You **covet** but do not **possess**.
You **kill** and **envy** but you cannot **obtain**;
    you **fight** and wage **war**.
You do not **possess** because you do not **ask**.
You **ask** but do not **receive**,
    because you ask **wrongly**, to spend it on your **passions**.

---

members arose because human ambition for leadership and control existed.

In comparison to those who would be filled with selfish ambition and those who might not be able to control the use of their tongue in teaching others, James speaks of those who show the fruits of wisdom active in their lives by their humility. In so doing, they can be identified as a lover of God, not a lover of the world (4:4–10). The passion of the lover of God is submitting to God (4:7) and the passion of the lover of the world is judging their neighbor. The former brings peace, the latter division.

Your proclamation of James' words is a timely reminder that amity can exist among peoples when they seek wisdom from above. They are also a reminder to you as you exercise your ministry as a lector to put aside any selfish ambition you might have and replace it with a humility that understands ministry as service.

GOSPEL   If the beginning of today's Gospel sounds familiar, it is! Jesus' prediction of his coming Passion, death, and Resurrection is the second time

in the Gospel according to Mark he foretells the events that are to come. The first prediction, given in similar words occurred in last Sunday's passage (Mark 8:31). In all, the Marcan account of the Gospel contains three Passion predictions, although the third one (Mark 10:32–34) is not proclaimed during the proclamation of Mark during Ordinary Time.

Whereas in the Gospel proclaimed last Sunday the only reaction of the disciples to Jesus' Passion prediction that is described is Peter's rebuke of Jesus, in today's Gospel proclamation, the disciples as a group are

GOSPEL Mark 9:30–37

A reading from the holy Gospel according to Mark

Jesus and his disciples **left** from there and began a **journey**
     through **Galilee**,
   but he did not wish **anyone** to know about it.
He was **teaching** his disciples and **telling** them,
   "The Son of **Man** is to be handed **over** to men
   and they will **kill** him,
   and three days after his **death** the Son of Man will **rise**."
But they **did** not understand the **saying**,
   and they were **afraid** to **question** him.

They came to **Capernaum** and, once inside the house,
   he began to **ask** them,
   "What were you **arguing** about on the **way**?"
But they remained **silent**.
They had been discussing among themselves on the way
   who was the **greatest**.
Then he sat **down**, called the **Twelve**, and **said** to them,
   "If anyone wishes to be **first**,
   he shall be the **last** of all and the **servant** of all."
Taking a **child**, he placed it in their **midst**,
   and putting his **arms** around it, he said to them,
   "Whoever receives one **child** such as this in my **name**,
      receives **me**;
   and whoever receives **me**,
   receives not **me** but the One who **sent** me."

Differentiate your proclamation between the narrative lines and what Jesus was teaching the disciples ("The Son of Man . . .") by pausing after the words "and telling them" and speaking Jesus' words in a more candid, direct tone of voice.

Capernaum = kuh-PER-n*m

Lower your tone of voice as you narrate the disciples' response to Jesus' question about what they were arguing about ("But they remained silent . . ."), as the disciples were no doubt embarrassed and ashamed about the reason they were arguing.

Let kindheartedness be heard in your voice as you speak Jesus' words ("Whoever receives one child . . ."). Make eye contact with the assembly as you proclaim Jesus' teaching.

said not to understand what Jesus was saying. Perhaps at some level, though, they understood because the evangelist tells us of the disciples' fear as they choose not to pursue Jesus' comments any further.

The second half of the Gospel provides us with the connection between the Passion prediction and the meaning of discipleship, similar to the order of last Sunday's Gospel. In each of the three passion predictions and the instructions on discipleship that follow, one or more of the

disciples do not grasp what it truly means to be a disciple. Today, the disciples are caught "red-handed," embarrassed because they were talking about serving their own self-interest by reaching the top of the human ladder of importance, exactly the opposite of what Jesus explains as the meaning of discipleship.

Using a child, a person in society without any legal status and who can do little on his or her own, Jesus illustrates that the role of a disciple in carrying on his work is one of service; status in society is

irrelevant to being a disciple. Rather, taking up one's cross and being of service qualify one as a disciple of the Son of Man. These instructions on what it takes to be a disciple continue through the Twenty-ninth Sunday in Ordinary Time, climaxing with the testimony of Mark 10:45.

26TH SUNDAY IN ORDINARY TIME

Lectionary #137

READING I   Numbers 11:25–29

A reading from the Book of Numbers

The LORD came down in the **cloud** and spoke to **Moses**.
Taking some of the **spirit** that was on Moses,
    the LORD **bestowed** it on the seventy elders;
    and as the spirit came to **rest** on them, they **prophesied**.

Now two men, one named **Eldad** and the other **Medad**,
    were not in the **gathering** but had been left in the **camp**.
They **too** had been on the list, but had not gone out to the **tent**;
    yet the spirit came to rest on them **also**,
    and they **prophesied** in the camp.
So, when a young man quickly told **Moses**,
    "Eldad and Medad are **prophesying** in the camp,"
    Joshua, son of **Nun**, who from his youth had been Moses'
      aide, said,
    "Moses, my lord, **stop** them."
But Moses answered him,
    "Are you **jealous** for my sake?
Would that **all** the people of the LORD were **prophets**!
Would that the LORD might bestow his spirit on them **all**!"

---

prophesied = PROF-uh-sīd

Pause before the narrative shifts focus to Eldad and Medad ("Now two men . . .").
Eldad = EL-dad
Medad = MEE-dad

Speak the young man's words to Moses reporting the actions of Eldad and Medad ("Eldad and Medad are prophesying . . .") in a quickened pace to convey the young man's concern.
prophesying = PROF-uh-sī-ing
Deliver Joshua's request to Moses ("Moses, my lord, stop them") in an emphatic tone of voice.
Proclaim the exclamatory statements in Moses' reply ("Would that all the people . . .") with conviction and zeal, making eye contact with the members of the assembly, as they are to also carry out the prophetic work of the Lord.

READING I Today's passage from the book of Numbers entails four parts. First, the Lord speaks to Moses and shares the spirit that was on Moses with the elders whom the Lord had previously asked Moses to assemble (11:16). The Lord's purpose in bestowing the spirit on the elders was to have them share in the burden of the people with Moses so that Moses no longer had to bear responsibility for the people's discontent on his own (11:17).

Second, the passage names two men, Eldad and Medad, who did not take part in the assembly. But the Spirit of the Lord still came upon them, enabling them to prophesy.

The third part of the reading tells that a young man reported Eldad and Medad for their actions and quickly got the support of Joshua.

The fourth and final part of the reading resolves the conflict. Instead of chastising the prophets who were not present at the "official" gathering, Moses recognized that they too were doing the Lord's work, while at the same time noting how the sin of jealousy stifles the Lord's prophetic work.

READING II At the outset, this reading appears only to be a condemnation of the rich for the misuse of their wealth and a prediction of the harsh judgment they will face at the eschaton.

Yet looking deeper into the context of the reading, it is clear the passage is meant to caution all Christians about the passing character of this world. Essentially, James instructs Christians that the importance the rich give to their wealth, a symbol of this world, will bring about their own destruction.

READING II   James 5:1–6

A reading from the Letter of Saint James

Come now, you **rich**, **weep** and **wail** over your impending
     miseries.
Your **wealth** has rotted **away**, your **clothes** have become
     moth-eaten,
     your gold and silver have **corroded**,
     and that corrosion will be a testimony **against** you;
     it will **devour** your flesh like a **fire**.
You have stored up **treasure** for the last days.
Behold, the **wages** you **withheld** from the **workers**
     who harvested your **fields** are crying **aloud**;
     and the cries of the **harvesters**
     have reached the **ears** of the Lord of **hosts**.
You have lived on earth in **luxury** and **pleasure**;
     you have **fattened** your hearts for the day of **slaughter**.
You have **condemned**;
     you have murdered the **righteous** one;
     he **offers** you no **resistance**.

Proclaim the commands ("Come now, you rich . . .") in a firm, even stern tone of voice. Try not to cross over the fine line to where your proclamation of this reading becomes chastisement of the assembly.

Pause before and after the words "You have stored up treasure" so as to isolate the sentence which is a key in understanding the central theological point of the reading: this world is passing away.

Impart the last verse ("You have condemned . . ."), which is a stinging indictment leveled against those in the world who misuse their riches, in a straightforward manner. Pause before the words "he offers you no resistance," and state them with acceptance in your tone of voice.

Thinking their wealth was a treasure to be kept until the end (see Matthew 5:22), the rich failed to give just compensation to employees and have selfishly prepared only themselves for the end time. As such, at "the day of slaughter," the time of the eschatological judgment, they themselves will experience destruction.

The reading concludes with the strong statement that the rich have condemned and murdered the righteous one who did not oppose his fate ("You have condemned . . ."). In this verse, the author may or may not

have had Jesus in mind, but could simply be referring to either Sirach 34:22 or Wisdom 2—3, both of which present the destruction of those who take the means of livelihood away from others, from a neighbor or from the poor.

As you prepare to proclaim this reading, spend some time also with James 5:7–12. These verses are not part of the reading you proclaim, but help complete the context for it. They extol Christians to be patient until the coming of the Lord, noting that it is most important to keep our hearts set on the Lord like the prophets

did, not the goods of the world that can corrupt if misused. Keeping our sights set on Jesus, who suffered, died for us, and leads us while on earth to use the gifts that God has given us would not bring about our destruction, but rather our life in communion with God.

GOSPEL   Last Sunday, in the Gospel account, the disciples were arguing about who among them was the greatest. This Sunday, the disciples appear

A reading from the holy Gospel according to Mark

At that time, **John** said to **Jesus**,
   "**Teacher**, we saw someone driving out **demons** in your name,
   and we tried to **prevent** him because he does not **follow** us."
Jesus replied, "Do **not** prevent him.
There is **no** one who performs a mighty **deed** in my name
   who can at the **same** time speak **ill** of me.
For whoever is not **against** us is **for** us.
Anyone who gives you a cup of **water** to drink
   because you belong to **Christ**,
   amen, I say to you, will surely not lose his **reward**.

"Whoever causes one of these **little** ones
   who **believe** in me to **sin**,
  it would be **better** for him if a great **millstone**
  were **put** around his neck
  and he were thrown into the **sea**.
If your **hand** causes you to sin, cut it **off**.
It is **better** for you to enter into life **maimed**
   than with **two** hands to go into **Gehenna**,
   into the unquenchable **fire**.
And if your **foot** causes you to sin, cut it **off**.
It is **better** for you to enter into life **crippled**
   than with **two** feet to be thrown into **Gehenna**.
And if your **eye** causes you to sin, pluck it **out**.
Better for you to enter into the kingdom of God with **one** eye
   than with **two** eyes to be thrown into **Gehenna**,
   where 'their worm does not **die**, and the fire is not **quenched**.'"

Speak John's words to Jesus ("Teacher, we saw someone . . .") in a concerned tone of voice.

After John's words, the rest of the Gospel is Jesus' words. Give Jesus' word at the beginning of his reply ("Do not prevent him . . . lose his reward") in a positive tone of voice.

Pause before the words ("Whoever causes one . . ."). Shift your tone of voice to one that is more serious and reflective of the warning Jesus is giving.

Gehenna = geh-HEN-nah

Deliver the first half of the words that conclude the reading ("Better for you to enter . . .") with some hope in you voice. Then switch to a more ominous tone of voice as you convey the second half ("than with two eyes . . .").

---

little better in the eyes of Jesus, as the disciples wish to judge for themselves who can do the Lord's work.

   The narrative thus begins with the disciples expressing their concern over seeing someone using Jesus' name to drive out demons. Not recognizing the goodness of the person's actions, because he was not part of their group, the disciples tried to stop him. Jesus, once again correcting the disciples, responds to the exclusivity they wish to maintain with regard to those who follow Jesus, with the principles of tolerance and acceptance.

Jesus' statement ("For whoever is not . . .") broadens his previous words ("There is no one . . ."). In doing so, it leads to the example that follows ("Anyone who gives . . ."). In contrast to the disciples' way of thinking, this example illustrates Jesus' teaching that even what might appear in human sight to be a small deed, done in Christ's name, does not lose its importance in God's eyes.

   Jesus' final words of warning to his disciples, an adaptation of Isaiah 66:24, tell of the seriousness of their desire to be exclusive in relation to whom they see

worthy of belonging to Jesus. To be guilty of the sin of excluding members from the community of disciples based on human judgment foreshadows a fate similar to the wicked who rebelled against the Lord in the final prophecy in Isaiah. Jesus' teaching also implies that if we welcome those who follow Jesus in their actions, although they might be outside the inner circle of disciples, we will experience the reward of the kingdom of God.

27TH SUNDAY IN ORDINARY TIME

Lectionary #140

READING I   Genesis 2:18–24

Genesis = JEN-uh-sis

Proclaim the Lord's words ("It is not good . . .") in a straightforward manner with certainty in your voice: the Lord is sure of what he is doing.
Convey the story in a narrative tone of voice, taking your time with the details, allowing the assembly to imagine the scene.

Proclaim the man's words ("This one, at last . . .") with conviction and excitement in your tone of voice.

Pause before imparting the final verse ("That is why a man . . ."), which explains the unity of man and woman and serves as the foundation for the theology of the Catholic sacrament of Marriage, in a more explanatory tone of voice than the one you used previously.

A reading from the Book of Genesis

The LORD God said: "It is not **good** for the man to be **alone**.
I will make a suitable **partner** for him."
So the LORD God **formed** out of the **ground**
    various wild **animals** and various **birds** of the air,
    and he **brought** them to the man to see what he would
        call them;
    whatever the man **called** each of them would be its **name**.
The man gave names to all the **cattle**,
    all the **birds** of the air, and all wild **animals**;
    but **none** proved to be the suitable **partner** for the man.

So the LORD God cast a deep **sleep** on the man,
    and while he was asleep,
    he took out one of his **ribs** and closed up its **place** with **flesh**.
The LORD God then built up into a **woman** the rib
    that he had **taken** from the man.
When he brought her to the man, the man said:
    "**This** one, at last, is **bone** of my **bones**
    and **flesh** of my **flesh**;
    this one shall be called '**woman**,'
    for out of 'her **man**' this one has been **taken**."
That is why a man **leaves** his father and mother
    and clings to his **wife**,
    and the **two** of them become **one flesh**.

READING I | The account of the creation of man and woman that is today's First Reading is paired with the Gospel according to Mark about Jesus' teaching on divorce. In this Gospel passage Jesus quotes the concluding verse from the first reading (Genesis 2:24).

The passage from Genesis is part of the larger second story of creation (Genesis 2:4b–25, or 2:4b—3:24 if the narrative of the Fall from grace is included). In the first creation story (Genesis 1:1—2:4), the one that is proclaimed at the Easter Vigil, God's creation of man (adam), male and female in the image of God, on the sixth day is the climax of creation. In contrast, in the second creation story, the creation of man and woman occurs sequentially. First, God makes man (adam) from the earth (adama). Then, the living creatures of the earth and sky are formed. After none of these is found to be a "suitable partner" for man, God forms woman from man.

Twice the phraseology "suitable partner" is repeated. It is best translated into English with the hyphenated expression "help-meet." The emphasis on partnership and mutuality evidenced in the Hebrew makes it clear that man and woman are made for each other, and that any literal interpretation which might see in the successive order of their creation a subordination of woman to man is mistaken.

The theology of the sacrament of Marriage in the Catholic Church, rooted in the Genesis creation accounts, begins from the basis of recognizing the equal personhood of both man and woman, who were both created in the image of God. In

READING II Hebrews 2:9–11

A reading from the Letter to the Hebrews

Brothers and sisters:
He "for a **little** while" was made "**lower** than the **angels**,"
    that by the **grace** of God he might taste **death** for everyone.

For it was **fitting** that he,
    for whom and **through** whom all things **exist**,
    in bringing **many** children to **glory**,
    should make the **leader** to their salvation **perfect**
        through **suffering**.
He who **consecrates** and those who are **being** consecrated
    all have **one origin**.
Therefore, he is not **ashamed** to call them "**brothers**."

Marriage, the equal personal dignity of both is to be respected and affirmed. Yet the Church also recognizes the difference and complementarity between the man and woman, in particular in relation to sexuality, which, like their equal personal dignity, is also evidenced in the divine act of creation (CCC, #2331–2336).

READING II Hebrews portrays Jesus as the "high priest" of the new covenant. The author of the letter argues for the superiority of Jesus over the angels

(1:4—2:18) and Moses (3:1—4:13), while building to the conclusions about the superiority of Jesus' priesthood (4:14—7:28) and his sacrificial ministry that established the new covenant (8:1—10:18).

The two brief verses you proclaim today come from Hebrews 2, a chapter that begins with a call to Christians to remain steadfast in belief. In order to provide encouragement in remaining faithful, the author develops his message around Christology.

Earlier in 1:4, God's Son is seen to be "superior to the angels" and in 2:9, the opening verse of today's reading, the author

acknowledges that for "a little while" (see Psalm 8:4–6) Jesus was made lower than the angels. Taken together, these two statements ground Christian belief in the full divinity and humanity of Jesus.

For the author of Hebrews, it was the fact that Jesus became human and suffered death that led to his exaltation with God. Through his obedience, which stands as an example to imitated by believers, Jesus made possible their salvation. It is because Jesus, God's Son and high priest, possesses fully both divinity and humanity

GOSPEL   Mark 10:2–16

A reading from the holy Gospel according to Mark

The **Pharisees** approached Jesus and asked,
  "Is it **lawful** for a **husband** to **divorce** his **wife**?"
They were testing him.
He said to them in reply, "What did **Moses** command you?"
They replied,
  "Moses **permitted** a husband to write a bill of **divorce**
  and **dismiss** her."
But Jesus told them,
  "Because of the **hardness** of your **hearts**
  he wrote you this **commandment**.
But from the **beginning** of creation, *God made them **male***
    *and **female**.*
*For this reason a man shall **leave** his father and mother*
    *and be **joined** to his wife,*
    *and the **two** shall become **one flesh**.*
So they are no longer **two** but **one flesh**.
Therefore what **God** has joined **together**,
  no human **being** must **separate**."
In the house the disciples **again** questioned Jesus about this.
He said to them,
  "Whoever **divorces** his wife and marries **another**
  commits **adultery** against her;
  and if **she** divorces her **husband** and marries another,
  she commits **adultery**."

Ask the Pharisees' question ("Is it lawful for a husband . . . ?") with a sense of cunning and deceit in your voice and making sure to raise your voice slightly at the end of the question.

Deliver Jesus' words ("Because of the hardness . . .") in a teacher-like tone of voice conveying a mild, but not harsh, confidence. Proceed in a moderate, unhurried pace as you proclaim the citation from Genesis ("God made them . . ."), allowing the assembly to make the connection with the First Reading.

Impart Jesus' words about divorce ("Whoever divorces . . .") in a pastoral tone of voice, presenting Jesus' teaching, but not sounding as if Jesus (and you proclaiming the words) are chastising the members of the assembly who are divorced and remarried.

---

that he consecrates us to the Father, the source of his life and ours.

The final line of the reading, although slightly apologetic in nature, is meant as loving encouragement to Christians. It testifies to our union with Jesus made possible because, although he is unique in his perfect divinity and humanity, still with him we share through our Baptism the same divine origin—the Father—and the same human nature. Through Jesus' act of consecration and our remembrance of it in the Eucharist, we are led by him back to our home with the Father.

GOSPEL   Today's Gospel passage has three basic parts: 1) the Pharisees question Jesus about divorce, 2) the disciples continue the Pharisees' line of questioning, and 3) Jesus invites the children to come to him.

First, surrounded by crowds who had come to hear him teach, Jesus is tested by the Pharisees who are interested in his knowledge of Mosaic law. Initially, Jesus responds to the Pharisees by turning the tables on them, asking them to tell him what Moses said about divorce. Jesus'

reply to their correct statement that the law of Moses permitted a husband to divorce his wife, gives the reason the law consented to divorce: the hardness of human hearts. In his response, Jesus cites a combination of Genesis 1:27 and 2:24 (the latter verse is part of today's First Reading), a strong statement on the permanence of marriage as God's intent from the beginning.

In the second part of the Gospel, the scene shifts to inside the house where the conversation is now between Jesus and his disciples. The Gospel passage only

Pause before the final section ("And people were bringing . . .") so that the new topic is clear.

Present Jesus' words to his disciples ("Let the children come to me . . .") in a firm but compassionate tone of voice.

Pause after Jesus' words and before delivering the final narrative line ("Then he embraced them . . .") in an affectionate tone of voice.

And people were bringing **children** to him
　　that he might **touch** them,
　but the disciples **rebuked** them.
When Jesus saw this he became **indignant** and said to them,
　"Let the children **come** to me;
　　do not prevent them, for the kingdom of God **belongs**
　　　to such as **these**.
Amen, I **say** to you,
　whoever does not accept the kingdom of God like a **child**
　　will not **enter** it."
Then he **embraced** them and **blessed** them,
　placing his **hands** on them.

[Shorter: Mark 10:2–12]

tells us that the disciples questioned Jesus again. It does not provide us with the questions the disciples actually posed to him, but simply gives is Jesus' response. His words appear as a stronger prohibition against divorce because they convict those of marrying again of adultery, thus breaking the sixth commandment (Exodus 20:14; Deuteronomy 5:18).

In the third and final section of today's Gospel, Jesus chastises the disciples for not allowing people to bring their children to him. The children are symbolic of all those who are open to God's presence in their lives. The receptivity and openness of children challenges those who follow Jesus to be open to his teaching, despite the challenges it poses.

Recognizing that his teaching, in particular with regard to divorce and remarriage as presented in this passage holds out an ideal, Jesus' compassionate response to the children also points to the compassion and empathy he holds out to those who attempt to be faithful to his teaching, but fall short due to their own human weakness or that of others. Following the example of Jesus' compassion, the Church, while holding the permanence and indissolubility of Marriage, calls upon the entire ecclesial community to respond to Christians who find themselves divorced or remarried to respond with an "attentive solicitude" (CCC, #1651).

28TH SUNDAY IN ORDINARY TIME

Lectionary #143

READING I Wisdom 7:7–11

A reading from the Book of Wisdom

I **prayed**, and **prudence** was given me;
    I **pleaded**, and the spirit of wisdom **came** to me.
I **preferred** her to **scepter** and **throne**,
and deemed riches **nothing** in comparison with her,
    nor did I liken any priceless **gem** to her;
because all **gold**, in view of **her**, is a little **sand**,
    and before her, **silver** is to be accounted **mire**.
Beyond **health** and **comeliness** I loved her,
and I chose to have **her** rather than the **light**,
    because the splendor of her **never** yields to sleep.
Yet all good things **together** came to me in her **company**,
    and countless **riches** at her **hands**.

Use a lighter, warmer tone of voice for the opening line ("I prayed . . ."). Then switch to a slightly stronger, firmer tone for "I pleaded . . . ."
scepter = SEP-ter

mire = mīr

Deliver the closing of the reading ("Yet all good things . . .") with gratitude in your voice, slowing your pace of proclamation a little.

READING II Hebrews 4:12–13

A reading from the Letter to the Hebrews

Brothers and sisters:
Indeed the word of **God** is **living** and **effective**,
    sharper than any two-edged **sword**,
    penetrating even between **soul** and **spirit**, **joints** and **marrow**,
    and able to discern **reflections** and thoughts of the **heart**.

Hebrews = HEE-br<u>oo</u>z

Proclaim the opening line ("Indeed the word of God . . .") in a strong and confident tone of voice.

READING I | The book of Wisdom, or the "Wisdom of Solomon," was written centuries after Solomon by an author of Jewish background who had knowledge of Greek philosophy.

The author's use of the first-person pronoun "I" makes this part of the speech appear as an account of the results of his (Solomon's) personal prayer for Wisdom (7:1–6; see 1 Kings 3:5–15). In these verses the author describes Wisdom in terms of understanding. The author also tells us that his prayer was answered by the "spirit of wisdom" coming to him.

Wisdom (*Sophia*, in Greek, a feminine noun) in the Greek philosophical tradition of the time represented prudence and was the basis for making intelligent decisions regarding life. In a Jewish religious context it was understood as guide for following the will of God in the way one lived life. Thus, Solomon prefers the "spirit of wisdom" he received from the Lord to such an extent that nothing compares to her. Moreover, wisdom will never leave Solomon; she is constantly present with him because her splendor "never yields to sleep."

READING II | As part of the fourth chapter of Hebrews, these two verses serve as a warning to Christians, appealing to them to remain steadfast in their faith by diligent testifying to the word of God at work in their lives.

Because Joshua, whose name is Jesus in Greek, spoke of a day when the Israelites would fully experience the Sabbath rest in God after he had led them into the Promised Land, the author of Hebrews puts forward that this rest still remains for the people of God (4:8–9). Although they might be tired and weary from the demands of the

No creature is **concealed** from him,
but everything is **naked** and **exposed** to the eyes of him
to whom we must render an **account**.

Pause before the words "No creature . . . ." Deliver them not as a warning, but as a reminder of our responsibility before God who sees all, using a reserved but strong and steady tone of voice.

GOSPEL   Mark 10:17–30

A reading from the holy Gospel according to Mark

Take your time with the opening ("As Jesus was setting out . . ."), which sets the stage for the entire Gospel.

As Jesus was setting out on a **journey**, a man ran up,
knelt down before him, and asked him,
"Good **teacher**, what must I **do** to inherit eternal **life**?"
Jesus **answered** him, "**Why** do you call me **good**?
No one is good but God **alone**.
You know the commandments: *You shall not **kill**;*
*you shall not commit **adultery**;*
*you shall not **steal**;*
*you shall not bear false **witness**;*
*you shall not **defraud**;*
*honor your **father** and your **mother**.*"
He replied and said to him,

Deliver Jesus' statement of the commandments not as if you are reprimanding the man speaking with Jesus, but in a straightforward manner, with certainty in your voice, clearly stating each one.

"**Teacher**, all of **these** I have observed from my **youth**."
Jesus, looking at him, **loved** him and said to him,
"You are lacking in one thing.
Go, **sell** what you have, and give to the **poor**
and you will have treasure in **heaven**; then come, **follow** me."
At that statement his face **fell**,
and he went away **sad**, for he had **many** possessions.

Offer the man's reply ("Teacher . . .") with disappointment in your voice. The man was probably expecting a different response from Jesus.

Christian life, they must be diligent in their efforts, cooperating with the word of God, so that others might see that the word is living and effective.

The word of God, the divine Word, judges in such a way that those who believe will indeed have to give an honest account of themselves. Because everything is exposed to the one to whom the account must be given, the faithful need be conscience of their thoughts, words, and actions, and truthful in their presentation of them to God (see Acts 1:24; 15:8).

The image of the sword used in reference to the word perhaps comes from Wisdom 18:16, which alludes to the word that carries out divine judgment (see Hosea 6:5; Jeremiah 23:29). As the end of the liturgical year approaches over the next month, this image illustrates the serious effect the power of the word can have in a person's life.

GOSPEL   Today's Gospel reading finds Jesus and his disciples continuing their journey toward Jerusalem and

encountering a rich man who asks what it takes to enter the kingdom of God. The passage can best be understood by dividing it into three sections.

In section one, a man approaches Jesus, desirous to learn what it takes to gain "eternal life." Jesus answers by citing six commandments from the second part of the Decalogue that deal with human relationships (Exodus 20:12–17; Deuteronomy 5:16–21). The man responds by defending

Make eye contact with the assembly and proclaim Jesus' words ("How hard it is . . .") emphatically, without any uncertainty in your voice.

Pause before the words "So Jesus again . . . ." Make eye contact with the assembly when you reach the word "Children." Continue the eye contact as you narrate the disciples' increased bewilderment with some agitation in your voice.

Impart Peter's words ("We have given . . .") with a little frustration in your voice.

Maintain optimism and hope throughout Jesus' reply ("Amen, I say to you . . ."). You are conveying his promise of eternal life to the assembly.

Jesus looked around and said to his **disciples**,
　　"How **hard** it is for those who have **wealth**
　　to enter the kingdom of **God**!"
The disciples were **amazed** at his words.
So Jesus **again** said to them in **reply**,
　　"**Children**, how **hard** it is to enter the kingdom of **God**!
It is easier for a **camel** to pass through the eye of a **needle**
　　than for one who is **rich** to enter the kingdom of **God**."
They were **exceedingly** astonished and said among themselves,
　　"Then **who** can be **saved**?"
Jesus **looked** at them and said,
　　"For human **beings** it is **impossible**, but not for **God**.
All things are possible for **God**."
Peter began to say to him,
　　"We have given up **everything** and followed you."
Jesus said, "**Amen**, I say to you,
　　there is **no one** who has given up **house** or **brothers** or **sisters**
　　or **mother** or **father** or **children** or **lands**
　　for **my** sake and for the sake of the **gospel**
　　who will not receive a **hundred** times more **now** in this
　　　　present age:
　　houses and **brothers** and **sisters**
　　and **mothers** and **children** and **lands**,
　　with **persecutions**, and eternal **life** in the age to **come**."

[Shorter: Mark 10:17–27]

---

himself, attesting to his lifelong observance of these laws. Jesus compassionately, but straightforwardly, tells the man that he must do one more thing.

By adding one more requirement for the rich man to enter the kingdom of God, Jesus does not deny the importance of following the commandments. Rather, he simply affirms both following them and serving others in need go hand in hand.

The second part finds Jesus explaining the meaning of his encounter with the rich man. He tells his disciples that his demand to the rich man to sell everything and give to the poor is as hard to follow as it is for a camel to go through the eye of a needle.

In the third and final section, Peter, reflecting on his own situation and that of the other disciples, states that they, in fact, have given everything up to follow Jesus (see Mark 1:18, 20, 2:14). Jesus' words in response acknowledge to Peter, first, that the disciples already experience now the rewards of following Jesus and, second, the fullness of eternal life is yet to come.

From the beginning of the Gospel according to Mark, the kingdom of God is seen to be present, already in the person of Jesus (1:15). Jesus' concluding words today are a restatement of that reality. They also look forward to the future of the disciples in the kingdom of God, but require the ongoing faithfulness of the disciples until that time of fulfillment comes.

29TH SUNDAY IN ORDINARY TIME

Lectionary #146

READING I   Isaiah 53:10–11

Isaiah = ĭ-ZAY-uh

Proclaim the line "The Lord was pleased . . ." in a secure tone of voice, allowing the word "crush" to sound like the action of crushing, but not in an over-exaggerated way.

Strengthen the confidence in your tone of voice as you proclaim the result of the servant's affliction ("he shall see the light . . .").

A reading from the Book of the Prophet Isaiah

The LORD was **pleased**
    to **crush** him in **infirmity**.

If he gives his **life** as an offering for **sin**,
    he shall see his **descendants** in a **long** life,
    and the **will** of the LORD shall be **accomplished** through him.

Because of his **affliction**
    he shall see the **light** in fullness of **days**;
through his **suffering**, my servant shall justify **many**,
    and their **guilt** he shall **bear**.

READING I   As we approach the final weeks of Ordinary Time, you might wonder about the suitability of the short two verses that make up today's First Reading. Taken from the fourth servant song in Isaiah (52:13—53:12), these verses focus on the suffering of the Lord's servant. Each year, the assembly hears them proclaimed as part of the First Reading on Good Friday (see this commentary for background).

Today's passage shows how God's will is accomplished in the suffering of his servant. The divine intent was the servant should give his life for the sins of many. In making this sacrifice the servant will know his descendants and will experience happiness forever with God.

The Greek word *lytron* that is used in the Septuagint for "offering" is the same word translated as "ransom" in the climactic verse of today's Gospel account (Mark 10:45). It connotes a transaction or purchase on behalf of someone who is held captive or enslaved. That the servant gained victory for many from their sin—as Jesus did through the ransom of his life—earned him a "portion among the great." The reward

he is to share with others in thanksgiving as God offers us a participation in the Resurrection of Jesus (Isaiah 53:12).

READING II   Today is the third Sunday of six at the end of the liturgical year that the Second Reading comes from the letter to the Hebrews. The letters of the New Testament are distributed for proclamation over the three-year cycle of Sundays in Ordinary Time. Hebrews itself is divided between Years B and C, during which the Second Reading is taken

READING II   Hebrews 4:14–16

Hebrews = HEE-br<u>oo</u>z

Pause at the commas so the main clauses of the opening verse ("Since we have a great high priest . . .") stand out.

Deliver the words "For we do not have a high priest . . ." in a warm and compassionate tone of voice, as Jesus our high priest understands our weaknesses because he himself has suffered.

Impart the final line ("So let us confidently approach . . ."), making eye contact with the assembly and using a strong, positive tone of voice reflecting the certainty of our faith in Christ.

A reading from the Letter to the Hebrews

Brothers and sisters:
Since we have a great **high** priest who has passed
    through the **heavens**,
  Jesus, the Son of **God**,
  let us hold **fast** to our **confession**.
For we do **not** have a high priest
  who is **unable** to sympathize with our **weaknesses**,
  but one who has **similarly** been tested in **every** way,
  yet without **sin**.
So let us **confidently** approach the throne of **grace**
  to receive **mercy** and to find **grace** for timely **help**.

from Hebrews 1—10 and Hebrews 11—12, respectively. The passages proclaimed are meant to be short and easily understood by the assembly (Introduction to the Lectionary, #107).

Today's selection from Hebrews formed part of the Second Reading on Good Friday, so you might want to see that commentary for more background. The two verses from the conclusion of the fourth chapter pick up immediately where last Sunday's reading ends. However, in contrast to last Sunday's reading, which served as a warning to Christians, this Sunday's

reading serves as a source of kindhearted encouragement. Far from being serious in tone, it is hopeful.

By presenting Jesus as the "great high priest" who is able to understand our weakness because he shares fully in our humanity—although without sin—and who passed through the heavens to God's throne, the author identifies Jesus as the mediator between heaven and earth—one with us in all things but sin and one with God in his divinity, thus one able to unite us with God. The "throne of grace," which

we can approach with confidence because of Jesus the high priest, is God's throne (8:1; 12:2) but also Jesus' throne (1:8), because he has forever existed as one with God. Our Christian hope for eternal life resides in this confidence we are able to have through Jesus the high priest enthroned with the Father as God.

While these two verses serve as the conclusion of Hebrews 4, according to the chapter and verse divisions that were delineated after the writing of the letter, they also serve as an introduction to the theme of Jesus' high priesthood. This

GOSPEL Mark 10:35–45

A reading from the holy Gospel according to Mark

James and John, the sons of Zebedee, came to Jesus and said
to him,
    "Teacher, we want you to do for us whatever we ask of you."
He replied, "What do you wish me to do for you?"
They answered him, "Grant that in your glory
    we may sit one at your right and the other at your left."
Jesus said to them, "You do not know what you are asking.
Can you drink the cup that I drink
    or be baptized with the baptism with which I am baptized?"
They said to him, "We can."
Jesus said to them, "The cup that I drink, you will drink,
    and with the baptism with which I am baptized, you will
        be baptized;
    but to sit at my right or at my left is not mine to give
    but is for those for whom it has been prepared."
When the ten heard this, they became indignant
        at James and John.

Zebedee = ZEB-uh-dee

State the words of James and John ("Teacher, we want . . .") in a matter-of-fact tone of voice. Make sure and emphasize the word "Teacher," pausing after it to set it off from the rest of the statement.

Convey the response of James and John ("We can") with reserved confidence, not exuberance or overconfidence. Use a more serious tone of voice to impart Jesus' words of explanation ("The cup that I drink . . .").

theme is central to the entire letter, but especially to Hebrews 5, the chapter from which the Second Reading is taken on the next two Sundays. In your preparation you might also want to look ahead a few Sundays to broaden your understanding of the textual context of the passage you proclaim today.

GOSPEL Today's Gospel comes immediately after the third Passion prediction (10:32–34). Its content is the third instruction on what is entailed

in truly being Jesus' disciple. Since the Twenty-fourth Sunday in Ordinary Time, the Gospel readings have been from the first and second instructions on discipleship (8:31—9:29; 9:30—10:31). Just when one might think it could not get any more difficult to follow Jesus, in today's Gospel we hear that being a disciple of Jesus means immersing one's self in Jesus' Passion and death.

The Gospel begins with the disciples James and John appearing rather immature. Their question to Jesus that opens the Gospel seems silly and childish—selfish

in its focus on what the disciples *want*, not what Jesus or others might desire. However, Jesus' reply, while showing Jesus wants to meet their needs, in turn places the onus back on James and John to take ownership of what they desire Jesus to do.

While the disciples wish to be seated next to Jesus in the kingdom of God, they find out through Jesus' reply to them that their request cannot easily be fulfilled simply through Jesus accepting his Passion and death. Rather, the disciples must take responsibility for their choice to follow Jesus. This means 1) drinking the cup

Gentiles = JEN-tĭls

Slow your pace somewhat as you proclaim the well-known conclusion of today's Gospel ("Rather, whoever wishes to be great . . .").

Jesus **summoned** them and said to them,
     "You **know** that those who are **recognized** as rulers over
          the Gentiles
     lord it over them,
     and their **great** ones make their **authority** over them **felt**.
But it shall not be so among you.
Rather, whoever wishes to be **great** among you will be
          your **servant**;
     whoever wishes to be **first** among you will be the **slave** of all.
For the Son of Man did not come to be **served**
     but to **serve** and to give his **life** as a **ransom** for **many**."

[Shorter: Mark 10:42–45]

Jesus drinks and 2) being baptized with the baptism of Jesus. The cup Jesus drinks is that of his Passion and death. For the disciples it is the cup of Jesus' own blood, the same cup that we as disciples of Jesus today drink from when we drink from the eucharistic cup. Similarly, the Baptism of Jesus is immersion into his death and Resurrection. Today we are plunged into the suffering and death of Jesus in the waters of Baptism, emerging from them to experience our new life in the resurrected Christ as his disciples.

After Jesus' response about the requirements for sitting next to him in the kingdom of God, Mark tells us the other ten disciples who were with James and John become angry, even offended. We do not know whether these disciples were upset with James and John for even beginning their discussion with Jesus or with Jesus for the response he gave.

Recognizing that the disciples were indignant, Jesus brought them back together. The Gospel then concludes with what is a—if not *the*—most important statement in Mark for understanding Jesus' Passion,

death, and Resurrection ("For the Son of Man . . .") Jesus, as the Son of Man, ruled through service, not the dominance of raw power *(katekyrieuousin)* of those who ruled over the Gentiles. That he gave his life as a ransom *(lytron)* for many provides the example par excellence of his humble service. Each disciple who wishes to be great and reign with Jesus must be a servant (in Greek, the word is *diakonos*, which literally means "one who waits on tables").

30TH SUNDAY IN ORDINARY TIME

Lectionary #149

Jeremiah = jair-uh-MĪ-uh

Pause after boldly proclaiming the opening statement: "Thus says the Lord."

Pause before the word "Behold." Lower your tone of voice slightly for this section, but still maintain hope and optimism.

Pause before the words "They departed in tears." Deliver the words of this section in a quieter, but still audible, compassionate tone of voice.

Ephraim = EE-fray-im

READING I   Jeremiah 31:7–9

A reading from the Book of the Prophet Jeremiah

Thus says the LORD:
Shout with **joy** for **Jacob**,
    exult at the head of the **nations**;
    proclaim your **praise** and say:
The LORD has **delivered** his people,
    the **remnant** of Israel.
Behold, I will bring them **back**
    from the land of the **north**;
I will **gather** them from the ends of the **world**,
    with the **blind** and the **lame** in their **midst**,
the **mothers** and those with **child**;
    they shall **return** as an immense **throng**.
They **departed** in **tears**,
    but I will **console** them and **guide** them;
I will **lead** them to brooks of **water**,
    on a **level** road, so that none shall **stumble**.
For I am a **father** to Israel,
    Ephraim is my **first-born**.

READING I | Today's passage from Jeremiah occurs immediately after the Lord announces the good news of the return the exiled people and the restoration of Israel (Jeremiah 31:1–6). Its verses begin with an imperative to "Shout for joy" for the Lord has saved his Chosen People. Jacob, whose name was changed to Israel in Genesis 32:29, is used to refer to Israel when she is in exile and persecuted, undergoing difficult times.

The "remnant of Israel" that the Lord has delivered refers to those who survived the fall of the northern kingdom of Israel to the Assyrians in 721 BC. Through the exile, they were cleansed and made whole to return to God with renewed faithfulness. Although "remnant" can be seen as a prediction of a small number of people God will deliver, the verses that follow depict an ingathering by God which brings together a larger number of people of all different backgrounds and abilities, an "immense throng" than "remnant" suggests.

At this point in the reading, the emphasis is on the miraculous event of the return from exile carried out by the Lord. The restoration of Israel is about the close relationship the Lord has with his people; the Lord consoles them for all they have been through; the Lord provides them with water (recall the complaints of the Israelites in the desert because they were dying of thirst).

In effect, the Lord's actions show that he is indeed Israel's father, and Ephraim, one of the 12 tribes of Israel, is his first-born. As Israel's father, the Lord is also the Father of all Christians whose heritage lies in the Israelite community.

Hebrews = HEE-br<u>oo</u>z

Proclaim the words "Every high priest . . . just as Aaron was" in a narrative tone of voice, one you would use if you were simply reading out loud, explaining an idea to a group of people.

Set off the quotations from the psalms ("You are my son . . ." and "You are a priest . . .") by pausing before them and delivering them in confident tone of voice that conveys certainty. Make eye contact with the assembly on the quotations helps to emphasize their importance in the reading as well.

Melchizedek = mel-KEEZ-ih-dek

READING II   Hebrews 5:1–6

A reading from the Letter to the Hebrews

Brothers and sisters:
Every **high** priest is **taken** from among men
    and made their **representative** before **God**,
    to offer **gifts** and **sacrifices** for **sins**.
He is able to deal **patiently** with the **ignorant** and **erring**,
    for he **himself** is beset by weakness
    and so, for **this** reason, must make sin offerings for **himself**
    as well as for the **people**.
No one takes this honor upon **himself**
    but only when called by **God**,
    just as **Aaron** was.
In the same way,
    it was not **Christ** who glorified **himself** in becoming high priest,
    but **rather** the one who **said** to him:
        You are my **son***: this day I have* **begotten** *you;*
    just as he says in **another** place:
        You are a priest **forever** *according to the order*
           of **Melchizedek***.*

READING II | In describing the role of the high priest as a representative of the people who offers gifts and sacrifices for sins, the author of Hebrews is referring to the Day of Atonement (Yom Kippur) in the Hebrew tradition (Leviticus 16:29–34). On this day, through the actions of the high priest on behalf of the Israelites, the Israelites are made pure and cleansed of their sins.

The two quotations from Psalms at the end of the reading underscore the belief that Jesus was the new high priest begotten by God who was called forth to serve from the beginning to the end of time through all eternity (Ps 2:7; 110:4). His priesthood was prefigured in that of Melchizedek who offered Abraham bread and wine in Genesis 14:18. In citing these two psalms, the author of Hebrews gives evidence for the superiority of Jesus' priesthood over the Levitical priesthood of Aaron, Moses' elder brother who helped lead the Israelites out of Egypt and was the first high priest.

As a high priest, Jesus has patience with the sinners he represents because he is fully human. However, his priesthood is superior because he did not give in to human weakness that leads to sin. Rather, his exalted death on the cross is the unique sin offering such that other offerings are no longer necessary.

GOSPEL | Like last Sunday's Gospel account in which Jesus asks the disciples "What do you wish me to do for you?" in today's passage, Jesus

Jericho = JAIR-ih-koh

Bartimaeus = bar-tih-MAY-us

Timaeus = tim-AY-us

State the words of Bartimaeus ("Jesus, son of David . . .") with pleading in your voice. On the repetition of the blind man's plea, deliver his words ("Son of David . . .") in a similar manner as you did the first time, but increasing the degree of intensity in your tone of voice.

From Jesus' command to "Call him" through Jesus' words "Go your way," build in hope and optimism, quickening the pace ever so slightly to convey the excitement of the healing that Jesus will perform.

Pause slightly before the words "Immediately he received . . . ." Then deliver this line in a slower pace and in a strong tone of voice, emphasizing the fact that the blind man now "followed him" by making eye contact with the assembly on those words.

GOSPEL   Mark 10:46–52

A reading from the holy Gospel according to Mark

As Jesus was leaving **Jericho** with his disciples and
        a sizable **crowd**,
    Bartimaeus, a **blind** man, the son of **Timaeus**,
    sat by the roadside **begging**.
On hearing that it was Jesus of **Nazareth**,
    he began to cry out and say,
    "**Jesus**, son of **David**, have **pity** on me."
And many **rebuked** him, telling him to be **silent**.
But he kept calling out all the **more**,
    "Son of **David**, have **pity** on me."
Jesus **stopped** and said, "**Call** him."
So they **called** the blind man, saying to him,
    "Take **courage**; get **up**, Jesus is **calling** you."
He threw aside his **cloak**, sprang **up**, and **came** to Jesus.
Jesus said to him in reply, "What do you want me to **do** for
        you?"
The blind man replied to him, "**Master**, I want to **see**."
Jesus told him, "Go your **way**; your **faith** has **saved** you."
Immediately he **received** his sight
    and **followed** him on the way.

asks a similar question of Bartimaeus: "What do you want me to do for you?" In both Gospel passages, those to whom Jesus asks the question respond with a direct request of him; the disciples ask to be seated at his right and left in the kingdom of God (10:37) and Bartimaeus wishes to see (10:51).

After Jesus responds, however, the disciples and Bartimaeus act in very different ways. In the Gospel proclaimed last Sunday, it is those who thought themselves to be disciples who seem to renege on their willingness to drink Jesus' cup and

be immersed in his Baptism after Jesus informs them this is what constitutes discipleship. In contrast, Bartimaeus, the beggar who can see because Jesus has healed him, chooses to follow Jesus as he travels on the road to Jerusalem leading to his suffering and death.

As we approach the end of the liturgical year in which we have journeyed with Jesus through the Gospel according to Mark, your proclamation of today's Gospel can offer an opportunity for the assembly

to reflect on their own faithfulness in following Jesus and celebrating the Paschal Mystery throughout over the past months. Will you and they be more like the disciples described by Mark, who balk at the requirements of following Jesus, or more like Bartimaeus, who eagerly and willingly follows Jesus—perhaps even participating in Jesus passion experience? If the latter, then the life we experience now in Jesus will be increased a hundred times at the end of this world, in the fullness of the kingdom of God (10:30).

ALL SAINTS

Lectionary #667

READING I   Revelation 7:2–4, 9–14

Revelation = rev-uh-LAY-shun

Enunciate the opening words ("I, John"), which identify the first person narrator of this reading, clearly observing the pauses at the commas.

"Do not damage . . ." is a lengthy sentence to proclaim in one breath without rushing through it and maintaining strength in your voice. Practice it aloud.

Pause before the words "After this." Build excitement in your voice from the beginning of this section through to "They cried out . . . ."

Pause at the semicolon after "They cried out in a loud voice" and then proclaim the words "Salvation comes . . ." boldly and confidently, increasing the volume in your tone of voice and making eye contact with the assembly.

A reading from the Book of Revelation

I, **John**, saw another **angel** come up from the **East**,
    holding the **seal** of the living God.
He cried out in a loud **voice** to the four **angels**
    who were given **power** to damage the **land** and the **sea**,
    "Do not damage the **land** or the **sea** or the **trees**
    until we put the **seal** on the **foreheads** of the servants
        of our **God**."
I heard the **number** of those who had been marked with the seal,
    one **hundred** and forty-four **thousand** marked
    from every **tribe** of the children of **Israel**.

After **this** I had a vision of a great **multitude**,
    which no one could **count**,
    from every **nation**, **race**, **people**, and **tongue**.
They stood before the **throne** and before the **Lamb**,
    wearing white **robes** and holding **palm** branches in their **hands**.
They cried out in a loud **voice**:

    "**Salvation** comes from our **God**, who is **seated** on the **throne**,
    and from the **Lamb**."

READING I This passage from the book of Revelation, which you proclaim as the First Reading, is difficult to understand because it is an apocalyptic vision. However, its appropriateness for the solemnity is obvious as it announces the salvation of those who have been chosen and faithful to the Lord.

The reading itself is actually a combination of two visions: the first comes from Revelation 7:1–8. In its use of the number 144,000, or 12 squared, representing the 12 tribes of Israel of the Old Testament, the vision is symbolic of the new Israel, the people of God, the Church, who have been sealed as the new community of those chosen by God.

Whereas the first vision seems to embrace symbolically a limited number of people who belong to the new Israel, the second vision ("After this . . . blood of the Lamb") extends the image of those who are made "white in the blood of the Lamb" (Revelation 7:9–17) to those of every nation, race, people, and language. Like the saints, these people are those who profess that salvation comes from God and from the Lamb, Jesus, who gave his life in the blood of the cross.

The Lord's description of them to John explains that the people of this multitude have experienced suffering, even persecution, and through their faithfulness to God and to the Lamb have been made pure. Through their own sufferings they have participated in Jesus' death and have been transformed into a new spiritual person, symbolized by the whiteness of their robes.

Pause after the words of the multitude and before the words "All the angels . . . ." Lower your tone of voice to the usual tone you use for proclamation.

Shift your tone of voice again to the exclamatory tone previously used for the words of the multitude as you proclaim the words "Amen. Blessing . . . ."

Pause before the words "Then one . . . ." Lower your tone of voice back down to your usual tone for proclamation.

Communicate the elder's words that conclude the reading ("These are the ones . . .") in a softer tone of voice that is not a whisper, but rather one that gets across the relief and contentment of those who survived distress and have been made new in the Lamb.

All the angels stood around the throne
　　and around the **elders** and the four living **creatures**.
They **prostrated** themselves before the throne,
　　worshiped **God**, and exclaimed:
　　　"**Amen**. **Blessing** and **glory**, **wisdom** and **thanksgiving**,
　　　　honor, **power**, and **might**
　　　　　be to our God for**ever** and **ever**. **Amen**."

Then one of the **elders** spoke up and said to me,
　　"Who **are** these wearing white **robes**, and where did they
　　　　come from?"
I said to him, "My **lord**, **you** are the one who **knows**."
He said to me,
　　"**These** are the ones who have **survived** the time
　　　of great **distress**;
　　they have **washed** their robes
　　and made them **white** in the Blood of the **Lamb**."

READING II　The emphasis of this passage from 1 John is the identity of faithful Christians as the "children of God." Because Christians have believed and accepted the sign of God's love in the gift of his Son (John 3:16), they are God's children. At the time of the writing of 1 John, there was division in the Christian community. Some believed Jesus was not fully human; others suggested that he was not fully divine. First John recounts that some of these members left the community. Indeed, the author of 1 John identifies

them as the antichrist (2:18–23). In contrast, those faithful—then, now, and in the future—who profess that Jesus is the Christ belong to the family of God's children.

GOSPEL　The Alternative Opening Prayer in the Sacramentary for the solemnity of All Saints reads in part: "God our Father, source of all holiness, the work of your hands is manifest in your saints, the beauty of your truth is reflected in their faith. May we who aspire to have part in their joy be filled with the

Spirit that blessed their lives, so that having shared their faith on earth we may also know their peace in your kingdom."

　This opening prayer connects with the Gospel proclamation of the Beatitudes in that the saints are those men and women who exemplified the living out of these teachings. Through their actions they carried forth the Father's work and reflected the truth of the Christian faith. As Christian faithful, we pray for their intercession as we too try to manifest the virtues of

READING II   1 John 3:1–3

A reading from the first Letter of Saint John

Beloved:
See what **love** the Father has bestowed on **us**
    that **we** may be called the **children** of **God**.
Yet so we **are**.
The reason the world does not know **us**
    is that it did not know **him**.
Beloved, we are God's children **now**;
    what we **shall** be has not yet been **revealed**.
We **do** know that when it is revealed we shall be **like** him,
    for we shall **see** him as he **is**.
Everyone who has this **hope** based on **him** makes himself **pure**,
    as he is pure.

As you proclaim this reading, take each line as it comes, consciously not rushing from sentence to sentence. All the lines of the reading are in the first person plural ("we" and "us") except for the final line ("Everyone . . ."), so making eye contact with the assembly for as much of the reading as you can do so with ease will enhance your communication of the close bond between the Father and his children.

the Beatitudes in our daily lives (CCC, #1716–1729).

There are two versions of the Beatitudes, the one in Matthew's account proclaimed today and the other in the Gospel according to Luke (6:20–26). Whereas in Matthew the Beatitudes are part of the "Sermon the Mount" and addressed to his disciples as well as the crowds, in Luke the Beatitudes are contained in the "Sermon on the Plain" and addressed only to his disciples. The first, second, fourth, and ninth Beatitudes in Matthew's account are paralleled, although with slight modifications, in Luke 6:20, 21b, 21a, and 22–23 respectfully.

Because Matthew adds the words "in spirit" to the first Beatitude, some scripture scholars have suggested that Matthew "spiritualizes" the teachings. Often this interpretation has been given as a negative one, as if Matthew did not recognize the material poor in his account of how Jesus announced the Beatitudes. Certainly, it is true that Matthew's version in some respects is less concrete than Luke's (Luke also recounts that Jesus adds a Beatitude for those who are hungry now in 6:21 and three "woe's"), but Matthew's version has Jesus' addition of "in spirit" that simply might mean it is those, no matter their economic state—rich or poor—who believe in God's presence in Jesus, who belong to the kingdom of heaven.

One of Matthew's goals in writing to a predominantly Jewish Christian audience around 80–90 AD was to show how the reward of the kingdom of heaven is open to

GOSPEL   Matthew 5:1–12a

A reading from the holy Gospel according to Matthew

When **Jesus** saw the **crowds**, he went up the **mountain**,
    and after he had sat **down**, his **disciples** came to him.
He began to **teach** them, saying:

"**Blessed** are the poor in **spirit**,
    for **theirs** is the Kingdom of **heaven**.
Blessed are they who **mourn**,
    for **they** will be **comforted**.
Blessed are the **meek**,
    for **they** will inherit the **land**.
Blessed are they who hunger and **thirst** for **righteousness**,
    for **they** will be **satisfied**.
Blessed are the **merciful**,
    for **they** will be shown **mercy**.
Blessed are the clean of **heart**,
    for **they** will **see** God.
Blessed are the **peacemakers**,
    for **they** will be called **children** of God.
Blessed are they who are **persecuted** for the sake
        of **righteousness**,
    for **theirs** is the Kingdom of **heaven**.
Blessed are **you** when they **insult** you and **persecute** you
    and utter every kind of **evil** against you **falsely** because of **me**.
Rejoice and be **glad**,
    for your **reward** will be **great** in **heaven**."

Proclaim the opening lines, which set the scene for Jesus' teaching of the Beatitudes, in a narrative tone of voice.

Pause after the words "He began . . ." and before beginning the list of Beatitudes. Because the Beatitudes are parallel in structure, you will want to be careful to practice your proclamation of them so it does not sound "sing-song," that is, containing the same rise and fall in inflection for each Beatitude. Rather, pause after each Beatitude and match your tone of voice to the descriptive words in each one. For example, on "poor in spirit" use a slightly lighter tone of voice and on "inherit the land" use a tone of voice that is fuller and firmer.

As you proclaim the final Beatitude ("Blessed are you . . ."), make eye contact with the assembly as the pronoun has changed from "they" to the personal "you." Maintain eye contact through "Rejoice and be glad" as you declare these commands of Jesus with joy in your voice, perhaps even with a smile that conveys happiness.

---

all—Gentiles included—who acknowledged Jesus as the Son of God as the kingdom of heaven was near at hand in their world. His version of the Beatitudes, and especially the particular beatitude "Blessed are the poor in spirit," serve his purpose of showing the kingdom of heaven is available to Jew and Gentile alike.

The future, passive tense in the second half of all but two of the Beatitudes announced in Matthew's account shows us an eschatological emphasis, meaning that the happiness which comes from living out the Beatitudes (*beatitudo* in Latin means "happy") is a reward that God *will* give in the future to those who have been, are, and will be faithful.

The first and tenth Beatitude, though, evidence that the kingdom of heaven is also available *now* to those who are dedicated to following Jesus, living as his followers (the crowds), even if they are not part of the inner circle of disciples, or are

Onot canonizes saints. It is from the latter that those who are part of the multitude of faithful can draw strength and inspiration, and thus grow closer to Christ (CCC, #956).

COMMEMORATION OF ALL THE FAITHFUL DEPARTED

Lectionary #668

READING I   Wisdom 3:1–9

A reading from the Book of Wisdom

Proclaim the opening line ("The souls of the just . . .") in a confident tone of voice. Then lower the intensity in your tone of voice as you continue ("They seemed . . .").

Communicate the line "But they are in peace" in a deliberate pace and with a gentle tone of voice, one slightly lower in volume than that used in the previous section.

Gradually build in intensity and confidence in your tone of voice as you proceed through this section so that when you proclaim the concluding line of the reading ("because grace and mercy . . .") the tone of your voice matches the one you used to proclaim the opening line ("The souls of the just . . .").

The **souls** of the **just** are in the hand of **God**,
  and no **torment** shall **touch** them.
They **seemed**, in the view of the **foolish**, to be **dead**;
  and their passing **away** was thought an **affliction**
  and their going **forth** from us, utter **destruction**.
But they are in **peace**.
For **if** in the sight of **others**, indeed they be **punished**,
  yet is their **hope** full of **immortality**;
chastised a little, they shall be greatly **blessed**,
  because God **tried** them
  and found them **worthy** of himself.
As **gold** in the furnace, he **proved** them,
  and as sacrificial **offerings** he took them to **himself**.
In the time of their **visitation** they shall **shine**,
  and shall **dart** about as **sparks** through **stubble**;
they shall judge **nations** and rule over **peoples**,
  and the LORD shall be their King **forever**.
Those who **trust** in him shall understand **truth**,
  and the **faithful** shall abide with him in **love**:
because **grace** and **mercy** are with his **holy** ones,
  and his **care** is with his **elect**.

The readings given here are suggestions. Any reading from the Lectionary for the Commemoration of All the Faithful Departed (#668) or the Masses the Dead (#1011–1015) may be used.

READING I This passage from Wisdom provides four main points that evidence God's love and care for the souls of those who have died. First, the opening lines convey the belief that "the wise"—those who trust in God now—can

be confident that the souls of those who were just are now with God.

"The foolish," on the other hand, who simply believe that physical death is the end of all life do not understand the peace in which the souls of the faithful reside.

Second, while the author states the souls of the just are at peace, there is some ambiguity about their state immediately after they die that is suggested in the words "For if in the sight . . . ." Some scholars see a reference to purgatory, the final purification of the elect in the slight chastisement that the souls undergo before they

enter fully into the joy of life with God, although this is not necessarily the intention of the author (see CCC, #1030–1032).

The third main point is the allusion to God's judgment that is experienced at some point after death contained in the phrase "In the time of their visitation." Whereas the souls of the just will live with God forever, those of the wicked will never be released from the snares of suffering and death (Wisdom 2:24; 3:10–12).

Fourth and finally, the reading concludes with a statement reiterating that

Address the assembly with the words "Brothers and sisters" by looking up and making eye contact. Continue your eye contact as you proclaim the words "Hope does not disappoint" slowly and in an optimistic tone of voice. Be careful not to drop the inflection in your voice too much as you proceed with the clause after the comma ("because the love of God . . .").

"How much more then . . ." can sound like a question, but it is a statement. Proclaim it emphatically and do not raise the pitch of your voice when you come to the end of the statement. Do the same as you come to the second statement ("how much more, once reconciled . . .").

READING II   Romans 5:5–11

A reading from the Letter of Saint Paul to the Romans

Brothers and sisters:
Hope does not **disappoint**,
    because the love of **God** has been poured **out** into our **hearts**
    through the Holy **Spirit** that has been **given** to us.
For **Christ**, while we were still **helpless**,
    died at the appointed time for the **ungodly**.
Indeed, only with **difficulty** does one **die** for a **just** person,
    though perhaps for a **good** person
    one might even **find** courage to **die**.
But God **proves** his love for us
    in that **while** we were still **sinners** Christ **died** for us.
How much **more** then, since we are now **justified** by his **Blood**,
    will we be **saved** through him from the **wrath**.
Indeed, **if**, while we were **enemies**,
    we were **reconciled** to God through the **death** of his **Son**,
    how much **more**, once **reconciled**,
    will we be **saved** by his **life**.
Not only **that**,
    but we **also** boast of God through our Lord Jesus **Christ**,
    through whom we have now received **reconciliation**.

Or:

the constant care of the Lord is always with those whom he has chosen ("his elect"). Its purpose is twofold: it comforts those who are concerned for their deceased loved ones who trusted in the Lord throughout their lives and it provides hope for those of us who remain on earth.

READING II | **ROMANS 5**. For Paul, the hope Christians have is genuine because it comes through the cross. Through Christ's death on the cross, while we were still unjustified sinners,

God's love was poured out on us. In this event, we see God sharing of His very self with us such that we might share in the divine life.

Indeed, Paul sees Christ's death on the cross in the example par excellence of God's love being poured out for us. It is for Paul proof of God's tremendous love for us because it occurred while we were still "ungodly." Paul makes his argument in steps by explaining first that, even for a just and righteous person, death is hard. Then, for a good person, one who cares for

others, death is still not easy, but it is easier to rationalize and thus find the strength with which to go through it. Finally, Paul's argument climaxes with his statement about the totally free and gratuitous nature of Christ's death. Christ died not on behalf of a just person or a good person, but on behalf of his enemies, those who were still sinful.

Through his death, Christ offered reconciliation—a reunification of sinners with God. According to Paul, then, by reconciling us to himself through his cross and resurrection, Christ saved those of us

READING II Romans 6:3–9

A reading from the Letter of Saint Paul to the Romans

Brothers and sisters:
Are you **unaware** that we who were **baptized** into Christ Jesus
    were **baptized** into his **death**?
We were indeed **buried** with him through baptism into **death**,
    so that, just as Christ was **raised** from the dead
    by the **glory** of the Father,
    we **too** might **live** in newness of **life**.

For if we have grown into **union** with him through a **death**
    like his,
    we shall also be **united** with him in the **resurrection**.
We know that our **old** self was **crucified** with him,
    so that our **sinful** body might be done **away** with,
    that we might no longer be in **slavery** to sin.
For a **dead** person has been **absolved** from sin.
If, then, we have **died** with Christ,
    we believe that we shall also **live** with him.
We know that **Christ**, raised from the **dead**, dies no **more**;
    death no longer has power over him.

Address the opening greeting directly at the members of the assembly by looking up and making eye contact with them. Because the reading is in the second person plural ("we") in its entirety, you will want to strive to make as much eye contact with the assembly as you can without distracting from the ease of your proclamation.

Let the confidence of faith be heard in your proclamation of the conditional statement "If, then, we have died . . ." through to the end of the reading. Keep your tone of voice strong through the final word. Then pause before saying, "The word of the Lord."

who were God's enemies. On this day when we commemorate the souls of all the faithful departed, the reconciliation that Paul tells us we can boast in is the source of our rejoicing. We joyfully profess that one day we will all meet together in Christ, and live reconciled with our brothers and sisters for ever (*Order of Christian Funerals*, #175).

ROMANS 6. Paul wrote this passage from Romans as a response to the question, why not do evil if God's gift of justification comes to those who sin, posed by those who thought the Gospel promotes moral leniency (Romans 3:5–8, 23–24). In this response,

Paul shows the foundation Baptism gives for a new relationship with Christ.

In Baptism, Christians are baptized "into Christ" *(eis Christon)*. This phrase denotes that Christians are incorporated into Christ's person and, as such, participate in his death and Resurrection. Because his death was death to sin, our unity with Christ in his death, for Paul means that our old, sinful body is washed clean, and done away with.

Being freed from sin, then, the baptized person also participates in the new

life brought through Christ's Resurrection. It is this life in Christ that now has power and control over the newly baptized. This new life, Paul believes, impels one to live uprightly in relation to God and our neighbor. Thus, moral laxity is no longer an option for the Christian's new self. While ethical behavior for the old self might not have had any qualifiers, for the new self it does. Christians must see to it that sin does not rule their bodies allowing them to give in to human desires (6:12).

Paul concludes today's passage with a statement of belief in our future life with

The first sentence is a lengthy one. Pausing at the commas and adding a minor pause after the words "own will" will help in your proclamation.

Communicate the reassuring line ("that I should not lose . . .") with a measure of hope in your tone of voice, making eye contact with the members of the assembly to convey that they will not be lost by him.

Proclaim this climactic line of the Gospel with unwavering strength in your tone of voice.

GOSPEL   John 6:37–40

A reading from the holy Gospel according to John

Jesus said to the **crowds**:
    "**Everything** that the Father **gives** me will **come** to me,
    and I will not reject **anyone** who comes to me,
    because I came **down** from heaven not to do my **own** will
    but the **will** of the one who **sent** me.
And **this** is the will of the one who **sent** me,
    that I should not lose **anything** of what he **gave** me,
    but that I should **raise** it on the last **day**.
For **this** is the will of my **Father**,
    that everyone who **sees** the Son and **believes** in him
    may have eternal **life**,
    and I shall **raise** him on the last **day**."

Christ. For Paul, it is our life on earth as those who were baptized into Christ's death and Resurrection that prepares us for the future. If we are interested in our future life with Christ, we must do our best to mitigate our sin now, for then we will know the fullness of life as God's gift to us.

GOSPEL   As today's passage begins, Jesus teaches the crowd that he will not turn away anyone who approaches him. Although earlier in John, "the Jews" cast out those who believe in

Jesus from the synagogue (9:34–35), Jesus will not turn away those who choose to believe in him. Jesus does not welcome those who come to him simply of his own accord, but he does so because he is doing the will of the Father who sent him. Moreover, he recognizes that all who come to him also come from the Father. On the last day, then Jesus will raise them up to be one with the Father so that they may have eternal life.

The gift of eternal life is anticipated in the Eucharist in which the faithful departed have participated. Through their

reception of the Bread of Life they have professed their belief in Jesus. At their death, their "soul goes to meet God, while awaiting its reunion with its glorified body" on "the last day," when Christ comes again and those who died in Christ will rise (CCC, #997, 1001).

32ND SUNDAY IN ORDINARY TIME

Lectionary #155

READING I   1 Kings 17:10–16

A reading from the first Book of Kings

In **those** days, Elijah the **prophet** went to **Zarephath**.
As he **arrived** at the entrance of the **city**,
    a **widow** was gathering **sticks** there; he called out to her,
    "**Please** bring me a small **cupful** of water to **drink**."
She left to get it, and he called out after her,
    "**Please** bring along a bit of **bread**."
She answered, "As the LORD, your God, **lives**,
    I have nothing **baked**; there is only a **handful** of flour in my **jar**
    and a little **oil** in my **jug**.
Just **now** I was collecting a couple of **sticks**,
    to go in and **prepare** something for **myself** and my **son**;
    when we have **eaten** it, we shall **die**."

Elijah = ee-LĪ-juh
Zarephath = ZAIR-uh-fath

Deliver Elijah's requests to the widow
("Please bring . . .") in a pleasant tone
of voice.

Offer the widow's answer ("As the
Lord . . .") with some regret and
disappointment in your voice.

READING I   The context of today's passage is Elijah's announcement of a drought to Ahab, king of Israel (1 Kings 17:1—19:21). After Elijah decreed the drought, the Lord told him to leave Tishbe in Gilead and go east of the Jordan, where he would find a stream of water from which to drink. However, after some time passed, the stream ran dry and the Lord told him to move to Zarephath, the site of today's reading and encounter with the widow. Zarephath was in the god Baal's territory. Yet even though the people worshipped Baal, the god of storms and fertility, in Zarephath, the drought occurred there as well.

Today's narrative begins with Elijah asking for a cup of water to drink and some bread to eat. In reply, the widow simply tells Elijah she has nothing baked because she has only a little flour and oil, enough to bake something for herself and her son, because they will both die soon. Elijah then consoles her and strangely—seemingly selfishly—asks her to first bake something for him. His justification for this request, though, is seen in the promise of the Lord that he offers to her, predicting the end of the drought. The widow and her son were able to eat, and eventually, although after a contest between the gods and the Lord, the people's confession that the "Lord is God!" (18:21–40) resolved the matter and it rained (18:41).

With only a couple of Sundays remaining in the liturgical year, the eschatological character of this reading is fitting. Like the widow, we might experience lean times in our earthly life, but the Lord will

Pause before the next section, which
is composed of only the prophet's words
("Elijah said to her . . ."). Proclaim
the prophet's words in a calm, reassuring
tone of voice. When you come to the
words of the Lord that Elijah speaks
("The jar of flour . . ."), proclaim them
with more depth and confidence in
your tone of voice, making direct eye
contact with the assembly for as much
of the Lord's words as possible.

Pause again before the concluding
summary section ("She left . . ."). Use a
more subdued, yet positive, narrative
tone of voice to communicate the miracle
that transpired.

Elijah said to her, "**Do** not be afraid.
Go and do as you **propose**.
But **first** make me a little **cake** and **bring** it to me.
Then you can prepare something for **yourself** and your **son**.
For the LORD, the God of **Israel**, **says**,
   'The **jar** of flour shall **not** go empty,
      nor the **jug** of oil run **dry**,
   until the **day** when the LORD sends **rain** upon the earth.'"
She **left** and did as Elijah had **said**.
She was able to eat for a **year**, and he and her son as **well**;
   the **jar** of flour did **not** go empty,
      nor the **jug** of oil run **dry**,
   as the LORD had foretold through **Elijah**.

always remain faithful. The Lord will triumph over other gods, now and at the end of time. In the interim, just as the widow had enough food to take her through for another year, the Lord provides us with the gift of his Son in the Eucharist to sustain us today so that we do not need to worry about what tomorrow will bring.

READING II Continuing the theme of Jesus' high priesthood, the author of Hebrews informs us that the sanctuary that Christ entered into at his death was not the sanctuary that the Jewish high priest passed through to the Holy of Holies, but was heaven.

Because Jesus entered heaven and now resides there with God, appearing on our behalf, other sacrifices are no longer necessary. For the author of Hebrews, Jesus' "once for all" (Hebrews 9:26; CCC, #571) sacrifice in the shedding of his blood on the cross served as the inauguration of a new age in which repeated sacrifices, such that the yearly sacrifice on the Day of Atonement, would no longer be necessary. In Jesus' sacrifice is the complete and lasting redemption for sin.

Yet there is also a fine distinction contained in these verses from Hebrews. While the author clearly rejects the idea that repeated sacrifice is necessary after Jesus' death, he does affirm the ongoing, eternal presence of Jesus' one sacrifice. Where is Jesus' sacrifice forever present? For Catholics, the "sacrifice of Christ and the sacrifice of the Eucharist are *one single sacrifice*" (CCC, #1367). Every time the Church celebrates the Eucharist, Christ's

READING II   Hebrews 9:24–28

Hebrews = HEE-br<u>oo</u>z

There are three sections in this reading containing lengthy sentences. Practice aloud so that you become familiar with the pauses at all the commas and semicolons. This will help to make the meaning of the passage clear to the assembly. Pause at the end of one section and the beginning of the next. The second section begins with "Not that he might . . ." and the third section begins with "But now once . . . ."

Proclaim the truth that Christ "will appear a second time" and the reason for Christ's second coming is "to bring salvation" with confidence, purposefully conveying the certainty of our faith as evident in the second main point of the reading.

A reading from the Letter to the Hebrews

Christ did not enter into a sanctuary made by **hands**,
    a copy of the **true** one, but heaven **itself**,
    that he might **now** appear before **God** on our **behalf**.
Not that he might offer himself **repeatedly**,
    as the **high** priest **enters** each year into the **sanctuary**
    with **blood** that is not his **own**;
    if **that** were so, he would have had to **suffer** repeatedly
    from the **foundation** of the **world**.
But **now** once for all he has **appeared** at the end of the **ages**
    to **take** away sin by his **sacrifice**.
Just as it is **appointed** that human beings die **once**,
    and after this the **judgment**, so also **Christ**,
    offered **once** to take away the sins of **many**,
    will appear a **second** time, not to take away **sin**
    but to bring **salvation** to those who eagerly **await** him.

---

sacrifice is remembered and made present. In her eucharistic liturgy, the Church does not literally reenact the Christ's bloody sacrifice of the cross, but rather Christ gives himself in the bread and wine in an "unbloody" manner (CCC, #1367).

Today's reading concludes with a statement of Christ, the high priest coming again a second time. This verse is reminiscent of the movement of the Jewish high priest remerging from the Holy of Holies on the Day of Atonement. The author's words attest to the Christian belief in the *parousia*, Christ reappearance at the time of

judgment. This time Christ comes, not to annul sin, but to bring the fullness of salvation. In the celebration of the Eucharist, we also look forward to Christ's coming again and anticipate our share with him in the heavenly glory (CCC, #1402–1405; see Memorial Acclamations A, B, and C).

GOSPEL   In today's Gospel, we find Jesus continuing to teach in the Temple precincts, which he has each day that he has been in Jerusalem.

In the first of two main sections in today's passage, Jesus warns the crowds about the scribes, teachers of the law of Moses, who use their role to gain honor and prestige for themselves and, in doing so, take advantage of widows. Widows in the Old Testament were powerless in society, but they were to receive kindness and care (see, for example, Exodus 22:22; Deuteronomy 14:28–29; 26:12–13; Isaiah 1:17; Jeremiah 22:3). In the New Testament they also were the subjects of special attention (Acts 6:1–3; 1 Timothy 5:3–16).

GOSPEL Mark 12:38–44

A reading from the holy Gospel according to Mark

In the course of his teaching Jesus said to the **crowds**,
    "**Beware** of the **scribes**, who like to go around in long **robes**
    and accept **greetings** in the **marketplaces**,
    seats of honor in **synagogues**,
    and **places** of honor at **banquets**.
They **devour** the houses of **widows** and, as a pretext
    recite lengthy **prayers**.
They will receive a **very** severe condemnation."

He sat **down** opposite the treasury
    and **observed** how the crowd put **money** into the treasury.
Many **rich** people put in large sums.
A **poor widow** also came and put in two small **coins** worth
        a few **cents**.
Calling his disciples to himself, he said to them,
    "**Amen**, I say to you, this poor **widow** put in **more**
    than all the **other** contributors to the **treasury**.
For **they** have all contributed from their **surplus** wealth,
    but **she**, from her **poverty**, has contributed all she **had**,
    her **whole** livelihood."

[Shorter: Mark 12:41–44]

Proclaim Jesus' words of warning ("Beware of the scribes . . .") as if you were giving serious counsel to the assembly. Look up and make eye contact as much as you can without taking away from the flow of the proclamation of the Gospel.

Deliver the consequence the scribes will face ("They will receive . . .") in a stern tone of voice, slowing your pace a bit on this line.

Soften your voice slightly as you proclaim Jesus' words to his disciples ("Amen, I say to you . . .") in an unhurried manner. Maintain firmness in your tone of voice so as to convey the authority in Jesus' teaching.

The actions of the scribes, Jesus tells the crowds, will lead to their "severe condemnation." Of this, the crowds are to want no part. To illustrate this point, the second section of the Gospel turns to the scene near the treasury. While rich people place a lot of money in the treasury, a poor widow gives two small coins (*lepta*), monetarily the smallest amount at the time.

Jesus gathers his disciples around him, for his teaching that follows is meant to explain what one must do to follow him. The widow, who made a true sacrifice, giving her "whole livelihood" exemplifies discipleship. The rich people, who only gave from "their surplus wealth," fail to measure up to the standards of being Jesus' disciples. But the widow, on the other hand, leaves no room for doubt about her commitment.

While the point of the Gospel is not that we all seek to become poor widows, you will want to proclaim this Gospel to the assembly so they can choose whether they want to follow the example of the scribes and the rich people or that of the poor widow. In choosing the latter, they will receive the promise of the Lord as the widow in the first reading did: they will be able to eat and not go hungry, for the Lord will take care of them, especially through the food of the Eucharist, which anticipates the eternal banquet in heaven (CCC, #1402–1405).

33RD SUNDAY IN ORDINARY TIME

Lectionary #158

READING I   Daniel 12:1–3

A reading from the Book of the Prophet Daniel

In those days, I, **Daniel**,
    heard this word of the **Lord**:
"At **that** time there shall arise
    Michael, the great **prince**,
    guardian of your **people**;
it shall be a time **unsurpassed** in **distress**
    since nations **began** until that time.
At **that** time your people shall **escape**,
    everyone who is found **written** in the **book**.

"**Many** of those who **sleep** in the dust of the **earth** shall **awake**;
    some shall live **forever**,
    others shall be an everlasting **horror** and **disgrace**.

"But the **wise** shall shine **brightly**
    like the **splendor** of the **firmament**,
and those who lead the many to **justice**
    shall be like the stars **forever**."

Pause noticeably at the colon after the introductory statement ("In those days . . .").

Narrate the words "At that time . . . until that time" in a subdued voice as you are conveying what will happen at the end times.

Change slightly from a hopeful tone of voice to a more pessimistic one as you convey the contrast between those who "shall live forever" and those who "shall be an everlasting horror." Pause before the words "But the wise . . . ." Proclaim them directly to the assembly making eye contact as much as possible. Place a great sense of optimism, confidence, and hope in your voice as you do so.

READING I Today's First Reading comes from Daniel's apocalyptic vision foretelling the future of the Jews. While they will be persecuted in the midst of the wars, they will be taken care of and watched over by the Lord. At the end of the difficult period, those who have been faithful to the Lord will survive. God's kingdom will triumph and those whom God has chosen will live forever. The prediction of the everlasting life is perhaps an early statement alluding to the Resurrection of the dead at the end of time. If so, the reference is probably more to a general Resurrection of the dead, than an individual Resurrection as the former not the latter was part of some early Jewish beliefs.

READING II Today's Second Reading begins by noting a couple of contrasts between the priests of the Old Testament who offered frequently offered sacrifices, not necessarily the high priest who offered sacrifice on the Day of Atonement and Jesus, the new high priest. First, Jesus' priesthood is superior to these priests because they offer sacrifices every day and still are unable to forgive sins. But Jesus, giving wholly of himself in his sacrifice on the cross—and only having to do so once, was able to take away sins.

Second, notice Jesus' posture as described in the line "and took his seat . . ." (see Psalm 110:1). His sitting at the right hand of God differs from the standing posture of the priests who offer repeated sacrifices. For many of us, standing may seem like a more powerful position. But the author's use of seated and our profession of belief in Jesus now being "seated at the right hand of the Father" in the creed

Hebrews = HEE-br<u>oo</u>z

Enunciate the words "Every priest" clearly, making sure the "t" on the end of the word "priest" is audible and does not elide with the word "stands" so it sounds as if "priest" is the plural "priests."

Look up and make eye contact with the assembly as you proclaim the words "For by one offering . . ." since the members of the assembly are part of "those who are being consecrated."

READING II   Hebrews 10:11–14, 18

A reading from the Letter to the Hebrews

Brothers and sisters:
Every priest stands **daily** at his **ministry**,
    offering **frequently** those same **sacrifices**
    that can **never** take away **sins**.
But **this** one offered **one** sacrifice for sins,
    and took his seat **forever** at the right hand of **God**;
    now he waits until his **enemies** are made his **footstool**.
For by **one** offering
    he has made perfect **forever** those who are being **consecrated**.

Where there is forgiveness of **these**,
    there is no longer **offering** for sin.

---

attest that Jesus is enthroned with God, sharing as he has from the beginning in the Father's divinity (CCC, #663; Hebrews 1:8; 4:16; 8:1; 12:2).

As we approach the conclusion of the liturgical year and the celebration of the solemnity of Our Lord Jesus Christ the King next Sunday, this reading gives hope to those of us who are consecrated by Jesus the high priest. Through our share in his priesthood begun through Baptism, we are able to look forward to the day when we will be one with him forever in God's kingdom. Made holy by Christ, we are also tasked with going forth from the liturgy and sharing our hope in the life to come with the men and women of the world.

GOSPEL   As the liturgical year draws to a close, the Gospel passage for today, taken from the chapter in Mark that precedes the beginning of the Passion narrative, turns to the eschatological theme that is proper to these Sundays (Introduction to the Lectionary, #105). Its main focus is the coming of the Son of Man in glory at the end of time.

Jesus uses the words from Daniel 7:13, although it is unclear whether or not he is doing so in reference to himself. On the lips of Jesus, the words are employed to speak of the glorious return of the Son of Man at the end of time. Later in the Gospel according to Mark, Jesus will also use them in response to the high priest's question (14:61–62): "Are you the Messiah, the son of the Blessed One?" Given this latter instance of Jesus applying Daniel 7:13 to himself, it

GOSPEL   Mark 13:24–32

A reading from the holy Gospel according to Mark

Jesus said to his **disciples**:
"In **those** days after that **tribulation**
   the sun will be **darkened**,
      and the **moon** will not give its **light**,
   and the **stars** will be falling from the **sky**,
      and the powers in the **heavens** will be **shaken**.

"And **then** they will see 'the Son of **Man** coming in the **clouds**'
   with great **power** and **glory**,
   and then he will send out the **angels**
   and **gather** his **elect** from the four **winds**,
   from the end of the **earth** to the end of the **sky**.

"Learn a **lesson** from the **fig** tree.
When its branch becomes **tender** and sprouts **leaves**,
   you know that **summer** is near.
In the **same** way, when you see **these** things happening,
   know that he is near, at the **gates**.
Amen, I **say** to you,
   this **generation** will not pass **away**
   until **all** these things have taken **place**.
Heaven and **earth** will pass away,
   but my **words** will **not** pass away.

"But of that **day** or **hour**, **no** one knows,
   neither the angels in **heaven**, nor the **Son**,
      but only the **Father**."

**Begin the proclamation of Jesus'
ominous words ("In those days . . .") as
if you were communicating bad news to
the assembly by using a serious tone of
voice and looking around at various parts
of the assembly.**

**Pause before the words "And then they
will see . . . ." Change from your serious
tone of voice to one that is brighter and
filled with more optimism.**

**Pause again before the parable of the fig
tree ("Learn a lesson . . ."). Deliver the
parable as if you are telling a story,
removing some of the brightness from
your tone of voice.**

**Resume the optimism in your tone of
voice as you proclaim the words "Heaven
and earth . . . ."**
**Pause before the words "But of that
day . . ." and declare them candidly.**

is plausible in today's Gospel that Jesus' use of this verse refers to himself.

This Gospel passage, like today's First Reading, contains some ominous images of the end times. Yet for those who are the chosen followers of God in Christ, the time when the Son of Man comes in glory will be a time of life. Creation itself will announce his arrival and all the elect will be gathered to witness his coming. To help the disciples understand this message he is conveying, Jesus illustrates it by using an example from nature appropriate to the time of year.

The festival of Passover was observed in the spring, and Jesus and his disciples were in Jerusalem to mark the occasion. Around the same time of year, the fig trees begin to be in leaf (Mark 11:13). This serves as a sign of the coming events of Jesus' Passion, death, and Resurrection, which themselves will herald a new age, the beginning of the *eschaton,* the end times.

All is not lost with the dark images of the dawning of a new age, because Jesus' words will not pass away. Those who have been faithful disciples, following Jesus and adhering to his words, will be with him in the kingdom of God, and one with him when he comes again. Yet they must also be faithful in the interim, as the disciples in Mark needed to be faithful in following Jesus even as they did not the exact day or hour when he was to suffer, die, and rise.

OUR LORD JESUS CHRIST THE KING

Lectionary #161

READING I   Daniel 7:13–14

A reading from the Book of the Prophet Daniel

As the **visions** during the night **continued**, I saw
    one like a Son of **man** coming,
        on the clouds of **heaven**;
    when he reached the **Ancient** One
        and was **presented** before him,
    the one like a Son of man received **dominion**,
        glory, and **kingship**;
        all **peoples**, **nations**, and **languages** serve him.
His **dominion** is an **everlasting** dominion
    that shall not be taken **away**,
    his kingship shall **not** be destroyed.

Pause after the announcement of the reading, making sure you have the assembly's attention. You do not want them to miss the line "I saw one like a human being . . . ." Proclaim it deliberately and in a reverent tone of voice.

Increase the intensity and strength in your tone of voice as you proclaim "the one like a Son of man received dominion . . . ." Maintain the confidence and energy in your proclamation through-out the reading to convey the optimism of his dominion.

READING I   Taken from the section of Daniel written in the first person (Daniel 7—12), the First Reading includes the phrase "one like a son of man coming," when, interpreted in light of the New Testament, is thought to refer to Jesus, Son of God and Son of Man. However, in its original context in this passage, it denotes "one in human form"—perhaps a human being—who received a share in the dominion and glory of the God, symbolized by the title "Ancient One." Only after the time of Jesus, and partly because of Jesus' unique use of the expression, did "son of man" become a messianic title.

The image in the phrase "one like a son of man coming" is the fifth in a series of images, the first four of which portrayed different beasts from the underworld. In contrast, the son of man comes not from below, but from the "clouds of heaven," an allusion to God's kingdom above from which God reigns.

On the solemnity of Our Lord Jesus Christ the King your excellent proclamation of this reading can assist the assembly in hearing that their belief in Christ as the Son of Man, who "is seated at the right hand of the Father," fulfills the vision of Daniel (CCC, #664).

READING II   Understanding Christ as the goal of each liturgical year finds consonance with today's passage from Revelation, which concludes with the "I am" statement spoken by God testifying that he is the beginning and the end of everything.

The use of "I am" shows that God is going to reveal something about his divine

READING II   Revelation 1:5–8

A reading from the Book of Revelation

Jesus **Christ** is the faithful **witness**,
  the **firstborn** of the **dead** and **ruler** of the kings of the **earth**.
To him who **loves** us and has **freed** us from our sins by his **blood**,
  who has made us into a **kingdom**,
    priests for his God and **Father**,
  to him be **glory** and **power forever** and **ever**. **Amen**.
  Behold, he is **coming** amid the **clouds**,
    and **every** eye will **see** him,
    even those who **pierced** him.
All the peoples of the earth will **lament** him.
    Yes. **Amen**.

"I am the **Alpha** and the **Omega**," says the Lord God,
  "the one who **is** and who **was** and who is to **come**,
    the **almighty**."

Look up and make eye contact as you proclaim the opening line in an unwavering voice, conveying the certainty of your own faith and that of the assembly.

Your proclamation of the clause "to him be glory . . . . Amen" should be given in a strong tone of voice, sustained through the "Amen." Remember to pause at the conclusion of the sentence "forever and ever" before proclaiming the "Amen," which functions as an affirmation of all the statements that come before it.

Communicate the final verse ("the one who is . . .") deliberately and purposefully, pausing slightly before each occurrence of the word "and."

Alpha = AL-fuh

Omega = oh-MAY=guh

identity. The saying in Revelation is similar to the "I am" sayings Jesus spoke in the Gospel according to John (6:51; 8:58; 10:11; 11:25; 14:6) that have as their Old Testament counterpart God's affirmation of his divine name to Moses in Exodus 3:14. Later in Revelation, Christ will use God's title ("I am the Alpha and the Omega") in reference to himself (22:13).

The use of "Alpha and Omega," the first and last letters of the Greek alphabet, like the English A and Z, attest to the vastness of God's reign throughout all time—past, present, and future. For Christian

believers, Christ's use of the title for himself reveals his divine identity.

GOSPEL   Pilate's question to Jesus ("Are you the King of the Jews?"), which opens today's Gospel account, highlights its appropriateness for the solemnity of Our Lord Jesus Christ the King.

Jesus' question in response to Pilate's initial inquiry ("Do you say this on your own . . . ?") personalizes the interaction between the two and implies that Pilate is

going to have to decide for himself who he believes Jesus to be, although he will eventually turn to "the Jews" to decide which prisoner he should release (18:38b–40).

Jesus' explanation of his kingdom, which follows Pilate's rhetorical question ("I am not a Jew, am I?") shows that Jesus is not a king according to the world's understanding of a king who brandishes political and military power. Frustrated that he has not received a direct answer from Jesus, Pilate follows up with another question, asking Jesus whether he is indeed saying he is king. Jesus' response

The opening question ("Are you the King of the Jews?") and the final sentence ("Everyone who belongs . . .") are the two most important lines of the Gospel. Ask Pilate's opening question slowly, pausing after it, allowing the question to resonate with the assembly. Proclaim the final line in a firm, reassuring tone of voice. The assembly of believers before you, having listened to Jesus' voice throughout the liturgical year, "belongs to the truth."

GOSPEL   John 18:33b–37

A reading from the holy Gospel according to John

Pilate said to **Jesus**,
    "Are **you** the King of the **Jews**?"
Jesus answered, "Do you say this on your **own**
    or have **others** told you **about** me?"
Pilate answered, "**I** am not a Jew, **am** I?
Your own **nation** and the chief **priests** handed you over to me.
What have you **done**?"
Jesus answered, "My **kingdom** does not **belong** to this world.
If my kingdom **did** belong to this world,
    my **attendants** would be **fighting**
    to keep me from being handed **over** to the Jews.
But as it **is**, my kingdom is not **here**."
So Pilate said to him, "Then you **are** a king?"
Jesus answered, "You **say** I am a king.
For **this** I was born and for **this** I came into the world,
    to testify to the **truth**.
Everyone who **belongs** to the truth **listens** to my voice."

("You say I am a king") is at most a lukewarm acknowledgment that in some way he is a king, although Pilate and others do not grasp the meaning of his kingship (see Matthew 26:64).

    Today's Gospel passage concludes with Jesus' statement that he testifies to the truth of his Father, the one who sent him. Pilate's response to Jesus' statement, while not a part of the Gospel you proclaim, is the question: "What is truth?" No answer is provided to his question at this

point in John's account (18:37). Earlier in John, however, the disciples of Jesus were described as being consecrated to the truth (14:6; 17:17, 19). The truth was identified as God's word (17:17). The word was God (1:1), became flesh, and was full of grace and truth as the Father's only Son (1:14).

    Having listened to Jesus' voice (John 18:37) throughout the course of the year and celebrated the events of his life through the table of the word and the Eucharist, we have been led by Jesus to the Father, and to a deeper share in his kingdom. Thus,

those in the assembly before you can answer *all* of Pilate's questions, proclaiming the kingship of Christ as they sing, "Christ, Jesus, victor! Christ Jesus, ruler! Christ Jesus, Lord and redeemer!" (the refrain from the traditional hymn "To Jesus Christ, Our Sovereign King") in praise of Jesus reigning as King for us through his death and Resurrection.